Strategic Management of Innovation and Design

There is now widespread agreement that innovation holds the key to future economic and social prosperity in developed countries. Experts studying contemporary capitalism also agree that the battle against unemployment and relocations can be won only through innovation. But what kind of innovation is required and what is the best way to manage, steer and organize it?

Grounded on experiences of innovative firms and based on the most recent design theories, this book argues that, instead of relying on traditional R&D and project management techniques, the strategic management of innovation must be based on innovative design activities. It analyzes and explains new management principles and techniques that deal with these activities, including innovation fields, lineages, C-K (Concept-Knowledge) diagrams and design spaces. The book is ideal for advanced courses in innovation management in industrial design schools, business schools, engineering schools, as well as managers looking to improve their practice.

Pascal Le Masson, **Benoît Weil** and **Armand Hatchuel** are Professors of Design and Management, Chair of Design Theory and Methods for Innovation at the Center for Management Science (CGS), MINES Paris Tech, Paris.

Strategic Management of Innovation and Design

Pascal Le Masson

Benoît Weil

Armand Hatchuel

Forewords by Paul Rivier and Marc Maurer
Afterword by Jacques Lacambre and Dominique Levent
Translated from *Les processus d'innovation* by Alison Bissery and adapted by the authors

CAMBRIDGE
UNIVERSITY PRESS

CAMBRIDGE UNIVERSITY PRESS
Cambridge, New York, Melbourne, Madrid, Cape Town, Singapore,
São Paulo, Delhi, Tokyo, Mexico City

Cambridge University Press
The Edinburgh Building, Cambridge CB2 8RU, UK

Published in the United States of America by Cambridge University Press, New York

www.cambridge.org
Information on this title: www.cambridge.org/9780521182430

First published 2010
Reprinted 2012

Printed at MPG Books Group, UK

A catalogue record for this publication is available from the British Library

Library of Congress Cataloging-in-Publication Data

Le Masson, Pascal.
  [Processus d'innovation. English]
  Strategic management of innovation and design / Pascal Le Masson, Benoît Weil, Armand Hatchuel;
forewords by Paul Rivier and Marc Maurer; afterword by Jacques Lacambre and Dominique Levent;
translated from "Les processus d'innovation" by Alison Bissery and adapted by the authors.
    p. cm.
  ISBN 978-0-521-76877-1 (Hardback) – ISBN 978-0-521-18243-0 (pbk.)
  1. Technological innovations–Management. 2. Industrial design. 3. Strategic planning.
4. Organizational effectiveness. I. Weil, Benoît II. Hatchuel, Armand. III. Title.
  HD45.L33 2010
  658.4′063–dc22

                                                                                    2010014311

ISBN 978-0-521-76877-1 Hardback
ISBN 978-0-521-18243-0 Paperback

Contents

PART I   From innovation to innovative design

Foreword by Paul Rivier

It gives me great pleasure to preface this book on innovation. In 1994, a young student contacted me because he wanted to do a PhD thesis on innovation at Tefal. I agreed, but on the condition that he took an active part in designing new products. Vincent Chapel was more successful than I had ever imagined. He managed some very interesting innovations for Tefal and then went on to create several innovative start-ups, one of which is described here. Also, his PhD, directed by Armand Hatchuel, gave me the opportunity to get to know and appreciate the research presented by the authors of this book.

As a company director, the necessity for innovation seems quite natural to me. It is not just one priority among others, as all the rest depends on it. First, economic survival, of course, but also the social well-being of the personnel, which, in my view, is the main purpose of firms. In the different companies I have managed over the years, I have always personally committed myself to exploring all the possible paths for new developments. I believe this is part of a manager's responsibilities. If all we have to propose are efforts to increase productivity, we can hardly expect members of staff to be really committed to the firm. It was doubtless this frame of mind which encouraged us to adopt design reasoning and business decisions in favour of innovation. To my surprise, people often failed to understand this approach, despite our growth record and continued success over a number of years.

Had we invented a 'model', as the authors suggest? It is not for me to say. Nonetheless, as I followed the work with the Ecole des Mines team, I became convinced that, once it was correctly analyzed and studied, our experience could be of benefit to other firms. Very wisely, the authors methodically confronted our solutions with those found in other firms, including some outside France. Their efforts in modelling and generalization also widened the scope, as their propositions go well beyond our particular context and business sectors.

The notions of innovation field, repeated innovation, lineage, reusing knowledge and prudent strategy that the reader will discover in this book are perfectly in line with the spirit needed to innovate in the current competitive environment. I also greatly appreciate the efforts made to clarify notions such as R&D, project, rule-based design and innovative design, because misunderstandings can arise due to the standard language of innovation and are often obstacles to cohesive action within firms.

I leave it to the readers and to researchers to discuss these propositions in more detail.

I would like to say how much I have appreciated the discussions I have had with the authors over the years. This book is a precious contribution to our collective capacity for innovation. It provides the firms and the scholars concerned with a better understanding of the notions and methods, which are fully up to date and present a remarkable, effective step forward.

I still have the privilege of helping firms which have been through major difficulties but which, thanks to these same values and approaches, are returning to growth, to everyone's benefit and through their joint efforts. Innovation based on solidarity is the best solution for maintaining employment.

Paul Rivier,
former CEO, Tefal

Foreword by Marc Maurer

Innovation and competitiveness

The impact of globalization goes way beyond the issue of relocations of manufacturing plants. It throws firms into a new arena where competition is no longer based on product performance alone but also on the overall effectiveness of their innovation strategies. The authors' experience and the numerous discussions we had the privilege of taking part in over the past ten years enabled us to be involved in and put into practice many of the recommendations found here. The notion of organizing intensive innovation, the structuring of lineages of innovative products and the organizing of constantly evolving technological sectors have become management methods that place this 'RID' at the heart of the firm's strategy. One of its main advantages is to structure the long-term view whilst also giving the management sufficient confidence to manage the short and medium term.

Until the 1990s, teams in charge of managing innovation – the R&D and marketing departments – were expected to deliver results whilst roughly keeping to the specifications, timetables and budgets. This operating method was often project-based; it brought new products onto the market in satisfactory conditions and helped to keep challengers at bay. In western countries, companies managed to maintain their growth and profitability. However, outsiders then started to improve their performance: they acquired technological capacities and were quick to learn, meaning they were able to almost catch up with the innovators, who were then obliged to speed up the rate of product renewals. At the same time, the growing number of new technologies that firms had to master led to an explosion in the financial burden of innovation, introducing the need for far more rigorous management of R&D resources. The management of innovation – in terms of both contributions and costs – is now an area where a firm's competitiveness is at play and where management methods have changed quite spectacularly. The good old recipes, where the CEO's intuition and the R&D managers' experience were sufficient for the firm to maintain its leadership, have been replaced by these far more structured methods, which use a more holistic approach to innovation.

The authors of this book, P. Le Masson, B. Weil and A. Hatchuel, have dissected a certain number of real cases. With a solid theoretical foundation, this comprehensive work provides a new formal framework for organizing Research-Innovation-Development. This book proposes a method which 'organizes' the interface between R&D (which delivers knowledge to the firm by consuming some resources), the market (the 'I' part) and the top management charged with organizing the strategic choices. This new method for managing RID puts into perspective a horizontal relationship between the technologies, at a given time, together with the notion of evolution over time. This helps optimize the synergies between projects and then build up the knowledge with a view to maximizing the results without consuming too many of the firm's resources. Those who take inspiration from this book and put its principles into practice will find it provides a powerful new competitive weapon.

Marc Maurer,
Head of R&D Centers,
Saint-Gobain Glass

Figures

Tables

Acknowledgements

This book is the result of a research project which lasted several years. It is often hard to say when projects began, but in this case it is easy to put a date on it. In 1994, the Mines ParisTech (former Ecole des Mines de Paris) created an option (a specific curriculum of the Master's Degree) in Engineering Design and Management, a combination of teaching and research areas that was quite unusual at that time. Under Armand Hatchuel's responsibility, a team of teachers was brought together, including Benoît Weil, Jean-Claude Sardas and Christophe Midler. Pascal Le Masson joined us a few years later.

Our aim was to combine design disciplines (engineering and industrial), innovation and project management and, in the longer term, to lead the design sciences to the same level of maturity as the sciences of decision-making and programming. In a few years, the research programme gathered speed at an unexpected rate. Most areas of teaching were gradually reorganized around an inspiring and unifying theoretical core, the C-K (Concept-Knowledge) design theory (Hatchuel 1996; Hatchuel and Weil 2001, 2003), which is now taught in a number of establishments. The programme was also in line with a major preoccupation, the necessity of strengthening firms' innovation capabilities. The progress made in this area helped us build up precious partnerships with many leading firms. This book owes a great deal to this original teaching and research project, although it looks at only part of the areas covered by it.

Our thanks go first to the teachers in the Engineering Design and Management option, and in particular to Christophe Midler (CRG, Ecole Polytechnique), who was involved in the project from the start and made an eminent contribution to this research. To Maurille Larivière (StrateCollege Designers), who provided remarkable industrial design experience for our work. And to Blanche Segrestin, Franck Aggeri and Philippe Lefebvre (MINES ParisTech), whose contributions often served as references for our research. Our warm thanks also to all the students who took the Engineering

Design and Management option and whose final-year projects were a source of progress and motivation for the teachers.

This book would not have been possible without the support of our many partners in firms. Our special thanks to Paul Rivier, former CEO of Tefal; to Marc Maurer, Director of R&D, Saint-Gobain Flat Glass; and to Jacques Lacambre, former Director of DARP, Renault, and Dominique Levent, Innovation Centre, Renault, who inspired this research and who were kind enough to write the afterword for this book.

We would also like to thank Georges Amar, head of the Foresight and Innovative Design department at RATP; Frank Batocchi, DRIA, PSA; Eloi Baudoux, DREAM, Renault; Vincent Chapel, CEO of Archimed Group; Pascal Daloz, VP of Dassault Systèmes; Philippe Doublet, preliminary projects, Renault; Yves Dubreil, DREAM, Renault; Billy Frederiksson, former VP for R&D, Saab Aerospace; Hubert Maillard, platform director, PSA; Gunnar Holmberg, SAAB Aerospace; Jean-Hervé Poisson, Renault; and Jean-Pierre Tetaz, CEO of Archilab, for their kind support and enlightening contributions to our research.

Our thanks also to Jean-Pierre Delhomme, Laurent Jammes, Philippe Lacour-Gayet and Yves Morel from Schlumberger; Alain Dieulin, R&D, Vallourec; Bernard Castan and Alex Kuhn, SAGEM; and Bruno Cozzati, Philippe Laporte Galaa and Jacques Merrien from Renault. And to so many others whom we must ask to forgive us for not being able to mention them here.

To Dominique Foray (IMD, Lausanne), Edith Heurgon (Cerisy-la-Salle cultural centre), Patrick Llerena (Beta University, Strasbourg), Pascal Petit (Cepremap, CNRS), Denis Clodic (Ecole des Mines), Iskander Gökalp (CNRS), Rami Shani (University of California), Susan Mohrman (University of California), Peter Magnusson (University of Karlstadt), Maria Elmquist (Chalmers Institute), Carliss Baldwin (Harvard Business School), Victor Seidel (University of Oxford), Alan MacCormack (MIT), Rafael Ramirez (University of Oxford), Annabelle Gawer (Imperial College), Francesco Zirpoli (University of Salerno), Markus Becker (University of Southern Denmark), Franck Piller (Aachen RWTH), Yoram Reich (Tel Aviv University), Jonathan Edelman and Ade Mabogunje (Stanford University), Eswaran Subrahmanian (Carnegie Mellon), Chris MacMahon (Bath University), Jean-François Boujut, Michel Tollenaere and Eric Blanco (Polytechnique Grenoble), Toshiharu Taura (Kobe University), Yukari Nagai (Tokyo University) and Ken Starkey (Nottingham University) for their inspiring research and for our stimulating discussions.

Many of the most fruitful exchanges were made possible through the meetings and conferences of leading academic communities: the Design Society, to which we express our grateful thanks for the creation of a Special Interest Group on design theory; EURAM (European Academy of Management), which hosts several tracks on design and innovation; and IPDM (International Product Development Management), a pioneering community in its field. We are most grateful to IPDM's Chairman, Christer Karlsson, and its board for welcoming the early pieces of our work.

Our most sincere thanks to all the researchers at MINES ParisTech's Centre for Management Science for their precious contributions. Warm thanks to Céline Bourdon and Martine Jouanon for their help. And to our colleagues at the Fenix Centre in Sweden, Niclas Adler, Flemming Norrgrenn and Bengt Stymne, and to all the centre's Executive PhD students for their welcome and for their contributions.

We are also most grateful to Alison Bissery for her rigorous and respectful translation. She joins us in extending our most sincere thanks to Maria Elmquist and Doug Robinson, who greatly contributed to improving this English version of the book.

We warmly thank Ken Starkey for his intellectual support in preparing the translation project. Four anonymous reviewers also gave us insightful comments to improve this English version and we are most grateful to Paula Parish, who was kind enough to include this book in her collection at Cambridge University Press. Finally, we would like to thank the partners of the Chair of Design Theory and Methods for Innovation, Dassault Systèmes, RATP, Renault, Thales and Vallourec for their help with this book and their ongoing support for the latest episodes.

Introduction: from R&D to RID

There is now widespread agreement that innovation holds the key to future economic and social prosperity in developed countries. Experts studying contemporary capitalism also agree that the battle against unemployment and relocations can be won only through innovation. It is *the* great challenge of the day and, for many specialists, the only possible solution to the problems facing western societies and to the current recession. Whether it is studied from a local or a global standpoint, innovation is the only way of satisfying the social, environmental and economic facets of growth, and of increasing levels of education whilst also creating value, jobs and purchasing power. It also seems to be the only way of reconciling, at least temporarily, employees, managers, consumers and shareholders.

In the face of such unanimity, governments in developed and in emerging economies have set up various incentive schemes designed to promote innovation, including special subsidies and aids for investment in R&D. Initiatives such as the EU common policy aimed at 'building a knowledge-based economy', notions such as 'lifelong learning and key competencies' and even the 'information society' all translate the same imperative for innovation. But is enough being done to meet the challenge?

A great deal of research has been carried out by firms and government departments, but what do we actually know about innovation? For instance, do we know which factors enhance a firm's innovation capability and whether financial incentives guarantee effective innovation? Can we use the traditional views of innovation to build the innovative firms and regions of the future? Are the current R&D organizations and the traditional engineering and marketing methods suited to a high pace of innovation? Do we have a set of management principles that can be taken as 'best practices' for managing innovation? It has to be said that, thanks to past and present interest in innovation, scholars from different disciplines (management, social studies, economics, etc.) have learned a lot about the importance of innovation and the stakes involved, but we still understand little about the relationships between 'knowledge', 'innovation', 'growth' and 'research'.

These are the issues we sought to address in the research project described in this book. In the course of our work, we made use of a number of international experiences in industry, together with new theoretical frameworks. Our first observation was that innovation has changed! Our second was that organizing an innovation process is neither simply a question of how much is spent on R&D, nor of better dialogue between the different functions and departments. Innovation needs more than just a good dose of courage and good forward planning. But above all, our observations led us to believe that fundamental, long-term changes are in store and that all organizations and professions must be prepared to face them. Actually, bearing in mind industrial and entrepreneurial history, this is not really surprising: innovation always involves more than just 'good ideas'. Each of the great industrial revolutions was linked to new forms of innovation, either in content, functions or organizations.

Innovation-based capitalism therefore faces a new challenge. The actors are aware of the stakes involved in innovation, but now they must be convinced of the need for a radical change in the place and the role of innovation in firms. And this change must be carefully prepared and organized. The following propositions clarify our point of view and sum up the general outline of the book:

1. Innovation is now *intensive*: it is systematic, repeated and oriented, instead of random and episodic. In its new form, it has become a major driving force for contemporary capitalism and it will determine the conditions of international economic competition in the future.

2. An intensive innovation process is *not the same thing as either research or development*, or traditional R&D, conceived as cooperation between the two. It is essentially based on *innovative design* activities, whose specific principles of rationality, efficiency, organization and management will be explained throughout this book.

3. Firms must make room for *innovative design and its organization* in their strategies and structures.

4. These wide-reaching changes can be expressed by a simple formula: *the transition from R&D to RID*. The new 'I' between research and development refers to the functions and competencies of innovative design. It is neither simply another structure or body, nor a simple coordinating function. It has an original, specific mission. We will see how innovative design activities are not only exploratory but *activate*, throughout the

firm, an *innovation-oriented metabolism*, i.e. a collective capacity to continually and simultaneously recreate *sources of value* (products, concepts, patents, environmental and social values, etc.) and new *competencies* (knowledge, expertise, rules, functions, etc.).

The transition from R&D to RID entails a drastic change in the way firms are managed and has economic, social and ecological impacts as it concerns all the different dimensions of innovation. The change is not confined to large international groups but affects all organizations. In fact, it could have the same universal thrust as Taylorism and Fayolism at the beginning of the twentieth century.

Before going any further, it is worth pausing for a moment to think about what we mean by 'innovation', as its different forms can be somewhat disconcerting.

1 Innovation, a victim to fashion?

Everything involves 'innovation' today, and its omnipresence emphasizes its natural ambivalence. It is such a vague, well-worn notion that it tends to leave people perplexed or to prompt an ironical smile.

Innovation is often synonymous with fashion, gadgets or illusions, witness expressions such as 'umpteenth reform', 'so-called novelty', 'patch-up job', etc. It is true that the notion has little substance if nothing is done to explain its content or the economic and social value it creates. The notion of 'innovation' *does not mean anything in itself*: the same innovative proposal will be assessed differently by any two observers. However, the same thing can be said of 'research': a new truth is not necessarily interesting. When companies began to set up research laboratories about a hundred years ago, there were always debates about the value of the research produced. It is interesting to study the mechanisms of innovation only because *the question of the value of the innovation is an integral part of it*. This means that the more a productive activity is innovative, the greater the need for methods to assess its value. This can be seen, for instance, in cultural or artistic creation where the critics are fully involved in the production process. Similarly, the most active consumer organizations are found in the most innovative markets (automobile, IT, etc.).

Innovation is always associated with change, uncertainty and risk. Unpleasant surprises can be found lurking in ambush behind the most brilliant ideas. By definition, innovation is unsettling and upsets people's habits. However, this implies that innovation is unintended and comes out of the blue, whereas in reality it can be intentional, prepared and organized to anticipate risks. This is the case for explorers, in sports or in science, who are all the better prepared and all the more organized in situations where they do not know what they are going to find. So it is not innovation as such that merits study but the ways and means, methods and mechanisms that design, elaborate and form the innovation process. Without such considerations, the term 'innovation' loses its substance and ends up provoking a mixture of enthusiasm, confusion and suspicion.

Commercial, technical or industrial innovations that create value are hardly a recent phenomenon. More than 200 years ago, during the Industrial Revolution in Britain, there were already debates about the advantages and disadvantages of 'industrial progress'; and the *Belle Epoque* before the First World War saw the birth of the car, Taylorism, electricity, bureaucracy, industrial design, underground rail systems, etc. But by now, in a civilization that has already undergone four or five major waves of social or technical change, are firms not used to innovation? Do they not already have well-organized, well-managed R&D departments, at least the largest among them? Everything seems to confirm a simple idea: there is nothing less innovative than talking about innovation. In which case, *why write yet another book about it?*

Why another book?

There were several reasons for undertaking the research project presented in this book. In the past twenty years, there have been great changes in the pace of innovation in the workings of contemporary capitalism and in its content. We put forward the idea of an emerging *innovation-intensive capitalism,* which obliges all organizations to invent functions based on innovation. Starting from this assumption, we developed a research strategy that differed from the usual orientations in several respects:

We did not study innovation, as such, *as a problem or a phenomenon,* but all the activities and organizations which, over the course of time, have been set up to *generate, direct and evaluate* innovations.

We therefore focused on the *design activities,* i.e. the activities used to conceive and formulate innovations. Traditionally divided into R&D, engineering and industrial design, these activities had increasingly been studied from different perspectives. It became more and more common for the notion of 'design' to be mentioned as a central resource for management thinking, yet no *adequate theoretical frame-work* emerged until recently.

Our approach *calls into question the central notion of R&D* and paves the way for developing a theory on *innovative design activities,* a major challenge for business history and theory.

Intensive innovation: constantly questioning the identity of objects

Contrary to a commonly held idea, innovation is not a natural, almost random phenomenon to be found in practically all organizations and firms.[1] Whether it takes the form of a new technique, new aesthetics or new work organization, innovation is above all *the result of the activity of communities that determine its form and its conditions of acceptability.* The history of architects, engineers, industrial designers and researchers illustrates this point. Although the need for innovation has taken different forms depending on the era or the sector of business, each time it has led to the emergence of new 'innovation professionals' with their own means of analysis and experimentation and with their own principles of action.

Intensive innovation: value creation through competition

In less than half a century, the process of generating innovations has become the major competitive playing field for contemporary capitalism and a vital source of sustainable development for contemporary societies. We will see in Chapter 1 that, as far as firms are concerned, it is a question of surviving in an innovation-intensive capitalist system. In societies that are used to regular changes in projects and lifestyles, it is even the fundamental way of creating value because, whether the value is judged on the basis of profits or on the progress achieved in terms of human, ecological or social development, it always requires innovative activities. This is one of the lessons to be learned from recent work on the role of innovation in sustainable development.[2] We must therefore stress a fundamental point in our work: innovation itself is not a new question, *but its place, scope and content have changed* and it is now characteristic of competition. Innovation has become intensive.

---

[1] Despite their sophistication, economic models of endogenous growth that try to take innovation into account still model the birth of innovations as random sequences.

[2] *See* the study on sustainable development policies proposed by Aggeri *et al.* (2005).

Today, innovation concerns more than ongoing industrial improvements or the updating of techniques and practices, or even fundamental research that might find applications without targeting them. The word 'intensive' implies that innovation covers more than just technical or aesthetic progress. All the visible or invisible characteristics of a product or service are potential fields for innovation. For instance, when the notion of 'service' was emphasized in the 1980s, an object's accessibility and ease of use were focused on as examples of innovation spaces. Similarly, the fact that car safety has become a key issue does not mean that today's drivers are more worried about accidents than their counterparts were in the 1950s. Above all, it means that the car manufacturers have decided to compete on this particular front and to let the consumers know about it with their continual references to Euro NCAP stars. As a result, consumers have increased their demands for enhanced car safety measures. The relationship between the notion of innovation and the notion of needs is complex: today's innovation will be tomorrow's need and vice versa. For firms, the challenge consists in being better than their competitors at navigating between the innovations and the needs.

In practice, this inevitably involves introducing new functions or new value spaces, which then stimulate the development of new techniques, which in turn give birth to new aesthetic qualities or new functions. In this way, intensive innovation extends and generalizes an inventive, self-producing, self-strengthening mechanism, whose most striking effect is first to question and then to renew the actual identity of given objects or values.

A key notion: the versatile identity of objects

For many firms, innovation is focused on products or services *with a relatively stable identity*. In general, these firms target well-identified customers and make regular improvements to products' known characteristics and functions. For example, computer manufacturers try to increase speeds and storage capacity because they know that their customers are expecting this. However, when they introduce networking functions, they are making *a significant change to the object's identity*. What was considered an advanced computer yesterday may be seen as a simple terminal tomorrow. New user patterns can also emerge: for example, the recent introduction of the MP3 format allows users to use their computers to download, store and exchange music, thus changing the way computers are apprehended as objects.

Contrary to what is often said, this is not only a question of nomad technology. As early as the fifteenth century, the first watches were nomadic objects, too. However, their identity could not be changed as it can today: they could strike the hour, mark the days and years or be hidden away in magnificent casings, but they could not be turned into walking libraries.

The specific characteristic of innovation-intensive capitalism is precisely that *it questions and then accelerates the renewal of the identity of objects.* It obliges firms and consumers to explore and discover new functions and new uses. *As employees or as consumers,* everybody must take into account unknown technologies and be prepared to develop or to appropriate them. Intensive innovation is therefore not just about changes in production methods or new goods. Traditional language does not account for the permanent need to build new systems of knowledge and of exchange and therefore fails to address the issue of the intense collective work involved in redesigning *the markets, competencies and user values that characterize contemporary capitalism.*

Recent history of computers, mobile phones or even household electrical goods provides particularly good examples of this new form of capitalism. Over the years, the functions offered by these devices and the ways in which they can be used have become more and more inventive. In the past forty years, the very nature of computers has changed; in less than ten years, the internet has completely upset communication systems worldwide; in five years, the mobile phone has become a commonplace accessory. In the latter case, the introduction of camera and video functions is one of the most striking examples of drastic changes in an object's identity. In short, the omnipresence, versatility and ambivalence of innovations are an inescapable feature of the changes in the identity of objects inherent to innovation-intensive capitalism.

More fundamentally, people are not used to thinking about the identity of objects and how this identity can change. This can be a dramatic source of social exclusion when common, practical knowledge becomes obsolete. Moreover, the greater part of our classic culture, both scientific and philosophical, is based on stable object identities: a house is always a house, a chair always a chair. Consequently, the great wealth of classic thinking does not provide mental or cognitive models to help us examine variations in the identity of objects. This is one of the key points we will be addressing, by proposing *design theories that enable us to study objects with unstable identities.*

Financial capitalism and innovation capitalism: avoiding the pincer effect

Even when firms are aware of the vital need for innovation, the global context makes their task difficult. They are caught in a *pincer effect* (Hatchuel 2004b): on the one hand, they need to enhance their innovative activities by stepping up capacities and resources, but on the other, they need to meet the demands of *financial capitalism*, i.e. the system that emerged from the recent globalization of capital markets. This system will no doubt be regulated more strictly after the recent crisis, yet financial efficiency will continue to be an important criterion for management: not only must firms meet stricter demands for returns on investment but they must also face up to competition from low labour cost countries. They are already competing in terms of production, but everything points to the fact that in the future they will also be *competing on the innovation processes as such*. Financial capitalism means that firms not only have to optimize the volume of innovations and the investments dedicated to them but also ensure that *the innovation processes are relevant, original and profitable*.

The combination of financial capitalism and innovation capitalism is a *formidable challenge* for all the current management doctrines and may prove to be an impossible equation for many firms. In some cases innovation capability will be sacrificed for short-term financial constraints, thus leading to slow suffocation; in others, the opposite scenario will prevail, with bankruptcy or unfriendly takeover bids around the corner. The solution is difficult but unavoidable: firms must *build new strategies combining innovation and financial considerations*. The art of management consists in the art of compromise, but if managers are to find original, value-added solutions, they must be able to control the different elements involved, reorienting them or shifting their emphasis as and when necessary. A wide range of management tools is now available for the financial aspects, but the same does not apply for innovation activities and functions, for which no appropriate tools exist. It is therefore difficult to combine a financial approach that can be controlled and measured, and an innovation approach that lacks the tools required to understand and manage it. Innovation capitalism hence runs the risk of being restricted and stifled by financial capitalism.

In our view, the pincer effect of these two aspects of contemporary capitalism leaves no doubt whatsoever about *the urgent need for research to identify the systems and practices required for strengthening innovation capabilities and activities*.

2   In search of a 'model firm' for innovation

Since the Second World War, several streams of research have addressed the question of innovation. A great variety of issues has been studied from a number of angles, each raising its correlative questions. For instance, innovation in terms of economic policy with questions about government incentives; as a risk for citizens, with questions about whether this was acceptable; as a commercial challenge, with questions about the best markets for the new products; as a technical challenge, with questions on the sort of research to be done and the experts to be consulted; and as a problem of creativity, with questions on where to find creative people and how to train them. And, of course, there were those who thought that innovation was and will inevitably continue to be unorganized. In short, in the past half a century, the different schools of thought have accumulated studies and work papers, fighting each other's ideas or ignoring them along the way. This book adopts an alternative stance.

Innovation as a management object: techniques and organizations

Our aim is to identify collective cognitive techniques that can be used to *manage, steer and organize innovation as an object*. We are concerned with everything that makes collective bodies aware of their innovation capabilities and enables them to increase their pace of innovation whilst keeping an eye on its general direction and the way it evolves over time. Despite constant efforts from economics, management and sociology, up until now academic research has made little progress in this respect.[3]

Silence from the major consultants

There is one particularly clear sign of the gaps in this subject: although there is an evident need to innovate, even the largest organization specialists and consulting firms seem very timid in their offers of services and hardly communicate at all on these issues. Apparently elementary questions such as how the innovation process can be addressed, which principles to use for action and management, whether innovation is the same thing as applied

---

[3] As shown in a recent overview of international research (Hage and Meeus 2006).

research or whether R&D activities are sufficient to build an innovation policy receive only prudent answers.

The current situation will not surprise those who know the world of industry. Innovation has been a driving force in industrial expansion for the past two centuries, *but doctrines have not been fully developed regarding the way it works and how it is managed and implemented.* In fact, innovative processes have often been developed secretly or at least in an unauthorized fashion, even in the most advanced organizations, with what is now commonly called 'skunk work'.

There are theoretical, historical and cultural reasons for these shortcomings that we will come back to later. Nonetheless, the idea of studying firms' capability to innovate and their management methods comes up against a sizeable obstacle that has tended to go unnoticed: for several decades now, we have not had a 'model firm' that managers, experts and employees all accept as the prime example of uncontested best practices in terms of innovation. This situation is very different from other periods and from other issues in the management sciences.

Management without a model?

After the Second World War, the major American firms embodied the most rational, most efficient organization model. Japanese firms then overtook them in the 1980s, demonstrating their supremacy in terms of flexibility and quality in the manufacturing industry. It must be said that Japanese production methods had an enormous impact on industrial executives and managers at that time, despite the fact that they used a variety of sometimes debatable methods that were not always applicable in other cultural contexts. During this period, Toyota was unanimously accepted as an example to study and sometimes to copy. Several authors even started referring to Toyotism, like Fordism in the past.

There is no equivalent in the field of innovation today. Innovation is seen as a survival strategy, *but there is no firm that everybody can immediately copy, imitate or simply use as an inspiration* and a reference for its innovation capability and for its methods. Of course, there are companies that are often mentioned for a particular, successful innovation: 3M for the Post-it, Sony for the Walkman, Renault for the Scenic, Apple for its iPhone, etc. However, the literature and above all the actors in the field have great difficulty relating these success stories to organizations, processes or procedures that they can copy or adapt. Similarly, the current ICT giants such as Microsoft, eBay and

Google are often given as examples of innovative firms, but there is no really stimulating or inspiring body of management doctrine rigorously associated with the action of these heroes of the moment.

What explains this lack of a model? One possibility is the state of firms. After all, even a quick survey of private or public companies – including the most advanced ones – is enough to realize that they can easily describe their project management systems, that they often have an R&D team and a protocol for new product launches, but *very few of them can describe their innovation process with any conviction or precision.* However, a completely different assumption can also be put forward for there being no best practices for innovation: could the lack of a model be due to *researchers' analytical frameworks and observation methods?*

The researcher's 'analytical glasses'

Putting innovation aside for the moment, let us look at the question in more general terms: *how do researchers recognize original management models?* To do so, they must be capable of:

identifying *original practices* and being able to recognize them as such;

interpreting these original practices in a *theoretical framework* that explains their originality, conditions of effectiveness and contingency criteria.

Returning to the field of innovation, what theoretical frameworks are available to complete these two steps?

Previous research on innovation has continued to rely too heavily on the functional divisions of management (strategy, R&D, audit, operations, HR management, etc.) and on the frameworks of contemporary economic and sociological thinking. The best research on innovation has been in the form of criticism. In management, the debate has focused on the contrast between 'mechanistic' (bureaucratic) structures and organic (adhocratic) structures (Burns and Stalker 1961), monodextrous and ambidextrous firms (Tushman, Anderson and O'Reilly 1997), closed and open forms of innovation (Chesbrough 2003), etc. In economics, the issue of innovation has given rise to fundamental criticism of the classic theories on markets and growth, but no appropriate analytical frameworks have yet emerged for economic action. In our view, this difficulty stems from the persistence of *a microeconomy built exclusively on production functions,* whereas innovation, as we shall see throughout this book, is based on 'design functions' (Hatchuel and Le Masson 2006). In sociology, research on innovation has above all stressed the need to mobilize networks of multiple players and very diverse institutions.[4] Overall, these studies have a major impact: they correct the fact that the traditional models in economics, management and sociology are too narrow, as they were originally built by observing bureaucracies, civil services, large factories or markets where there was relatively little innovation or, in any case, that were not well suited to innovation-intensive capitalism with its rapid renewal of object identities.

Yet it seems that we still know little about the reasoning, the collective learning processes or the management tools that can be mobilized to help communities increase their capability to innovate.

A discovery-oriented research methodology

These observations led to the specific *research approach* described in this book. Generally speaking, management researchers try to identify the principles of organization found in 'best practice' firms, but this implies that the latter are easy to identify. The fact that no one company is acknowledged as a reference in the area of innovation meant that our research followed a somewhat original path as *it had to look for the empirical facts and for the theory at the same time.* We can distinguish between three phases in our work: empirical discovery, theorization identification and intervention enrichment.

a) **Empirical discovery: original practices**. A series of long-term 'intervention research' projects (David and Hatchuel 2007) enabled us to highlight *original practices*, particularly well adapted to innovation. Some of the firms studied and accompanied from the inside (Tefal, Avanti, Saint-Gobain Sekurit, Saab Aerospace, etc.) proved to be particularly *original in their ways of managing innovation*. These firms were ultimately chosen for this study because they had managed to maintain strong innovation capability, sometimes over several decades, even though they were not always particularly well known for this.

b) **Theorization identification: modelling innovative design**. The original practices were then theorized, formalized and analysed to highlight the reasoning behind *innovative design activities* and their organization. The theoretical models were based on the *C-K design theory* (Hatchuel 1996a;

---

[4] Our colleagues Michel Callon and Bruno Latour at the Ecole des Mines Centre for the Sociology of Innovation developed an actor-network theory, which criticizes classic diffusionist views of innovation in sociology. However, such criticism is not valid for management research, which has always focused on the development phases of new products and innovations.

Hatchuel and Weil 2003, 2009) and not on the traditional methods used in the management or social sciences. The use of non-intuitive, formal models that require an effort of abstraction was justified in this case because they are highly interpretative and explicative. They confirmed our assumption: *innovation capability is based on reasoning that is not easy to understand with ordinary approaches.*

This is not all that surprising, considering that everyday life does not provide us with many opportunities to try our hand at designing new objects. Any thought given to creative activities is more or less limited to the arts and usually tends to be in the form of a judgement or comment on the work rather than on the design process itself.

c) **Intervention enrichment: validatory experience**. The emerging models of innovative design then served as a reference framework for intervention research projects[5] in several companies (Renault, RATP, Schlumberger, Rhodia, Air Liquide, etc.) that had expressed an interest in studying and enhancing their capability to innovate. The results of this work validated *the principles of a transition from R&D to RID*, i.e. confirmed that the methods of innovative design make a decisive contribution, distinct from research and development, whilst strengthening the overall innovation capability.

Management research as an actor in business history

By putting a focus on discovery rather than on confirmation, the traditional objectives of management research are set in a different context and change on several levels.

a) It is generally accepted that discovery and observation in the 'field' cannot be separated from *theoretical and conceptual invention*. We can only 'see' what can be 'thought'; this is the condition of scientific research. Nonetheless, this 'law of nature' seems less rigorous in management or in the social sciences, where rigorous and well-documented empirical observations appear to suffice for the production of knowledge. However, this 'natural' approach is no longer sufficient when the

---

[5] Most of this research was carried out by the authors, but we should also point out the contributions made by our students of the Design Engineering Option at the Ecole des Mines de Paris, under our direction. Work by students from the Ecole Polytechnique for the Master's Degree in Project, Innovation, Design (under the direction of C. Midler) and students from the INA-PG, option Innovation and Management, Life Sciences (under the direction of M. Nakhla), also made precious contributions to the research on these questions.

actors under observation mobilize reasoning and actions that are not fully understood or that cannot be identified using *ordinary descriptions*. This is precisely the situation with innovative design activities. They move away from the most natural notions of thought and language and can be studied only using a theoretical framework to help identify their approach.

b) This type of investigation no longer assumes that management history has already taken place for research to be able to study it. Management research is not exclusively *ex post*, but can have an impact on the changes taking place in firms. It cannot determine the course of industrial history on its own, but it can change it by extending the range of models available to the actors involved.

c) Finally, this approach fits in with *a foundationalist perspective of the management sciences*. Discussed in length elsewhere (David, Hatchuel and Laufer 2000; Hatchuel 2009), this perspective suggests that rather than studying 'innovation' as a universal notion defined using standard disciplinary hypotheses, it should be studied *as a specific type of collective action in which practical and organizational methods evolve over time*. For our research, this consists of focusing on the collective capabilities for innovation that correspond to the current forms of competition and capitalism.

3   Outline of the book

The following pages present the layout of the book with a brief summary of each chapter.

Chapter 1 illustrates the phenomenon of intensive innovation with a series of situations encountered during our research projects. The tricky questions they pose in terms of strategy, methods and steering processes have been partly addressed in previous research but have not been convincingly solved, which explains why we chose to adopt a different approach. Our demonstration is, of course, based on an analysis of the different streams of research on innovation, but, for easier reference, we have included our main summary of the literature in a separate appendix.

Chapter 2 describes our approach, which looks at the management reasoning, tools and practices that have made the activity of innovation possible throughout history, as 'rule-based' collective action in firms. We show that the specific nature of competition through intensive innovation poses a theoretical enigma for traditional models of innovation.

Chapter 3 solves the enigma with a change of angle. On the basis that innovation is inevitably the result of a design process, we demonstrate that new design models and theories offer useful frameworks for deriving instruments to support and manage innovative action. This different focus provided us with an object to study and the tools to explore it, and paved the way for our work at the heart of the innovative activities of several firms.

Chapter 4 plunges into the universe of Tefal in Rumilly, at the beginning of the 1990s when the company was headed by Paul Rivier.[6] The experience was as abundant as the miraculous draught of fishes. We discovered a firm whose strategies were entirely focused on the simultaneous renewal of products and competencies. The study was made possible by the total immersion of a PhD student (Chapel 1997), who later used the model discovered at Tefal to develop several ranges of innovative products and a number of patents.

Chapter 5 draws up the key notions of the 'Tefal' model, describing *a system of repeated innovation* that stimulates growth despite harsh competition. The model is based on *prudent design strategies*, built on 'product lineages', which organize a powerful *metabolism* of knowledge within the company. Tefal provided an initial 'model' for our research, with processes that are rarely seen or at least scarcely developed in other firms. But is it really a model, i.e. does the reasoning describe practices that could be effective in other contexts?

In Chapter 6, we follow the team of a start-up, Avanti, which provided a good answer to our question. The company was founded by our former PhD student and we gave it our support. By adapting the rationale of the Tefal model to its own context, the start-up won the national trophy for innovation. This convinced us that the model had solid foundations and a logical framework that was far more than a simple management 'recipe' or a superficial invention. To understand the possible consequences for large firms, we then had to take another look at the traditional notion of R&D.

Chapter 7 describes some of the ways in which R&D was historically built up in large firms. At its beginnings research (R) was not related to innovation except in some rare, though particularly instructive, cases. Above all, it helped introduce scientific methods for validating manufacturing processes. Development (D), meanwhile, was historically a remarkable invention for domesticating innovation through rule-based design. However, by upsetting

---

[6] A firm is studied at a specific point in time and the analyses are valid only for the period of observation in question. They can obviously not be taken to illustrate the company's present situation.

the identity of objects, competition through intensive innovation under-
mines the very foundations of *D*. How can R&D be adapted to suit intensive
innovation? The problem of combining innovative activities with R&D has
not been clearly formulated until now, which explains the recurrent crises
suffered by research and development departments in large firms.

In Chapter 8, we compare the Tefal model with the traditional R&D
concept and come to the conclusion that innovative design activities are
neither *R* nor *D*. A third system for renewing value in firms is proposed, the
'*I*' function, which has not been clearly identified in industrial history
before. This chapter describes the missions and structures of this function,
which is dedicated to innovation. In more scientific terms, we call it an
'innovative design function', thus rigorously designating its activity and its
methods. This leads to the RID triad, which replaces the former R&D. Does
it already exist in certain firms or can it be said that innovative firms move
spontaneously towards this type of operational system?

Chapter 9 returns to the world of firms for further debate on this point.
This time we look at a major French glassmaker for the car industry, Saint-
Gobain Sekurit, a firm which has a long tradition in innovation. Over the
years, the firm's R&D has undergone remarkable changes. We show that they
can be easily understood and interpreted using the RID model, which
provides a series of highly coherent results. The notion of innovative design
therefore confronts us with a radical change that could have serious repercussions for industrial firms. A rigorous formal framework and operational
tools are required to cater for this change.

Chapter 10 examines the theoretical problems involved in building a
formal framework. In order to study the empirical facts, which can be better
understood using theory, a solid methodological grounding is given to RID
by introducing the C-K theory (C for concepts, K for knowledge), initially
proposed by A. Hatchuel and further developed with B. Weil, then with
P. Le Masson. This theory serves as a formal framework for the operations
that guide innovative design work. We then demonstrate the distinction
between traditional project management and the process of managing an
innovative design activity carried out by the 'expansion' of 'innovation
fields' in several original, interdependent 'design spaces'. This results in the
elaboration of pertinent management tools.

Chapters 11, 12 and 13 illustrate, on the basis of a series of industrial
experiences, how innovation fields can be structured and managed.
A distinction is made between three main sorts of innovative design – Type 1:
innovation fields where new values are added (e.g. a new approach to

comfort or to the environment); Type 2: innovation fields with technological changes and regeneration of functions (e.g. mobilizing new energies); and Type 3: innovation fields resulting in the design of products with a high scientific content.

Chapter 14 studies the transition from innovative design to rule-based design from a practical standpoint, looking at the need to make the concepts resulting from the innovative field more concrete by gradually turning them into product lineages destined for commercial use. We demonstrate that this change cannot be made through a simple transfer but is a question of concerted engineering work carried out in a series of stages. In this way, the functions can be reorganized, often an indispensable condition for a smooth transition to rule-based design.

Chapter 15 explains that innovative design is often not restricted to activities within a single firm, as shown by the large increase in exploratory partnerships in the past ten years. However, the experience is often disappointing for the simple reason that innovative design imposes a style of cooperation that combines two distinct approaches, the first consisting of exploring and revising the objects of the innovative design and the second consisting of the need for cohesion in the partners' interests and expectations. Based on recent work, we demonstrate how this process can be managed in such a way as to limit the risks for the partnership. This provides some key points for understanding and managing multi-firm projects for innovative design.

In the conclusion, we return to the consequences of RID in firms and the changes it implies in terms of management. We distinguish between three eras in modern management history. The first era dealt with the major operating parameters: sales, production and structural and functional organization. The second era took into account projects and functions; firms managed product renewals but kept to their core professions. Besides the globalization and financial orientation of contemporary businesses, a third era of modern management may be emerging with the introduction of RID. It must cater for changes in the identity of products and services and inevitably has different missions, methods of intervention and approaches from those used in the previous eras. Although it is hard to imagine how management will evolve during this third era, future developments are bound to have an important impact on the survival of organizations and firms if innovation-intensive capitalism persists.

PART I

From innovation to innovative design

1 What do we know about innovation? Testing the economic and social sciences

What do we know about innovation? Apart from inherited ideas and a host of scientific articles on the subject, do we now have a clear picture of the problems raised by innovation in firms today? To introduce the issue from a concrete foundation, we shall begin by describing a number of real case examples in which the authors have been personally involved and which became the starting point for several of the 'innovation adventures' described in greater detail later on in the book.

1.1   Contemporary innovation: received ideas versus facts

1.1.1   Mad ideas? Yes, but well-managed ones!

In the early 2000s, at Linköping University, Sweden, several research teams were working on a project to design unmanned aerial vehicles (UAVs) for traffic surveillance. For the project's promoters, the WITAS project was a 'blue sky project', i.e. aimed at stimulating the researchers' imaginations rather than designing a commercial product. The researchers' first objective was to venture off the beaten track usually trodden within their disciplines in the hope that such explorations would lead to the discovery of new concepts and alternatives for products or technologies. The research project had a substantial budget, sufficient to last several years, even though it did have a specific target for direct industrial application.

One of the key elements in the project was the steering committee. Far from being an administrative formality, the carefully prepared meetings were attended by the project manager, his team and the main stakeholders, which included the former director of the Swedish Space Agency and the Vice-President of Corporate Technology at Saab Aerospace, Billy Fredriksson. Although he was in charge of the Swedish firm's most important aeronautical programmes, Billy Fredriksson was quite prepared to spend several hours in these meetings, several times a year.

There were fears that the project would get lost in bureaucratic meanderings, as is often the case for projects financed in this way, but the steering committee meetings certainly did not give this impression. The members examined all the results in detail, studying the experimental approaches and the targets to be set. Their recommendations could be cutting and, at times, unexpected. For instance, at one stage in the discussions on alternative prototypes, the discussions were so fierce that the project manager resigned and the research teams were completely reshuffled.

There could be no doubt that WITAS's conceptual explorations were imaginative and prolific, but the project's managers decided that strict, frequent management interventions were required to ensure really fruitful, varied and innovative work. The results were convincing and in fact the WITAS project was an archetype of innovative design management. The project is studied in more detail in Chapter 10.

1.1.2   Good ideas or good organization?

Our second case is Tefal, a specialist in the highly competitive small electrical goods sector, based in Annecy. In 1995, when we first became interested in the company, it produced all its products in France. It had the best profit record in its sector and its employees sometimes received the equivalent of up to twenty-three months' salary per year.

The CEO, Paul Rivier, met Vincent Chapel, a young engineer from the Ecole des Mines. 'Mr Chapel, I was very interested to receive your request to do a PhD thesis on innovation management in our firm. As I am sure you are aware, Tefal is a highly innovative firm and innovation is not a problem for us. Look at this prototype, for instance, or this product that will be launched next week. If you work with us, you will no doubt discover good practices, but this is not what I want your doctorate to be about. What I am looking for is a formal framework of how innovation is organized at Tefal. Tefal innovates, but needs a model. This may seem surprising, but good practices are not enough. Tefal needs to explain what is behind its success to its shareholders, before they decide to impose traditional management rules which, I am convinced, would be harmful to the firm's innovation capability. I hope your work will help us explain a model that is specific to Tefal.'

This approach was not new, as many industrial champions (Ford, General Motors under Alfred Sloan, Toyota, etc.) developed theories from their own models. In the past, it was enough to implement 'good practices' for innovation, but at Tefal, innovation had become the key to performance and conditioned the firm's very survival. The firm's efficiency was linked to efficient processes. Although its performance seemed to stem from what other sectors such as the pharmaceuticals industry would call 'blockbusters' – leading products that account for the bulk of a firm's profits – Tefal's success went far beyond its flagship products, non-stick frying pans. In fact, at that time, the patents for the pans had already been in the public domain for many years. Could the firm's performance be linked to its ability to keep up a high rate of repeated innovation?

How did it sustain this repeated innovation and make it profitable? What resources did it employ and were they used 'efficiently'? R&D intensity (a firm's expenditures on R&D divided by its turnover) is often used as an indicator of a firm's innovation capability, but this ratio was so low at Tefal that it raised questions about its R&D.

In 1997, three years after this interview, Vincent Chapel defended his thesis (1997) entitled: 'La croissance par l'innovation intensive: de la dynamique d'apprentissage à la révélation d'un modèle industriel, le cas Tefal' [Growth by intensive innovation: from learning dynamics to the revelation of an industrial model in the case of Tefal]. We will come back to Tefal in Chapters 4 and 5 to help illustrate performance and efficiency in the context of intensive innovation.

1.1.3   Managing innovation: choosing or guiding?

The first steering committee for a major project on 'comfort in the car interiors of the future' took place at a leading automobile manufacturer's premises in Paris in 2000, grouping the product manager, the engineering managers, heads of research, the head of front-end innovation and representatives from the industrial design and purchasing departments. The project manager had been preparing for this meeting for several months and had wanted to mobilize the company on an issue that was a key source of innovation with high added value for the customers. He enthusiastically described several architectural innovations, explaining how technical problems could be solved in each case. He also gave a review of all the vehicles due to come onto the market in the following ten years, pointing out the windows of opportunity for innovation. He had carefully prepared the different alternatives which the managers could choose between, describing the solutions and demonstrators for each of the possible themes of innovation. He concluded by asking the participants to say which of the demonstrators should be given the highest priority.

However, the meeting did not go as he had planned. After listening to all the other actors' opinions and the discussions, instead of choosing between the three alternatives, the front-end innovation manager suggested a new path for the explorations, 'thin-seat' technology. The designers were baffled by this recommendation. Why should they explore what seemed to be a secondary subject compared with other aspects of comfort in car interiors? Why should they give up the other research paths and, moreover, did this recommendation actually fall within their remit?

After a meeting of this sort, it is easy to imagine the innovation team's confusion and frustration, and yet there had been no lack of communication between the various actors involved. How could the front-end innovation manager have explained the reasoning, based on his long experience and expertise, which had helped him identify the seat as the linchpin of any new features for car interiors? How could he have described the organization entailed by his recommendations, i.e. an organization that was no longer based on project management with clearly defined objectives set after a preliminary choice but on quick, one-off searches, exploring a vast, previously unknown territory beyond the profession's usual perimeters? The problem was not a lack of communication but a lack of basic tools to explain the reasoning and the organizations required.

What role can managers play in the context of innovation? Are they still decision-makers with the prerogative to choose between several carefully studied alternatives, or should they serve as guides to explore new territories?

This raises the issue of the cognitive challenges of innovation. In situations of innovation, the actors are naturally obliged to go beyond the usual organizational divisions and frontiers between functions; but apart from multifunctional meetings, which ideally bring all the players together, the problem is to find the modes of collective reasoning and the appropriate organizations to explore the concepts and create new competencies. We will return to this crucial question often throughout the book and will see in Chapters 10 and 11 how the problems were solved in the case we have just sketched out.

1.1.4   Can clients be more creative than their suppliers?

In the mid-1990s, the Saint-Gobain Sekurit research centre in Germany finally decided, after much hesitation, to launch a solar control windscreen project. Nonetheless, many people in the company, which specializes in glass for the automobile industry, were sceptical about the project, wondering why they should be studying something that would substantially increase the product's price but with nothing to show that the user would notice a significant improvement in thermal comfort.

An obvious answer was that one of the firm's leading clients, a car manufacturer, had been persistently asking the firm to work on the project and so there were fears that some of its competitors might be ready to respond to the demand. Yet clients often made strange demands and one of the roles of a competent supplier is to guide them towards areas of innovation with obvious value creation. Saint-Gobain Sekurit is renowned for its capacity to supply glazing in the most complex shapes, much appreciated by automobile designers, so why should it embark on a project that did not make the most of its competencies in shaping and might even encourage other car manufacturers to turn to solar control features rather than complex shapes? As specialists in development in the traditional competitive environment, it was quite reasonable for Sekurit's experts to be sceptical.

However, in the end, when Saint-Gobain Sekurit decided to go ahead with the solar control project for Renault it was probably not because of the car manufacturer's insistence, or to do with the competitors, but rather that some of the designers realized at that stage that the nature of competition was beginning to change. Instead of working on the best price/quality ratios for known functions, should they not be exploring new functions? Instead of constantly fine-tuning well-identified areas of expertise, should they not be trying to create new functions and competencies? Not only did Saint-Gobain Sekurit have great success with the solar control project, but five years later the firm had been transformed and was marketing multi-functional glazing products based on technologies that had never been used on such a large scale before. In a period of just five years, the research laboratory became a centre for innovation whose work stimulated and protected the development departments and the other research centres. In Chapter 9, we will see how all this came about and look at the new organizations that emerged during that period.

At this stage, this short example serves to show that it was not a question of innovating with the client or of imitating competitors. The two alternatives can be equally risky: clients can be changeable and uncertain and 'followers' can lose out if they follow the wrong path and are always late if they follow the right ones. It is a question of finding the right forms of organization to maintain a high rate of new product launches, combining functional exploration and the regeneration of competencies, and also to cater for novel client demands, to counter competitors' proposals and even launch new proposals to attract clients.

1.1.5   Perseverance? Yes, if it means learning

In 2002, a meeting took place at the Ecole des Mines in Paris with managers from Schlumberger, a world leader in oilfield services with a solid reputation for innovation. However, even its specialists were sometimes puzzled by the form taken by their innovative projects. 'In this study on innovation, we would like you to analyse a strange project: we have spent a great deal of money on it, mobilizing a large number of designers, for development and research, we have carried out a host of different trials, mainly in partnership with clients. But after several years' work, with lots of ups and downs, the project is coming to an end. And yet we have the impression that we have tried out a new form of organization that was actually very effective.'

Who could deny that innovation is a mixture of ups and downs, setbacks and perseverance, or to paraphrase Edison, '1 per cent inspiration, 99 per cent perspiration'? Schlumberger's project was a good example of this. The problem is to find the right impetus and the right organization to deal with long research projects, teeming with ideas. Also, however good the projects may be, at some stage they have to be evaluated. The development department will assess whether the teams were effective and whether or not they had supplied the product in question in the required time. The research department will look at any work that has been published. In both cases, the setbacks will be judged as inexplicable and costly, and put down to the designers' incompetence.

Does this mean that there should be no evaluation? Should projects take the form of skunk work, carried out by a few enthusiasts on top of their normal activities? And is it wise to resort to such limited, high-risk ways of working, now that competition through innovation seems to be the norm? There is another possibility: could it be that the evaluation criteria need to be revised, given that innovative design reasoning has its own specific criteria, thus making it different from research or development reasoning? Innovative design prefers variety rather than convergence, originality rather than routine, the production of new knowledge rather than existing expertise. When it was judged on the basis of these criteria, Schlumberger's project could be seen in a completely different light: a variety of directions had been explored, original paths had been uncovered and new competencies had been developed. This confirmed the designers' vague impressions that the project had indeed been a successful innovative design project (*see* Chapter 13). We will come back to these evaluation criteria in Chapters 10 and 13.

These anecdotes, which are all based on real cases although we have simplified them here, serve to show how original and sometimes surprising management approaches can be hidden behind incumbent ideas. Perseverance, best practices, blue-sky projects and user relations are all traditional watchwords in innovation, but their practical implementation involves managing the economic, market, cognitive, organizational and managerial aspects of innovation.

1.2   Innovation seen by the different disciplines

What do we know about these different aspects of innovation? Each of them comes under a different scientific discipline and has given rise to a wealth of literature. In the following pages, we give a brief overview of the current state of the art, before seeing to what extent the disciplines are able to propose models of collective action to foster innovation. A more detailed study can be found in the bibliographical appendix, which describes the concepts proposed by each discipline, how they came into being and their impact, placing them whenever possible in the genealogy of research work.

1.2.1   Economic policy and innovation

The relationships between innovation and economic policy go back a very long way. For example, the emergence of new industries played an enormous role in the economic policies of Colbert, French Minister of Finance from 1665 to 1683. More generally speaking, the policies of patents and privileges practised in both France and England in the seventeenth and eighteenth centuries favoured inventors, entrepreneurs and the growth of new economic sectors (Hilaire-Pérez 2000). With the arrival of the railways, which required concessions and forms of State intervention, each new project gave rise to debates on whether the new techniques were really 'progress', as Booth described one of the first railways, the Manchester–Liverpool line, when it was opened in 1831 (Booth 1831). The first 'technical economists' demanded State intervention to support science in the name of industrial progress. For example, Charles Babbage questioned the British authorities on their scientific policies and on the 'decline of science in England' (Babbage 1830, 1833), speaking of the threat for the 'future development of industry' and proposing compensations for people carrying out scientific investigations.

At that time economic policy addressed innovation in many different ways, including setting up training programmes, financing research, making laws covering inventions and protecting inventors and regulations on monopolies (concessions, privileges, competition laws, etc.), creating factories and launching major infrastructure programmes. Public policies on innovation sometimes also sought to assess the impact of innovation. For instance, the introduction of planned public policies – such as the New Deal after the 1929 crisis – meant that States began to wonder about the impact of scientific discoveries on the nation in terms of new products, new risks such as unemployment, infrastructure planning, etc. (Susskind and Inouye 1983). The innovations or the inventions – the distinction was not clearly made at this stage – were analysed like given facts and the consequences of their dissemination were studied.

When viewed in terms of economics and the stakes of economic policy, innovation was seen as a challenge or at least a powerful means of questioning the traditional economic theories. First, innovation finds fault in the general equilibrium theory as it is a dynamic force whereas general equilibrium describes a static equilibrium; second, it calls into question the theory of pure, perfect competition; and third, it means that forms of knowledge production and exchanges of skills, and not just products and services, must be taken into account.

Work on these questions led to a series of now widely used concepts: innovation typologies (product/process, radical/incremental, invention/innovation), the notion of R&D and investment in R&D, notions of technological trajectory, of national systems of innovation, etc. These notions cannot be separated from the economic contexts in which they came to life, whether it be the Great Depression of 1929, planning and massive State intervention in scientific research after the Second World War, the rise of Japan in the 1980s, etc.

Dynamic streams of research on economic policies and innovation seem to infer that new questions have appeared which also result from changes in the economic context. There are three main trends:

> *The question of knowledge*: the use of the term 'knowledge-based economy' underlines the importance attached to the production and exchange of knowledge. This is not an easy question from a theoretical standpoint. What is a knowledge market? What are the advantages and disadvantages of barter or of contractual exchange? What are the

different forms of appropriation: public goods, patents, etc. (Foray 2000, 2003)? From the point of view of economic policy, these questions reflect the major challenges of legislative changes to contract and intellectual property laws in the face of new forms of partnership and collective production of knowledge (Segrestin 2003). In addition, although knowledge is an essential variable, the relationship between knowledge production and innovation is far from deterministic (Jones 1995a), implying that there are other variables which have still not been correctly modelled (Hatchuel and Le Masson 2006).

The question of the actors: all the above-mentioned research was inevitably based on certain representations of the innovation process and of the actors involved. The authors were often obliged to discuss these representations, as illustrated by the success of Kline and Rosenberg's article (1986), which proposed a new representation of the innovation process for economists. Today, there seems to be a need to reassess these representations. On the one hand, evolutionary works have come to a point where authors claim that 'research has to reach a much finer analysis at both the empirical and the theoretical levels, and to move from the statement that everything is changing with everything else' (Malerba 2006). On the other hand, microeconomists, whose theories of endogenous growth were based on a traditional representation of the firm as a production function, are once again discussing the status that firms should hold in a theory of endogenous growth designed to take into account the characteristics of 'innovative firms' (Pakes and Ericson 1998; Klette and Griliches 2000). More heterodox works, which had discussed the modelling of firms very early on (Cohendet 1998), are observing an apparently growing number of actors involved in the innovation process. Does this mean that new models are required for firms? How can the different actors' collaboration be modelled (Foray 2003)?

The question of the nature of innovation itself: new phenomenologies on industry lifecycles (Grebel, Krafft and Saviotti 2006) and on sociotechnical regime transition echo recently discovered works on novelty by Schumpeter (1932 [2005]). Schumpeter defined development as 'a transition from one norm of the economic system to another norm in such a way that this transition cannot be decomposed into infinitesimal steps', wherein the norm represents 'all the concrete relationships of the concrete data that correspond to the Walrasian system'. Hence development is the renewal of both production functions and utility functions in the whole economy. This goes much further than the classical Schumpeterian growth models. Contemporary works on growth and innovation are now studying how to endogenize Schumpeterian 'development'.

In this context, it is still hard to define the characteristics of an innovation-friendly economy without having a clearer understanding of the processes and the actors in innovation and the way they develop new knowledge and share it. This is the aim of this book. Based on a study of design activities, we will present a new model of the firm as a design model (Chapters 4 to 6), which will then help to analyse forms of economic reasoning in innovative design situations (Chapters 10 to 15).

1.2.2   Social networks, market and innovation

Merchants in the Middle Ages were probably the first to think about the relationships between new products, markets and society, one of their primary concerns being to supply customers with products they wanted to buy (Renouard 1949).

Later, the arrival of mass consumer goods led to the invention of new ways of interacting with the market. For instance, at the end of the eighteenth century, Wedgwood pottery was sold to the burgeoning urban middle classes in showrooms and in illustrated catalogues (Forty 1986, Chapter 1); at the end of the nineteenth century, Lever used a brand strategy combining packaging and advertising and targeting low-income households to sell its soap products (Forty 1986, Chapter 3). When the food processing industry launched its first products, it used famous scientists to vouch for the quality and reassure customers that there were no health risks. For example, in 1865, George Giebert, founder of the Liebig Extract of Meat Company (LEMCO), a world leader in meat extracts, appointed a famous organic chemist, Justus von Liebig, as director. With great media coverage and for a comfortable salary, the company used Liebig's name – on the products, on calendars, recipe books, etc. – and entrusted him with the task of controlling the products (Brock 1997).

At the beginning of the twentieth century, new market relations developed as production became more concentrated, major centres of production emerged and transport capacities grew. The need arose for scientific tools capable of targeting advertising campaigns, improving the organization of sales forces and adapting products to the specific needs of local markets (Freeland 1920, 1926; Cochoy 1999). A series of concepts was gradually drawn up to describe the relationships between social networks, markets and innovation.

The approach was similar to the one adopted for the economic sciences. Innovation raised some fundamental questions in the field of economic science; the same applies to markets and social networks. As Norbert Alter (2003) pointed out, it is a paradox to talk about sociology applied to innovation as the aim of sociology is to analyse the stable systems of rules on which social relations are built, whereas innovation poses the question of the dynamics of these systems of rules. For markets, innovation raises the question of how markets can be established when there is no obvious demand or when the customers are not yet familiar with the products being offered. For society, innovation brings up the question of the plasticity of social groups and systems of rules.

Several key notions were developed as a result of these questions, including needs, adoption and diffusion, lead-user, sociotechnical network and community of practice. These studies on social networks affected by innovation also result in representations of the innovation process itself. The question of needs led to the idea that they should be analysed before finding an answer to them; the lead-user theory encouraged von Hippel (1988) to recommend an innovation process consisting of identifying the lead-users' inventions and marketing them; the notions of actor and of sociotechnical network represent innovation as a whirlwind process that is hard to manage, in which points of convergence are difficult to find; communities of practice develop innovation through an emerging process consisting of providing and sharing solutions to new problems. It is the social analyses that result in the different representations of the innovation process, often confusing the way in which the innovation is diffused with the design process itself.

This research also highlighted three key trends:

A marker for the nature of new products and new services: behaviourism ignored the products, apparently assuming that they could be sold to anyone; needs analysis used simple vocabulary to describe products; niche analysis, product differentiation and the analysis of sociostyles have provided an enriched vision of products (defined by their utility value but also their hedonic and symbolic values) (Holbrook and Hirschman 1982; Laurent and Kapferer 1985). Today, research on the difficult problem of describing product quality and diversity, on the need for mediators and on the personalization of products through customer service relations underlines a current trend in new products and services: products are not only diverse but also pose a problem of 'qualification' (Callon, Méadel and Rabeharisoa 2000).

The growing presence of organizational issues: when the authors renewed their interest in organizations, they treated them as if they were societies with specific properties (hierarchy, established order). New 'figures' were introduced, as inventors were joined by deviators, communities of practice, functions, instrument makers, etc. In adding these descriptions, the authors also explained the specific features of the 'organizations', with a special emphasis on firms' ability to create links between different communities of practice. More recent works have also analysed the social phenomena relating to companies' organizations for intensive innovation (Minguet and Osty 2008).

Growing use of the notions by firms: most of the research referred to above concerned innovation, but without establishing an explicit relationship to firms. However, more and more firms today are using research of this sort in their innovation processes. For instance, Brown (1991) described how Xerox used anthropological studies on users of photocopiers, on practices in accounting departments and on repair technicians' work to help the company develop new products and services. Questions such as analysing current uses, exploring new uses, for instance through virtual communities on the internet (Kozinets 2002), and even customers' involvement in design processes (Magnusson 2003; Piller *et al.* 2003) have become highly strategic issues in many companies.

In this context, we shall begin by analysing the new forms of competition through innovation, the new organizations which design new products and the new activities which organize relations in companies. We shall then look at the issue of designing value (Chapters 4 and 5), changes in marketing when large R&D firms are transformed (Chapters 7 and following) and the new practices that consist of involving the client in the design process much earlier (*see* the Telia case study, Chapter 11).

1.2.3   Cognitive process and innovation

Knowledge and reasoning are major challenges in all innovation processes, as shown by the wealth of architects' manuals, encyclopaedias, engineering science treatises, theories on machine construction, etc. that has been written over the years. During the nineteenth century, doctrine was gradually built up on experimental methods and their relations to scientific discovery and there were great debates on how to train engineers, especially regarding theoretical versus practical training. Issues such as how new knowledge is produced and transmitted and how methods for innovation are passed on became almost national debates.

However, in the past few decades, progress in research into individual and collective decision-making processes and the new concepts proposed by the theory of information have brought innovation to the foreground once again, but from a different perspective. On the one hand, progress in modelling decision-making processes encouraged researchers to look at the process of invention and individual discoveries and the question of collective decisions in the face of unusual, new situations. On the other, the success of information theories opened a new field of research on the transfer and accumulation of knowledge. More recently, this research converged on questions of knowledge production in action.

Similarly to economic policy and to markets and social networks, the question of innovation poses a problem for research into cognitive processes, but it is also the source of progress.

The main problem is that very little work has been done to date on one of the most vital issues for the cognitive sciences, i.e. how to describe creative reasoning. The question of innovation has led to progress as work on knowledge in action has gone beyond the paradigm of information to concentrate on new fields: first, the nature of knowledge (the distinction between tacit and explicit) and, second, the production of knowledge (typology of knowledge in action: 'doing know-how', 'understanding know-how', 'combining know-how' and experiential learning).

Two key trends are currently emerging:

A change in context: the main reason why current work on modelling is interested in not only communication channels but also the nature of experts' knowledge and how it is produced is that the knowledge and its production are undergoing a major crisis. Although it is not always clearly stated, what is really being studied in this research is the way the work of engineers, researchers, designers, strategists and marketing specialists is changing in firms today.

Merging of work on reasoning and on knowledge: there were two main streams of research: first, work on individual and collective reasoning (Simon, March, Argyris and Schön, etc.) and, second, work on knowledge (its nature, relation to action, etc. – see Nonaka, Blackler, Cohen, etc.). The authors in the first stream faced the issue of ill-defined problems which they could not address, where imagery must be used and the production of knowledge is hard to control. The second stream went through several stages. The authors began by looking at the nature of the knowledge used (tacit/explicit), then at the way in which knowledge production was influenced by innovation (dynamic evolution of core competencies, analysis of forms of activities: experiential learning, trial and error, etc.) and finally how a form of knowledge production could be more or less innovative, more or less 'enacting'. How can a knowledge production process be organized in such a way as to lead to innovation? At this stage, the authors came back to the question of reasoning. It is therefore not terribly surprising that, precisely on this issue of innovation reasoning, the authors were obliged, once again, to raise the question of intuition and 'flashes of insight'. We should also point out that the question is also raised in the more technical field of knowledge engineering, the descendant of artificial intelligence and expert systems: how to move from static to dynamic representations of ontologies.

There seems to be a vital gap concerning cognitive processes in the context of innovation, i.e. how can reasoning and knowledge be combined, or more precisely, how can innovative reasoning and knowledge production be combined? Which forms of reasoning should be used and how can they be implemented collectively, that is without being limited to creative contributions, or flashes of insight, from individuals?

This is a fundamental question and an integral part of our approach. We shall begin by studying the issue at the level of innovative firms (Chapters 4 to 6), then for the organization of R&D firms (Chapters 7 to 9) and finally for innovative design reasoning for teams charged with exploring innovation fields (Chapters 10 to 15). At that stage, we shall discuss the relationships between innovative design reasoning and creativity. Note that a formal answer to the question is proposed in Chapter 10, which outlines the C-K theory for design reasoning.

1.2.4   Organizational theory and innovation

In the past, organizations have been continually modelled by innovation, which often acted as a stimulus but sometimes upset and disorganized their activities. At the end of the nineteenth century, innovation-related issues played a key role in the creation of research laboratories, whether in terms of providing support for new product design, of controlling innovations made by independent inventors or even of blocking the competitive environment by means of patents. When planning departments appeared in Taylor's time, one of their main aims was to match the levels of innovation achieved with Taylor's high-speed steel processes. Engineering departments came into being because they distinguished between new work and routine work, and manufacturing units were developed to enable joint innovations

(Lefebvre 1998), i.e. innovations at the interface between two trades, made possible by their physical closeness and the opportunities for making mutual adjustments.

However, literature on organizational theory was less interested in these historical issues than in more general questions. Can innovation be organized? What is the place of innovation in organizational theory? What are the characteristic features of innovative organizations? Which organizational forms suit which systems of innovation?

Similarly to questions of economic policy, social networks and cognitive processes, it is clear that innovation has had an incredibly corrosive effect on organizational theories. The latter now seem extremely fragile, with their boundaries being disputed by the sociology of networks, by economics (especially by evolutionary theorists), by work on organizational learning and by all sorts of managerial currents, each trying to find a definition for the innovative organization.

Nonetheless, a large number of concepts have emerged from this conjunction of innovation and organizational theory: the distinction between product innovation and organizational innovation, notions such as organic organizations, ambidextrous organizations and continuously changing organizations, using complexity theory to analyse 'pink noise' or 'white noise' phenomena, core competencies, dynamic capabilities, etc.

Two major trends can be found in this abundant, complex body of research, the first concerning the nature of innovation and the second the languages that describe organizations.

Over the years, the term 'innovation' has been used to refer to different forms of innovation. From the 1960s to the 1980s, the authors were mainly interested in *organizational innovation*, or how organizations managed to take on new forms. They addressed organizational change and changes in structures and processes. Product innovation was touched on only to underline that different types of product renewals required different organizational structures.

There was an important change of course at the beginning of the 1990s, following Brown and Eisenhardt's work. The authors no longer looked at *product design* as one situation involving change among others (product innovation, organizational innovation, market innovation, etc.) but as the means of *adapting to change* par excellence.

The authors who studied innovation challenged the notions of universal organization theory on the grounds that it failed to take organizational change into account. They therefore proposed a new language to describe organizations. One of the best examples was organic organization (together with adhocracy and mutual adjustment in large organizations). However, this solution was in fact more problematic than initially thought: instead of proposing a new structure, organic organizations in fact opened up a new dimension, that of the actors' behaviour. This element was then implicit in all the work on ambidextrous organizations and organizations undergoing continuous change.

Other research projects then sought more radical means of avoiding the traditional language of structure and process. In particular, the Innovation Journey and work on strategic competencies proposed new languages to describe the inner workings of innovation; the first identified the natural laws of organizations using statistical data on 'events'; the second identified hybrid objects (dynamic capabilities and core competencies) that combine elements of structure, process and behaviour (dynamic capabilities are both organizational routines and hypotheses on the actors' behaviour; core competencies are both specific entities in the structure and the inner secret of its metabolism).

Other research concentrated on organizational behaviour and, instead of trying to reduce it to structural forms, tried to deduce its specific mechanisms. For instance, Weick suggested that jazz improvisation was an excellent metaphor for organizing creativity (Weick 1998), while Starkey *et al.* showed that the UK television industry was based on organizations that were neither in the form of networks nor hierarchies but could be considered as latent organizations (Starkey, Barnatt and Tempest 2000).

1.2.5   Innovation and management

Heads of laboratories, engineering departments, marketing departments and design studios have been developing management techniques in one way or another for a very long time now. For example, engineering departments invented most of their management techniques in the period from 1880 to 1900; planning departments, industrial research and marketing developed theirs in the period from 1900 to 1920. Taylor made an important contribution not only to the doctrine of shop floor management but also to the techniques that were used (the famous time and motion studies and, more generally speaking, the scientific analysis of production activities). The same techniques were sometimes used to organize industrial research laboratories (*see* Charpy 1919; Chevenard 1933), often considered to be the planning and management departments for the process industries (*see* Le Châtelier 1930). Scientific organization also had a major impact on sales and, later, marketing departments (*see* Freeland 1920, 1926). Until the 1970s, these management techniques remained relatively stable, to such an extent that they were even considered 'natural'.

In the context of stable functions, management tended to focus on processes, with two contrasting approaches: first, managing product development processes, i.e. coordinating and integrating the different functional experts mentioned above; and second, managing the innovation process, i.e. going beyond product development as such by recognizing opportunities for innovation and acquiring new knowledge. It is only very recently that there has been renewed interest in management techniques for the different functions themselves, i.e. research, marketing, engineering, etc.

In recent managerial literature, there is often less sense of being attached to a specific discipline. The authors come from very different backgrounds (consulting firms, academic research and practitioners): either an author plays on two different fronts, or different authors group together to publish their work. They often seem to take their inspiration from other disciplines (cf. radical vs. incremental innovation, tacit knowledge, routines, etc.) and use these theoretical devices to analyse 'phenomenology' that is new to firms. In fact, it is this phenomenology that is then used in turn in the disciplines in question (see, for example, Eisenhardt's work using Clark's research on project management). One point that characterizes all this work is that the approaches are very fragmented (processes, strategy, functions, activities, etc.) due to the lack of a unified framework.

The second remark is a paradox: putting these authors into a wide category of innovation management is not really controversial and yet it is surprising to note that many of them do not mention innovation at all. They either prefer the new product development perspective or the traditional organizational breakdown (R&D, marketing). This is more important than it may seem. The management perspective adopted by most of these authors led them to abandon the term 'innovation' which, in its classic sense, is not an actionable notion.

These works were written following consultants' and analysts' reports on trends in firms or the emergence of original practices in specific firms (see the studies by the consulting firm Booz Allen Hamilton in the 1950s) and therefore explain certain transformations in firms. Two major trends can be noted, which we will study in more detail in the following chapters:

Managerial approaches have changed drastically in the past few years. We have moved from the coordination of major functions – stage-gate organization, project management – to a transformation of the activities themselves (new research, new marketing and the appearance of new activities).

As we said, innovation is not really mentioned as a result, but it has emerged as a specific activity, which must apparently be distinguished from traditional activities, involving not only a form of 'discipline' but also tools, missions and special forms of interaction with other partners.

1.3 Innovation: from a phenomenon to a new management object

This brief summary shows that a large number of notions have come to light as a result of work on innovation: product innovation, process innovation, radical versus incremental innovation, communities of practice, organizational innovation, organic organizations, ambidextrous organizations, core competencies, tacit versus explicit knowledge, etc. However, all these notions are diffracted by the prism of the disciplines which created them. They do not provide a direct answer to the issue that concerns us in this book: finding a way of collectively managing and organizing actions aimed at leading to repeated, sustainable innovation. More specifically, they do not help us to understand the enigmas illustrated at the start of this chapter. For example, how can we manage blue-sky projects? How can we manage communication on innovative issues? Which organizational models provide firms with growth by repeated innovation? How can firms assess the efficiency of their R&D? How can they interact with innovative clients? How can they manage and evaluate their strategies for experiments and prototypes?

There is clearly a gap between the questions posed by the management of repeated innovation and the notions proposed in the literature. So, how can we use the different notions? We could try to summarize them, but the problems subsist. We prefer to show that, despite the fact that they start from very different positions dictated by the disciplines in question, all these approaches try to account for recent evolutions. They therefore tend to converge and propose new characteristics of contemporary innovation. However, it is precisely these new characteristics that call for a radical change in perspective and in methods, as we shall see in the following chapter.

1.3.1   Innovation, a critical stance for the social sciences

One point that is clear from an examination of the work: innovation is not an independent subject. There is no discipline that directly studies innovation. On the contrary, the different contributions came from very varied disciplines, which sometimes adopted quite contrasting positions.

However, all the approaches – with the exception of the managerial approach – initially adopted a quite similar rhetorical stance to innovation: it served to criticize the established theories in each of the disciplinary fields. By looking at innovation, the researchers were able to adopt a particularly good tactical position for highlighting the weak points in these theories, whether it be the social theories, or theories on economic exchanges, organization, cognitive mechanisms, etc. The initial question was often to find out what happened to the theories when they were confronted with innovation. As innovation was frequently a blind spot, new notions such as the ones presented above were usually introduced to deal with it, and the disciplinary theories were revised or added to in consequence. As a result, although the new notions relate to innovation, they are often part of complex disciplinary genealogies and it can be difficult and risky to take them out of context.

1.3.2   Innovation crosses the boundaries of the disciplines

Nonetheless, this does not mean that the disciplinary fields are completely watertight, and in fact it is surprising to see how the issue of innovation seems to be helping to gradually bring them together. For instance, it is becoming increasingly difficult to categorize the authors in the most recent work, which seems to move easily from economics or sociology to management. This may be as much the result of changes in the questions dealt with by research as of changes in the activity itself (a state of crisis for certain players, new forms of innovation, etc.).

This interplay leads to a common field of research on the subject of innovation which, after being a pretext, is now becoming an independent object of investigations. It appears to have all the characteristics required, i.e. knowledge, organization, process, tools, value spaces, etc.

1.3.3   Managing innovation: from a phenomenon to a field of action

This common field of research involves more than simply bringing researchers together to work on the same subject. In fact, it implies a relatively profound change of paradigm. In the past, researchers were interested in questions that concerned an object x in an innovation situation, 'x' being the economy, the organization, social relations, knowledge, values, etc. Today, they have come closer together because a different issue has been raised: managing innovation by means of x. This transforms the perspective mentioned earlier: it is no longer a question of showing how certain theories (of x) are contested in a specific critical situation (innovation), but of designating a new object, the management of innovation, which knowledge of x can help to understand and to practise.

In other words, the original question was about the impact of a phenomenon, innovation, on the major disciplinary notions of growth, social relations, knowledge, etc. The new question is different: innovation is no longer a phenomenon but has become the object of the action. However, whereas it is widely accepted that there is a relationship between a firm's innovation and its growth, there is still much uncertainty as to how innovation can be managed in order to obtain this growth.

Questions for further study and discussion

What impact does the definition of innovation have on research trends and on methodology?

What impact do the disciplines' different approaches have on the definition of innovation?

How can we define skills which are 'useful' in terms of innovation? Which stakeholders are involved?

Compare research on innovation with other fields of management research: structure of the firm, culture of the firm, human resources management.

2 Management sciences and innovation: identity of objects and innovation capability

A number of practical questions immediately arise when we look at innovation as a field of action rather than purely a phenomenon. Take the case of the new 'innovation management' function that has been introduced in many firms in recent years. What exactly do innovation managers or directors do? What is the scope of their activities and how do they organize their teams and divide the work between the different members? How do they interact with the other functions in the firm, the factories, research laboratories and engineering and design departments? How is their work evaluated, on what basis and with which criteria?

Confronted with the issue of managing the 'action of innovation', we can begin by seeing whether or not the notions mentioned above can be considered as *means of action*. Should innovation managers organize 'communities of practice'? Should they collect ideas and consult lead-users? Should they finance R&D by allocating optimal budgets and resources? Should they distinguish between incremental and radical innovation? Should they consider new business specializations for radical innovation? For innovation managers, and indeed for all the other players concerned, are these notions *actionable*? Before that question can be answered, we need to know the aim of the action itself. What is the innovation in question? Are we talking about changing the colour of a product or introducing a new technology? Who will judge the 'novelty', the customer or the professionals? What is 'good' innovation? How can the efficiency of processes be evaluated? Is the aim to minimize investments or to maximize profits? Or should the focus be on the brand image or on promises and resources for future developments?

All these questions underline that managing innovation is not just about finding the right 'means' and the best 'solutions'. We need to find *a model for action* that describes not only the ways and means but also, to a certain extent, the aims pursued, as the latter condition the nature of the performance. The questions also explain the position of management research into innovation: the management of innovation is the simple application of neither the economics of innovation nor the sociology of innovation, but poses the question of a comprehensive theory of action which can lead to innovation.

In this chapter, we will describe some basic characteristics of action models that meet contemporary economic challenges relating to innovation. We shall begin by looking at the key elements of contemporary innovation. Innovation is not a new subject, of course, but the issue is particularly acute today because it takes such specific and unusual forms that the traditional methods are no longer able to deal with it. We will show that the present-day challenge is competition by innovation in a situation of unstable object identities and limited resources. We will then go on to see that the action models found in the literature are not suited to these two constraints: they either manage unstable object identities but are unable to control resources or, on the contrary, they control resources but only on the assumption that the objects remain stable. Finally, we shall see that this apparently insurmountable contradiction in fact stems from the actual term of innovation itself. Bearing in mind the limits of existing models, we can propose the principles of an action model adapted to what we call *innovation capability management*.

2.1   Innovation capability: transforming the identity of objects

Is there anything really new about the current research on innovation or have we always come back to the same questions over the past 150 years? The literature outlined in the previous chapter seems to indicate that there have been changes in the realm of innovation. For example, we pointed out that, by focusing on evolutions in new products, sociological work on innovation is currently studying difficulties in product 'qualification', whereas in the past it examined mass production and then variety. The products themselves have apparently changed. As for economics, it is currently studying the sound use of resources; it is also focusing on the fact that one resource, knowledge, has not been taken into account sufficiently in previous models. In the past, management research, meanwhile, discussed the structuring and coordination of the major functions of organizations, with a view to optimizing the use of resources in terms of quality, cost and time. At present, it is looking at how to transform the activities themselves (innovative research, innovative marketing, etc.), with new debates on both resources and performance.

The literature therefore echoes a number of profound changes that we will focus on in the following pages.

2.1.1   Crisis in the identity of objects and innovation capitalism

Let us take a close look at the 'new' products. What makes them new? Sometimes the reasons are so obvious that nobody sees them.

2.1.1.1   The notion of crisis in the identity of objects

First of all, we should note that products are constantly being renewed. For instance, cars rarely last for more than eight years on the production chain; the mobile phone market, like the watch market before it, is becoming a market dictated by fashion, where collections have to be renewed every six months. This rapid renewal is a first feature of 'new products'. However, it could also be simply an indication of constant progress in a dominant design.

A second prominent feature relates more to one-off innovations: products have appeared that did not exist a few years ago. Digital cameras, personal digital assistants (PDAs), portable computers and internet connections, for instance, cannot be classified under pre-existing dominant designs.

In addition, these new products have spread throughout the world at a speed that has never been seen before in industrial history. Take the telephone market: at the beginning of 1996, barely 2 per cent of the French used a mobile phone; five years later, at the beginning of 2001, nearly 50 per cent of the population was equipped with one. In comparison, there were four million fixed telephone lines in France in 1967; eight years later, there were still only seven million. A special programme was launched by the French authorities that year to make up for the low penetration rates: the aim was for everyone to have a telephone by 1982, i.e. 21 million telephone lines seven years later. Is the answer to try to combine these two processes, one-off innovation and new product development?

This brings us to a third characteristic, perhaps the most original. These new products pose a really difficult problem to their designers and their users, the question of their *identity*. Whereas no long explanations are required to understand the identity of a mobile telephone, the same cannot be said for a PDA, for instance. The name of the object, personal digital assistant, is so vague that many of its potential users quite naturally wonder what it is supposed to be used for. The same applies to many other products, such as WiFi, USB keys, Bluetooth telecommunications, to name but a few.

And yet it is at this level that the challenges of new product design are to be found today. Product identity is no longer the stable starting point for product design. In the past, the product's performance, the major architectural alternatives and the nature of the functions were decided in advance, but all these points are now open questions.

Let's take the example of mobile phones, which we described perhaps a little hastily as having a clear identity. Just a few years ago, in 2001, mobile phones were already being launched every month with new, original interfaces. When designers tried to imagine the next generation of products, they could not simply think about improving the life of the batteries, the quality of sound, the phone's compactness or the quality of the screen, they also had to imagine future hybrids, such as telephone and PDA, or telephone and portable computer. Also, how could radio, music, images, positioning tools and maps be added to the phones? What place should be given to games, to business uses or to personal development? And what about the good old pen? The development of pens that digitize people's writing in real time suggested that this traditional object might also make a comeback. As we can see, in 2001 it was certainly not an easy task for designers to predict that, among all the possible hybrid solutions, the main winners two years later would be text messaging and digital cameras.

2.1.1.2 Identity crisis in many sectors

The same symptoms can be found in many sectors, not just the computer and telecommunications industries. For example, the concept of 'nutraceuticals' fits somewhere between food and pharmaceuticals, but no satisfactory definition has yet been agreed on. There are similar uncertainties concerning the relationships between cosmetics and health, and high-tech evolutions in textiles.

It is difficult to find examples of industries that have been spared the phenomenon. Take the case of the automobile industry, which is often considered the archetype of a dominant design industry, with a relatively watertight industrial environment in which functional features evolve slowly. The sector is currently showing symptoms of a redefinition of its value spaces. For instance, certain manufacturers are studying the concept of 'steering', although it would be reasonable to suppose that its value was already fully understood and controlled. The most conservative among them are also addressing car safety from the point of view of other road users and not just the vehicle's occupants. Also, new data communication services and on-board internet put an end to the industry's compartmentalization.

Environmental concerns are also having a considerable impact on one of the core functions, the engine, with the likely adoption of hybrid and/or electrical solutions in the future. It is already clear that electric cars will not be simply today's cars with an electric engine, as car manufacturers and new entrants to the car industry are seriously studying concepts such as 'collective cars', 'urban vehicles' and other new business models based on electricity. The crisis in the identities of products seems to be spreading to a wide range of different industrial branches, and in fact the very notion of 'industrial branch' is suddenly becoming more fragile. It is perhaps not a coincidence that some of these sectors are also the most turbulent in the market and regularly provoke 'high-tech' bubbles (the internet, telecommunications, organic products and pharmaceuticals, energy, etc.).

2.1.1.3 Not just a passing crisis

Is this just a passing trend, resulting from a phase where new technologies have spread throughout industry? Will identities become stable again once this phase is over?

The example of accessories for the new mobile solutions seems to prove the contrary; the situation that left designers perplexed in 2001 had not become any more stable by 2003, although various alternatives had of course been explored. For cameras, for instance, the competition seemed to have agreed to focus on the number of pixels. However, there were also some new alternatives: should the instrument's architectures be broken down into earphones, power units, information units, screens and other accessories? Should telephones focus on leisure activities and games? What was the future for DVD players? Should car navigation systems be added? Could USB keys be the solution, as a convenient way of carrying information without having to carry a computer? And the digital pen was still making progress, after signing agreements with paper and notebook suppliers, etc.

The main concerns two years later, in 2005, were new iPod hybrids, the success of Blackberry (in the business world), new clever phone hinges (flip covers, pivot and sliding flaps, etc.), the difficult beginnings of television on mobile phones, questions about high-speed connections (UMTS, WiFi, WiMax, etc.), a new software market for mobile phones (first for ringtones and then for GPS navigation systems) and new integrated services (a mobile phone with numerous services relating to mobility, including payment, hotel and car key cards, airline loyalty cards, etc.). It is clear that object identities did not become any more stable during this period and that competition was growing on two different levels at the same time. First, there was competition around momentarily stable dominant designs (e.g. regarding cameras' weight and resolution), with fierce price wars that eroded margins and suffocated the competitors, and second, competition that consisted in continually shifting the object's identity, so that profits could be made at least for a short time if the idea met with success. Two years later, the competition continues: the incumbents are surprised by the success of Apple's i-Phone and App Store, and Google's Android is another radical alternative.

It may seem reasonable to assume that the users and the consumers themselves will push for new stability. However, it should be noted that western societies have become extremely receptive to these new forms of innovation. Consumers are more and more highly educated (Thélot and Vallet 2000; Nakamura 2001) and, even if they may not want to, they are capable of learning how to use specialized technology and become familiar with it. In this context, it is vital for firms to know how to encourage and develop user learning processes.

Living in a world where objects' identities are constantly changing is perhaps not such a major challenge for societies that have been capable, in just a few decades and sometimes with great strife, to face up to massive unemployment, to experience the breakdown of the family unit and the growing numbers of reconstituted families, to invent civil contracts to replace marriage vows and to challenge ways of giving birth or of coping with death. Western societies today are looking for new values (cf. sustainable development) and for objects that can give substance to them.

The economic sustainability of such repeated, radical innovation is also questionable: is such intense innovation possible in capital-intensive industries? There is no definitive answer to this question, but there are some surprising examples. For instance, the microelectronics industry is highly capital intensive but has managed to organize continuous innovation and to follow (and reinforce) the particularly demanding Moore's Law. Moreover, today it is no longer sufficient to 'shrink the microprocessor': several companies are exploring 'More than Moore' innovation fields, in directions still not well defined (communication, data storage, sensors, biochips, etc.) but encompassing the coordination of all the actors of the systems on a chip and likely to involve high investments in the future.

Nevertheless, it is possible that the firms themselves may not be able to cope with the uncertainties regarding the objects to be designed. In practice, competition through intensive innovation will spread if certain firms or communities (inter-firm partnerships, consumer associations, public authorities, etc.) develop suitable forms of organization and of action to meet the challenges of this new form of innovation. We shall see later in the book the work that is being done in this respect.

It is therefore not unrealistic to assume that the current situation, in which object identities are uncertain, will continue to be the case.

2.1.1.4 Innovation-intensive capitalism

This plasticity in objects' identity and the resulting uncertainty for manufacturers are major symptoms of current economic trends. For the actors concerned (designers, manufacturers, distributors, salespeople, consumers and prescribers), all the points of reference disappear when product identities change and they no longer know which functions to work on, or where to look for improvements in performance. New areas are currently being opened for smart, but also high-risk, explorations and inventions: new value spaces, new features, new technologies and new functions, new business models and new forms of market relations.

Nearly all firms are affected by these transformations. This is why innovation is no longer a luxury but has become a form of competition. In economic and financial terms, it is now vital to launch new products regularly, preferably ones that shift the emphasis of performance to hitherto unexplored aspects with added value for the customers. A study from the consulting firm Deloitte-Touche-Tohmatsu showed that this dependency on new products has speeded up considerably in recent years. In 2004, an average of 29 per cent of the turnover of 650 European and American firms from all sectors of business came from products that were less than three years old, compared with 21 per cent in 1998 (Deloitte, Touche and Tohmatsu 2005). In certain cases, 80 per cent of the companies' profits, i.e. its oxygen (whereas the turnover is more a question of the size of the organization), can come from products less than three years old. These figures also mean that the products are attacked very quickly as the competitive advantage never lasts terribly long.

Finally, there are more and more different areas where competition can take place. Not only must the products be enhanced all the time but also the promises they make and their innovation capabilities. Awards, trade fairs and shows, publications, demonstrations and communication are all key tools that must be used in a new, effective way in any innovation strategy. Volvo's YCC concept car is a case in point. The car was 'designed by women for women' to target the most demanding premium customer, the independent professional woman. It made the headlines of the general-interest press, particularly in the United States, with the most intensive media coverage in the entire history of the automobile industry. However, for Volvo, the concept car was a means not only of announcing a stylish new line but also of exploring a value space, working on its brand image and even, as an employer, of attracting female candidates to the company.

2.1.2 Spectacular rise in resources devoted to innovation

How can firms face up to these challenges? They seem to demand an increase in investments. But another important aspect of competition is that resources must be controlled. This is in fact the second characteristic of competition through innovation, in a context where firms are confronted with a spectacular rise in the share of their resources devoted to innovation. For example, statistics from the CNISF (National Council of French Engineers and Scientists) provide data on trends in engineers' activities for the period from 1958 to 2002. Figure 2.1 shows the trends in three types of activities carried out by engineers (production, research and design) as percentages of the total number of engineers employed (dotted line) and in absolute value (continuous line). We have adjusted the data to give a 'homogeneous' category that is not simply R&D (Hatchuel and Le Masson 2004).

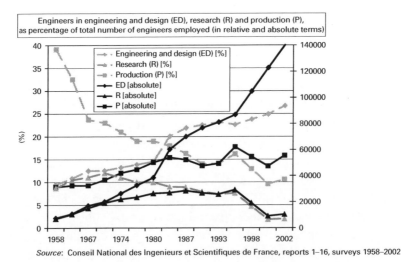

Source: Conseil National des Ingenieurs et Scientifiques de France, reports 1–16, surveys 1958–2002

Figure 2.1 Rise in the number of engineers working in design (*see* engineering department curves – diamonds, continuous and dotted lines)

The number of engineers working in design and in research departments was multiplied by twenty in this period of less than fifty years (the total number of engineers was multiplied by only six during the same period). The data clearly show that engineers moved towards activities relating to innovation. It should be noted that the same factor of twenty applied to staff in the engineering and design department at Renault from 1960 to 1995, when the number of engineers and technicians rose from 500 to 10,000 (Weil 1999).

This dramatic increase in firms' resources devoted to innovation seems to be speeding up still further since the mid-1990s. The trend means that these 'investments' are being changed into visible 'costs' that must be carefully controlled. After outsourcing production, many firms are now outsourcing their engineering and design departments. In this way, the 'costs' are controlled and there is less and less skunk work.

2.1.3   The obligations of innovation capability

As we have seen, the increasing number of questions on innovation is far more than just a passing trend. It is the symptom of a profound transformation in contemporary capitalism: *the emergence of innovation-intensive capitalism.* In this form of capitalism, firms face two contradictory obligations:

Designing in a context of uncertain object identities: from the nineteenth century, firms learned how to harness innovation, as long as it concerned products with stable identities. Customer expectations were known and codified; they were translated into product functions. These sometimes needed to be updated or required research into new technologies, but in this case the latter were well identified too. New identities did sometimes emerge, but they became stable very quickly and there were no changes in the form of competition involved. In the current situation of unstable object identities, it is precisely the form of competition that poses the problem. Firms are not only obliged to make minor improvements to known functions, they must also explore new identities, either to guard against competitors' offers or to avoid harmful price competition. However, if the products' identities are not set from the start, this means that firms have to work on a host of different aspects at the same time. Who are the customers, where is the market, what are the needs, features, functionalities, technologies, processes, references, costs, suppliers, etc.? All these elements now have to be designed and this appears to involve all the more activities and resources.

Controlling the rise in resources devoted to innovation: this second characteristic of innovation-intensive capitalism, the spectacular increase in
costs, illustrates the drastic economic changes taking place at present.
However, this increase also helps tighten the constraints because,
although more and more aspects must be taken into account in order
to obtain commercial success, it obliges firms to control the numbers
of staff in their R&D and marketing departments. After years of
continuous growth, the staff numbers in the automobile industry's
engineering and design departments are levelling off, and many other
companies are trying to follow suit. Indeed, this ability to control R&D
expenditure is becoming a key aspect of performance. As a result, new
product developments are no longer used as an opportunity for
innovative experiments; many 'fundamental' research laboratories have
disappeared or redirected their work to short-term applications, for
which they are judged in terms of execution times; as for skunk work,
the growing complexity of products and systems means that obstacle
races are getting longer and longer for 'intrapreneurs'.

The leading issue for innovation management today is therefore to look for
models for collective action that deal effectively with these two obligations,
transforming the identity of objects and controlling resources.

2.2 The conflict between transforming identity and controlling resources

We must now see whether there are already action models to deal with this
issue, but before we do so, we will start by explaining what we mean by
'model for collective action'.

2.2.1 The four components of a model for collective action

As we said in the introduction, a model for collective action cannot be
limited to means of action. Building on work conducted by Armand
Hatchuel and Benoît Weil (1992; *see* box below), the action model adopted
here comprises four components.

The first is a model of the activity and the reasoning. It serves as a basic
language to elaborate the three following parts and designates the
objects to be managed.

The technical substratum: all the techniques and tools needed to manage the objects highlighted by the model of activity (i.e. the 'means').

The type of performance: the nature of the target performance and the appropriate evaluation criteria, which must be adapted to specific industrial situations. They emerge on a local, temporary basis, step by step, and depend on the corresponding models of activity and the means of action.

Finally, forms of organization. These are essential given that collective action implies a certain number of actors, often from heterogeneous backgrounds.

These components will be referred to throughout the book as we gradually build an appropriate action model to face the challenges of innovation-intensive capitalism.

Managerial technologies and the four components of an action model

The above definition of an action model is based on the latest theories on collective action (Hatchuel 2001b). The four components stem from the managerial techniques put forward by Hatchuel and Weil (1992). By analysing expert systems at the end of the 1980s, the authors showed that the latter were rationalized in a similar way to the scientific management of work, operational research (OR) and computer-assisted production management (CAPM). In the authors' view, all these rationalizations can be qualified as 'rational myths' (Hatchuel and Molet 1986), as they have the potential of myths to mobilize action, whilst also containing the properties for reflection and learning inherent to reasoning.

The rationalizations in question are 'modelling projects': modelling people's movements in scientific management, modelling flows in CAPM, modelling decisions in OR and modelling expertise in expert systems. They are guided by potential material and relational stakes, which they gradually make more credible. This is why all techniques have three components:

A technical substratum, i.e. all the modelling techniques required for the objects in question; in the case of Taylorism, this involved using experiment plans and time and motion studies; OR, CAPM and artificial intelligence (AI) use computers and their respective algorithms. The vital point here is that, historically speaking, these foundations 'all belonged to the arsenal of mathematics, logic and physics' (Hatchuel and Weil 1995).

A management philosophy, i.e. a system of concepts that describes the objects and objectives targeted by the rationalization. For scientific management, the underlying philosophy is labour productivity, for operational research it is optimizing decision-making, for computer-assisted production management it is coherent, intelligible flows and for expert systems, the automation of knowledge. This component corresponds to the 'type of performance'.

> A simplified view of organizational relations. Management techniques also describe collective roles and situations. For instance, in scientific management, this could be a time and motion man who becomes a methods engineer, interacting between 'the management' and 'the workers'. This component corresponds to 'forms of organization'.
> We can add a fourth component here, which is the modelling of reasoning. In the previous cases, the objects were defined and mathematical models were therefore suitable. Production management was based on a representation consisting of products and tasks, on series of operations and production schedules. However, in cases where the identity of the objects is uncertain, the minimum language traditionally employed (projects, functions, techniques, markets, etc.) must be built up as the action takes place. It cannot therefore be used as a foundation. We shall see that probability, optimization and planning models are no longer suitable. Hence, we do not have a reference model to build managerial technology. This fourth component is in fact a precondition for the other three components to be deployed.

As we underlined earlier, authors who wrote about innovation in the past did not necessarily do so with the intention of finding a model for collective action. Nonetheless, the different elements found in the literature generally correspond to more or less implicit, coherent action models. We shall now discuss four such models.

2.2.2 Laissez-faire and black box: the traps of action at a distance

The first two models for managing innovation have the advantage of not making restrictive assumptions about object identities. Let us examine them in turn.

2.2.2.1 Laissez-faire: the limitations of incentives to action

The laissez-faire model considers that the processes that gave rise to the 'happy surprise' of creating an innovation are beyond the abilities of collective management and are in fact unmanageable.

Take the example of an economic policy designed to promote innovation and based on the idea of not hampering entrepreneurs in their actions. It will not try to specify exactly what this action is, or how to give support to it or try to improve it. Policies of this sort can be adopted within firms, in which case it is assumed that there is a capacity for 'intrapreneurship' and the action simply consists of not hindering it and perhaps even favouring its development.

Considerations on technologies, how they are to be distributed and stabilized, and the phenomena of competition and substitution that they seem to entail are also forms of laissez-faire: innovation managers using these notions are reduced to writing a list of the technologies, then deciding which to follow and which not. In this case, the technologies have their own dynamics and the innovator has no impact on them.

In addition, communities of practice emerge as natural groupings of the players concerned. Innovating with communities of practice simply consists of not preventing them from flourishing, in the hope that new, useful knowledge and concepts will result from the process.

These notions make a separation between what can be achieved by the manager and the sphere of innovation. The manager can only manage things in a favourable context in which initiatives are taken by 'enterprising' or 'innovative' actors. This tends to encourage the manager to take a passive role. As for the entrepreneurs or innovators, they have to count on their own energy, creativeness, tenacity and savoir-faire.

This model is extremely open regarding object identities and is relatively limited when it comes to controlling resources.

The laissez-faire model

Model of activity and reasoning: innovation is produced by a process outside the action model itself. The model describes the actions of managers who are not the innovators, and describes the action model for innovators in the vocabulary used for entrepreneurial action (mobilization, enrolment, motivation, etc.). The model's fundamental hypothesis: the managers' actions have very little impact on the innovators' actions (and any impact they may have is mainly negative).

Forms of organization: the model distinguishes between two types of actors: first, the entrepreneurs, communities of practice, intrapreneurs and other reference figures that carry out the innovation and, second, the managers (when they exist).

There is no technical substratum (freedom given to entrepreneurs, communities of practice, creativity, technology, etc.).

The performance stems from the 'success' of the entrepreneur or the community concerned. This performance is uncertain, random and one-off.

As already mentioned, the literature rarely describes a full action model. However, some authors follow the model, more or less implicitly: the classical literature on lead-users, on creativity, on communities of practice, on the sociological approach to the entrepreneur, etc.

2.2.2.2 **The mysteries of the black box: the paradox of R&D**

A second model also considers that innovation is a happy surprise, again with no constraints on the identity of objects, but in this case it also deals with the question of the resources invested. The model's fundamental hypothesis is that it is possible to act on the innovation process as if it were a black box, i.e. without describing the process itself.

Theories on public action for innovation often fit into this model. For instance, in discussions on questions such as the level of financing for public research, how it can be financed or how to encourage private research, it is assumed that the means of action can be mobilized without having to go into details about the actual subject of the research in question or the exploitation of its results (cf. competitive clusters and national research agency programmes).

The question of how resources are allocated is also relevant to firms, which can address the problem of the optimal level of R&D investments without necessarily knowing how the R&D work contributes to the innovation process. Firms often use a random model, where investing in R&D simply consists of taking part more often in a lottery (incidentally, with very little chance of success).

The innovation process is seen as a black box which reacts to incentives (at least partially) in a deterministic manner. The black box model need not be criticized as such, as it provides a form of simplification that can be very useful. The problem is knowing whether this simplification is not too simplistic. In other words, does the black box react positively to the levers for action in question, and how effective is it?

We are fortunate to have an excellent source of data to help examine this question, as economists have been carefully monitoring evolutions in R&D expenditure by states and firms for more than thirty years. Their findings are coded and presented in the *Frascati Manual*, which is updated on a regular basis. However, although there has been extremely strong growth in R&D expenditure (which we will come back to later), it is not easy to demonstrate its impact on economic growth. These findings have sparked off a great deal of research (see box below). A survey of the studies, carried out by Mairesse and Sassenou (1991), came to some fairly severe conclusions: 'The studies are not sufficient to show the existence of a significant relationship between R&D and productivity.' They go on to say that the impact is uncertain, especially because time-lags are often long; results vary from one sector and from one company to another, change depending on the period and are hidden by the impact of other factors governing production and productivity.

The paradox of R&D

The authors are particularly circumspect concerning the returns to R&D. For example, Boyer (1988) asked: 'Given that R&D expenditures are growing, how can we explain that productivity has not, with a few exceptions, been significantly increased?' The survey by

Mairesse and Sassenou (1991) confirmed the difficulties in assessing the contribution of R&D to growth.

The comparison of the R&D staff in the working population and growth in total factory productivity is also significant (*see* Figure 2.2). This was demonstrated by Jones (1995a), who used these statistics to show the limits of endogenous growth models that assume that R&D staff numbers are proportional to technical progress. As the figure shows, growth in factor productivity does not follow the same curve as R&D staff.

The impact of R&D investments therefore remains puzzling. There is a real impact (differentiation between firms, social returns, etc.), but it is difficult to correlate a 'quantity' (financial investment, research staff, etc.) to a performance (economic growth). In other words, quantity is apparently not the only lever for action.

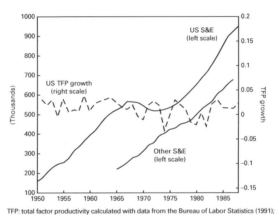

TFP: total factor productivity calculated with data from the Bureau of Labor Statistics (1991);
S&E: scientists & engineers; Other = France + Germany + Japan
Sources: National Sciences Foundation (1989) (*see* Jones 1995) and statistical abstract of the US economy.

Figure 2.2   Growth in R&D staff and GDP growth in the United States (1950–1989)

To illustrate the difficulty in correlating R&D investments and growth, we analysed data from the British Department of Trade and Industry (DTI 2004) on the top 700 international companies by R&D investment. To see whether such a correlation could be made for these 700 companies, Figure 2.3 shows investments in R&D (represented by the classic ratio of R&D over turnover) and the growth rate of turnover. The data are smoothed over a relatively long period (four years). The 'cloud' form of the data points shows that it is hard to make a correlation.

A number of objections can be raised concerning calculations of this sort. For example, could it be that the effect is deferred? Would it not be

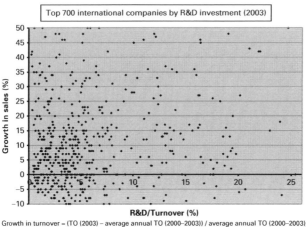

Growth in turnover = (TO (2003) – average annual TO (2000–2003)) / average annual TO (2000–2003);
R&D/TO = average annual R&D (2000–2003) / average annual TO (2000–2003)
Source: DTI R&D Scoreboard, 2004.

Figure 2.3   The paradox of R&D in large companies

preferable to examine the impact on profits or stock exchange rates? In 2005, a study from the consulting firm Booz Allen Hamilton (*see* the bibliographical appendix for details of its historical role in work on innovation management) obtained similar results from a sample of 1,000 companies. Its work also tested the objections we have just mentioned, showing that there was no correlation, whatever the timescale and performance indicators used (Jaruselski, Dehoff and Bordia 2005).

Another objection could be that the results were obtained in very different sectors. In fact, calculations sector by sector reflect the same heterogeneity. But above all, as soon as we mention the word 'sector', we are in fact distinguishing between different ways of using research for product developments. Thus, more fundamentally, an explanation of the relationship between R&D investments and growth must take into account the forms of organization adopted by the firms.

We cannot confirm the hypothesis of a deterministic relationship between R&D investment and its impact on companies in terms of innovation and growth. By restricting the means of action to the intensity of investments in R&D, we obtain only a low or even doubtful correlation with the firm's growth. In other words, models of this sort are not sufficient for controlling resources and we must look for other significant action variables.

Retaining the hypothesis of the black box, one potential variable to be considered is intellectual property (IP). This is a form of incentive for the production of knowledge and for innovation, but it is clear that little is known about the processes involved in using IP in firms. Whatever the case may be, there is the same controversy concerning the impact of IP on innovation as there is for R&D. Does IP favour or inhibit innovation? In fact, is there actually any link between IP and innovation? Which type of regulation would favour innovation, and what type of innovation? There is wide debate on these issues (*see* Howells 2005). It has become clear that they require more precise modelling of the nature of the innovation in question, which in turn raises the issue of the object's identity, thus moving away from the black box model.

We cannot review here all the cases in which the innovation process is treated as a black box; however, its efficiency is debatable in all the cases we know, mainly due to the assumption of ignorance concerning the innovation processes. A theory of innovation management must include reflection on the organization that contributes to the innovation.

The black box model

Model of activity and reasoning: innovation is again produced by a process outside the action model itself. The model describes the actions of managers who are not the innovators, and does not describe the innovation process. This process is considered to be random; its probability of success is influenced by external factors.

Forms of organization: the model distinguishes between two types of actors, those in the innovation process and external managers.

Technical substratum: R&D investments, public aids for research, industrial property, etc.

The performance is represented by the firm's growth or by economic growth, including the notion of return on investment.

As noted earlier, the literature rarely describes a complete model of action. We can find only a partial description in the economic model of innovation, based on incentives or R&D investment.

2.2.3   Innovation and the identity of objects: the limits of product policies

Other models have focused on describing and controlling the resources devoted to innovation. However, we shall see that these models are in fact based on restrictive hypotheses concerning the identity of objects. There are two families of models of collective action. In the first, innovation is radical and the result of a random process based on regular, but independent, projects. In the second, the innovation is a 'new product', which marginally improves well-identified performances.

2.2.3.1 Is innovation a stroke of luck?

We can begin by looking at processes targeting one-off, radical innovation. They aim to discover a product or service that will give the firm a strong competitive advantage and sometimes a 'rent'. Performance is assimilated with a unique product or service, which breaks away from the types of products existing in the industry and provides the firm with profits that make up for past failures.

The archetypal case is that of nylon. Du Pont de Nemours' 'discovery' of nylon stockings offered the company an exceptional market position for several decades in the period following the Second World War.[1]

Two means of action are associated with this approach to managing one-off innovation:

First, new technologies. High-tech solutions increase the chances of discovering a profitable innovation. The technology can be 'acquired' by purchasing specialized companies, by investing in R&D or by developing new industrial capabilities. A large number of research laboratories tried to imitate 'new nylon' because, according to the myth, the chemical molecule on which nylon is based had been synthesized for the first time by the firm's fundamental chemical laboratory. We must stress that this sort of approach makes the implicit assumption that *the technologies to be invested in have been identified*: investments must be made in nanotechnologies or biotechnologies in the same way that Du Pont invested in research into long organic chains.

Second, an original product. There must be the basic 'good idea', which matches market needs and has original uses (e.g. the hula hoop, Sony Walkman, nylon stockings, Facebook, etc.). The means of action are therefore employed to obtain this mythical 'good idea'. They can involve lead-users, suggestion boxes and sometimes even purchases of patents or companies. Another means of action involves project management, giving a 'heavyweight project manager' the resources to give the product a high profile. Again, we must stress that this approach implicitly assumes that the competencies are accessible and that the idea or the profile in question can be given intrinsic value in the market. In other words, *the value can be identified fairly early on in the process.*

These processes have been described in very different contexts, such as an entrepreneur with a 'good idea', a firm identified for its founding product or

---

[1] We will come back to the case of nylon in Chapter 8.

a random model in which the research laboratory is financed in the hope of finding a 'new nylon'.

How effective are these processes? In practice, the hope of acquiring a leading competitive position on the basis of blockbuster products or new technologies has shown its limitations in the past. In the best of cases, the 'rent' provided by the new products was eroded very quickly, but more often the 'new nylons' were not discovered quickly enough and R&D investments proved too costly and unprofitable. This was the case at the beginning of the 1980s and then in the 1990s when it led to drastic cutbacks in fundamental research budgets.

This historical fact can be explained by the exacting demands of processes designed to create one-off innovations, particularly because the innovation must be profitable enough to pay for its own development but also for any past failures. It has to pay for any investigations into technologies that led nowhere and for products that were failures. A number of authors have stressed how difficult it is to coordinate the 'right product' and the 'right technology'. Failure rates are therefore high. Moreover, these means of action – new technologies, an original product – assume that the technologies have been identified or that the value is confirmed early enough in the process. The means of action are therefore unable to manage cases where there are uncertainties as to the value and the competencies. The process must thus target innovative products with a high profit-earning capacity in order to finance all the probable failures, so making it a high-risk lottery.

Given this context, one might ask whether firms actually use this model of one-off innovation. Surely companies tend to be multi-product, with a view to smoothing out the risks and amortizing the investments by proposing product families? In this case, it would be misleading if not dangerous to isolate one-off projects, given that performance is precisely the ability to offer variations, to play several successive moves and even to learn from failures. Note that the 'rent' from nylon resulted, to a great extent, from the firm's capacity to develop different offers and to make continual improvements in the performance of both the product and its manufacturing process. Another problem: what chance do holders of one-off innovations have in the face of other firms which are prompt to imitate, explore alternatives and change and improve performance? In a way, it is precisely the fact that certain firms have been able to control the notion of repetition that has made one-off innovation strategies obsolete (we will come back to this in Chapter 6 regarding entrepreneurs and Chapter 7 regarding design tradition in large firms).

This underlines the ambiguity in the model itself. Is the organization actually targeting a one-off innovation, or is this an *analytical bias*, with the analyst isolating a single element in what is actually a far longer process of action? The second hypothesis seems to be true today in cases where this sort of model is applied to contemporary firms. Paradoxically, it is relatively rare to find cases where entrepreneurs or complex organizations of firms act on a one-off basis. A good example would be unique events such as organizing the Olympic Games. Entrepreneurs seldom act on isolated cases and are in fact assessed on their successive successes and failures. Even in the case of one-off innovations, underlying mechanisms of repetition have been identified, for instance in the 'latent organizations' described by Starkey *et al.* (Starkey, Barnatt and Tempest 2000). One-off innovation thus seems to be a fairly limited category of collective action.

One-off innovation is therefore a possible lever for action, but it targets a particular form of performance and is used in only very specific situations. The current forms of competition between firms and the resulting types of product renewals mean that the model is no longer appropriate for companies today.

The one-off innovation model

Model of activity and reasoning: the innovation breaks away from a known reference (dominant design, stable object identities). The existence of this identity forms a basic language (performance, technology, etc.).

Forms of organization: one-off project, in a single firm or an extended framework (partnership).

Technical substratum: new technology, new performance (the 'good idea'), new processes, new architectures, etc.

The performance consists in a one-off innovation that breaks away from the norm and is sufficiently profitable to pay for past failures.

A large number of works have studied one-off innovation (*see* the bibliographical appendix) and insisted on the break with previous products and organizations (*see* management of technology acquisition, 'ideas' management, open innovation, heavyweight project management, fuzzy front end, the management of discontinuous innovation, radical innovation, etc.).

2.2.3.2   Innovation and planning

For a long time, firms have sought to *plan* repeated innovation, considering that performance is no longer to be found in 'providential' innovation but by regular new product launches. Their aim is to keep up a high rate of product renewal, whilst increasing performance from one generation to the next.

Once again, two main families can be distinguished in the means of action employed to obtain this performance:

Competency: in a perspective of repetition and renewal of the product range, new technologies are less important than the mastering of core competencies or 'functions'. Once again, the focus here is on knowledge enhancement and the building of ontologies that we mentioned in the previous chapter (*see* the bibliographical appendix for further details).

The product: in this case the 'good idea' is less important than the right tools for product development, which include market surveys to position the product, value analysis, division of tasks, concurrent engineering, process validation, planning, etc.

How effective are these different means of action? Mastering a competence is obviously an effective solution, but only if it is possible to say in advance that the products to be developed actually use that particular competency. Similarly, market surveys are all the more appropriate if the targeted market already exists. In other words, these means of action are effective for certain types of innovation. In fact, the literature tends to speak of new product development rather than innovation. This is more important than it may seem: in these cases, the product's customers, functions, features, architecture and technologies are known, as are the professional groups involved. The product is nonetheless 'novel'. In fact, repetition favours improvements in performance in areas such as quality, cost, features, etc. However, it fits into the same line as its predecessors and there is no radical change of identity. The *nature* of the features is stable and the underlying technologies change very little. The 'innovators' therefore have quite a precise idea of the expected characteristics and of the competencies to be used to design and produce it. In this context, the means of action in question – the competencies, the product – are relevant and well suited to the circumstances.

These means of action correspond to a well-known type of market (and of competition), i.e. markets in which there are *dominant designs*. Given that the product identities, performance, architectures and functions are stable, it is possible to divide the work among firms. Very large R&D and marketing departments can be built and the product design function can be delegated to first-, second-, third- or even fourth-tier suppliers. This is the domain of the R&D-based firm, which is capable of organizing a continual increase in performance, both in technology and in functions (we will study this model in Chapter 7).

However, the model no longer works in cases of unstable identities because the basic language disappears and functions and products can no longer be used as a basis for organizing the development.

The planned innovation model

Model of activity and reasoning: the innovation is a change, but within a stable reference (dominant design, stable object identities). The change is 'parametric': the nature of the performance is given, only the level changes (increased speed, compactness, dB, consumption; precision of models, speed of development, etc.). The existence of this identity forms a basic language (performance, technology, etc.).

Forms of organization: the organizations charged with product development in the firms (engineering, research, marketing, industrial design, etc.).

Technical substratum: the tools used for good project management (specifications, identification of resources, division of work, etc.).

The performance is incremental progress in a dominant design, achieved at the lowest possible cost.

Knowledge management techniques and the methods of engineering (value analysis, Houses of Quality, portfolio management, etc.) are different facets of this model.

2.2.4   An action model for innovation management: contradiction or enigma?

None of the four models given above is sufficient to cope with the challenges of innovation-intensive capitalism. In the literature, some works recommend flexibility in two areas, competencies and products, on the grounds that flexibility of competencies can be obtained through competency dynamics, i.e. competency in acquiring competencies, and agility in products can be achieved through the designers' creativeness and their ability to listen to market trends through empathic design (*see* the bibliographical appendix). However, this takes us away from 'actionable' processes and back to laissez-faire. The ambidextrous organization, for example, consists in steering dominant design processes whilst at the same time giving freedom to the actors working on potential new markets.

It does not seem possible to avoid this opposition: models in which identities are free to change have difficulty in controlling resources and, on the contrary, models that try to control resources are inevitably based on descriptions of stable identities. Is innovation management, in the sense that object identities are not stabilized *ex ante*, an inescapable oxymoron or simply an enigma?

2.3   Building innovation capability: which model for collective action?

We believe that innovation management is indeed an inescapable oxymoron, but that managing innovation capability is an enigma. Although the enigma cannot be solved at this stage, we can at least suggest some key elements to be found in the solution.

2.3.1   The traps of innovation as a value judgement

Managing innovation involves an impossible contradiction that stems more from the words employed than from difficulties in carrying out appropriate action in situations of innovation by competition. The term 'innovation' itself is a hazardous trap for managers.

What is innovation? The word is so common that it seems unnecessary to define it and yet many of the difficulties arising from the notion are in fact due to the definition we give to it. Innovation is *a judgement made on an existing object*. A product or service is *qualified as innovative* by experts in the field or by the customers.

This simple definition has major consequences. First of all, the innovation is always judged in a subjective manner, but this is not nearly as serious as the fact that innovation is only spoken about *ex post*: a judgement can be made only once the object has been designed. In this perspective, 'managing innovative products' amounts to 'managing products that x considers innovative'. This means that the notion of innovation is not 'actionable' as the innovation can be characterized only once the action has been completed.

Any model designed to manage innovation must make its position clear regarding this definition, as the key characteristic in any model is the way it models activities. There are two alternative stances:

In the first case, the definition is respected to the letter and the hypothesis of *ex post* judgement is retained. *Ex post* judgement offers great freedom on the question of identity, but means that there are always great difficulties in controlling resources. This is the case of our first two models:

Strictly speaking, *the innovation process can only be known ex post* and therefore it is not possible to control the action (hypothesis of uncontrollable process). This is the laissez-faire model.

An alternative consists in identifying the environments in which the phenomenon is the most likely to be produced. The action then consists of preserving these environments or, more generally speaking, of identifying conditions that do not hamper and may improve the emergence of an innovation. This is the black box model.

In the second case, the definition is circumvented so that the resources concerned by the innovation process can be identified *ex ante*. The conditions of judgement are built *ex ante:* there is a reference against which the degree of innovation will be assessed. A product is judged to be innovative if it *breaks away* from the existing technologies or products, or if its performance or technology are *progress* compared with the established references. These are cases of the one-off model of innovation and the product development model respectively. Once again, the hypothesis on what is called innovation leads to the hypotheses on the underlying action model:

In the first case, the action consists in voluntarily exploring new technologies or new functions compared with given references. In this context of a break from the past, it is hard to think of forms of continuity and of extension because the reference is not supposed to change in the course of the explorations. The trials are therefore considered to be independent and the repetition is only the result of a probabilistic approach. This is the model of random exploration.

In the second case, the product's identity is the reference that constitutes the action. It defines the product's competencies and functionalities, the type of performance and the organization (project, functions).

In these conditions, the means of action to be used are intrinsically related to the hypotheses on the product's identity.

2.3.2   From innovation to innovation capability

In this new context, it is the actual definition of innovation that has become an insuperable obstacle. As we have seen, a simple *ex post* observation is not a satisfactory solution, but it is not possible to build an *ex ante* reference either, given that, in cases of objects with unstable identities, the reference needed to make a judgement on the innovative nature of the object is not available.

The immediate result of this analysis is that we can no longer talk about managing innovation. In the context of unstable object identities, we cannot take a stable initial reference; and the new demands for efficiency stemming from competition by innovation mean that it is no longer possible to consider innovation as a stroke of luck, observed *ex post*. On the contrary, it is important to focus on the *resources* devoted to this activity and on the characteristics of the *competitive context*.

Hence, after our study of the challenges of innovation-intensive capitalism, we must reformulate our question: we are looking for forms of collective action to manage innovation capabilities in the context of unstable object identities.

2.3.3   Elements of a new model

We have shown in this chapter that the previous action models identified and examined by the literature on innovation have been highly dependent on a certain understanding of the term innovation. Innovation was seen as a value judgement on a result, meaning that the models were limited either by trying to favour the spontaneous development of innovation or by planning the renewal of products in which the innovation concerned only limited, predictable characteristics. We have also explained the limits of these models in the current context where the stakes of innovation have changed. In particular, none of the action models described above appears to be appropriate when an object's identity is not given at the start but, on the contrary, becomes one of the major challenges of the innovation process. The inexorable rise in resources devoted to development and to innovation activities also means that thought must be given to whether or not they are efficient and potential action models must prove that they are sustainable for the firm. Therefore, what we are looking for is an action model for managing innovation capability. What can we say at this point about this new action model? Let us take the four components of an action model mentioned above and see how they apply to managing innovation capability.

1) The activity and the reasoning: the fact that the actual identity of the objects is in the balance leaves us with an extremely challenging problem. What forms of reasoning and activities can lead to such revisions whilst also respecting the constraints relating to economizing resources? One thing is certain, the reasoning can no longer be based on a prior representation of the object in the form of functions and technologies, as was the case in the past. The very idea that useful competencies can be defined in advance must be abandoned. Great efforts must therefore be made on the language used to describe the activity and more precisely concerning the reasoning made in these situations. The first criterion in the specifications consists in *explaining a model for activity and reasoning* without the assumption of stable object identities, i.e. with the assumption that the products and competencies are flexible.

2) The objects to be managed: the means of action for managing innovation capability will not be based on stable functions and performance.

This is a key point. We have seen that in the traditional models (one-off innovation, product development) the means of action concern either the competencies or the product, the implicit assumption being that the other dimension is available. In these cases, high-tech processes automatically generate products, original ideas find the relevant competencies and product development has known functions for an identified performance. When product identities are unstable, we can no longer represent these two dimensions separately. Growth in competencies is based on product concepts, which in turn are worked on in relation to the growth in competencies. It is essential for a repeated innovation strategy to look at how these two elements can be linked and separated.

3) Concerning the performance, the function of managing innovation capability is to ensure growth in a context of unstable object identities. At this stage, we can say that the innovation will be repeated, as one-off innovation has already shown its limits.

4) Three remarks can be made concerning the context and the forms of organization:

The project-based organizational framework often used in the past is no longer valid as it is based on the assumption that the object identities are stable.

In the new context, we are looking at the innovation capabilities of a community or collective body. Although it restricts the scope, we have limited our study to cases in which this collective body is a company (other studies have analysed the issue of innovation in inter-firm partnerships (Segrestin 2003) – see Chapter 15). This means that we are looking for a model to manage the innovation capabilities of firms, or a model for the *innovative firm*.

Our aim is not to focus on particular types of firms, such as start-ups, and to condemn others, such as the 'old' R&D-based firm. It is not enough to carry out a contingency study to explain why certain forms of organization work (why the champions are successful) and why others fail. Indeed, if the hypothesis of a general evolution in the competitive context is right, a contingency analysis can lead only to severe selection, as the forms adapted to the new context will be extremely rare and atypical. On the contrary, the aim of the theory is to increase the capacity for action of the largest possible number of firms. In particular, this means that it will address the issue of the forms of transition from an organization adapted to competition based on

Table 2.1. Summary of 'innovation management' models and specifications for managing innovation capabilities in the context of unstable object identities

	Laissez-faire model	Black box model	One-off innovation	Planned innovation	Specifications for innovative firm
Models of activity and reasoning	Innovation hypothesis: innovation = *ex post* judgement; two distinct models of action (the manager's, the innovator's)	Innovation hypothesis: innovation = *ex post* judgement; action model = non-innovative manager; innovation process = black box	Innovation hypothesis: innovation = a break with a known reference (dominant design – stable object identities)	Innovation hypothesis: innovation = incremental change within a dominant design which serves as a reference (stable object identities)	A model of activity without stable product identities (flexibility for products and competencies)
Objects to be managed – technical substratum	Manager does not influence entrepreneurs Communities of practice, individual creativity, technology, etc.	Industrial property, investment in R&D, public aids to research	New technologies, select and back a 'good idea'	Management of functions (core competencies, etc.), product development management	Structure innovation capabilities without basing them on 'functions' or 'performance'
Type of performance	Entrepreneur's 'success' Uncertain, random, one-off performance	Firms' growth, economic growth with return on investment made	A one-off, 'breakaway' innovation (technology or product), which pays for all past failures	Competition on a given dominant design (known product identities)	Growth by repeated innovation, in a context of unstable object identities (no one-off projects)
Forms of organization	Two types of actors: innovator 'figures' and managers	Two actors: the manager and the innovators (inside and/or outside the firm)	One-off project – in the firm or with a wider scope (multi-partner)	Organizations charged with product development (often projects within the firm)	At the firm level, including major R&D-based firms, without being limited to a project framework

dominant design (R&D-based organization) to an organization adapted to competition based on repeated innovation strategies.

These specifications are summarized in Table 2.1.

In these specifications, the greatest difficulty is to be expected on the issue of the model of activity itself. We have explained the limits of technology management and product development, but what are the underlying processes in a context of uncertain object identities? What reasoning can be employed? Which model or types of activities can be used for support?

In the following chapter, we will explain why we decided to use the *design activity* as the reference framework for the rest of the study. We shall see that the innovative design perspective enables us to propose a set of notions that is coherent with the specifications given above.

Questions for further study and discussion

What is intentional in an innovation process?

What is an 'actionable' theory from a managerial standpoint?

Key notions – Chapter 2

Intensive innovation

Crisis in the identity of objects

3 The design activity and innovation capability

In the preceding chapters, we have shown that innovation must be seen from a different angle, i.e. as the result of an actively sustained, voluntary process that can be organized, rather than as an *ex post* judgement. Firms wishing to innovate must manage 'innovation capabilities', but what exactly does this mean? Which activities are involved, who should lead them and how can their performance be evaluated?

The aim of this chapter is to show that firms which try to develop their innovation capabilities must place a new *emphasis on design activities*. These must be carefully organized and managed, especially in the case of innovative design. Although they play a central role in most major industrial firms today, relatively little is documented about these design activities, which leads us to believe that they have not been studied in any great detail.

There are several reasons for focused exploration and analysis of design activities. If we try to identify the actors who contribute to innovation capabilities, we automatically think of the researchers and engineers in R&D departments, whose mission is indeed to contribute to innovation by designing products and processes. However, unless we want to restrict our study to technological innovation, we should also include industrial designers, a rapidly expanding category which has an increasing influence within firms today.[1] We should also mention specialists in communications and semiotics, such as advertisers, brand designers, etc., and in certain cases user groups should also be included. All these actors have one thing in common: they design things.

The literature on innovation also points us in this direction, as it frequently uses metaphors based on design and often focuses on characteristic, design-oriented features (Hatchuel, Le Masson and Weil 2006a).

---

[1] We take the notion of 'design' in the broadest sense (*see* a formal definition in Chapter 10). We do not limit design to the specific profession of industrial designers – we consider it as a way of thinking and acting; it is a form of collective action. Design can involve many different actors: engineers, marketing experts, researchers, industrial designers and users can all be designers.

Several authors have pointed out that innovation requires active intervention from several networks of participants which help transform
the initial ideas to make them more practical and viable, and that
customers can sometimes be useful participants too (Callon 1986; Van
de Ven *et al.* 1999; Whitley 2000). It is precisely the role of design to
start with 'initial ideas' and gradually make them more concrete.
Innovation apparently requires an active, collective design process in
which all the designers are not necessarily identified *a priori.*

Other authors have indicated that innovation requires a complex learning
process in contexts of uncertainty, using a variety of knowledge types,
ranging from tacit to explicit, already existing or yet to be created
(Nonaka and Takeuchi 1995); it can be directed through intensive
experimentation (Leonard-Barton 1995; Thomke 2003a). These features
are common to all design processes, whether in the artistic, architectural
or engineering fields.

Innovation requires forms of 'mapping', 'guiding patterns' and 'framing'
(Van de Ven *et al.* 1999). All these notions are additional metaphors for
design paths, design rules and briefs.

Other results show more directly that design cultures and rules encourage
creative behaviour. We can give two examples:

The metaphor of jazz and organizations. Karl Weick suggested jazz improvisation as a metaphor for describing new modes of organization
favouring autonomy and creativity (Weick 1998). Jazz improvisation is
a good example of local design work (the improvisation itself) embedded in a set of design rules (theme, harmony, rhythm, musical genre,
etc.) and an organizational process (the band, rehearsals, instruments,
etc.). All these elements combined enable the jazz soloist to be 'innovative' within accepted, shared limits. Jazz musicians can improvise freely
as long as they respect these rules. The design rules for jazz also enable
the creation of innovative organizations in the form of professional
orchestras, organized and trained for imagining creative variations.

Latent organizations in cultural organizations. Starkey *et al.* (Starkey,
Barnatt and Tempest 2000) showed that cultural enterprises (in the
world of television) presented distinct forms of networks and hierarchies, which they called 'latent organizations'. Although television companies appear to manage independent projects and *ad hoc* teams for
each project, over the long term they almost always rebuild the same
teams over and over again. These latent organizations can be explained
by the fact that the teams are recognized for their design capabilities.
In these cases, latent organizations operate with a form of periodic

collective employment agreement, instead of using the free job market. Such teams promote design cultures that are recognized by the companies concerned.

This converging evidence encourages us to take a closer look at design activities that are often seen only in the background, and often only as a metaphor in work on innovation. In this chapter, we will explain a few of the essential properties of design activities, taking inspiration from the great historical design traditions of the architect, the artist and the engineer. However, we shall see that this perspective is interesting here only if we can go beyond the usual restrictive representations of design. We show that the current trends in design activities support this wider view and that the challenges of innovation-intensive capitalism correspond to major transformations in the world of design today.

3.1   Design: an activity underlying all innovations

Is there a risk that we will find the same pitfalls within design as we did within innovation? Is design an activity that can be organized and managed? Can it deal with situations in which object identities are uncertain? In truth, since antiquity, design has been considered as a *conscious activity* (Alexander 1964), whether on the individual or the collective level, and therefore as an organized activity. In this respect, design can be a management object.

As a collective activity, design has often been identified with (or even reserved for) certain major historical figures who built the main design traditions, i.e. architects, artists and engineers. A rapid examination of these traditions highlights several specific features of the design activity that relate to the issue of innovation (Hatchuel and Weil 2002).

3.1.1   Architectural and artistic traditions: reasoning, knowledge and expansion

Architects offer a perfect example of innovation capability management. Each new construction is an innovation, but a host of treatises and theories on architecture is available to help architects exercise their profession. The oldest surviving treatise on architecture, *Ten Books on Architecture*, was written by Vitruvius in the first century BC (Vitruvius 1999). In Chapters I and II of the first book,[2] the architect provides a conceptual framework for

---

[2] Chapter I: *De architectis institiendis, The education of an architect*; Chapter II: *Ex quibus rebus architectura contest, What does architecture consist of?*

the creation of buildings, based on a science of architecture comprising, on the one hand, '*knowledge* of so many arts' and, on the other, the *reasoning* that helps extract what is needed from the vast amount of potentially useful knowledge. This architectural reasoning is based on a model of the major functions of the object to be designed, which must respect the Vitruvian criteria of 'fitness, arrangement, eurhythmy or proportion, consistency and distribution or economy'.

As for artists, it must be said that artistic tradition has a more complex relationship with the notion of design. Artists, like architects, claim paternity for their creations, but they do not feel that they must take into account any predefined functions or that they are designed to solve old and well-articulated problems. The contemporary artist strives to create 'new worlds'. Artists are well aware that the future of their work depends entirely on other people's judgement of it; they know that their 'worlds' can be seen in a unique way by each observer, or '*regardeur*', to use Marcel Duchamp's expression. Artistic tradition therefore offers us *an extreme view of design and of innovation*, an act that creates worlds, each one unique and all the richer as they are perceived as such by the people receiving them. The philosopher Nelson Goodman gave a precise summary of this approach: 'How an object or event functions as a work explains how, through certain modes of reference, what so functions may contribute to a vision of – and to the making of – a world' (Goodman 1978).

This design tradition results in unexpected events. In fact, this comes back to an element that we pointed out as a stumbling block for the cognitive theories, i.e. creative reasoning. Hatchuel and Weil called the design process's aptitude to generate 'new things' its *expandability* (Hatchuel and Weil 2002). Design therefore helps to maintain, but also to explain, an essential notion in work on innovation.

Artistic tradition also shows that it is impossible to claim that an artist's work is finished as it is the starting point of another design process, the work accomplished by the observer. We could say that spectators are offered the opportunity of continuing on from the artist's process of expansion by their own means. The tradition thus helps us find another essential notion of innovation, but this time in the perspective of action: the role of the 'reception' of the design, by users, customers, the observer, etc.

Finally, the construction of new worlds also involves elements that help provoke them or structure them. The most extreme case was perhaps Marcel Duchamp's 'readymade' concept, but perspective also played a role in creating worlds, as a 'symbolic form', which 'rationalises the visual impression of the subject' (Panofsky 1975). Knowledge and reasoning, the two elements found in architectural tradition, are therefore found in the artistic tradition too.

3.1.2 Engineering tradition: a process of expansion based on the production of knowledge and experimentation

Although it is more recent, the engineering tradition has historical ties with architecture and the arts, particularly during the Renaissance. It differs from them in several respects, however, particularly with its unique relationship to knowledge. Engineers build up a new process of expansion by developing their knowledge; they adopted scientific approaches early on as a central element of their profession, thus distinguishing it from architecture. The expansion of scientific knowledge is obtained by observation, experiment, calculation and 'modelling', and it is precisely on this level that engineering design became collective.

Design reasoning was an essential part of engineers' activities. They adopted some of the Vitruvian 'functions', particularly when designing machines and instruments, but as they were confronted with a wider range of systems than architects, they adapted their reasoning to different objects.

This variety of objects, together with the collective nature of the activity, called for a system of reasoning to define the different steps to be followed, with control and validation tests at each stage to improve reliability. Proto-types, tests, demonstrators, etc. were proposed. The system had to be based on language that was sufficiently abstract and universal to be adaptable to all industries and all techniques. One of the most successful models was the German systematic design model (Pahl and Beitz 1977), which distinguished between three main stages: functional design, in which the object's main functions are identified; conceptual design, in which the scientific principles and architectural options are selected; and 'embodiment', in which the system is physically brought into service (*see* Chapters 7 and 8). The systematic design model, which is still a widely studied reference today, is based on a set of tools and methods that all engineers have a duty to know about (Duchamp 1988; Aoussat, Christofol and Le Coq 2000; Minguet and Thuderoz 2005). It served to elaborate increasingly powerful tools (in CAD in particular), which in turn have resulted in major changes in collective activities (Blanco 1998; Jeantet 1998).

This design tradition has a complex relationship with innovation: the engineer is always torn between applications and inventions. Engineering tradition is inseparable from the idea of invention, improvements and innovation. On this point, it comes close to the tradition of expansion found in the art world. However, engineers do not necessarily invent things in all their projects. They memorize past 'expansions' and can reuse them, as things that 'worked' yesterday may be a resource for tomorrow. Depending on their talents and the needs of the moment, engineers can go back to past solutions, adapt them or perhaps try to renew them. They then run the risk of technical failures or, like artists, the risk of their propositions being refused. A design-based approach therefore highlights a vital aspect in innovation capability: the engineer must be able to think about innovation and imitation of the past at the same time.

3.1.3   Design, a promising approach

These three major design traditions of architects, artists and engineers highlight some critical properties of design activities and sometimes of design reasoning:
   the exploitation of existing knowledge;
   the modelling of objects, for example to define the properties of the object
      to be designed;
   the extension of knowledge (notably through science);
   the acceptance of innovative expansion of the original propositions
      (cf. artists' creation of new worlds).
We should stress that these properties match our requirements for a model of activity as they are not based on static object identities that determine in advance the competencies and the objects to be designed. In a design-based perspective, there is not necessarily a predefined identity; similarly, an existing identity may be no more than an element of 'knowledge' that can be changed by an innovative expansion. In addition, the production of knowledge is not restricted by a given identity but can take place in a variety of directions. However, the object's identity may represent a stable model of the object to be designed (cf. architectural tradition), meaning that the design-based perspective can also include restrictive forms such as planned innovation.

Design also opens pathways for the other aspects of innovation capability management (objects to be managed, type of performance, forms of organization). 'Action models' can be found behind all these design activities, particularly in architects', artists' and engineers' strategies of *repetition*.

Although each piece of work is new, original and unique, architects, artists and engineers try not to repeat everything for each project, but to use a framework that helps them go back over the design and improve on it. The framework can, of course, be shared with many others, as in the case of the architectural orders, for example, or it can be an *ad hoc* system, like those imagined by artists. In this way, individual 'innovations' are never radically new as, far from being generated spontaneously, they are always attached to a genealogy, whether in the world of artists, in the classic architectural orders or more generally speaking in the scientific knowledge and functions called on by engineers.

However, this must not be confused with the linear model of determinism: each design also entails metamorphosis and change; artists play and tinker with their worlds, go beyond them and explore them; architects use the orders to explore new proportions and to solve new problems; engineers study, often in a highly controlled manner, alternatives between 'applications' and 'inventions'. All past explorations feed future explorations.

The design-based approach therefore helps highlight the *embryological* aspects of the activity. New products, technologies, values and competencies emerge, but at the same time this is based on past products, technologies, values and competencies.

A key factor in organizing the design activity is to structure the often collective process of embryogenesis, by structuring product families, playing on established values, reusing well-structured competencies and well-controlled technologies, tests, prototyping, division of work, prescription, reciprocal prescription and horizontal learning processes, etc. This process can target different types of performance: designing without restrictions on the knowledge to be produced or, on the contrary, trying to use only existing knowledge, i.e. designing whilst producing the minimum amount of knowledge; designing rapidly or with large expansions. In the above, we can identify 'objects to be managed', 'types of performance' and 'forms of organization' which are relevant to the question of managing innovation capability. We can also see that there can be different managerial techniques, corresponding to different types of performance.

3.2   Design: few studies and limited representations

Although the great traditions of artists, architects and engineers show that design is a promising approach, it is nonetheless true that their representations of design have sometimes been restrictive. A brief study of these limitations will help understand why it is important to overcome them.

3.2.1   Design and product development

A good example of a restrictive interpretation of design can be found in the classic definition given by the French Standards Association, AFNOR, in norm FD X 50–127, dated January 1988: 'Design: creative activity starting from expressed needs and existing knowledge and ending in the definition of a product which satisfies these needs and which can be produced industrially' (international reference: NF EN ISO 9000:2000).[3]

The definition is highly restrictive in that the needs have to be expressed, the knowledge already exists and the aim is to design a 'product'. Moreover, the fact that it must be possible to manufacture the product places the definition firmly in engineering tradition.

In this frequent sort of limitation, only the most systematic and most routine parts of engineers' design activities are accounted for. The tradition of new product development (NPD) concentrated on this aspect (Wheelwright and Clark 1992). It focused on coordination with the other functions (marketing, manufacturing) and provided very few descriptions of designers' work, the activity of product design or the difficulties in exploring functional spaces (which were limited to standard specifications completed using Houses of Quality (Hauser and Clausing 1988)).

In this case, innovation is limited to situations in which object identities are stable. Any expansion of knowledge is voluntarily reduced on the grounds that it implies extra costs, and any expansion of propositions is limited to the identity of reference objects.

It is interesting to note that recent trends in product development add a 'creativity phase' before the development process (Goldenberg and Mazursky 2002; Pahl and Beitz 2006) (*see* the bibliographical appendix, Section 3, for further references). However, the works tend to consider creativity as an external, extraneous process, largely independent of the design process itself and allowing for only limited combinations between creativity and engineering design. In Chapter 10, we present a design theory that accounts for creativity in design thinking (C-K theory).

---

[3] It should be noted that the norm was recently changed. The new definition is as follows: 'A set of processes which transform requirements into specific characteristics or specifications for a product, process or system' (FD X 50–127 from April 2002). We would like to thank Fabienne Flin for this information.

3.2.2 Design and industrial design

More recently, several authors have focused on the importance of industrial design for innovation management (von Stamm 2003; Best 2006; Utterback *et al.* 2006; Verganti 2008; Dell'Era and Verganti 2009). They underline that designers are more sensitive to the users, to emotions, to symbols, to creativity and the arts and to fashion. This helped identify a new type of innovation, 'design-driven innovation' (Verganti 2008), which radically changes the emotional and symbolic content of a product.

This approach sheds light on a very important aspect of the nature of design. However, in this book, design is not limited to industrial design. Industrial design is just one tradition in design, close to art tradition. Limiting design to industrial design tends to arbitrarily restrict the circle of designers to industrial designers.

It should be stressed that the rise of interest for industrial design is an interesting symptom of changes in the approach to product development. We see this as a symptom of the rise of 'innovative design', which we will study later in the book. Innovative design refers to a form of design which concerns all the traditional design functions (R&D, marketing, industrial design) and even new actors (in particular users: in industrial design tradition, users are people whom industrial designers must take care of, whereas in the broader perspective of innovative design users themselves can also be in the position of designers).

3.2.3 Design and classic organizational theories

In a completely different respect, design was often restricted in organizational tradition too. In Henry Mintzberg's major synthesis (1982), organizational configurations were essentially based on different types of coordination: mutual adjustment, direct supervision, the standardization of work processes, the standardization of outputs and the standardization of skills. Each of these coordination mechanisms dominated in an 'ideal' organization structure, i.e. respectively a simple structure, an adhocracy, a machine bureaucracy, a divisionalized form and a professional bureaucracy. Hatchuel (2001a) showed that these five types of structure are based on two specific approaches to design:

> On the one hand, the three latter types, machine bureaucracy, divisionalized form and professional bureaucracy, are based on past design work: standards *have had to be designed* for work, tasks and processes,

products and competencies, meaning that design work was essential. However, we have no idea how the standards were designed, who designed them, how they were revised or what knowledge was required. The design activity is assumed to have taken place but is not actually mentioned.

On the other hand, the first two types, simple structure and adhocracy, were in fact explained very little, except to say that the simple structure is purely hierarchical and that adhocracy is a horizontal structure. In this case, they are purely relational systems and there is no mention of the issue of design.

In short, either design is described by its results alone, with little mention of the activity itself, which is considered obvious and natural; or design is not described at all.

3.2.4   Design and problem-solving

A third type of restriction concerns the design reasoning. In previous research, design has often been grouped with task planning, calculations and optimization, particularly in work on product development and in the engineering sciences.

In the 1960s, Simon made an interesting although somewhat limited attempt to link design reasoning and problem-solving. He was the first to insist on the need to build a science of design. To do so, he employed most of the tools from decision-making theory in situations of so-called bounded rationality. However, he restricted the notion of a specific design theory somewhat, by stating that it would be close to problem-solving theory: 'When we study the process of design we discover that design is problem solving. If you have a basic theory of problem solving then you are well on your way to a theory of Design' (Simon 1995). As Hatchuel pointed out (2002), the difficulty is that traditional problem-solving theories do not give a specific place to the notion of 'expansion'. In his attempts to propose a theory on 'creative thinking', Simon (Simon, Newell and Shaw 1979) defended the idea that this thinking was no different from reasoning in a context of bounded rationality.

In this case, how are innovation, invention and expansion possible? Simon explained this by the intervention of 'imagery', when new solutions come to mind, but this approach has its limitations. He also showed that a clever combination of all the knowledge available could make new solutions emerge. However, although this second approach is quite acceptable, it is still restrictive as it is impossible to distinguish between two types of situation: either the solutions already existed and the expansion is limited to an exploration, or the solutions did not exist at the beginning of the process and the design activity must elaborate them. In this case, the expansion is far more than just a combination.

The notion of design has therefore often been seen in a restrictive manner (we shall see in Chapter 8 that these restrictions in fact correspond to a specific design regime, systematic design, as organized in R&D-based organizations since the beginning of the twentieth century). Certain vital aspects of design are nonetheless coming to the fore. For instance, new types of designers are emerging other than engineers, notably industrial designers. There is also now talk of designing new values and not just products; of creating business and not just developing products; of expansion in propositions and not only decision-making and problem-solving. It is all the more important to overcome these restrictions since the elements that were hidden behind them, but are now emerging, represent the current challenges in the world of design. We shall now take a closer look at these challenges.

3.3   Innovative design: a fruitful approach for transforming the identity of objects

In the following sections, we will describe the four main trends in the design world today and show that they correspond to contemporary transformations in innovation-based competition.

3.3.1   Rise in staff numbers and new actors: organizing collective design

We have already mentioned the increase in resources devoted to innovation, i.e. design resources. The corresponding rise in staff numbers obliges organizations to carry out major transformations, which the classic, restrictive approaches to design can have difficulty in accounting for.

The transformation is not only quantitative, the designers' functions are changing too. For example, at Renault in the period from 1950 to 1990, not only were staff numbers multiplied by twenty, but also new specialities emerged among the engineers in the engineering and design department (acoustics, electronics, new materials, etc.) and a strong product department and a large industrial design studio (employing nearly 300 people) were also set up. We have seen that design traditions, particularly among artists and engineers, differ enormously from one field to another. Given that one of the crucial challenges today, in industry in general and in the automobile industry in particular, is for designers and engineers to work together in design activities (Hirt 2003), what can be done to avoid misunderstandings, or, worse, confrontations, when there is a restrictive view of design?

3.3.2   The changing identity of objects

The second trend is that the uncertainty surrounding object identities is causing profound changes in the profession of engineering. Many of the efforts to construct systems that we noted in engineering design tradition were based on stable object identities. It was this stability that led to stable functional languages, that guided the production of scientific knowledge, that led to convergence at the end of the long collective design process and that ensured that the intermediate validation phases were reliable indicators of this convergence.

Today, a large amount of scientific knowledge must be produced to design new products, not only in sectors such as pharmaceuticals but also in aeronautics and in seemingly more traditional disciplines such as thermotics. These science-based products require new forms of organization that go way beyond the restrictive frameworks mentioned above (Hatchuel, Le Masson and Weil 2004b). In a completely different field, it has become a crucial challenge for some industrial design studios to design coherent, shareable sign systems using semiotic models (Le Bail and Oussaïffi 2004). In certain situations, the market itself has to be designed. In the past, there were often cases of products that generated needs, but today it is a question of finding methods that go much further than 'strokes of luck'. How can customers be trained? How do we find out about a future 'partner' or a potential market that does not exist yet when there are no products or transactions to study, or even general recognition of the roles of customer and supplier? This may seem an extreme example and yet sectors such as automobile telematics and electronic tyres are in fact very close to this case today (Barrois and Lindemann 2004; Midler 2004).

In contemporary design situations such as these, the only way to manage the design activity is to adopt a design approach that takes into account the joint expansion of knowledge and propositions.

3.3.3   Trends for design organizations

The third trend concerns design organizations. Many new organizations have been added to the traditional functional divisions of marketing, engineering and design, research and industrial design. Some have become stable, as in project management, with its relatively well-controlled cross-functional teams and matrix-based organizations. But other new organizations are emerging today.

The increase in problems relating to innovation has given birth to many embryonic *innovation departments* charged with building new means of interaction with the existing actors, and new forms of partnerships are emerging to respond to new challenges. These are no longer simple co-development partnerships in which two companies work together on a case where the object's competencies and functions are more or less identified in advance; they are now exploratory partnerships in which the actors have no certainties regarding their own interests or the shared interests and where the identity of the object to be designed is far from stable (Segrestin 2003). Many studies have focused on the spectacular growth in partnerships of this sort, which are crucial in helping firms invest in new value spaces (Hagedoorn 2001), but they have also noted their very high failure rates.

3.3.4   The new challenges of design reasoning

The fourth trend concerns the current challenges regarding design reasoning. Providing a formal framework for design reasoning has become a vital issue, which goes well beyond academic circles as industrialists are also voicing their concerns. For example, at the opening of the 2003 International Conference on Engineering Design in Stockholm, the vice president of Saab AB in charge of technology called for generic theories on design reasoning to help elaborate new methods and tools (Fredriksson 2003). For the world leader in design assistance tools, Dassault Systèmes, today's challenge is also to propose tools for innovative design and, once again, a rigorous formal framework is essential (Prevéraud 2003).

3.4   Conclusion: design, an analytical framework for innovation capability

In the previous chapters, we have examined the specific nature of present-day competition by innovation, characterized by uncertain object identities and the need for strict controls on the resources devoted to innovation.

Table 3.1. Specifications for managing innovation capability

	Specifications for innovative firm	Perspective offered by design activities
Models of activity and reasoning	A model of activity without stable product identities (flexibility for products and competencies)	Forms marked by reasoning and expansions of concepts and knowledge
Objects to be managed – technical substratum	Structure innovation capabilities without basing them on 'functions' or 'performance'	Ability to generate new objects to support (collective) design
Type of performance	Growth by repeated innovation, in a context of unstable object identities (no one-off projects)	Historically varied types of performance (knowledge-based economy; strong expansion, etc.)
Forms of organization	At the firm level, including major R&D-based firms, without being limited to a project framework	Variety of forms currently grouped in the R&D-based firm

When these two factors are combined they produce a scissor effect, with the result that companies today are obliged to invent new forms of organization for their innovation capabilities and in particular for all their design activities (research, development, marketing, industrial design, strategy, communication, etc.). New rationalizations are currently under way that are likely to lead to a new industrial model. However, at present, no 'one best way' has been found that companies can simply follow. Nonetheless, it is possible to highlight the key conditions that an action model of this sort should fulfil (*see* Table 3.1).

We have seen that design activities are a promising path for constructing a management model for firms' innovation capabilities, i.e. a model for the innovative firm. To summarize, the objectives are as follows:

Propose a model of activity that is not based on a set object identity, i.e. not based on *a priori* typologies for functions, competencies, needs, etc. On the contrary, a model of this sort should account first for the expansion of competencies, and second for the creation and exploration of 'new worlds' or new 'value potential'. Design activities and theories are deeply affected by these two dynamics.

Propose new objects for which new 'management techniques' can be invented that are not the traditional objects: specifications for features, functions, etc. However, in the case of uncertain object identities, these 'features' and 'functions' have to be designed. It is therefore hard to identify the objects to be managed. Nonetheless, this is no reason to go back to a form of laissez-faire. Over the years, the traditional figures in design have been capable of inventing objects to cater for their own capacity for 'innovation' (cf. the architectural orders, the artists' 'worlds', the engineers' functional languages and conceptual models). Today, too, design communities could therefore be the right place for new means of action to be invented.

Propose types of performance that are neither simply competition on a dominant design (i.e. based on 'cones' of performance fixed by the objects' identities) nor a 'bet' on one-off innovations. The performance therefore consists in organizing repeated growth by innovation, without stabilizing the object identities. In the past, design activities have targeted different types of performance (rapid design, design with no production of new knowledge, design by strong expansion, etc.) and the question of design without stable object identities is not unheard of in certain design traditions.

Propose suitable forms of organization, with a special focus on their compatibility with the traditional R&D-based firm. Does the new model make the R&D model obsolete or, on the contrary, does it help make the most of research and of development in the context of competition by intensive innovation? This question is already posed in the design organizations of the major R&D-based firms which have to integrate designers from different backgrounds with very different traditions.

Questions for further study and discussion

What are the received ideas about design?

What can be qualified as 'innovation capabilities'? Compare them with 'capabilities' for change.

PART II
Design capacities in innovative firms

4 Highly innovative firms – Tefal 1974–1997: the wizards of Rumilly

Innovation from the inside

In Chapter 1 we mentioned a number of real cases of players directly involved in innovation. In this chapter, we introduce an imaginary Innovation Manager who has just been appointed to a large firm and who will serve as a guide for the concrete problems facing managers on an everyday basis. He begins with some very practical questions. 'In the current system of innovation-intensive capitalism, how can we manage our firm's design capacities when we have uncertain object identities and limited resources? My company has just created the job of Innovation Manager and knows that there is an urgent need to address the issue, but how do I go about it in practice? Where can I find the new techniques we need to manage innovation?'

To answer these questions, we needed to study innovation 'from the inside', but the first problem was to decide where to look and what to describe. There were hosts of examples of workshops with state-of-the-art prototypes, of open-plan offices with the muffled hum of CAD workstations. There were also scores of visionary leaders and distraught managers, not to mention the thousands of anonymous engineers and doctors designing the cars, microprocessors, drugs, food products or services of the future. They could tell us about their successes and failures, the palace intrigues and all that went on behind the scenes, but were their experiences relevant to the problem of managing design capacities? The greatest prudence was required. In most firms, it was easy to find stories of innovations through skunk work and the language describing projects, portfolios and function/project matrices. But it was far more difficult to identify the new practices that helped the firms face up to competition by intensive innovation.

New vocabulary and new models were needed to bring these original practices to light and then to explain them and assess their value for implementation elsewhere. It was essential to go right to the heart of innovation to develop the appropriate vocabulary, but this had to be done in the right firm, in the right conditions.

4.1   What is a 'model' firm?

4.1.1   Why use a case study?

How could we study innovative design situations – i.e. situations where the identity of the objects is uncertain – when we did not have the basic language to identify the objects to be managed or the nature of the performance, or to describe their organization? We were confronted with an extremely difficult problem: the methods usually employed in the management sciences were not appropriate. For instance, take the example of statistical surveys based on questionnaires: how could we formulate the questions for the selected sample of firms? How could we recognize what was new and describe the original ways of operating invented by certain firms?

We were seeking to bring to light a class of phenomena and to describe original innovative design processes. In the same way as biologists studying a mysterious metabolism, we needed a model organism, i.e. an organism that could be observed, with surprising characteristics that could provide a wealth of information about it. This is what the management sciences call a case, which is used to deduce the laws governing the phenomena in question. The question of 'generalization' will be covered in the next chapter.

How did we choose the case and what were its essential characteristics? Contrary to the many stories of innovation, we were not looking for a unique case of an innovative product, because it was precisely the notion of repetition that interested us; nor were we looking for a long history of an 'innovation' or 'technology' that led to several products (such as the cases in *The Innovation Journey*, by Van de Ven *et al.*). We were interested in the innovation capability, i.e. the collective work of the design teams in action, which in some cases work on several technologies and several innovations at the same time. We preferred to focus on situations where there was lasting, organized, collective design. In short, our idea of an interesting case was a firm that was capable of repeated innovation over a relatively long period of time.

4.1.2   Choosing a case

In the following pages we will study the case of Tefal. It may seem paradox-ical that we looked for a model of growth by repeated innovation in a relatively low-tech industry – the small household electrical goods sector – but in fact it is a sector where there are extreme tensions, as illustrated by the case of Moulinex.[1] Tefal would probably not have been able to stand up to competition from Asia or to pressure from the large supermarket chains if it had not implemented innovative design strategies, which bolstered growth during the three decades during which the model was used (end 1960s to end 1990s)[2] (*see* figures in the box below). Tefal therefore provided us with a prime example of a 'model organism' for our study.

Tefal, key figures 1961–1997

Tefal belongs to the SEB Group, which specializes in household electrical goods and also owns the brands Calor (essentially for irons) and Rowenta (for vacuum cleaners). In 1997, Tefal accounted for 30 per cent of the group's total turnover of 9.1 billion francs (€1.39 billion)[3] but more than 50 per cent of the group's profits.

From 1961 to 1995, Tefal's staff increased from 35 to 2,300 and turnover rose from 30 million francs to 2.7 billion francs (approximately €4.6 million to €410 million) (*see* Figure 4.1). Despite economic crises, the firm experienced strong, sustained growth in staff numbers, turnover and profits throughout the period. As a general rule, its employees received the equivalent of eighteen months' salary per year, sometimes even twenty-three months'. The products were manufactured in France – mainly in Rumilly, located near Annecy – at a time when competitors were beginning to sub-contract their produc-tion to Asia. In 1997, the firm had the best profit record in its sector and had maintained average profitability of around 14.5 per cent of annual turnover for twenty years. Our aim was to explain the phenomenon and see whether it could be used as inspiration for other firms to find new means of action.

---

[1] Moulinex became a household name in France through its kitchen and household appliances, the first of which was launched in 1932. It enjoyed great success until the mid-1980s when competition became stronger, and was then particularly hit by low-cost labour/products from emerging countries in the 1990s. After months of high-profile protests and demonstrations, the firm went into bankruptcy in 2001 and thousands of employees were made redundant. The firm was eventually taken over by its main competitor, the SEB Group.

[2] After 1997, major organizational reforms – in particular the introduction of business units – led to profound changes in the Tefal model.

[3] 1997 figures.

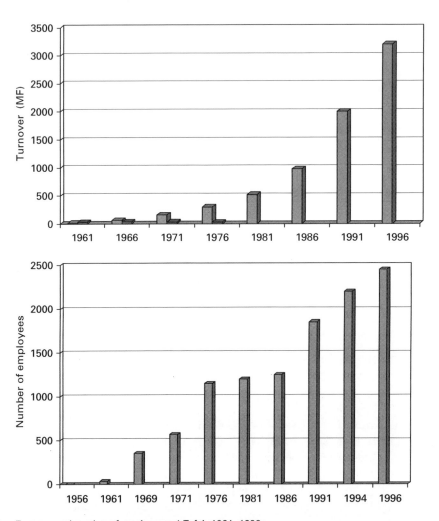

Figure 4.1   Turnover and number of employees at Tefal, 1961–1996

4.1.3   Context and research methodology

The first step in our research was to ensure that the 'model organism' could be studied and to find a suitable methodology. It was not enough to just visit the company and describe what we found there, as an audit at Tefal in 1994 had come to some severe conclusions about the firm: its organization was not clear, logistics and stock management could be improved and project-based management left much to be desired. The project managers' responsibilities were not clearly defined and the targets even less so, given that specifications were not defined at the beginning of projects. All this hardly gave a clear picture of Tefal's success.[4] It was not easy to explain – at least with the usual management criteria – and called for a more detailed study.

This study was carried out by Vincent Chapel. As we saw briefly in Chapter 1, Vincent was extremely interested in innovation mechanisms and asked the CEO of Tefal, Paul Rivier, whether he could examine the case of Tefal for his management PhD thesis. Mr Rivier agreed, but on the condition that he worked directly with the design teams as a designer. During the three years spent at Tefal, Vincent Chapel therefore worked as a design engineer and took part in a number of product design projects. He helped create the baby care range and registered twenty-seven patents during his PhD, no doubt a unique case in the management sciences.

Why was it important to work with the designers? Because it wasn't enough to simply ask them for a hypothetical secret recipe: the 'wizards of Rumilly'[5] were incapable of explaining how they did things or how they were organized, a fact that incidentally made their relationships with their parent company, the SEB Group, relatively complicated. Vincent Chapel's work consisted of inventing and drafting an illustrative model for the work of the virtuoso players who performed the music so magnificently without being able to explain their secrets. Apart from taking part in the design activity, one of the main difficulties was that, as the basic organizational language was unsuitable, a new, consistent language had to be developed to describe the activity, a language able to highlight the acute phenomena found at Tefal and not elsewhere. This work on conceptualization had to be done for the model to come into being.[6]

4.2 Non-traditional recipes for growth by innovation

None of the traditional reasons put forward to explain a firm's success is capable of fully explaining Tefal's sustained growth for more than twenty years. In the following paragraphs, we look at the main proposals suggested

[4] There are indeed serious grounds for thinking that if traditional management criteria had been applied it would have been the end of the Tefal model.
[5] This is an adaptation of the famous expression used by American journalists at the end of the nineteenth century to describe Edison, 'the Wizard of Menlo Park'.
[6] See 'La croissance par l'innovation intensive: de la dynamique d'apprentissage à la révélation d'un modèle industriel' [Growth by intensive innovation: from learning dynamics to the revelation of an industrial model], Vincent Chapel's PhD thesis in Engineering and Management, presented in 1997 at the Ecole des Mines de Paris under the direction of Armand Hatchuel and Benoît Weil (Chapel 1997).

in the literature (cf. Chapter 1), as this helps highlight several of the original features of our model.

The literature reviewed in Chapter 1 and in the bibliographical appendix puts forward a series of reasons to explain growth in firms: an exceptional invention, mastering a key technology, the statistical model, the providential entrepreneur, creativity and good project management. Can Tefal's success be explained by one of these principles?

4.2.1   Why Tefal's success involves more than an exceptional one-off invention

Tefal first became known in the 1950s for inventing the non-stick frying pan. Could it be an exemplary case of a firm that has built its growth on a revolutionary one-off invention, and is this product enough to explain its success? This would make it an ideal case of 'innovation': the transformation of an 'invention' into a product on the market, which then ensures the growth of the firm to which it gave birth. It would be an exemplary case of the linear model (the innovation being a process going from the invention or scientific discovery to the development of a product and its introduction on the market – cf. the box below and the box later on in this chapter on how the Grégoire family invented the non-stick frying pan).

Literature: the linear model

The linear model is mentioned in several traditions:
- the economic tradition of business creation (cf. Schumpeter's modelling of the firm with business cycles (Schumpeter 1964) and its econometric application by MacLaurin (1953));
- the managerial tradition, particularly for fundamental research management in the 1950s, the linear model serving in this case as a foundation for the creation of central laboratories and research departments in many large groups (see the reference work at that time, written by Mees, Research Director at Kodak (Mees and Leermakers 1950));
- the critical tradition for science and R&D, showing the difference between an invention process (of a linear nature with a key emphasis on the individual inventor) and research (Jewkes, Sawers and Stillerman 1958).

However, Tefal does not simply produce 'magic frying pans', as other families of products are just as innovative and contribute to the company's turnover and profits. These include appliances for raclettes and fondues, electrical barbecues and Crep'Party pancake machines in the 'informal meals' product family; a range of bathroom scales in the 'personal care' and kitchen scales in the 'food preparation' families; a range of domestic appliances; bottle-warmers, sterilizers and baby monitors in the 'baby care' family; and not forgetting the extremely profitable odour-proof cheese preserver in the 'food storage' family. The products vary in terms of commercial success, but they all make a significant contribution to the company's growth, which can thus be explained by two factors: permanent renewals within existing product families and regular additions of new ones.

This variety of products invalidates the hypothesis of a success built on one single innovation.

4.2.2   Why Tefal's success involves more than mastering key technologies

Although the company's success is not due to a single original idea, many of the products responsible for the firm's growth are nonetheless partly based on one key competency: an ingenious process for making a layer of PTFE (Poly Tetra Fluoro Ethylene), the famous non-stick Teflon, adhere to an aluminium surface. This appears to make it an example of a business that has concentrated on a 'core competency' to build growth.

Literature: the core competencies model

In the literature on innovation-based growth, the authors often underline the importance of mastering a technology or a 'core competency'.

In the appendix, we explain that this idea refers to the resource-based theories (Penrose 1959), which had two major offsprings, first in heterodox economics (evolutionary economics) and second in strategic management (Barney 1991; Pavitt 1992; Hamel and Prahalad 1994a; Leonard-Barton 1995; Teece, Pisano and Shuen 1997; Tidd, Bessant and Pavitt 1997).

However, Tefal's innovative products are not based on a single technology. The great variety of products is matched by the variety of competencies required to design them. The non-stick frying pans are produced using PTFE coatings technology but also require aluminium spinning processes, whereas saucepans involve stamping technology. Similar examples apply for all the products, which involve electricity, electronics, assembly, plastics processing, etc. Could it be that these technologies are so simple that they are negligible compared with the core competency? This does not seem to be the case, since certain products owe their success to technologies that are just as sophisticated as PTFE coating, such as thermal control by fuzzy logic for the bottle-warmer, or the thermo-spot temperature indicator on the base of the frying pans.

Can we assume that Tefal acquired these technologies and simply combined them with its own competencies? In fact, the designers at Tefal master these other techniques extremely well, to such an extent that they are recognized in the international community for their expertise in each of the areas in question. Moreover, in most cases they have had to adapt them and add to them to make them suitable for the small household electrical goods sector.

Tefal is therefore characterized by its great agility in adopting different technologies, its ability to master them very quickly and adapt them to the context of household electrical goods. It is this agility that enables the firm to sustain a high rate of product launches (several hundred each year).

4.2.3   Why Tefal's success involves more than a statistical model of repeated innovation

Could it be that Tefal's success lies in its ability to multiply the number of trials made, thus multiplying the chances of finding successful products through strokes of luck? Is the success based on a simple statistical model, where innovation is a random phenomenon and success is guaranteed by simply multiplying the number of attempts?

Literature: the random model

In economics, the random model is still a basic model for work on the growth and size of firms in population studies (*see* Jovanovic 1982; Sutton 1997 (synthesizing Ijiri and Simon, Gibrat, Jovanovic and Pakes-Ericson); Pakes and Ericson 1998).

The model is also widely used in management literature (Stalk and Hout 1993; d'Aveni and Gunther 1994; Eisenhardt and Brown 1998). From the 1960s onwards, it became one of the reference models for research management (Mees 1916; Benusiglio 1966–1967). The *Harvard Business Review* presented a rigorous overview of the model more than twenty years ago, explaining how economists view R&D (Mansfield 1981). Since then, it has remained one of the leading paradigms on the subject of management, particularly with the idea of 'tolerating failures' (Farson and Keyes 2002; Thomke 2003a).

Could the success be due to an exceptionally long series of strokes of luck? The regularity of the repeated successes seems to invalidate this hypothesis.

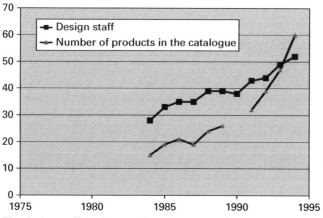

The design staff work on engineering, research, tests, prototyping, methods, industrialization, norms and quality

Figure 4.2   New products and design staff in Tefal's household electrical goods division

Or did the firm simply increase the probability of success by increasing the number of trials?

If we adopt the idea of a statistical model of innovation, the number of designers should be roughly proportional to the number of ideas produced; as there was a constant growth in Tefal's product ranges, the staff numbers should therefore have increased in the same proportions. We have figures for evolutions in the numbers of design staff in the household electrical goods branch from 1984 to 1994 and also for the number of products present in the catalogue for the same period. The figures give a minimum estimate of the number of products launched as products regularly left the catalogue and certain products launched never reached the catalogue due to lack of success. The number of designers grew far more slowly than the list of products (*see* Figure 4.2).

The idea of statistical success can also be seen from another angle. It is quite reasonable to assume that the statistical model requires just as many designers at Tefal as it does in other industries. In principle, there seems to be no reason why the constant increase in design staff found very generally in the active population (in absolute, but especially in relative, terms) (see data on French engineers in Chapter 2) should not also be found at Tefal. But, contrary to all expectations, the percentage of designers is remarkably stable (*see* Figure 4.3). Whereas the numbers of executives and employees

| | Renault | | Tefal | |
	1984	1994	1984	1994
Blue collar	63	46	71	74
White collar	37	54	29	26
Turnover (billions of French Francs, 6.67FF = 1€	72	146	0,78	2,54
Base 100	100	202,78	100	325,64

Sources: V. Chapel, thesis, Ecole des Mines, 1997; B. Weil, thesis, *Conception collective, coordination et savoirs*, Ecole des Mines, 1999; Renault's turnover (automobile branch) 1996

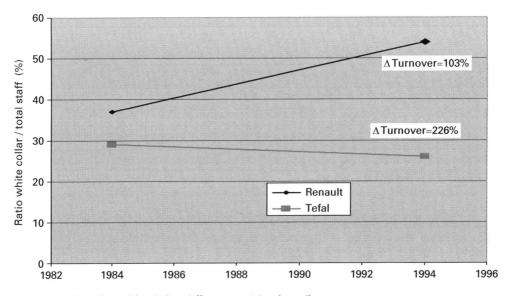

Figure 4.3 Renault vs. Tefal, design staff management and growth

increased substantially during this period at Renault, the proportion of white-collar workers remained the same at Tefal. This is one of the great mysteries surrounding the firm: far from relying on a statistical model of innovation, the firm had a surprisingly economical way of managing its designers. We will return to this key point later.

Apart from increasing the number of trials, another hypothesis regarding the statistical model of innovation involves a more careful selection of the products to be developed and knowing how to find the necessary design resources. It is a question of selecting the right opportunities and then organizing the business rigorously and rapidly.

Literature: the rigorous selection/organization model

This is the argument put forward by Drucker on innovation and entrepreneurship (Drucker 1985) and also the conclusion made by Tidd *et al.* on managing innovation (Tidd, Bessant and Pavitt 1997). It puts the focus on rigorous selection of the products to be developed followed by rigorous business organization.

Certain authors focused on the ability to recognize opportunities (Kim and Mauborgne 2000); others put more emphasis on 'absorptive capacity' (Cohen and Levinthal 1990) and on dynamic capabilities (Teece and Pisano 1994), i.e. the ability to find the necessary competencies as quickly as possible.

The notion of open innovation suggests that firms source innovation ideas and competencies outside the firm to lower costs and extend their knowledge base (Chesbrough 2003).

Once again, these explanations do not describe precisely the way Tefal operated. The firm was capable of entering new fields of knowledge and of course it had an exceptional ability to recognize business opportunities; however, it is also true that the relationship between the business opportunities and the competencies is relatively complex. For instance, it was the research on an odour-proof raclette machine (opportunity) that led to the acquisition of competencies on catalysis. But the odour-proof raclette machine was a commercial failure; it was the reusing of catalysis for the cheese preserver that finally led to the creation of a profitable product line (*see* the box on the odour-proof raclette machine later in this chapter). Thus, there are close, complicated relationships between market opportunities and the acquisition of competencies. It was by playing on and building up interdependency that Tefal managed to produce growth.

4.2.4 Why Tefal's success involves more than a providential entrepreneur

It is tempting to think that Tefal's success is due to one or perhaps a handful of providential entrepreneurs. Could Tefal's success be due to its managers' exceptional creativity, their ability to invent innovative products, their vision of the market, their ability to see consumers' needs and their specialized knowledge of household goods? If so, this confirms the long-awaited return of the 'entrepreneur' (Giget 1998; Van de Ven *et al.* 1999).

Literature: the model of the providential entrepreneur

The tradition of the providential man goes back a long way. It was already present with Schumpeter (1964) and Jewkes *et al.* (Jewkes, Sawers and Stillerman 1958) in their work on inventors, or Penrose (1959), who believed that entrepreneurs and 'entrepreneurial services' create growth (as opposed to administrative services which tend to deal with day-to-day support, i.e. managing existing business).

It re-emerged briefly with Peters and Waterman (1982) and is now back in the spotlight, although the need for new types of visionary managers is also evoked (Cusumano and Selby 1995). Schön (1969) argued against the idea on the grounds that, since we do not really know how to find or to train providential men, it is a poor way of managing innovation.

Two key points go against this claim in the case of Tefal. First, Vincent Chapel's experience in the firm showed that design was very much a collective affair. Far from concerning just a few individuals, everybody was involved. For instance, he tells the story of how the warp-resistant frying pan was invented. An employee on the stamping press had the idea of adding a small stainless steel disc to reinforce the aluminium base and talked to his foreman about it. Tests were carried out soon afterwards and a first prototype was then submitted to the main designers and managers. The project was then improved on, the patent drafted and the processes established. More generally speaking, the design routines comprised a fairly wide range of design functions including engineering, testing, prototyping, methods, industrialization, work on norms and quality and sometimes some research. As for managing the design process, a product committee attended by the CEO and the division heads, plus several dozen other people (product managers, project managers, prototype managers, etc.), was held once a month to review all the innovations being designed at that time.

Second, it was difficult to find a pre-existing 'vision' at Tefal that guided innovation (*see* the box on the beginnings of the baby care range). When the products came onto the market, a 'vision' for future product ranges gradually emerged. For instance, there was no overall vision behind the launching of the waffle machine in the 1970s, but it was this product launch that led to the idea of the 'informal meals' concept and helped *build* a key 'vision' for designing a large number of other successful products.

4.2.5   Why Tefal's success involves more than managing creativity

We have seen that Tefal's success was due to the multiplication of projects, without this being a result of a planning process, and that the ideas for new products sprang from a collective process rather than an individual entre-preneur. Could Tefal be an example of growth by innovation due to good creativity management?

Literature: the creativity management model

This notion is somewhat vague in the literature (we come back to this in more detail in Chapter 10), although there are several studies on the subject: creativity in business (Amabile 1998), ordinary creativity for all (Alter 2000; Robinson and Stern 2000), creativity with systems such as suggestion boxes (Fairbank and Williams 2001) or factory quality circles (Lawler III and Mohrman 1985). Creativity management means that managers leave the designers their autonomy and creativity without harnessing their inventiveness and let the right networks and communities of informal practices be built up to enhance innovation (Bailyn 1985; Stewart 1996; Amabile 1998; Alter 2000). Hargadon and Sutton (1997) described the model of creativity management at Ideo to underline that efficient creativity management actually requires very specific management skills and a capacity to combine different factors (work on incentives, on auction, on cognitive capacities, on knowledge production procedures, etc.). This empirical case presents several similarities with Tefal.

Tefal did have very 'organic' ways of operating, with a rudimentary organiza-tion chart that did not really reflect the actual work relationships. However, if this were the only explanation for Tefal's success, this would take us back to the idea of probabilities: the experiences of creativity did not result in growth in the relative share of good ideas but rather growth in the total number of ideas (Magnusson 2001). The methods based on creativity tend to make the assumption of a constant (or even decreasing) 'rate' of good ideas depending on the number of ideas, with a final filtering to ensure that only the best ones are retained. Tefal's success seems to be better than the statistics given that the percentage of successful products compared with all the products launched was quite high. This can be explained by the fact that it had a capacity to filter that did not rely solely on the market, and yet the hypothesis of creativity says nothing about this capacity to filter.

In fact, practices at Tefal were richer than anything described in the theory of creativity. There were, of course, forms of organized creativity (cf. the box on the history of the odour-proof raclette machine). However, there was also *an exceptional capacity to filter*, organized collectively with the monthly product committees attended by the main managers and the designers in charge of the projects in progress. The filtering was done on the basis of past learning processes and accumulated experiences, and the questions to be treated had already been investigated in the form of rapid, varied prototypes. These skills must be taken into account when describing Tefal's success and not just the creativity of its designers.

Apart from the filter, the 'ideas' formulated by the designers were themselves limited in number and their 'quality' tended to be better than for simple creative work. In other words, the designers themselves were more than just creative and their proposals were already more elaborated than 'ideas'; they were more like new concepts that already contained the knowledge provided by everybody else. At Tefal, contrary to creativity sessions where designers are asked to put their knowledge aside as it might harness their creativity, work on drawing up concepts was very strongly influenced by all the players' knowledge. The ideas were the starting point in a process where they were reworked and transformed and where developments and interdependencies were organized (creativity and ideas will be dealt with later in Chapters 10 and 11).

4.2.6   Why Tefal's success involves more than good project management

Having ruled out the main traditional theories on growth by innovation models, it remains for us to examine the idea that Tefal's success may be due simply to good project management, i.e. a large group of visionary managers capable of giving good project objectives to competent, closely knit teams. This idea could fit in with the collective nature of design, as certain members of the group of visionary managers could also be project managers.

However, once again the theory does not really explain how things operated at Tefal. Although Tefal did practise some forms of project management, they had surprising features that were often contrary to the rules of 'good' project management:

Project management was two-headed: instead of the single project manager, Tefal had product project managers and technical project managers. The product project manager was in fact in charge of a product family to be developed; he was far more concerned with adding to this family than with managing identified projects. He defended ideas more than specific projects and his work consisted of helping to make progress with a large number of 'projects', often with ill-defined objectives.

The specifications were implicit. They were not given at the beginning of the 'project' and the aim of the design process was precisely to prepare them. The two-headed project management system had the advantage of enabling a 'client' representative and a 'technical' representative to take part in drawing up the specifications.

Table 4.1. Some of Tefal's specific features

Traditional explanations	Specific to Tefal
One-off invention	Product variety. Product families expanded continuously
Key technology	Variety of functions. Competencies expanded continuously
Random model	Control of total number of designers
Providential entrepreneur	Collective design work with ability to build a common vision
Creativity	Expertise and prototyping, the basis of the product committee
Project management	Two-headed project management, implicit specifications

There were no detailed timetables, but time-based objectives such as home exhibitions, etc. served as points of reference and major meeting places. At the start, no resources were allocated, no QCT (quality, cost, time) objectives or sales objectives were fixed and no details were given about the entrance ticket, except that it had to be as low as possible. There was no projected timescale either. Development speeded up or slowed down depending on the potential and on external events echoed by the product committee.

Although some forms of project management could indeed be identified at Tefal, the above differences cannot be neglected. Could it be that the specific nature of Tefal was precisely its surprising ability to speak of 'management' even before the 'project' actually existed, i.e. before there was either a target object or a specific time limit? This is a characteristic feature of what we have called innovative design: the ability to put up with instability of object identities and to make new identities emerge.

This discussion on the traditional explanations enables us to highlight several original elements found at Tefal, which are summarized in Table 4.1.

4.3   A surprising 'metabolism'

Despite its success, Tefal seems to 'deviate' from the usual theories on innovation management. What driving forces and 'mechanisms' have led to its success? We shall see that these 'mechanisms' are such that it is difficult to talk about them in terms of 'mechanics' and that in fact it seems easier to describe Tefal using biological-style processes. We will show that it is a *metabolic model*. It is the nature of the things it metabolizes, or transforms, and the way in which this metabolism is produced, that enable us to describe the way Tefal operates.

This notion of metabolism, which we describe in detail below, is the first element of the new language we were looking for. It offers a new way of describing how innovative design is organized. In the following pages, we describe this metabolism by presenting its main characteristics one after the other, but it is important to stress that all these elements come into play at the same time. This is indeed one of the essential features of a metabolism: it contains its own systems of reinforcement and interaction (circular causalities) with forms of conditioning and regulation that are inseparable from the transformation processes themselves. It is the way the model itself works that ensures its survival and its structuring. This may seem tautological, but at Tefal, it is the repeated innovation that enables the repetition of the innovation and it is difficult to isolate one element rather than another in the origins of growth by innovation.

How can a metabolism be described? Biochemistry refers to 'metabolic pathways' to describe series of chemical reactions that build metabolic products (to be used or stored in cells) and initiate or control other metabolic pathways. We will examine certain 'metabolic pathways' that form the basis of the Tefal model.

Literature: metabolism vs. organic organization

Burns and Stalker (1961) described firms and products which presented the characteristic features of innovative design: products with new identities appeared in the electronics industry in the post-war period, mobilizing new competencies. In this context, Burns and Stalker were particularly concerned to show that mechanistic firms had difficulty in changing to more organic systems. As Hannan and Freeman (1989) pointed out: 'It is instructive to note that B&S found only one instance of an organic structure in a situation in which this should have been the appropriate form of organization. Their book is essentially an analysis of why organizations that ought to change to organic systems fail to do so, even when there is high agreement among their managers that they should move in that direction.' The 'mechanistic model' describes structures, division of work and delegation of responsibilities, whereas the organic model is characterized by the absence of these traditional characteristics, which are replaced by a general concern for innovation on the part of all the actors in the firm.

There was no doubt whatsoever that this concern for innovation existed at Tefal, but our aim is to provide a detailed description of the 'metabolisms' of this organism. The notion of metabolism helps describe the collective action in an organic firm. We shall see that the innovation-intensive metabolisms in innovative firms such as Tefal comprise processes which go way beyond the behaviour of the actors involved.

For a more detailed discussion of the notion, *see* Hatchuel, Le Masson and Weil (2006a).

4.3.1   Discovering and exploring value spaces

The designers at Tefal had always been attentive to changes in values resulting from social transformations stretching over several decades. The products matched their concerns to 'simplify housewives' tasks', 'lessen the chores' or 'offer new forms of conviviality' in a period when so many changes took place in terms of social, family and domestic behaviour. The profound changes that have taken place in western societies in the past half century, such as the generalization of work for women, later marriages, massive urbanization and the increase in single-parent families, have had major impacts in the home. These changes in values were all opportunities for innovation. Tefal's products represent transformations in society's values.

However, this was not just another manifestation of the notion of 'strategic vision': the space for values and innovations was not identified *ex ante*, but coincided with the gradual introduction of the innovations themselves. All the new appliances and devices designed by Tefal – or its competitors – thus helped give material form to these new values. In some respects the designers made possible these transformations to home life and helped to express the associated value space.

The story of the origins of the Tefal frying pan illustrates this first essential feature of the model (*see* box below). It is an almost archetypal combination of a 'technical' invention and the identification of new values.

The origins of the Tefal frying pan

The story of Tefal frying pans seems to be the story of an invention, but appearances can often be misleading.

Immediately after the Second World War, Marc Grégoire worked as an engineer at ONERA, the French national aerospace research centre. He was also very keen on fly fishing. During his spare time, he spent long hours trying to make a fishing rod out of the then new, highly elastic and resistant fibreglass materials. But he encountered a major difficulty: freeing the fibreglass rod from the mandrel used to give it its shape. The problem was that the coatings available at that time did not cater for making finely tapered items such as the fishing rod. One of Grégoire's colleagues at ONERA suggested that he should try a new material, recently put on the market by the American firm Du Pont de Nemours under the trade name Teflon®: PTFE. It had surprising wetting properties that made it non-stick and was therefore a potential solution for coating moulds. But a problem remained: how to make the non-stick coating adhere to an aluminium mould.

Grégoire worked on the subject for several months, multiplying his experiments and exploring numerous alternatives. One day, he noticed that when acid attacked the aluminium it provoked small cavities with the strange characteristic of being narrower on the surface than deeper down. This gave him the idea of making the PTFE adhere mechanically and not with primers or chemicals. He took an aluminium surface attacked by acid, deposited a layer of PTFE on it that filled in the pores and, once cooked, adhered to the support (*see* Figure 4.4).

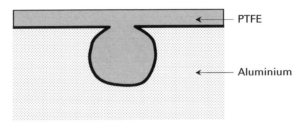

Figure 4.4   Schematic diagram of how PTFE adheres to aluminium

It was at this point that Colette Grégoire, Marc's wife, intervened. She was tired of her husband spending all his time buried in his experiments and asked him whether he could make something that would be useful in the house instead. They had three young children, their milk had to be boiled every day and that meant lots of saucepans to be scoured: couldn't he make her a saucepan with his non-stick system? Grégoire went to his local Prisunic store but there were no saucepans. Anxious not to go home empty-handed, he decided to buy a frying pan instead. And so the first non-stick frying pan was invented.

Grégoire later protected his invention with several patents before trying to sell the idea to the manufacturers of the time. But they took no notice of him, explaining that the saucepan market was a capital equipment market: people bought a set of pots and pans when they set up house and had them recoated as and when necessary, they were passed on from mother to daughter, so what need was there for cheap aluminium frying pans? Tefal frying pans were born when Grégoire decided to produce them himself, the name Tefal being a contraction of Teflon and aluminium. We know how successful the entrepreneur proved to be.

It is easy to recognize these stereotypes: the inventor, science, leading-edge materials, rebuffs from the established manufacturers. But there is also Colette Grégoire's role: it is she, in the end, who best represents a vital element in Tefal's genes, the relation to value. She brought to light the new values in the home and expressed women's demands for household equipment to make their work easier. It was Colette Grégoire who contradicted in advance the kitchen utensil manufacturers' words. Tefal came into being and was developed because it had identified this value space.

Source: V. Chapel was fortunate enough to hear the story of the origins of the non-stick frying pan from Marc Grégoire himself, shortly before he died.

We should point out that this relation to value is not a relation of evaluation, as if the value was given and served to 'evaluate' the quality of the product. It is a relation of discovery: the product's success is a symptom of the emergence of potential new values. The case of the waffle machine is a good illustration of this point.

The waffle machine and the value of informal meals

In 1975, Marc Grégoire's patents for Tefal fell into the public domain, so the firm sought to diversify its products. One such product was a family waffle machine. At the time, metal waffle machines were reserved for professionals. As they did not have non-stick coatings, it took long preparation and several dozen trial runs to find just the right balance between the temperature, the batter and the amount of fat on the hotplates to make the perfect waffle. These lengthy preparations could be justified only for commercial use, at fairs, etc. Its non-stick coating brought the Tefal waffle machine into the home: housewives could make excellent waffles on the first attempt. The machine's enormous success surprised its designers.

    At this point, work began on discovering and exploring the value. Studies carried out at the time on how the product was used showed that it was not so much the waffles that were popular but the idea of new ways of having meals: the waffle machine was a medium for informal, easy-to-prepare meals, where the cook was not separated from the other guests and where everybody took part in the cooking. It was this study that enabled them to pinpoint the value of 'informal' or 'convivial' meals. The value space was then explored, leading to the famous raclette and Crep'Party pancake machines.

4.3.2   Prudent explorations

The creation of the baby care range, a completely new product line for the company, illustrates how the Tefal model is based on prudence. We begin by examining the case in the box below before coming back to this notion of 'prudence'.

The creation of the baby care range

The baby care range was developed in the period 1995–1997. Although the product line was new, the problems involved were not. As early as 1976, Tefal had presented a heated fabric baby bottle-warmer at a home exhibition, but it was not a commercial success. Ten years later, the bottle-warmer was seen as one of the possible diversifications for the firm's successful range of kettles. In 1990 another rapid study of the child care market indicated that the market was in regular expansion, that products had low technical levels, that brand awareness was all-important and that the brands present were not terribly innovative. However, the competitors had extensive product ranges covering all the aspects of baby care and not just a single product, which would have been the case for the Tefal baby bottle-warmer. Another important characteristic was that they were mainly distributed by specialized retail chains and not via the supermarket outlets used by Tefal. Finally, competition took place in the global arena.

The baby care range was developed on the basis of this study. There was no 'strategic project' and no long additional preliminary studies were carried out. The prior knowledge and the way Tefal operated meant that a simple 'brief' could be given to develop a range of baby care products, whilst maintaining the usual objectives, i.e. to simplify housewives' – or, in this case, mothers' – tasks, to differentiate themselves from the competitors and to use the firm's key competencies (which at that time were electronics, weighing, plastics, telephony). There were no specifications. The designers worked on the ideas received in particular during the product committee meetings. Four products were developed at the same time by the most competent departments (the sterilizer and the bottle-warmer in the household electrical goods department; the baby scales and baby monitors in the weighing-telephony department).

We can focus on the development of the sterilizing products and the bottle-warmer. The project management was two-headed, for the technical side and the marketing side, with one of them following all the stages of the product development and mobilizing the necessary expertise. The idea was to explore several worlds at the same time, including the competition, industrial property in the domain, technical alternatives, technology watch and prescribers (meetings with paediatricians, visits to maternity hospitals, etc.). They were also keen to identify the essential marketing landmarks, such as the Home Exhibition in summer 1995. This represented a massive production of knowledge for the firm. For instance, in the case of technical alternatives, the designers explored very open, extremely heterogeneous issues. The alternative methods of sterilization included refrigeration, chemicals, autoclave, UV rays, etc. The alternative methods for heating included electrical resistance, bain-marie, induction, microwave, etc. Several technologies were available or in the process of being developed concerning temperature regulation, including electromechanics, electronics with fuzzy logic, etc.

The development process was completed in a few months: it took six months for the prototype centre to produce a functional prototype, including technical discussions and unforeseeable events (the project was postponed at one point for several weeks because of an emergency on another project that was given priority). The prototype was used for tests 'in the kitchen' (on the Tefal premises) and also to make a stereolithographic model, to make detailed plans and to calculate the economic profitability (cost price, investments, etc.). The tooling was ordered at the end of 1994. The industrial design and the packaging were ready in March 1995. As for all developments, modifications were made: one major change involved adding a function for heating jars of baby food, which the tests had identified as being an essential feature. The question of the diameter of the jars of baby food obliged Vincent Chapel and the head of the household electrical goods department to carry out an epic survey in just a few days, to find all the different dimensions for the jars sold in all the European markets. The product was launched in August 1995.

New applications were studied as early as March 1995 and were launched the following year. The designers had worked not just on a new range but on an evolutive range.

This case study highlights several interesting aspects of the firm: its ability to reuse existing knowledge; to develop original, robust solutions very quickly; to think from the start in terms of product families; and to do rapid but thorough overviews and to produce new knowledge. However, we would particularly like to underline the designers' efficiency and ability to limit the risks: relatively few people were involved in the project and the investments were fairly low; the project lasted only a few months; and a limited range was brought onto the market as quickly as possible whilst preparing additions to it. As far as possible, they worked with resources that were already available, in the framework of existing departments. It was not a major strategic project, financed at a loss, with heavy investments over a period of several years. The issue of the level of technology and the amount of knowledge produced must also be addressed. It was probably far less than for science-based projects (*see* Chapter 13), but it is clear that a large amount of knowledge was nonetheless produced (cf. the regulator for the bottle-warmer or, more generally speaking, knowledge regarding the baby care sector).

The process of exploring a value space in this case is characterized by the behaviour of 'prudence' on the part of the firm when it comes to innovation. As Vincent Chapel underlined in his doctoral thesis on Tefal, this prudence was not a question of limiting innovation because it involved risk-taking. On the contrary, Tefal's managers believed that they would be running a major risk if they did *not* innovate, and that innovation, far from being a costly artifice, was one of the conditions of the firm's survival. Nonetheless, this absolute necessity did not solve the problem of the risks and uncertainties always inherent to developing innovations. The attitude adopted by the managers at Tefal was to reduce the risks as much as possible and in particular the consequences of the risks for the firm. Their priority was to minimize the risk of the company's failure by ensuring that, even if an innovation was not a success, it could not threaten the company's survival or even its good health.

The innovation process followed what Vincent Chapel calls a 'prudent model' of innovation. This legal term used in bankruptcy law refers to the firm's risk of failure. The model was prudent as it combined two complementary aspects, essential for a firm's survival:

First, as we saw above, it was 'prudence' itself that imposed innovation, in terms of the firm's survival.

Second, that the risk imposed by the innovation was not neglected. All the risks, including the financial risks, the risk of immobilizing design capacities or risks for the brand image, were taken into account carefully in the model and minimized as far as possible. By minimizing the risks, Tefal's investments for a new product were ten times lower than those made by its direct competitor at that time, Moulinex.

The term 'as far as possible' was guided by a simple rule: in order not to jeopardize the repeated innovation model, the conditions of repetition had to be assured, i.e. no individual innovation could be capable of putting the company at risk. This is why one of the characteristics of new product developments was the concern for a 'low break-even point': investments in a new product were not to be too high, so that in the event that sales failed this would not threaten the firm's survival. Easier said than done! It required a long-term policy and constant efforts, particularly with respect to the industrial system itself, which was extraordinarily flexible and easy to re-engineer. It should be noted that design costs were also kept very low: limited resources and high-speed new product development – just a few months for the entire development process for the new baby care range – were also part of Tefal's prudent innovation policy, given that no one product development was ever allowed to monopolize the design capacities.

This prudent model, the second feature of the Tefal model, made it possible to obtain the other characteristics detailed below.

4.3.3   Obtaining a high rate of product launches and learning from the market

We have explained the origins of several of Tefal's leading products. However, we have not forgotten our aim of studying the firm's innovation capability. The odour-proof raclette machine will help us explain the approach, which goes beyond the classic product development frameworks. This machine illustrates the capacity to launch products and also the processes involved in repeated innovation.

The odour-proof raclette machine

During a product committee meeting attended by Vincent Chapel, the CEO expressed his concern about a drop in the sales of raclette machines. Was it a worrying signal that Tefal's products no longer suited current tastes? As usual, the company wanted to respond quickly. There was no time to launch a market survey to understand the phenomenon, which was in fact only at the stage of a slight warning. In any case, could a market survey help understand how the raclette machine was used?

The CEO decided to organize a raclette party on the following Saturday and invited the main designers. Whilst eating, they asked questions, analysed and discussed their ideas. They agreed that eating a raclette was always a treat and involved having a good time, but one problem was that it was difficult to stand the smell of stale cooked cheese lingering in the curtains and carpets the following day. The odour, or rather the lack of odour, would hence be a way of offering a unique selling point for raclette machines.

The designers set to work immediately. They quickly realized that there were various alternatives for reducing odours but that the most promising method was offered by catalysis. The head of the household electrical goods branch asked Vincent Chapel to organize a two-week tour of Europe for him to find out everything about catalysis from factories, laboratories, experts, etc. In a few weeks, Tefal's designers became as competent on the subject as experts from the automobile industry who had been using catalysis for their depollution systems for years.

A solution for an odour-proof raclette machine gradually emerged but came up against a sizeable obstacle: the high cost of catalysis. In the car industry, a catalytic exhaust system costs the same price as an engine. How could they use catalysis in a product sold for €30 including tax? A surprising solution was found when a member of Tefal's staff visited a car factory and asked about the containers marked 'rejects'. The answer was that the automobile industry was extremely demanding and the production process for catalytic converters was still not fully mastered. Many monoliths presented unacceptable geometrical defects. But these 'rejects' were perfectly acceptable for use outside the automobile industry. Tefal bought the 'rejects' at a cheap price. The odour-proof raclette machine was then produced respecting, as in the previous cases, the prudent nature of the Tefal model.

In fact, this prudence was particularly important in this case because the odour-proof raclette machine quickly proved to be a commercial failure. Sales in the supermarket in Annecy failed to take off, so the managers went to see for themselves, to listen and talk to the customers, who pointed out a major problem with the product: the odour-proof filter was located on the top of the hotplate, the same place that serves for keeping the potatoes warm during the meal.

The first thing most developers would have thought of doing would have been to design a new architecture for the raclette machine. However, they did not choose this option because the designers had realized that new habits were gradually developing in the way raclette machines were being used. 'Raclette parties' were becoming more sophisticated. So they proposed a completely different concept, a combined machine. Tefal was the first company to propose machines that made greater use of the top of the hotplate, particularly with its raclette + pierrade (stone grill) machines. This time they were a great success. They also opened new possibilities for hybridization and multi-functions that could be offered in a multitude of combinations, thus giving a new lease of life for products in the 'informal meals' range.

What about the work on odour-proofing? Should it be labelled amongst the explorations and acquisitions of knowledge that were failures? On the contrary, the knowledge gained about catalysis was reused in a study on refrigerator odours; it also served as a basis for work on membranes that led to one of the most profitable products ever, the cheese preserver; and it was used again a few years later to develop the odour-proof chip pan.

This short history illustrates many of Tefal's characteristics: learning from the market, radical incrementalism on the raclette machine lineage, the role played by the 'expert managers' and the relation to knowledge production. We will come back to these elements in the following paragraphs.

The third essential feature to be found in the case of Tefal is the high rate of product launches, linked to forms of learning. Not only was innovation 'repeated' but the frequency of innovations was high. This was related to the exploratory dynamics of the innovation space: each product launch was a means of getting to know the market better. Its success or failure provided information on the trends, needs and values that were declining or emerging. The fact that Tefal did not carry out any market surveys is significant. It was the product launches that represented the best possible survey. There are several reasons for this:

- Tefal managed to keep design costs so low that a product launch was hardly more expensive than a market survey.
- The rate of innovation was not compatible with the time needed to carry out a market survey: the product would have been on the market before the survey was finished.
- But above all, Tefal paid great attention to learning mechanisms about the market. It was not just a 'go to market' strategy but rather an original and elaborate way of analysing market trends: all Tefal's staff members went to the supermarkets or markets and sold the new products themselves.

4.3.4   Following the path of radical incrementalism

The fourth feature is that innovation is incremental, but radically incremental. None of the individual innovations involved a fundamental change. For instance, the new baby care range was designed using an available knowledge base. However, the incremental 'step' was non-zero for each of the products: even for an apparently stable product such as the non-stick frying pan, innovations were found from one product to the next.

As shown in Figure 4.5, it was the succession of these small steps that built the important changes observed in retrospect. What do the first raclette machines have in common with today's multi-function machines? The genealogy of these products' design helps reconstruct the incremental trajectories that led from one to the other. It should be noted that the 'incrementalism' exists not only within a given product family but also between product families. Product spaces were separated gradually. For instance, the 'informal meals' products were a direct result of applying a non-stick coating to kitchen accessories other than frying pans and saucepans (a waffle machine, as we saw earlier).

Tefal is characterized by the fact that it never followed either trajectory 1 or 3. It avoided radical projects (3) on the grounds that they were not prudent in the sense that they required large investments with high risks.

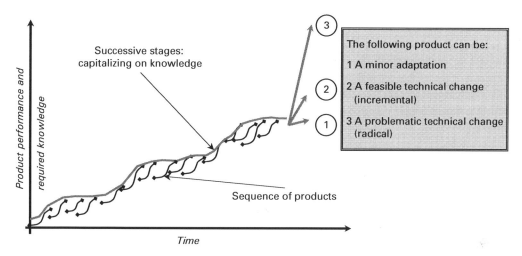

Figure 4.5   From incremental to radical

But Tefal also avoided minor projects (1) because they did not enable the company to acquire sufficient knowledge to maintain innovation dynamics. This is the other side of a prudent nature.

4.3.5   The role of expert managers

Finally, Tefal's durability appears to be linked to the special profile of its managers with, as we have seen, a CEO who organized raclette parties, a department head who visited European laboratories specializing in catalysis, or the habit for all the managers to go out and sell the products themselves. These managers were also experts, who knew the products, the technologies and the customers. This is why Vincent Chapel christened them 'expert managers'.

Although they were not alone in contributing to the firm's success, these expert managers were nonetheless essential to the way it operated. They managed the innovation processes, developed products themselves or added their precious ideas to the developments under way, they thought up the future ranges and sparked off certain original developments, such as the work on the baby care range.

4.3.6   A metabolic model

Having examined the major features of the Tefal model and its essential 'metabolic pathways', we can return to the model itself. None of the elements taken separately explains the firm's success, but they all appear to be essential to the way Tefal operated. There was a form of dynamic balance that meant that the repeated innovation was possible and that it was the repetition itself that enabled the model to survive. Like riding a bike, it is the dynamics that keep the balance. The dynamics are an element of the metabolism and regulate the way it functions.

If the rate of innovation slackens, the model enters a crisis: competition becomes stiffer for the existing products; there is a risk of competition becoming cost-focused, with the threat of cutbacks in design staff; feedback from the market becomes scarcer, making innovations more random; the incremental approach could disappear to the profit of risky radicalism; and the expertise of the expert managers is no longer updated, with the risk of cutting them off from technical evolutions and trends in values.

Conversely, the coexistence of expert managers, a rapid, cheap development method for products with low break-even points, the dynamics of exploring a value space and forms of learning from the market enables a sustained rate of innovation.

As for all organisms with complex metabolisms, this general coherency seems to have been elaborated by a form of embryogenesis. Although Tefal's balance only appears to be maintained by dynamics, this balance also seems to be an inheritance of past growth. The company generated its own 'organs' during its 'growth'. In the case of Tefal, economic growth has all the features of biological growth. The managers became experts as they gained experience working at Tefal. They had all been with the company for a long time and became heads of divisions which they had in many cases helped create as and when products were designed. It was the gradual acquisition of competencies and technologies that made each innovation incremental whilst being non-zero; and the introduction of production systems, prototypes, tests and specific design projects over time that enabled rapid, cheap product developments with low break-even points.

There are therefore two aspects to the metabolic nature of Tefal. The firm is a system whose balance involves the interaction of a large number of variables and this system is the result of a long growth process.

4.4 Conclusion: can Tefal be considered a 'model' of growth by innovation?

In his thesis on Tefal, Vincent Chapel suggested that Tefal was the archetype of a new industrial model. We need to remember that this term is to be taken in the biological sense, in that Tefal was an exceptional 'organism' with special characteristics that could not be identified with the traditional theories and therefore called the latter into question. However, the conditions for survival are so numerous and so harsh that there are serious grounds for doubting whether the species will ever comprise more than a very limited number of individuals. To what extent can this exceptional 'model' really serve as a model, i.e. as a set of principles for action that can be appropriated and controlled, to guide transformations in other firms? This is a key point in the reasoning: how can the status of the model be transformed? How can it be changed from an exemplary but dangerously original model into a guide for action?

By examining the factors that might explain Tefal's success, Vincent Chapel's work revealed a complex system that was self-generating during growth. These two characteristics are a great challenge if the case of Tefal is to be used in other contexts. The complexity of the system is a sign that it might not be robust in other conditions. The fact that it is self-generating suggests that only an organization that has followed the same growth trajectory would be capable of reproducing the same types of repeated innovation. In other words, a company wishing to innovate repeatedly could not simply import structures but would have to try to 'start from scratch' in order to copy Tefal's style of development.

If we are to use Tefal as a 'model', we must therefore address the following two problems:

First, we must use the 'model organism' – and its complexity – to derive a model of the inter-relationships between the minimum number of variables required to describe the phenomena, the results and the different means of action and control: can the apparent complexity be reduced to a small number of essential propositions? Is it possible in this way to explain the links, not between innovation and growth but between certain innovative design practices and the firm's growth? Is it possible to explain the essential interactions and their effects and to understand the major balances in the firm's 'system of rent'? (*See* Chapter 5.)

Second, we must study the possible duplication of the model. If we manage to discover the essential processes and levers for action in the Tefal model, we can then see whether they are completely foreign to practices in less innovative firms, or whether they are 'latent' but inhibited. (*See* Chapter 6.)

Questions for further study and discussion

Criticize the Tefal model. What are the potentially negative effects of devices paradoxically used by Tefal, such as the lack of specifications, the apparently informal nature of communications, the product committees attended by a very large number of people including the CEO and two-headed project management (product/technical) rather than having a single project manager?

In the light of the Tefal case, is it possible to help firms wishing to introduce strategies for growth by repeated innovation? If so, what recommendations should be given?

What contingent aspects can there be in the Tefal case?

Key notions – Chapter 4

Growth by repeated innovation
Inadequacy of traditional models:
    Not only one-off invention
    Not only a key technology
    Not only a statistical model
    Not only a providential manager
    Not only creativity
    Not only good project management

Metabolism
Prudent model
Radical incrementalism
Expert manager

5 A model of the innovative firm: design strategy, metabolism and growth regime

5.1 Introduction: Tefal, from the firm to the model?

5.1.1 An Innovation Manager's questions

As in the previous chapter, an imaginary Innovation Manager will serve as a guide to the practical issues involved in adopting the potential model.

'The Tefal model is of course very attractive, but I can see lots of reasons why it wouldn't work in our company. For example, I like the idea of two-headed project management and agree that it is really important to make sure that technical experts and product experts work together and communicate well. But there are also very good reasons for keeping separate departments and letting them work on precise, well-defined objectives. Isn't it risky to change specifications all the time to keep up with the latest market information? I'm concerned that a two-headed management system might mean too much to-ing and fro-ing, with difficulties in controlling variety and with high coordination costs. I'm not convinced that designers will be any more productive working together just because there is a two-headed project management team.

'The same applies to the specifications. Having less restrictive specifications will of course improve flexibility, but once again, I'm concerned about things going too far, with problems regarding excessive variety or simply nonconformity.

'The product committee seems attractive too on the face of it, but how do you organize a meeting of nearly eighty people – including the top management – and ensure that there are healthy discussions and not just sterile debates about major strategic options that always end up being too vague?

'However attractive they may seem, if Tefal's practices were adopted elsewhere, wouldn't this lead to problems in terms of cost, quality and lead times, result in badly targeted products and be a source of confusion and "wars of religion" in the firms in question? And, apart from the organizational changes, what about all the other aspects? For instance, how does the firm find the right level of industrial flexibility if the processes require heavier investments; or flexibility in competencies if the design process requires scientific research into fundamental phenomena associated with the product; or finally, flexibility of product architectures, given that they are often extremely complex and cannot be completely redesigned each time?'

5.1.2   Which sort of 'model'?

Can the Tefal model stand up to all these arguments? We must begin by distinguishing between two possible interpretations of the term 'model'. In the first meaning, it takes the form of a 'master model' or reference to be imitated or reproduced. It is a set of devices, mechanisms (rules, tools, processes) to be duplicated as faithfully as possible. However, as the Innovation Manager's comments show, the 'rules' to be duplicated could have a negative impact in certain cases. This implies that we have to *find* the very specific domain in which duplication is possible. Could it be that the Tefal model is useful only in the case of relatively simple consumer goods or perhaps only for products requiring low investments? Or in companies with no R&D departments, or in medium-sized companies? These questions are based on general contingency variables (type of product, type of organization, size of firm, etc.), but the case of Tefal does not help us judge whether or not they are pertinent. How sensitive is the 'model' to the size of the firm or the type of product? To answer these questions we would have to re-examine the major variables themselves.

It is therefore the second meaning of 'model' that is more appropriate here. We can define it as a set of relationships between variables that may be abstract, new and original.

5.1.3   Tefal: components for a management theory on innovative design

Could it be that Tefal's environment was so specific and so different from other environments that any theories developed there cannot be applied to other contemporary firms? On the contrary, Tefal echoed the major tensions of innovation-intensive capitalism:

Are there uncertain object identities? Although the identities of Tefal's products are less astonishing than those found in the world of mobile telephones, constant work was nonetheless done on the objects' identities and a number of changes were made, often radical ones. For instance, Tefal took waffle machines from fairgrounds into the home; the firm transformed raclette machines, which were initially used only in restaurants, and launched the idea of individual grilling trays; and it introduced the home 'pierrade' stone grill and the cheese preserver, both of which were the result of unusual hybrids. Existing product lines also had this characteristic of uncertain identity, as illustrated by the raclette machine, which evolved from an odour-proof solution to a multi-functional concept. Tefal's products illustrated and accompanied trends in the kitchen (who will use them, in what circumstances, on what occasions?), trends in 'informal meals', trends in baby care (safety, health) and trends in food storage (health but also organoleptic qualities).

Are there changes in design activities? We have already pointed out that Tefal was atypical in that the percentage of designers did not grow compared with total staff and that R&D was not organized (it had no clearly identified research, engineering and design or marketing departments). However, Tefal did have certain fundamental characteristics: work on products' industrial design; the challenge of collaboration and partnerships with suppliers and, above all, with research laboratories; and intensive work on knowledge acquisition (e.g. trip organized to study catalysis; and the fact that the firm's CEO was an assiduous reader of publications from the French National Centre for Scientific Research, CNRS).

We can ask another series of questions to see whether the Tefal model fits our specifications for models to manage innovative design (*see* Section 3.4).

'A model of activity without stable object identities'? Tefal was indeed in a situation in which the innovation process consisted of exploring new technologies (e.g. electronics, new materials) and new value spaces (e.g. informal meals).

'Structure innovation capabilities without basing them on product functions or performance but without resorting to laissez-faire'? The challenge of Vincent Chapel's thesis on Tefal was precisely to highlight means of collective action which went beyond the too simplistic traditional explanations (cf. invention, technology, providential entrepreneur, etc.).

The type of performance: 'Growth by repeated innovation'? The Tefal case provided an opportunity to analyse innovation that was repeated over a twenty-year period but, as we have seen, was not a random process based on a series of one-off, independent projects.

Organization: 'At the firm level, without being limited to a project framework'? Tefal provided the opportunity to study the functioning of a firm that was capable of multiple innovations (and not just a mythical 'frying pan project').

Hence, work on Tefal as a 'biological' model should help to construct a theory to manage innovative design.

Having removed the obstacles, we can now construct our theoretical model based on the Tefal case. The model will be based on the four components outlined in Part I and reviewed above: model of activity, objects to be managed, type of performance and forms of organization.

5.2   The combined dynamics of competencies and products

5.2.1   Inputs and outputs of a design function

The initial analyses of the Tefal case showed that growth by innovation resulted from the dynamics of the design activities. We shall now examine the inputs and outputs of this design activity, modelled as a *design function*.[1]

What are the resources of this design function? First, as we have seen, the design activity demands *competencies*. Taken in the widest sense of the term, competencies are therefore inputs of the design function. Second, in the case of firms, i.e. of economic activity, the design activity is set in a context of a series of existing products (to be continued or broken away from). Thus, the inputs of a design function are existing goods and competencies.

What are the results of a design function? At least one of its outputs is *the definition of the firm's products*. This involves a revision of the list of existing goods (withdrawal, modification, extension, etc.) and a definition of the processes required to produce and distribute these goods. This is the clearest output. It should be noted that it is very different from the usual representation of a firm's output in the formal framework of the production function, in which the output is a quantity of a good of a known nature with a known production function.

---

[1] *See* Hatchuel and Le Masson (2001) and Le Masson (2001) for further explanations on modelling design activities. The issue is also covered in Encaoua *et al.* (2001) and positioned with respect to other economic approaches. The model is different from the microeconomic approach which consists of modelling the form as a production function with quantities of production factors as inputs and with quantities of goods or services whose nature is known and established *ex ante* as outputs (finalized list of goods).

However, this was not the only output in the case of Tefal. One of the firm's major strengths was to fully exploit *all* the outputs of a project. Vincent Chapel noted that every project, from design through to the market launch, always produced more knowledge than necessary for the target product. The outputs were not only products but also new competencies that were not necessarily used for that particular product. Hence, the outputs included not only the competencies which were 'useful' for the project but *all the competencies* produced during the project.

5.2.2 Outputs: excess knowledge

The knowledge produced during design projects has often been mentioned in the literature. Studies include work on research laboratories and knowledge production (Roussel, Saad and Erickson 1991; Miller and Morris 1999; Buderi 2000), on experimentation techniques (Thomke 2001), on exploring alternatives in parallel in engineering and design departments (*see* the Toyota case in Sobek 1996), and on exploring markets (Leonard and Rayport 1997; von Hippel, Thomke and Sonnack 1999; Prahalad and Ramaswamy 2000; Le Masson and Magnusson 2002; Piller *et al.* 2003).

From an economic standpoint, these learning processes represent costs. Can they be limited, for example by 'optimizing' and 'planning' design? In practice, planning processes of this sort require knowedge of the form of the final result. Intensive innovation is, however, characterized by the exploration of new, open-ended object identities. In this case, any new design for a product or process involves creating more knowledge in the firm (or with its suppliers) than the first new product needs in the end. 'Over-learning' or 'excess knowledge production' generally takes place because it is extremely difficult to adjust the amount of knowledge produced to the exact amount that will actually be useful to the one-off project.

It is important to note that firms do not only have to manage the costs of their own learning processes; if a market is to exist, they must also manage the customers' learning processes. In a context of uncertain object identities, the customers' learning capacities (user values, functions, underlying technologies, etc.) are vital to ensure that the economic dynamics continue. If these dynamics are not managed by the firm itself or by the industrial environment, entire areas of industrial growth can be under threat, as customers are not necessarily prepared to go through costly learning processes for each new product. There are already examples of management of this sort, for instance in mechanisms such as prescription-based markets

(Hatchuel 1995) and in the apparent continuity and degree of stability in user values that can be noted in products based on dominant designs (Abernathy and Utterback 1978).[2]

5.2.3   Outputs: 'learning rents'

How can these costs be managed other than by making adjustments on a project-by-project basis? In a system of repetition, previous costs can be changed into *rents*. In the context of repeated design, outputs from the design function mean that investments in a new product create two different sources of rent: first, a classic rent (CR) coming directly from product sales and, second, a rent that we call a 'learning rent' (LR). The learning rent comes from ideas of improvements that emerge during the design process for product n and that will be used for products developed at a later stage (n+1, n+2, etc.). It is a rent in the sense that the project n helps make the following projects more successful. Tefal gradually adapted its organization in such a way as to obtain the greatest possible benefits from its learning rents.

We can distinguish between two different types of rent depending on the source of the learning, i.e. those from marketing (learning rent from the market, LRM) and those from the design activity itself (learning rent from design, LRD).

Hatchuel *et al.* (1998) explained LRM as follows: as Chapel pointed out, in Tefal's area of activity, *ex ante* market surveys do very little to reduce commercial uncertainties. The only reliable way of validating a product is to market it. This is a key point in the analysis and several authors have focused on the importance of 'going to the market' (Peters and Waterman 1982). This is not just a question of rapid execution but is important because the market is a precious source of knowledge for positioning future development projects.

However, in practice, this strategy is very demanding because the market does not always 'speak' for itself. Apart from recommendations from the distributors, it is important to study the way the product is received and to interpret the results. To be really productive, going *to* the market must be followed by feedback *from* the market. The customers' reactions must be analysed in a clear, critical way, as this generates far more information than the traditional sales figures and can provide knowledge that can be used to redesign the following products. The feedback sometimes calls into

---

[2] We come back to this point in Part III.

question the firm's capabilities on certain points. The results obtained from this process of building and maintaining the firm's capacity to learn from the market are what we call the LRM.

We can now examine the notion of LRD. Before reaching the marketing stage, product development is already an opportunity to learn many new things. It involves an intensive exploration process. On the one hand, known techniques are reassessed and work is done on how they can be applied in new contexts. On the other hand, new techniques are put forward, examined, mobilized and then either retained or abandoned. Each development project therefore transforms the firm's competencies. Once again, it is important to note that these learning processes are not necessarily spontaneous and must be encouraged, if only by the flow of demands coming from new projects.

These competencies in terms of the market or regarding design cannot be separated from the people who acquire them. The development work acts simultaneously on each actor's knowledge and on all the actors' capacity to coordinate their work. This coordination is far from a simple exercise in human relations as it has an impact on the content of the competencies. For example, when a specialist in aluminium developed a frying pan with a specialist in Teflon, they not only got to know each other but both extended their competencies in such a way as to serve the specific interaction required to design the frying pan. *Coordinated competencies* were therefore developed. Rather than 'path-dependency', the notion here is 'interaction-dependency', i.e. the interactions required for the development process to guide the emergence of explorations and competencies.

5.2.4 Innovation martingales

The challenge is to transform any excess knowledge produced into real learning rents that can then be reinvested. Excess knowledge is lost if financial constraints (bankruptcy, demands for high returns on investment for the initial product before designing the following ones, etc.) prevent this reinvestment. This brings us back to the notion of the prudent model of innovation, in which the risks are limited to ensure that repetition is always possible.

However, the notion is not limited to a simple financial criterion as the value of these rents depends on the succession of developments and on the way the designers take advantage of this succession, i.e. their ability to capitalize on knowledge and memorize past developments.

This is what Hatchuel *et al.* (1998) qualified as an 'innovation martingale', that is 'a development strategy designed to put to good use the learning rents resulting from a predictable series of associated developments'. The martingales are therefore a means of following profitable, robust paths of innovation.

We thus have the key elements for describing the basic metabolism: the inputs (goods and knowledge), the outputs (change in the list of goods and change in the knowledge available) and the way the design functions follow on from one another. This gives a simple process: a design function is a function describing the expansion of the space of competencies × products. This provides a minimum description of the activity. We also have a new objective, which is to develop innovation martingales in order to reuse excess knowledge produced in previous design processes in the best possible way.

We shall now turn to the second component of the model: what were the objects to be managed in the case of Tefal? Using the notion of 'lineage of competencies and products' we shall now model these mechanisms for managing learning.

5.3   A new management object: product lineages

5.3.1   Coevolution of competencies and products

How can these learning rents be organized and put to good use? Past research on product development and technological trajectories has already provided some precious indications (see Chapters 1 and 2 and the bibliographical appendix). We have already mentioned two classic approaches:

Several studies have shown *the permanency of products*: to organize the rent, there must be continuity in the products themselves. There are two advantages: first, the customers do not have to relearn the product's user values and, second, the firms can reuse stable architectures, product validation techniques, forms of division of work, etc. Technical economists had indeed pointed out that whole sectors of industry were structured by what they called dominant design, i.e. a design shared by all the competitors, which resulted in stable architectures and product values, and organized competition around a small number of functions considered essential by the customers (*see* the bibliographical appendix for the positioning of this stream of research and its main authors: Abernathy and Utterback (1978) and Utterback (1994)). Techniques such as value analysis, functional analysis, market analysis and specifications on the model of Houses of Quality (Hauser and Clausing 1988) are all direct consequences of the phenomenon of dominant design.

Other works focused on *key competencies*. In this case, the rent is put to good use by designing products that can be designed using existing knowledge. The main advantage is that this saves having to produce additional knowledge. Another important element concerns the firm's positioning, as the core competency is defined as the competency that enables a firm to distinguish itself from its competitors (*see* bibliographical appendix Section 4.1 for this stream of research and its main authors: Burgelman and Rosenbloom (1989) and Hamel and Prahalad (1994b)).

Detailed analysis of design processes then showed that a good product development process combined these two forms of continuity. The reference works on the subject (Clark and Fujimoto 1991; Wheelwright and Clark 1992) insist on the importance of already having competencies and of positioning the product in existing markets, in relation to customers' needs. This provides us with a first model for exploiting learning rents. However, it is a restrictive model that is not suitable in all circumstances:

First of all, the system for developing new products intrinsically *minimizes knowledge production*. The aim is to exploit existing resources as much as possible and to avoid having to produce new ones. Several authors have even underlined that the project management approach has had a harmful impact on functions and the building of competencies in firms (Weil 1999).

Second, even though the NPD approach enables the different functional groups to learn project after project (Benghozi, Charue-Duboc and Midler 2000; Charue-Duboc and Midler 2000), it does not allow for the complete revision of the products' identities, no new value spaces are created and no new functions are built.

The case of Tefal illustrates a different approach, with two main properties. First, contrary to the previous cases, the aim was not so much to minimize the knowledge produced as to organize the learning rents. Second, the two dynamics – of products and of competencies – were considered at the same time, so that the innovation martingales were forms of coevolution of competencies and products.

As the dynamics linking products and competencies were unstable, they required specific forms of management depending on past learning and future requirements.

Tefal's success stemmed from its ability to play on the innovation martingales, i.e. to ensure that each development project was not carried out in isolation but also took into account future projects. In fact, the firm's principal action consisted of organizing *the coevolution of products and knowledge* as and when the design actions took place. At the heart of the Tefal model was the firm's ability to build what we call design lineages in which competencies and products became more and more closely linked in a process of mutual enrichment.

5.3.2   Innovation martingales at Tefal: product families, design lineages, hybrid lineages

5.3.2.1   Product families as simple martingales

The notion of 'innovation martingale' can take simple, well-known forms such as the gradual development of products designed from the outset on the basis of a 'common family' concept.

Some examples of product 'families'

Today, many manufactured products are based on the notion of 'common family'. As we shall see in the next part of the book, it is inseparable from traditional R&D-based organizations, whose design regimes (so-called 'systematic design') never design one-off products but always a family of products. These families can be structured in many different ways (shared architecture, modular architecture, range, etc.).

Some classic examples are the A320 family of aircraft: A320, A319, A321 and A318. More generally speaking, aircraft in the Airbus range (A320, A340, A380, etc.) share various functional and architectural principles (cockpit, nose cone, limitations on direct operating costs, etc.). Also, car models are proposed in a number of variations, not only in the colour but also in the engine, the equipment and features, and the more recent notion of platforms has made it possible to design different types of car – people carriers, hatchbacks, notchbacks, coupés/convertibles, etc. – on the same platform.

Methods for the management of such product families and platforms have been studied by Meyer and Lehnerd (1997), Meyer and Mugge (2001) and Meyer and Dalal (2002).

This concept helps meet customers' demands for customized products and is possible in terms of cost, investments, tooling, etc. because this has been planned in advance. In fact, it is a question of planning forms of marginal flexibility for the products, as in the classic view of product 'families' and 'ranges'.

In formal terms, this means that design at level n enables n+1, n+2, n+3, etc. products to be designed at low cost. 'At low cost' implies that little new knowledge is needed during the successive development projects and conversely that it will be relatively difficult to put learning rents from project n to good use in the following projects. In other words, in a family-based formula, it is difficult to take advantage of learning that opens up alternatives outside the family.

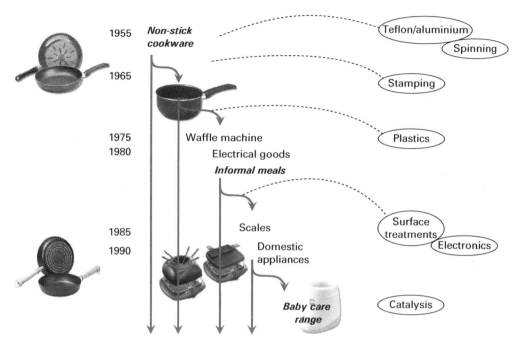

Figure 5.1   Co-generation of products and competencies at Tefal: product lineages as innovation martingales

5.3.2.2   The lineage, a martingale for Tefal

There is, however, a more sophisticated type of martingale, which involves anticipating the progress accomplished in developing a first product, thus creating what Hatchuel *et al.* call 'lineages'. For the first product, the 'head of the lineage', knowledge is explored and accumulated; this helps define and design the following products that are better adapted to the market and also cheaper, and therefore more competitive, because they exploit the learning acquired by the head of the lineage.

In formal terms, learning from level n is reused immediately for n+1; design efforts are greater at level n+1 than they would be for a simple product family. Project n+1 is a source of learning for n+2 and so on.

Although Tefal may seem to base its design work on 'families', its specific innovation capability in fact stemmed from its concern to systematically look for lineage effects. For instance, developing the household electrical goods division demanded a great deal of knowledge on plastics; this was accumulated in particular for the waffle machine. The learning was then mobilized and developed in a completely new range of products, informal meals. The dynamics of Tefal's lineages are illustrated in Figure 5.1:

Lineage 1: in 1955, the frying pan was head of the lineage of non-stick cookware; competencies were acquired on welding Teflon® to aluminium and on spinning and stamping processes for aluminium, the knowledge being built up gradually as other products were developed.

Lineage 2: in the 1970s, the waffle machine prefigured the electrical goods and informal meals lineage following the acquisition of competencies in the domain of plastics.

Lineage n: in the 1980s, the electronic scales prefigured electronic accessories in the domestic appliances and telephony ranges but also, at a later stage, the baby care range, by their acquisition of competencies in electronics and surface treatment.

Some examples of coevolution in the literature

The notion of coevolution between product and competence has been described in the literature. The notion of dominant design itself is implicitly a model of coevolution of product and competence (R&D emerges when the main features of the product are stabilizing) (Abernathy and Utterback 1978).

Sanderson and Uzumeri (1995) give a particularly interesting illustration of this type of coevolution between the nature of competencies and the products. Analysing the Sony Walkman family they demonstrated that, first, the Sony 'family' was different from that of its competitors and, second, that there were strong design dynamics within the family, suggesting that Sony had developed a form of lineage, at least in the case of the Walkman. Unfortunately, their article does not enable us to discover the design dynamics in the family. We find similar dynamics in Penrose's (1960) paper on Du Pont or in the notion of product sequencing (Helfat and Raubitschek 2000).

5.3.2.3   Hybridization between lineages

Finally, apart from the 'family', which is a simple group of similar products, and the lineage, which involves the combined dynamics of competencies and products, there is a third type of formula for innovation which consists of transferring specific competencies from one lineage to another. This is the process we call 'hybridization'. The mechanism was one of the key foundations of Tefal's strategy and tied in well with the firm's prudent approach. Each new lineage required a comprehensive basket of competencies (Teflon® on aluminium, plastics, electronics, etc.), but only one of these competencies was missing when the lineage emerged, as the others had been acquired for existing lineages (*see* Figure 5.2).

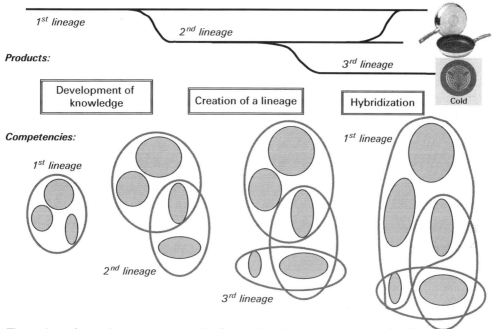

The pockets of expertise are represented by forms which increase in size as the 'level' and 'quantity' of available knowledge increases

Figure 5.2   The lineage versus the concept of dominant design

It should be noted that this mechanism of exchange between lineages went both ways, as lineages could 'import' and 'export' competencies. By exporting competencies on stamping and non-stick coatings, the frying pan lineage gave birth to the electrical goods division; in return, the latter imported techniques on plastics and silk-screen printing that helped transform the frying pans (*see* Figure 5.3).

5.3.3 The lineage: intentionally creating dominant designs and markets

In this model, growth is obtained by the virtuous coevolution of the firm's products and knowledge; the externalities created consist of knowledge which serves to design product families and then new externalities, etc. It is not only the dynamics that are important but, above all, the strong links between the competencies and the products. The competencies are generated by the needs of product design and are then used to design the following generations of products.

Hence, an apparently obvious outcome can in fact be built up gradually: a firm has the competencies of its products and the products of its

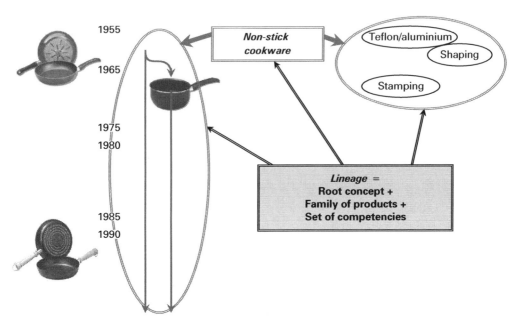

Figure 5.3   The three static characteristics of a lineage

competencies. We deliberately used the word 'apparently' because the outcome is often difficult to obtain. So many firms complain that their research departments produce knowledge which cannot be used, that nobody knows how the existing products were made, or what can be done to make them evolve.

The lineage is a matching of competencies and products (product family and key competencies) which is a principle of evolution and of stability (innovation paths). To summarize these key points:

At first view, and particularly from the customer's standpoint, the lineage is seen in the form of a family of successive products which seems to undergo only minor modifications over time. We mentioned earlier the notion of dominant design (Abernathy and Utterback 1978; Utterback 1994), which is a stable form of a product, common to all the competitors. This relative stability allows customers to accumulate their knowledge of the products and to follow the changes. For instance, cars have seemingly evolved very little in the past few decades: the main architectures (body and platform), the main parts (engine, axle system, seats, etc.), the functions (freedom of transport, comfort, etc.) and the methods (driving wheel, pedals, gears, etc.) have remained stable. This has simplified the demands made on the customers (comparing vehicles, learning how to drive them), but also those made on the designer to design the successive vehicles.

But the lineage can also call into question the dominant design. Whereas the latter concept insists on the similarity of products over time, on the contrary the concept of lineage highlights the fact that small variations in products can hide large renewals of knowledge. Although a car is still a car, it is clear that Volkswagen's new Beetle required completely different competencies from those needed to design the original Beetle. Products' dominant designs are only apparent. They evolve continuously, but these slight changes can lead to complete reversals in well-established compromises and competencies. The notion of lineage explains that the underlying learning dynamics are made possible by a certain form of stability. The lineage is therefore a sustainable regime for the coevolution of a series of products and a corresponding sub-set of competencies held in the firm.

At Tefal, this feature of evolution within a dominant design was crucial in understanding the dynamics of the lineages. In fact, the lineage was a way of intentionally building a dominant design.

It is also a way of creating a form of stability in the dynamics of products launched on the market. This stability can be seen from two standpoints:

First, for the customers, it facilitates the learning processes concerning the product; new products are never radically different from the preceding ones but are more of a response to a criticism concerning the latter. It is in this sense that the notion of lineage builds endogenous customer learning processes.

Second, for the firm, the lineage illustrates permanent efforts in exploring value spaces. Each new product is a way of learning about customer 'user values', i.e. an opportunity to widen a pocket of knowledge about a market, with a view to improving the following product concepts in the lineage.

Hence, the notion of lineage gives a different view of the market, which is no longer seen as a matching of supply and demand, defined *ex ante*, but as the dynamics achieved by collectively building this supply and demand.

5.4 A new performance criterion: to maximize learning rents

The notion of lineage is therefore a central focus of our work. We shall now explain its properties and the types of performance that become possible with this approach.

5.4.1   Lineages: no stable product identities and prudent growth

From a descriptive point of view, at a fixed point in time t, a lineage constructed by Tefal presented the three following characteristics:

A set of well-identified competencies, whose 'nature' was relatively stable – these could be referred to as a 'function'. Within a given pocket of competencies (of a fixed nature), the competencies grew as the products were developed for the lineage. The level of expertise therefore grew and a lineage could also be regularly enriched by new competencies.

An expanding family of products. In terms of their 'nature', these existing products had recognizable common traits stemming as much from their uses as from their functions and technologies. However, the products evolved enormously within the family.

A guiding concept, of which each product was a unique example that also guided the successive design processes. The guiding concept itself was relatively stable, but could also evolve over time. For instance, the concept of 'informal meals', which was central to Tefal's design of innovative products for several decades, emerged only once several design processes had taken place.

These three characteristics were illustrated in Tefal's first ever lineage, non-stick cookware (*see* Figure 5.3).

These characteristics are also one of the foundations of the performance: they enable a prudent approach by combining low exposure (avoiding massive investments in new knowledge, encouraging small steps, exploring robust value spaces, etc.) and capacities for change (no stabilization of object identities, or of the list of technical skills).

Lineage and business units

A lineage is not a business unit. The distinction has nothing to do with accounting but concerns the expansions allowed (i.e. authorized and made possible) in each case.

A business unit is defined by the space occupied by the products and competencies it is charged with exploiting. Products and competencies are resources, of course, but they also determine the limits of the business unit's action, for example to avoid competing with other business units' products. Hence, a business unit has something of a *territorial approach*. It does not go beyond the territory it exploits and, conversely, the firm gives it responsibility for any new activity in this territory (from an acquisition, for example) that would otherwise result in internal competition.

By comparison, a lineage is built on the basis of the expansion and the evolution of the territory itself:

> The guiding concept, product families and shared competencies represent a coherent set of means (not just 'products', 'competencies' or 'visions') and not 'territorial resources'.
>
> This set of means does not restrict the capacity for action but represents *a potential for expansion*, in terms of both knowledge and product concepts. Although there are some constraints regarding the expansion (cf. 'Maximizing learning rents by building lineages', below), expansions are never refused on the grounds that they are 'outside' the product family, the lineage's basic competencies or the initial 'vision'.
>
> Expansions of knowledge or concepts that occur for one lineage can be reused by any of the firm's other lineages. Once again, the resources are not shared according to people's respective territories, but the lineages themselves are redefined to improve the potential for expansion. The lineage's vision, product family and knowledge are changed regularly to ensure that they remain coherent and to keep their potential for expansion.
>
> We can illustrate this point with the specific case of Tefal's thermo-spot temperature indicator and the non-stick cookware lineage. Previous work on other lineages meant that Tefal had mastered screen printing of active polymers (in this case, colour changes depending on temperature). This competency helped give birth to the thermo-spot, a temperature indicator on the bottom of Tefal's frying pans, which changes colour when the frying pan reaches the ideal temperature for frying. This is a good illustration of how expansions from other lineages resulted in the redefining of the guiding concept in the non-stick cookware lineage – it became intelligent – and the lineage's competencies space – it integrated processes for polymer deposits.

5.4.2   Maximizing learning rents by building lineages

As we have seen, the lineage is not decided in advance but is gradually built up as and when the products are designed. Three dynamics are involved in the emergence of a lineage: learning in each of the 'functions' concerned, gradual explorations of the user value space and the gradual elaboration of a guiding concept.

The explorations are not random: without neglecting learning processes during the successive projects, the idea is to 'think several projects ahead'. The guiding concept of the lineage illustrates the way in which the successive product designs are guided by an abstract concept; the latter is also the result of a substantial design effort and is reviewed at regular intervals. It is not a question of observing a set of core competencies *a posteriori*. On the contrary, the designers identify and stabilize competencies as they go along, reinforcing them product after product and trying, as much as possible, not to go beyond them.

The dynamics involved in building lineages are vital, as to a great extent they determine the firm's actual perimeter. Broadly speaking, lineages gradually become stable first by minimizing the learning that is necessary (and predictable) at each stage – for the designer and for the customer – and second by maximizing the potential innovation in this context by making the best possible use of the knowledge acquired during previous learning phases.

However, we must qualify the idea of 'minimizing' and 'maximizing'. Minimizing the necessary learning involves measuring, adjusting and limiting the efforts made, but at the same time ensuring that there is some growth in knowledge, however small, if only to ensure progress or a competitive advantage. The process is therefore conditioned by the product's lineage. At the same time as minimizing, the designers must constantly pay attention to any new knowledge that becomes available even if it does not apply directly to their project. As for the notion of maximizing innovation, at Tefal this consisted above all of maximizing the rate of innovation: an innovation had to be ready for the next trade show; it would be as good as possible, provided that knowledge was acquired. The notion of 'rate' of innovation does not imply frantic short-term action but rather the ability to anticipate several development projects in advance and to assess the action over time, without brutal 'updating'. It is also the ability to take into account knowledge concerning the market that is gradually acquired as the products are launched. The designers think several projects ahead and are on the lookout for anything that might feed the series of projects to come. Thus, the process of maximizing is conditioned by the learning acquired.

The lineage is therefore built in such a way as to maximize the learning rents. It maximizes the ratio between profit expectations for the future products – over a period of time that depends, for example, on the firm's ability to build fruitful, long-term guiding concepts – and the cost of the learning required to design these products. For one-off products – without an innovation martingale, therefore with no lineage – this means that the firm chooses the profitable product that it knows how to design with a minimum amount of learning. For successive product development projects, it means that the firm maintains competencies in the domains where the smallest element of learning can have an impact on the products designed. Meanwhile, it will pull out of domains in which little is learned and where learning has little impact on the products, illustrating that it is essential to maximize learning rents in order to build the competencies required for each lineage.

The notion of maximizing learning rents describes Tefal's 'prudent' approach and it could even be said that it made it possible and manageable.

Maximizing learning rents has several consequences that lead to prudent management:

First, it means that the firm has to innovate. This is a key point, as a prudent strategy does not mean giving up innovation but innovating in a controlled manner.

Second, maximizing throughout the lineage means that there is always a concern to maintain the ability to carry out several development projects; this is also a feature of the prudent approach.

Third, it also means that there is a prudent strategy concerning the acquisition of knowledge, as there is no question of investing everything in a key competency requiring heavy investments (a laboratory, time, a factory, etc.).

Fourth, the market strategy is profitable. The prudent approach involves exploring new value spaces, without taking unnecessary risks on a one-off product, but without being content to simply offer existing features in different forms.

Design economics theory: the different returns of a design function (Hatchuel and Le Masson 2006)

Modelling the firm as a design function serves to synthesize different types of returns (and therefore different types of performance).

The classic notion of returns on factors must be reclarified for design functions; in addition, by introducing learning as an output, a condition of innovation, there is a risk of generating returns that grow to infinity. Constraints must therefore be put on the design function by explaining the different returns that can be defined using the formal frameworks described above, in particular the notion of lineages. Take a lineage of innovations $fc_1 \, o \, fc_2 \, o \, \ldots \, fc_k$ for a single good g. Four different returns can be indicated, depending on whether we consider the design function whose returns increase with the firm's profits, or the production functions whose returns increase with the quantities produced; also depending on whether we reason in static terms (returns defined at each stage of innovation) or in dynamic terms (returns defined over the entire lineage). The following returns can thus be defined in qualitative terms:

1. **Static returns to production**: each production function generated is a classic function, hence giving diminishing returns to its factors.
2. **Dynamic returns to production**: the transition from one production function to another through a design effort can produce growing returns for a production factor that is common to a lineage, e.g. regular reductions in the energy used to manufacture a product lineage.
3. **Static returns to design**: these are evaluated for a given competency, but for which output? We have seen that, by nature, design functions have many different outputs (nature of goods, production functions, knowledge, etc.). They can therefore be

defined more globally with respect to the benefits derived at a stage of the innovation. In this case, we can accept the hypothesis of growing returns, at least in an area in which the competency varies. For example, making greater efforts to improve the style of a new product can transform mediocre sales into spectacular sales. Also, the marginal gains can increase over a large area of the investment made.

4. **Dynamic returns to design**: when there is repeated innovation, we can also define one (or several) notions of dynamic returns to design. The notion can be evaluated for a level of competency that is set but whose return to design improves by repetition (for instance, a firm which hires young people with the same level of education for one-off projects, but makes better and better use of their competency). It is also possible to evaluate dynamic returns to design that take into account the evolution of a competency throughout the lineage. For example, improved knowledge concerning a material makes it possible to propose added value functions for a product. The same functions can then be used by the designers to further increase the value of the following products. This sort of virtuous circle makes growing dynamic returns to design. For example, when improvements were made to the steam engine, this was also of benefit to the machine manufacturers. Can we assume that the impact that the growth of competencies has on profits continues to increase indefinitely over time? This implies that lineages are viable indefinitely and can always be improved by learning. At the very least, this is forgetting the issue of competition. It is therefore more realistic to assume that the dynamic returns to design can grow up to a certain level in the lineage but will then decline. The notion of diminishing dynamic returns to design can be called the 'competition effect on the lineage', which means that the longer the lineage, the more intense the competition becomes. New lineages must therefore be launched when additional learning is not sufficient to face up to the competition effect on the lineage.

The formal framework for the design function thus identifies specific management approaches for the design activity. For example, even a small static return to design can make up for the diminishing nature of static returns to production by provoking dynamic returns to production. It is therefore advisable for a firm to repeat innovation during the strong learning periods at the beginning of the lineage, as the learning will become less effective if the lineage lasts for too long. The design function therefore opens up a whole range of possibilities stemming from the enormous potential to be found in the effective organization of repeated innovation.

5.5　Ring-based organization

We have specified three components of the Tefal model, i.e. modelling activity as a design function (describing the expansion of the space of competencies × products); identifying the objects to be managed, with lineages to manage the coevolution of competencies and products; and identifying the types of performance, by maximizing learning rents. We can now look at the different forms of organization it developed to encourage learning and to combine the lineages.

5.5.1 How organization favours learning: learning by doing versus learning from doing

The notion of 'learning by doing' is often used in the literature (e.g. in economics (Arrow 1962)). This type of learning is usually defined by contrasting it with more active forms of learning, for instance from R&D activities. Following the empirical study of the Tefal case, Hatchuel *et al.* (1998) considered that substantial revisions should be made to these notions.

In their view, the notion of learning by doing is too much inspired by the 'learning curves' found in industrial organization. In widespread use, particularly in the aviation industry, these curves set the level of performance for a given task, for operators, workshops and factories, depending on the number of times the task is performed. They give the impression that productivity gains can be made simply by repeating the tasks. However, a closer study of the notion shows that there is nothing mechanical about it and that it results from the actual way the learning is organized, i.e. by defining a reference method, through a period of free experimentation, by designing process sheets and through the presence of observers (Hatchuel 1994). In the aviation industry, it sets performance targets for learning.

A classic example of 'learning from doing': learning curves in the aviation industry

In the aviation industry, the learning curves are not drawn *a posteriori* (i.e. by observation after the event) but *a priori*. They serve as targets to be met by the workshops and are used to negotiate unit prices depending on the volume of the order.

The supposed 'learning by doing curves' are in fact an incentive to organize 'learning from doing'. Given the context, it is not surprising that *a posteriori* evaluations show almost perfect learning curves (although not absolutely perfect, as this would mean that they had not been ambitious enough).

For Hatchuel *et al.* (1998) this is not really a case of 'learning by doing' but of 'learning from doing'. The action itself creates an infinite amount of possible learning. If the action is to teach people how to 'do things better' or to give 'new ideas', it must include selective practices that enable the players to question the effects, sort the causes and formulate new knowledge. This means that feedback from experience must be organized and above all that the knowledge must be used; active measures must also be taken to identify and encourage learning rents.

This notion of 'learning from doing' has two consequences:

With respect to human resources management, two points were particularly marked in the case of Tefal:

The concern to maximize learning led to great stability in the technical teams and to exceptional continuity in the management team.

Specific actors and particular roles in the organization were responsible for the learning rents stemming from repeated innovation: expert managers and product managers not only looked after existing products but also managed innovation and accumulated learning on design and marketing.

The organizational structure focused on maximizing learning rents from the lineages; it was therefore built around the principle of lineages. Consequently, the organization was the result of designs in progress in the firm. It in fact had two components: the first, which we have just mentioned, concerned organizational groupings in the individual lineages, but the second concerned the 'trans-lineage' dimension, obtained through new competencies.

5.5.2   A ring-based organization reflecting the design dynamics

Tefal's organization model was indeed structured by the design processes. Although from the outside it appeared to be a traditional firm with a classic functional organization chart plus certain matrix-based elements, closer observations revealed what Hatchuel *et al.* (1998) qualified as a 'ring-based organization' (*see* Figure 5.4):

- In the centre, the circle of expert managers.
- Next, a circle of project managers who managed developments on a 'radial' basis.
- Finally, an outer circle of the functional departments – production, maintenance, quality, trials, prototypes – whose managers were at the service of the lineages and who also ensured cross-disciplinary circulation. The rate of circulation was determined by product design issues which were a constant driving force for innovation.

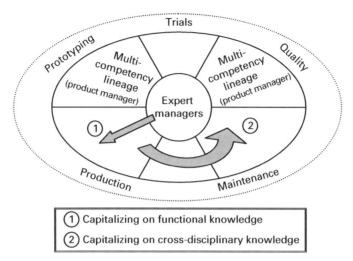

Figure 5.4 The ring-based organization

5.6 Conclusion

This chapter has shown that Tefal can serve as a source of inspiration for a management model for innovation capability (in this case, in innovative firms).

We can summarize the main results on the basis of the four components required for a new model for managing innovative firms (*see* Table 5.1):

We have a *model of activity* to describe the design economics within the firm: the firm is a *design function* that transforms the space (products × competencies) during each design exercise; the repetition of these exercises can be managed in such a way as to develop innovation martingales. It should be noted that this model of the economics of the activity is very general and can in fact be applied to all firms. It is entirely independent from predefined object identities.

We also have indications of *what innovative firms manage as a priority, i.e. lineages combining products and competencies.* The aim is to encourage the emergence of a number of lineages exploiting learning rents and then to structure them, set them up and possibly create hybrids. The notion of lineage serves to model what is managed by the firm without being trapped in the language of 'functions' or 'performance'. However, this notion does not explain *how to* manage.

Table 5.1. Summary of theoretical contributions of the Tefal model

	Specifications for innovative firm	Model of the innovative firm from the Tefal case
Models of activity and reasoning	A model of activity without stable product identities (flexibility for products and competencies)	The firm as a design function = coevolution of competencies and products
Objects to be managed – technical substratum	Structure innovation capabilities without basing them on 'functions' or 'performance'	Lineages and learning rents
Type of performance	Growth by repeated innovation, in a context of unstable object identities (no one-off projects)	Prudent growth by reusing excess knowledge without stabilizing object identities
Forms of organization	At the firm level, including major R&D-based firms, without being limited to a project framework	Metabolism (ring-based, with conceptual core)

The lineage is not 'natural' or given from the outset but has to be designed. We can list a number of properties to be found in a lineage, representing the *type of performance*: length, maximization of learning rents, flexibility regarding object identities, i.e. regarding the value and the competencies, durability, etc.

However, questions remain, such as how to make lineages emerge and how to structure and manage them. Collective efforts can be made to manage lineages, but the actors must also decide on their perimeter, on certain initial competencies, on the terms of the value to be studied, etc.

Using the case of Tefal, we have drawn up a 'simplified portrait of an organization' (Hatchuel 1996a) with a few figures of key players: a conceptual core[3] responsible for the emergence of new lineages, expert managers in charge of setting up the lineages, etc. This provides us with a new organizational language.

Once again, we must stress an important limitation, which is the absence of the traditional organizational language, in particular the language used in design. In other words, as we have not used the notions of

---

[3] The conceptual core includes the people who work on the concepts for the lineages (i.e. the expert managers at the heart of the ring-based organization) and the conceptual notions resulting from their work.

R&D, marketing, etc., what happens in cases where the activity is organized around these functions? This is one of the points which we deal with in Part III.

Questions for further study and discussion

Compare the notion of product lineage and the classical notion of technological trajectory: what are the differences?

Discuss the notion of acquiring competencies or absorptive capacity in the perspective of design strategy and repeated innovation.

What are the relations between repeated innovation and classical notions such as radical and incremental innovation? Can incremental innovations be repeated? Use examples such as mobile phones, television and CDs, studying not only the objects themselves but also the firms that developed them.

Key notions – Chapter 5

Notion of 'design strategy': coevolution of competencies and products

Reusing excess knowledge produced

Lineages

Product lineages: from product families to the genealogy of products

Lineages of competencies: from technological trajectories to the genealogy of competencies

Learning rents: learning rents from design, learning rents from the market

6 Grafting the Tefal model: astonishing performance from an innovative start-up

Before trying out our model for innovative firms on cases that are very different from Tefal, we shall begin by putting it to the test in the specific context of an innovative start-up, Avanti.

Avanti was created by Vincent Chapel using the Tefal model. He had been fascinated by his work with Tefal and by the model he had discovered there; he was keen to test the model's coherency, efficiency and feasibility and to see whether, by putting it into practice, he could 'manufacture' a new Tefal. In 2000, just two years after its creation, Avanti won a National Trophy for Innovation. In this chapter, we shall see how this came about and how Avanti used the model to fit its own circumstances.

6.1   Innovative design: a key growth factor for start-ups

Start-ups go hand in hand with innovation, at least in the literature. The new economy provides plenty of stories of lively start-ups outperforming sluggish organizations in the old economy, although there are, of course, a few counterexamples too. Nonetheless, start-ups do seem to be a form of organization that can compete with large firms in terms of innovation, and this is reason enough to study them here.

There are in fact two reasons for taking a closer look at start-ups. First of all the question of innovation in a new company comes down to the question of innovative design. Second, many authors believe that small start-ups are more conducive to innovative design than large firms, although the issue of management methods remains allusive. A small, potentially high-growth firm is therefore an interesting first test for the Tefal model.

6.1.1   Innovative design: an obligation for start-ups

The literature on 'innovation' in start-ups describes situations of innovative design, i.e. situations in which object identities are being called into question. According to the authors who have worked on the subject, start-ups are obliged to adopt strategies of innovative design as they have an advantage when they change the rules of competition. However, in the case of head-on competition, i.e. based on dominant designs, young companies are always in a position of inferiority compared with more mature firms.

Entrepreneurs replaced by large firms

Since the second half of the nineteenth century, the literature has often remarked on the disappearance of the entrepreneur, unable to compete with large firms and their powerful organizations.

As early as 1833, Charles Babbage advised the sons of the major manufacturers, i.e. the second generation of entrepreneurs, to engage in scientific careers rather than follow their fathers, for the benefit of the future development of industry (Babbage 1833). But perhaps the most perceptive study on the subject was by Valéry (1957), writing on methods in German industry in the aftermath of the French defeat of 1870, and showing that the inventor had been replaced by smooth-running collective organizations 'without genius'. Alois Riedler, a great professor at the Technical University of Berlin, made a similar observation at the time, describing the evolutions in industrial organization for electro-technologies (Riedler 1916).

We have already mentioned Schumpeter's work, which showed on the one hand that it was entrepreneurs who 'reform production routines by exploiting inventions' and on the other that 'innovation itself is being reduced to routine' by 'teams of trained specialists who turn out what is required and make it work in predictable ways' (Schumpeter 1942, Chapter 12). Jewkes made the same observation in the 1950s, noting the relative decline in 'individual invention' in industries where large research laboratories are usually found (Jewkes, Sawers and Stillerman 1958, pp. 89–90).

More recently, Abernathy and Utterback's studies of 'patterns of industrial innovations' in the 1970s revealed very large reductions in the number of firms in mature industrial sectors and the strong growth in medium-sized firms (Abernathy and Utterback 1978; Utterback 1994). These studies have recently been confirmed by new economic studies on failure rates for firms (Suarez and Utterback 1995).

In the 1960s, Cooper (1966) gave the following list of handicaps for small firms: difficulty in obtaining high-level expertise, short-term pressure, difficulty in exploiting new products developed by the firm on a large scale, inability to cope with runs of bad luck and rapid competition from large firms which copy successful products.

For all these reasons, often evoked before and since Cooper, small companies seem to be viable only for new product lineages, in the 'interstices' left by large firms. This expression was used by Penrose (1959), who studied the place of the entrepreneur in the growing bureaucratization experienced in firms at that time. She emphasized the fact that large companies cannot cover all the opportunities that arise (which, incidentally, they help to extend, particularly by constantly creating resources) and they therefore abandon certain territories to the small firms.

6.1.2   Which management method for what sort of growth?

Small firms are *obliged* to place an emphasis on innovative design, as they are unable to compete against larger firms on dominant designs. Small firms also seem to be very capable of focusing on innovative design. The literature reveals this as different forms of flexibility:

Small firms have the ability to maintain the capability of the inventor/ entrepreneur: whereas large firms organize explorations methodically, small firms can take advantage of the qualities of the inventor/entrepreneur. In the 1960s, the literature insisted on this point. For instance, in Penrose's view, entrepreneurs are versatile, flexible, do not have to wait for market demands, can raise their own funds, are ambitious and seek either to make their fortune or to become empire builders. Similarly, Jewkes pointed out that organized research rushed to 'fill the obvious gaps', whereas in the past invention went hand in hand with independence, a fact that, even in the twentieth century, allowed many inventions to be made (Jewkes, Sawers and Stillerman 1958).

Small firms have flexibility in relation to technology and to the market: having no previous investments to worry about, start-ups are not restricted by their production systems. Instead of trying to improve the performance of their products in a particular direction (and sometimes before customer demand even arises), start-ups explore new customer demands and new uses (Christensen and Rosenbloom 1995). Entrepreneurs (or 'mentor capitalists', in the words of Leonard and Swap 2000) work to 'shape a prototype to show to venture capitalists. The sculpting is an iterative process of opening up and exploring multiple alternatives and then focusing on one or two that appear to create a sustainable advantage'(p. 77).

Start-ups are obliged to seek opportunities in a prudent yet active manner (Drucker 1985; Bhide 1992, 1994; Christensen 1997): as they do not have large financial resources, they must seize the first opportunities that come up and be satisfied with 'small gains'. Christensen even recommended that innovation should be entrusted to teams that are 'small enough to get excited by small gains'.

Small firms therefore seem to be more flexible than large ones when it comes to exploring alternatives and making new markets emerge. However, these descriptions of 'favourable conditions' do not provide ways of managing the firms. What do start-ups have to manage? Is it a question of leaving providential entrepreneurs to flourish, as they did in the past? As there are no existing product lines and no current expertise on which to base the division of work and learning, how can the design work be organized? What do we mean by 'seizing opportunities' and is this sufficient to ensure growth? Is it enough to restrict resources and to work in small teams? It is this second point that explains our interest in start-ups: in the 'favourable conditions' described above, does the Tefal model support a firm's growth?

6.2   Grafting the Tefal model: selected principles

As Vincent Chapel, co-founder of Avanti with his friend Jean-Pierre Tetaz, liked to say: 'Avanti is a start-up in the old economy'. It was a start-up because Avanti was started from scratch with high growth ambitions; and it was in the old economy because, at a time when everyone was dreaming of high-tech, internet and virtual worlds, Avanti targeted the down-to-earth world of do-it-yourself (DIY) tools. In a very short period of time, Avanti became highly successful, in fact just as the internet wave began to break.

> In 1999, Avanti made a name for itself at the INPI, the French National Institute of Industrial Property, when it came top of the list of French companies for the number of patents and brands registered per employee (twenty-two patents and sixteen brands registered in 1999).

> The same year, Avanti won the Castorama prize for DIY tools for women, as precious recognition from one of the sector's largest retailers, also its leading client.

> The following year, Avanti was presented with the Trophy for Innovation by the French Minister for Industry, rewarding the exceptional performance of a firm that had built its growth on repeated innovation.

The situation was particularly interesting because Avanti maintained close links with Tefal and its model. This was mainly due to Vincent Chapel, of course, as he had studied Tefal and knew the firm well. The relationship was all the closer since he set up Avanti in Alby-sur-Chéran, in the region of Annecy, close to Tefal's main site in Rumilly, and remained in close contact with Tefal's network of suppliers.

But that was not all: when he founded Avanti, Vincent Chapel's aim was not only to create a successful firm in the DIY sector but also to prove, through practical experience, that the Tefal model could be used to manage a start-up and provide satisfactory results. In this respect, the demonstration was convincing and gave us an exceptional opportunity to study how the Tefal model was implemented and how it helped manage growth in a start-up. We shall see how the basic metabolism of Avanti was set up using the Tefal model; how Avanti focused on designing lineages combining products and competencies; and finally, how the new firm evolved from the initial closely knit relationships to form an organization that was also inspired by the Tefal model.

6.2.1   Organizing an effective design function

Based on the example of Tefal, the founders' first job was to bring to light potentially high-growth value spaces. They began by working on watches, then tried to specialize in designing objects such as pens, notebooks, etc. for businesses.

They worked on a host of ideas until one day Jean-Pierre Tetaz, following a bad experience the previous weekend, put forward the idea of working on a device to help hammer in nails without hitting one's fingers. He worked on it for a few days, trying different alternatives, analysing present and past devices and exploring various systems and methods for holding the nails in place, such as pliers or elastic bands. There were a large number of patents for nail-holders, some of them dating back to the end of the nineteenth century (*see* Figure 6.1).

After several explorations and several prototypes, he designed a version that was close to the current nail-holder. The device, which holds the nail with a magnet, guiding it into a vertical groove in the head of the tool, has an ergonomic handle (inspired by frying pan handles, of course) and two flat surfaces at the head and the base of the handle that enable the tool to be placed firmly on the work surface (*see* Figure 6.2). The new nail-holder was an immediate success.

As observed in the literature mentioned above, we can see that the designers worked by trial and error, but the successive explorations were always prudent. They were neither too long nor too costly, meaning that

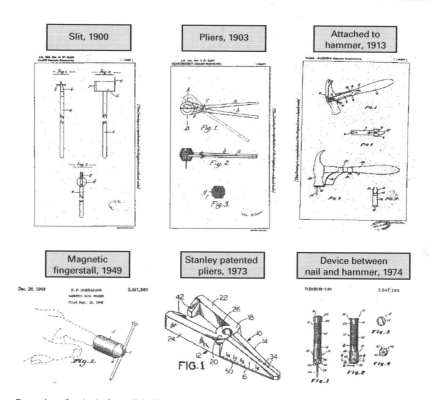

Figure 6.1   Examples of patents for nail-holders

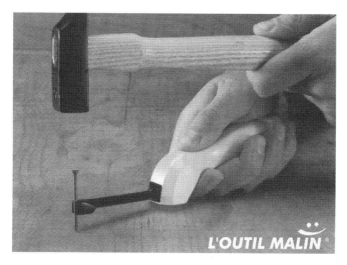

Figure 6.2   The Avanti nail-holder, the first in the 'smart tools' range

the designers kept their capacities for action and enhanced them for the following development project. The products had to be profitable, had to help them learn about the market and, above all, had to involve only low levels of resources. The break-even point was low, so that very few products needed to be sold to recover the initial investment. Relatively quickly, Avanti built up relations with major retailers in the DIY sector and limited its financial risks still further by asking its clients for firm commitments on the volumes of products ordered.

We should note that the strategy was not to minimize excess knowledge but always to maximize a learning rent, i.e. to maximize the relationship between the potential for action and the knowledge produced.

We can see other elements of the basic metabolism. First, its relationship to knowledge production: as Avanti considered that the heart of the firm was design, it outsourced production on the basis that it did not contribute sufficiently to learning. The Avanti team was therefore entirely devoted to design, which included relations with the suppliers. It was a closely knit team, documents were disseminated rapidly, and a large number of rough prototypes were made and used as a basis for collective explorations.

More precisely, Avanti organized both learning rents from design and learning rents from the market. For learning rents from the market, members of Avanti went to the DIY superstores where the products were sold to try to understand the motives for purchase (or non-purchase). They quickly learned that the market enjoyed sustained, continuous growth; it was dominated by the DIY superstores; and at that time it was boosted by tax incentives that cut the cost of renovation work in homes and also by the impact of the gales that hit France at the end of December 1999. Several major product brands were market references in terms of quality (Black and Decker, Bosch, Facom), whereas the other manufacturers competed on price. They identified classic trends such as the notion of the products' back-up services. Customers needed to know not only which product to buy but also how to use it, which explained the increasing numbers of demonstrations carried out at the points of sale.

As Vincent Chapel explained, one day in a DIY superstore he was suddenly struck by the contrast between the rows of shelves stocked with shiny, professional-looking tools and the smartly dressed men and women walking up and down the aisles looking a little lost. These were the people who would buy the nail-holder: women and white-collar workers without any real knowledge of DIY, but who were not ashamed to admit it, who were prepared to buy a 'tool to make them smart' in an area where they were keen to invest their time and money. This anecdote was the start of the 'smart tool' concept.

As for learning rents from design, although at first sight the work appeared to be disorganized as it mainly involved trial and error and numerous prototypes, the designers' learning capabilities gradually became more organized and improved in quality. For instance, the *ergovis* (an ergonomic screwdriver), one of the following products in the 'smart tool' range, was designed by recruiting industrial designers whose task was initially to 'prototype' and 'let them see' rapidly what the product concepts could look like. This helped avoid certain phases of costly prototyping. Nonetheless, prototyping and trials using prototypes were essential stages: they allowed the designers to manipulate the tools, work on their uses and find new functions. In fact, the trials played an increasingly important role and the team worked hard to maintain them and extend them.

Trial and error was not the only means of learning, as the team carried out frequent, swift work to establish the state of the art (access to databases for patents, brands and models, rapid surveys in the retail outlets, etc.). Another important element was variety, in that each design project resulted not only in a product but also in many other concepts. For instance, the nail-holder gave birth to a large number of concepts for different nail-holders. This idea of identifying and exploring alternatives in fact represented 'excess knowledge' that was then used either to protect the field if the expected growth materialized, or to propose other alternatives to other clients (a disposable version of the nail-holder was purchased by a furniture specialist and included in its assembly kits).

The above elements illustrate how Avanti managed to create a metabolism combining evolving knowledge and concepts by using the Tefal model and avoiding simply carrying out costly, sterile trial and error processes. We can now look at the second component, the management of lineages.

6.2.2   Setting up lineages

Avanti was built on the notion of repeated innovation. There was never any question of the nail-holder being a unique product, a 'blockbuster' responsible for the firm's entire growth. The team was therefore rapidly confronted with the problem of how to set up lineages. Should they find other nail-holders by systematically exploiting the variations identified initially? Should the business be extended to cover all the products in the

DIY market? Finally, how could they use past learning to support future growth, without restricting their explorations?

First of all, the information about the market helped highlight the potential value of tools which targeted non-experts rather than professionals, particularly white-collar workers tempted by DIY solutions. This gave birth to the *smart tool concept*, which served as a guiding concept for the lineage (*see* Chapter 5). The explorations therefore focused on situations where tools of this sort could be the most useful. DIY novices do jobs like laying carpets, wallpapering, putting up pictures, etc., so these areas seemed to have potential. New products gradually emerged as a result of their findings. They were always designed with the potential users in mind: the cut-angle (designed to cut wallpaper without tearing it and without having to use a square), the *proxivis* (a cylinder containing different types of screw heads that fixes onto an electrical or hand screwdriver so that it can be adapted quickly to different sorts of screws), the *ergovis* (an ergonomic screwdriver in the form of a handle) and the *arrache-tout* (a tool for removing nails without marking the support surfaces). An innovative range was gradually

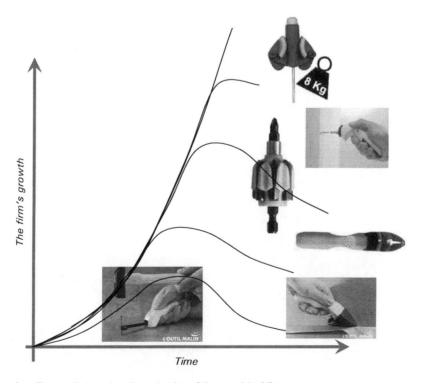

Figure 6.3   Avanti's growth, based on the extension of the smart tool lineage

built up, allowing the firm to grow by repeated innovation (*see* Figure 6.3). The firm distributed 300,000 units in 1999 and forecast 1 million by 2000. In 2001 the firm was sold to a larger company.

We should note that the firm's growth was also virtuous in terms of finance, a point that is often insisted on in the literature on start-ups. Although it is an important issue, we have not mentioned this aspect so far, for the simple reason that the lineage approach partly helped overcome the obstacle. Indeed, Avanti's initial difficulty was not in raising large sums of money but, on the contrary, in raising only a relatively small sum, because investors did not consider such a low initial investment to be credible. However, it was perfectly in line with the prudent model, and growth by repeated innovation did the rest. As each new product required only a small investment, with a very low break-even point, it was profitable. Even if the profits were small – the quantities were kept relatively low to limit risks – the repetition of the innovation ensured a regular growth in turnover and in income.

After a few months, they had the idea of organizing more specific lineages. For example, would it be possible to imagine a range of tools based on the notion of 'fastenings and fixings'? Once again, work was done to structure a lineage. Explorations were launched to find out about existing products and their uses. A first product was brought onto the market fairly quickly. Called 'clipper', it was a clip system inspired by the cleats used on sailing dinghies and windsurfing boards and was designed to help keep tools neat and tidy. Avanti's designers organized the work between them. Investigations into different fastening methods revealed a host of specialized products (fixing objects/surfaces; walls/floors/ceilings; inside/outside; different types of surfaces; one or two-sided, etc.). The typology became so complex that it was difficult to know how to continue the design process. The designers decided to work on the action of fixing and fastening things and on the range of operations involved. They discovered an interesting value space: tools used in the preparation phase prior to fixing. Preparations such as taking measurements, marking and preparing the surface are all considered thankless tasks by non-experts, although they often guarantee the quality of the final result. Several concepts were proposed in what became a new value space for smart tools (*see* Figure 6.4).[1]

---

[1] The work was carried out with two Design Engineering students from the Ecole des Mines, Gilles Toulemonde and Aude Tuchendler, in a period of work experience at Avanti. See the public report (Toulemonde and Tuchendler 2000).

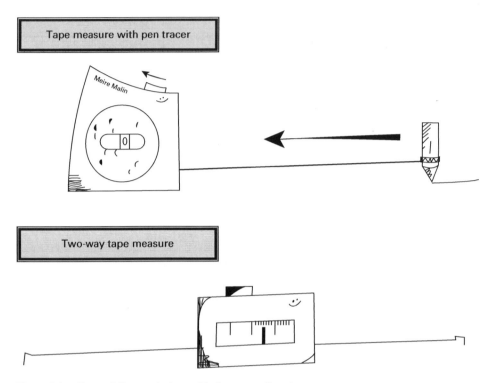

Figure 6.4   Two variations on tools used in the preparation phase

This illustrates how management by lineage resulted in the firm's growth by repeated innovation through efforts in two directions, i.e. the launching of the lineage with a first product and the elaboration of a new lineage.

6.2.3   Setting up the organization

It may seem strange to talk of organization in the case of such a small structure, but as the business grew, the question of how the collective work was to be organized obviously had to be dealt with. Once again, the Tefal model was a source of inspiration.

Avanti rapidly began to use 'support functions' to back up the design activities of the strategic core, as they had done at Tefal. Although its organization was in a relatively embryonic state, within just a few months the firm put someone in charge of monitoring technological developments, particularly patent rights. Later on, the team included a communications manager, a CAD manager and a professional industrial designer. They also used outside support functions. With a view to minimizing the initial investments and sharing risks with the suppliers, Avanti often worked on designs with partners who were also its suppliers. The latter could also be described as support functions for the core activity. The firm gradually compiled a list of reference suppliers and built up relationships with privileged distributors. Special attention was paid to a very special sort of supplier: the suppliers of ideas. Avanti's success with the nail-holder meant that its name became known in the business and several independent inventors approached the firm with proposals. These inventors nonetheless stayed outside the firm as 'support functions' and were not integrated into the conceptual core. In practice, their ideas were usually substantially reworked to fit into the lineages that were being built at the time (value as smart tools, minimizing production costs, coherency with emerging brand image, etc.).

The support functions in fact represented an outer circle of the ring-based organization. How did the lineages fit into the organization? As they were still in their early stages, the lineages did not usually entail strict division of the work. Nonetheless, a form of structuring did take place around the lineages when it came to training. Training the young designers was a major challenge for Avanti's growth prospects. They had to be integrated into the team and made familiar with the firm's specific model. An original form of training gradually emerged in which the young designers joined to help design tools in the existing lineages (the *ergovis*, for instance, was mostly designed by young industrial designers). The experienced managers, meanwhile, spent more of their time on building new lineages; whilst keeping an eye on the development of the *ergovis*, they were extremely attentive to the initial exploratory work on fastenings and fixings. The conceptual core began to generate lineages which, as they grew, could generate their own business managers. The conceptual core therefore focused chiefly on the main activity, i.e. the emergence of new lineages.

The first lesson to be learned from this brief history of the first few years of Avanti is the role played by the model of growth by innovative design. Beyond the classical characteristics of start-up innovation (interstitial, radical, agile), Avanti history shows what the start-up was managing. The designers did not rush to exploit all the opportunities in a disorderly fashion, but tried to channel the firm's exuberance and dynamism by directing it towards certain activities. The management focused on four main points:

> *The basic metabolism*: prudent design capacities were set up after careful consideration. The firm managed an economic system producing knowledge and concepts.

Management by lineage: confronted with a flow of 'good ideas' and profit opportunities, Avanti concentrated its efforts on establishing a lineage. This meant that the firm began by working on the guiding concept for the lineage (the notion of smart tools) by multiplying learning (about the market, studying uses, etc.). It was not until the concept had been clarified that the designers began to work on setting up the new lineage. We also saw how, once the exploitation of a lineage was well established, the Tefal model encouraged Avanti to rapidly organize a new lineage (this time in the field of fastenings and fixings).

The type of performance: Avanti maximized learning rents on the lineages and between the lineages, whilst keeping to its prudent economic approach based on a very low initial investment, risk-sharing and endogenous growth stemming from the new products.

Finally, the start-up had a real organization although, far from the traditional functional breakdowns, this mostly consisted of a series of design support functions (monitoring, industrial designers, etc.) on the edges of the conceptual core. Nonetheless, the roles within the conceptual core began to be differentiated, with the heart of the core working on the emergence of new lineages, whereas the following ring dealt with the previous ones.

It is clear from this discussion that Avanti could not guarantee its growth by simply applying the model – it had to overcome a series of difficulties and invent original devices in order to implement it. The managers set up a 'balanced', prudent design function, which focused on certain activities only (no production; partnerships with distributors). However, the major difficulty was to initiate and structure lineages. Organizing alternatives was all the more difficult since it gradually became a collective process, involving a great deal of learning, forms of creativeness and an ability to organize explorations in a hierarchical, structured manner, to avoid the risk of being drowned in a sea of original ideas. This is a key element in innovative design situations, as we shall see in the following chapters.

Questions for further study and discussion

Can you find other examples of innovative firms? What information is required to recognize and understand the behaviour of innovative firms?

Imagine how to design simple products conducive to preparing a repeated innovation strategy.

Are platform design or modular design strategies necessary for repeated innovation?

Analyse some famous cases of growth by repeated innovation. In the eighteenth century, Wedgwood and Watt and Boulton. In the nineteenth century, Edison and Eiffel. In the twentieth century, Sony, Swatch, Accor and Dassault Systèmes. In the twenty-first century, Apple.

PART III

Rebuilding innovation capabilities

7 Large firms and intensive innovation: the recurring R&D crises

'Is the model of the innovative firm close or radically opposed to R&D?'
Can the model derived from the Tefal case be used in other firms? Let's imagine our Innovation Manager's reaction.

'The model is highly instructive and confirms some of my intuitions. But above all, it gives me a language to help understand and explain to my colleagues that traditional solutions, however attractive some of them may still seem, cannot be used in a context of intensive innovation. For instance, take the case of "blockbusters", miracle products or services that are supposed to secure a firm's growth for many years ahead. The idea is really tempting for innovation departments like ours. But the blockbuster model focuses solely on static returns to design, with no question of reusing excess knowledge. It is therefore a risky model as it ignores learning rents.'

'The same applies to the random model, where the innovation department simply tries to balance a project portfolio between large and small and long-term and medium-term projects. Once again, the model manages the returns to each project but does not take into account learning rents and possible interdependencies between the different projects.'

'The Tefal model also shows the limitations of a model based purely on expertise. It shows that growth is always the result of a combination of expertise (in expansion) and a design process. Innovation departments can't just manage experts and knowledge, but must address the problem of how to combine knowledge management and the process for designing products and services. Your model shows how important it is to manage product and competency dynamics at the same time.'

'But I'm not sure about this last idea. Aren't R&D functions already supposed to organize this interplay? There is a strange paradox here: why has so little been said about R&D, although it is omnipresent in our firm? Come to think of it, it is striking to see that neither Tefal nor Avanti had an R&D function. Anyone would think that R&D belongs exclusively to large firms and that there is a sort of contradiction between innovative design and R&D. Isn't R&D supposed to be the function in charge of innovation? Isn't innovation one of the objectives of R&D activities? And, in fact, doesn't R&D already manage innovation by lineage, with clear product ranges and well-identified functions and disciplines? Isn't R&D a derivative of the model developed from the Tefal case?'

'Are the Tefal model and R&D radically opposed or in fact very close? This is a key issue for my department because it has only been set up recently and we feel a bit small compared with the powerful troops in R&D. Are we radically different, in which case we must find a way of working together; or are we very similar, in which case, why did we set up a new department?'

In response to the Innovation Manager's questions, in Section 7.1 we will study the origins and the main characteristics of R&D and give some examples of successful R&D-based firms. We show that the model of the R&D-based firm is a specific version of the innovative firm illustrated by Tefal (7.2), but is based on certain restrictive assumptions. Finally, we examine a recent case to show why these restrictive assumptions mean that the R&D-based model is ill-suited to situations of competition by intensive innovation (7.3).

7.1   Traditional R&D: initial domestication of innovations

To understand the current crises in R&D, we must start by understanding its past achievements. Today, it is impossible to imagine a large firm without design engineers, grouped in a 'research' or an 'engineering and design' department. This did not just happen 'naturally'; on the contrary, the organization model can be dated back to a specific period when engineering and design departments were invented by a few, often highly successful vanguards. One of the first historical examples will help us understand the strength of the model which they invented to manage innovation.

7.1.1   The invention of systematic design at the Baldwin Locomotive Works

7.1.1.1   The origins: Stephenson and Son or 'wild' innovation

In a book on innovation, it is more common to find the story of the famous English inventors of the steam engine, George Stephenson and his son Robert, rather than the American inventor Matthias Baldwin. So we shall start with the Stephensons as they help understand Baldwin's work and the superiority of the forms of design organization he introduced.[1]

The Stephensons were the great heroes of the beginnings of the railways. In 1825, they inaugurated the first ever railway line, which ran from the Tyne coalmines near Darlington to the port of Stockton. The machines were prototypes, little was known about the economics of the system and there were few competent engineers working in the domain at that time. The Stephensons used the Stockton–Darlington line as a test field, which helped them improve the models of locomotives and study the economic viability of the line. Robert Stephenson explored new concepts for locomotives that gave birth to the famous Rocket, which won the Rainhill Trials, a contest held in 1829 to find the best locomotive engine for the Liverpool–Manchester railway line.

Baldwin moved in a similar environment of 'inspired amateurs', but in the United States. The Rainhill Trials had aroused enormous interest from mechanical engineers throughout the world and, shortly after the contest, Baldwin started by reproducing the Stephensons' Rocket. He then added a number of different innovations: a front wheel mounted on a swivel truck that improved the locomotive's steering in the tight bends of the American railways (1832), and a new axle and new suspension (1838).

The two firms then followed very different paths. From the 1850s onwards, Robert Stephenson & Co. gradually lost its leadership and became just another competitor among others, with a limited export market as the British railway companies designed and built their own machines. Baldwin, however, experienced impressive growth.

7.1.1.2 Rationalizing the design activity

The Baldwin Locomotive Works was confronted with several difficulties during this period, including the fact that it received specific, extremely varied demands from specialized customers and was therefore unable to impose a single product. The market was also very volatile: every ten years or so, speculation on the railways led to a financial crisis, which dried up cash flows and had a severe impact on the firm's turnover. The firm needed flexible design capabilities if it was to seize the opportunities as and when

---

[1] This case study is drawn from an extremely well-documented book by John K. Brown (1995); it is also based on Booth (1831); Stephenson, Stephenson and Locke (1831); Warren (1923); Chapelon (1952); Rolt (1960); and Hindle and Lubar (1986). For a more detailed study, *see* Le Masson and Weil (2004, 2008).

they arose, but how did it manage flexibility, variety and cost control, not to mention innovation?

In several successive stages that we can only summarize here, the Baldwin Locomotive Works gradually introduced highly original methods of reasoning and organization which enabled it to achieve remarkable levels of performance. A good example was that it managed to reduce the time required from taking an order to delivering a locomotive to just eight weeks, only three of which were taken up by the design process.

Baldwin began by moving away from 'wild' design, characterized by cottage industry-style product development, and gradually began to invent tools and methods that established three different ways of describing objects, or three languages corresponding to (i) functions, (ii) conceptual models and (iii) parts, components and manufacturing processes. Mass design was then possible, as clear roles were given to salesmen, engineers and technicians in engineering and design departments and those in the factory. He had in fact invented systematic design and laid the foundations for major R&D firms.

Baldwin's three languages can be described as follows:

Language No. 1: functions. Baldwin began by producing standard product catalogues to help guide clients' choices. The firm then proposed standard specifications, which served as a framework for the sales negotiations, and provided a list of the main components and their dimensions. In this way, when the order was placed, the client was 'free' to specify the performance required for each of the corresponding elements.

Language No. 2: conceptual models. The catalogues contained reference models that served as a basis for designing new variations. The conceptual models speeded up the design process as the designers could draw up lists of the machine parts to be designed more quickly.

Language No. 3: the parts and the detailed design process. The engineers introduced standard components that reduced the time required to design the parts and made them easier to produce. The components were presented either in the form of a catalogue for the clients to choose from, or in the form of 'drawing cards', i.e. patterns for parts that were used from one project to the next. As a result of these standardized parts, the production departments had to respect the plans provided by the designers (this led to the reintroduction of piecework, i.e. wages based on pieces produced rather than on time worked).

The three languages gradually came to correspond to specific players and functions in the firm: the marketing department, which drew up the specifications; engineers and technicians in the engineering and design departments, who designed the conceptual architectures; and the draughts-men charged with the detailed studies.

This organization was an extremely effective way of rationalizing design as it served as a basis for dividing out the design work and helped coordinate the actors and support the individuals' learning processes. The resulting 'linear model' was neither costly nor unproductive and was a way of routinizing design. And above all, it domesticated innovation. Each of the languages was a means of exploring and structuring an innovation space; they maintained independent spaces for exploration whilst fitting together in such a way as to be easily coordinated.

This rationalization led to significant growth in the production and productivity of engineering and design departments. The system was introduced in many large firms, particularly in Germany and the United States, and gradually became more sophisticated. 'Revisers' were recruited to check that the norms were respected and that the production did not deviate from a firm's specific design standards; calculations of profit-earning capacity became the rule; and design staff increased in numbers and became more specialized, using new design rules and new ways of capitalizing on previous design projects.

This often had spectacular results. For instance, from 1902 to 1909, the machine manufacturer Borsig increased production by 170 per cent and productivity by nearly 30 per cent following reforms to its engineering and design departments and achieved a rate of 92 per cent of standardized pieces per machine (Neuhaus 1910). When Westinghouse reorganized its engineering and design departments in 1902, this had a massive impact on productivity: design lead times were reduced from 34 days to 6.3 days within four years and the firm designed twice as many products whilst increasing the number of designers by only 17 per cent (Koch 1908).

7.1.2   Domesticating innovation through R&D: the case of Airbus

R&D is still an extremely efficient way of domesticating innovation even today. A good example of this is the aviation industry, whose organization and design reasoning are based on the languages of systematic design:

Functions: the industry makes great efforts to organize its production into ranges. Just as Baldwin designed families of locomotives and not just single steam engines, the aviation industry's systematic design strategy is also based on *ranges* of aircraft. These are organized by range (i.e. distance) and by number of seats, the two key elements determining airlines' needs. Manufacturers also offer standard functional specifications,

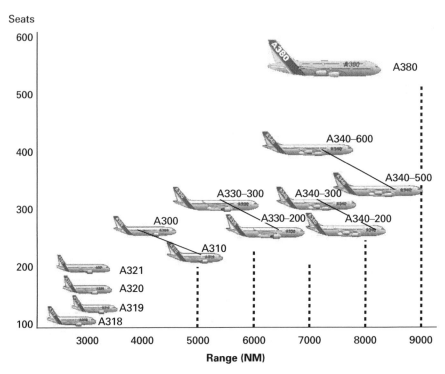

Figure 7.1   Airbus and the domestication of innovation: designing ranges of commercial aircraft (special thanks to Eric Ballot for this figure)

indicating the reference features for all the aircraft in the range. Very early on, Airbus made direct operating costs (DOCs) (maintenance, crews, etc.) a priority, another criterion being to reduce the time (and cost) of the training required for a pilot to qualify to fly a new aircraft in the range.

Conceptual models: work on the specifications involves a series of construction principles used for the entire range, such as standard cockpits to reduce training costs, electric flight commands and more automatic functions (to enable crews of two pilots and reduce DOCs), reusable modules (nose cone) and the introduction of families to cover the needs. This last point can be explained as follows: in Figure 7.1's diagonal 'range × seats' we find the family (A320, A300–310, A330, A340, A380) and each family is then split into models by adding or taking away a flight leg. The figure shows the progression from the A318 to the A321 by adding flight legs, which reduces the flight range and increases the number of passengers. These construction principles are based on modelling capabilities provided by research work in different scientific disciplines (fluid dynamics, materials, mechanics, etc.).

Embodiment: the components are designed using a series of stable, reusable technologies. Due to the strict certification requirements in the aviation industry, these technologies are mastered well and evolve relatively slowly.

One of the keys to Airbus's success in civil aviation today is that it was able to identify the relevant functional specifications, to make them match the construction principles and to design the necessary components.

On the basis of these two examples, can we say that R&D-based firms innovate and, if so, why does innovation still raise so many questions? The two examples show that the strength of R&D is its ability to repeat the design process, but it is also clear that, far from being opposed to innovation, this repetition in fact seems to favour it. Better still, some elements seem to indicate that R&D-based firms follow the Tefal model. There is a metabolism of knowledge, the knowledge produced is reused from one development project to the next and there are strictly managed product lineages (cf. Baldwin's ranges of locomotives and Airbus's ranges of aircraft). Perhaps there is no antagonism after all, as large firms seem to be models of innovation, too.

It may even be that it is precisely for this reason that the model prevailed over other options in the past. As we saw at the end of Part II, at the end of the nineteenth century many observers noted the inexorable decline of small enterprises, which were being replaced by large R&D-based firms. What factor was strong enough to impose technical departments, engineering and design departments and research departments in all large firms throughout the world? These highly demanding, extremely costly forms of organization would certainly not have been adopted if they had not offered an extraordinary capacity to domesticate innovation.

However, the model of the R&D-based firm in fact requires very specific conditions before it can develop, as shown by the two crises experienced in the late twentieth century.

7.2 First crisis: R&D threatened by suffocation in the 1960s

7.2.1 Economic and social changes, 1960s–1980s

Profound economic and social changes had an enormous impact on industry from the 1960s onwards, which can be summarized in four major trends:

The growth due to reconstruction in the aftermath of the Second World War began to slow. International competition grew as trade became more international and new markets opened.

The consumer society, which had begun to appear between the two wars, particularly in the United States, spread rapidly and arrived in Europe in the 1950s. The middle classes acquired household equipment (refrigerators, radios, cars and then televisions, etc.) on a massive scale. Tefal's non-stick frying pan was launched during this period. Another important change was that people started to throw things away, meaning that products' renewal rates increased significantly (particularly in textiles and clothing). Product variety increased rapidly and markets became more and more segmented.

New concerns also arose as consumers became increasingly aware of issues such as the quality and safety of the products they were buying (consumer associations were formed and new prescribers emerged) and began to worry about the environment (debates on the atom bomb, on major industrial accidents – Bhopal, Amoco Cadiz – on acid rain, etc.). Numerous norms and regulations were drawn up on these subjects.

The fourth key trend was the emergence of new forms of distribution. Mass marketing changed the relationships with the final customer, imposed pressure on prices and introduced new forms of differentiation (brand, packaging, advertising, etc.).

These trends led to a rise in competition and there was an explosion in the variety of products on offer. Industry was divided into sectors and a profusion of performance criteria was drawn up for products in response to consumers' new demands.

7.2.2   The R&D model, victim of its own success

How did the R&D model face up to these challenges? It was robust in handling variety and therefore seemed well suited to the new industrial context, but at the same time it appeared to be suffocating:

In the face of growing demands, the R&D model was capable of adopting an approach based on constant improvements. However, in the end, technical solutions show their limits for a given element of performance. The R&D model is not a model for exploring new technologies and does not prepare for situations where performance peaks have reached their limits.

The R&D model sought to normalize, standardize and regulate with a view to facilitating coordination, reducing design and production costs and improving market organization (ranges, labels, prescription, etc.). However, this process generates a more restrictive environment and regulatory systems can block favourable technical or commercial alternatives.

The refrigerator market and energy consumption norms

In the 1990s, the European Commission introduced two directives (94/2/EC and 96/57/EC) concerning energy consumption for refrigerators, domestic appliances which, of course, have to be plugged in all the time. The first stipulated that the appliances should be labelled to indicate their consumption and the second banned appliances that did not have satisfactory performance in terms of energy consumption.

These norms clearly oriented the competition towards appliances with low consumption. The labelling policy also made the domestic refrigeration sector far more dynamic as it encouraged people to buy new appliances. The label was seen as proof of quality in terms of energy but also, through an illusion deliberately maintained by the retailers, as proof of the quality of the product as a whole.

It was these regulations and the system of labelling that then prevented the manufacturers from exploring new value spaces, particularly concerning food storage (quality in terms of health, organoleptic properties, etc.), because the energy restrictions were such that it was difficult to propose new functions that consumed even the slightest bit more energy.

R&D was organized to allow for a wide variety of products to be produced. However, the mechanism for identifying and refining competencies, reference components and quantified features also has pernicious effects because, as the process advances, performance variables are multiplied, functional specifications become longer and longer and functional layers build up one after another; expertise is increasingly specialized but also more and more fragmented, sometimes to the point of outsourcing (see box below on the automobile industry).

Fragmented design in the automobile industry

Automobile design is one of the most extreme cases of fragmented design. First of all, there is a profusion of features in areas such as safety, anti-pollution, communication systems and x-by-wire. Design is often delegated to suppliers, or even suppliers' suppliers, and all the systems and components are gradually being refined and becoming more complex.

Car manufacturers are adding more and more layers and divisions so that cars have become like a series of jigsaw puzzles stacked on top of each other. The vehicles are divided into four different areas: area of architecture (the driver's immediate environment, front unit, etc.), major system (chassis, electronics, etc.), elementary function group (dashboard, braking, air-conditioning, etc.) and features (acoustics, passive safety, etc.).

The R&D model was suffocating and went into crisis. How could it manage so many functional features and integrate so many rules, good practices and technical principles? Whereas in the past it had been possible to divide work into sub-tasks, R&D firms could no longer share out design work and distribute it over a period of time. Constraints often appear late on in a design process and final validations sometimes call the entire design process into question. For instance, in certain cases, details in the production (glues, a fastening system, a car bonnet, etc.) can invalidate architectural choices or prevent certain functional requirements from being met. Where there had been a smooth hierarchy of quantified features, reference architectures and standard components (components that made it possible to produce the reference architectures, which in turn made it possible to provide the features), there was now the need to reinvent hierarchies and *ad hoc* divisions. They had to find creative compromises to do away with the apparently inevitable contradictions between features and technical constraints, but such compromises tended to be project-specific, difficult and precarious, in that the slightest change, during a project or from one project to another, called them into question.[2]

Project management was developed in this crisis situation (Clark and Fujimoto 1991; Wheelwright and Clark 1992; Midler 1993; Weil 1999). Its aim was to provide management tools and organization models that could find the most appropriate QCT compromises on the basis of precise specifications and available competencies. New CAD techniques also facilitated interactions between designers: it was easier to adjust components' dimensions when changes were made, to manage technical data and integrate existing models more rapidly, to validate designs and to coordinate the designers' work using virtual scale models.

7.2.3   The limitations of the R&D model: a restrictive view of lineages

As we have seen, the R&D model adapted to the new context, but the first signs of the scissor effect (cf. Chapter 2) began to appear: on the one hand, new values meant that a growing number of elements had to be designed (due to variety, new regulations, new constraints, etc.) and, on the other, design staff numbers were increasing all the time.

This first crisis highlighted a major limitation of the R&D model compared with the general model of the innovative firm found in the case of

---

[2] *See* Weil (1999) for the notion of creative compromise.

Tefal: the forms of lineage employed. We have defined a lineage as a combination of the dynamics of a set of product concepts and the dynamics of a set of competencies. In fact, the R&D model is built on a very specific combination, based on stable object identities, given that the functions, construction principles, industrial processes and technological solutions are known in advance. In the R&D model, a product lineage is therefore structured, often on the level of an industrial sector, with:

   a set of reference functions, which guide competition between the firms;

   a set of functions and scientific results forming validated construction principles, which transform functional specifications into technical specifications. These construction principles are disseminated by the professional groups, schools and technical sectors;

   a set of available technologies, which serve to meet the demands of the technical specifications. They are disseminated by the process designers or the suppliers.

Innovations can be made in these three aspects, in which case performance increases, the models are better controlled and technologies are improved. This represents one of the models studied in Chapter 2, i.e. planned innovation. The literature on this model in fact describes organization by systematic design in large R&D-based firms.

At first sight, this model of a lineage appears to be very general, the idea being to start by exploring a reference functional space, then to mobilize construction principles and finally to find the right processes and technologies to suit them. It does not seem to introduce many restrictions.

However, the first crisis of the R&D model showed that this model of lineage can in fact exist in only very specific circumstances: the functions, construction principles and technologies must be practically stable and fit in with each other. Progress from one stage to the next must not involve costly steps backwards; there must be what we can call 'downward compatibility'. However, when dominant designs evolve and become more complex, designers must imagine new functions, integrate new construction principles, which are often very different from the previous ones (if not completely contradictory), and master new processes, although they often know very little about the constraints in terms of their impact on the product. It is no longer possible to structure lineages in such a way that functional language, construction principles and technologies remain independent and set in strict hierarchies.

The challenge for project management and CAD tools was therefore to extend the R&D model to situations in which upward independence is not guaranteed (a detailed design has to be tested to validate architectural choices), where it might be necessary to introduce a new function late in the process and where the construction principles are too immature for a strict division of the work and require intense efforts to coordinate the different waves of prototypes and trials.

7.3   Second crisis: R&D on the critical path of innovative projects

The second crisis of the R&D-based firm, which highlighted other limitations of the R&D model, concerned innovative design.

The economic and social context that we described in detail in Chapters 2 and 3 resulted in a major contradiction: competition through innovation implied massive investments in design, but at a time when it was also vital to make stricter controls on design costs, which had risen dramatically. These two contrasting phenomena had never been experienced on such a large scale before:

As far as competition by innovation was concerned, we must remember that it was no longer simply a question of variety or rapid renewals – which an R&D model could have dealt with – but of growing uncertainty regarding object identities. The aim was no longer just to introduce a new function for an object (e.g. acoustics in cars), but to make significant changes in the functional space or even to design objects based on imprecise briefs with no identified functional spaces. The designers therefore had to design a growing number of elements (value, business model, functions, conceptual models, etc.).

As far as design staff were concerned, we must remember that the increase reflected a strong trend resulting from efforts made to counter the difficulties of systematic design in the 1980s and 1990s. Many companies had more white-collar than blue-collar workers and were confronted with engineering and design departments with tens of thousands of engineers and technicians and research centres with several hundred research scientists. New problems arose as firms began to realize that the challenge no longer consisted of outsourcing production but outsourcing design. For example, when the internet bubble burst, Ericsson halved the number of R&D staff in just a few years.

To help understand the impact of this crisis, we shall now look at the case of an R&D-based firm confronted with new, intensive innovation in its sector.

7.3.1   Discovering that a bagless vacuum cleaner is still a vacuum cleaner

The vacuum cleaner industry is a prime example of the shock produced by the emergence of a sudden change of object identity in an environment in which R&D is well organized and capable of managing product changes as long as they stay within well-established dominant designs.

In the 1990s, the vacuum cleaner sector was hardly renowned for its innovations. Upright and cylinder vacuum cleaners had been the two reference architectures for several decades; ranges were organized by motor power, which was assimilated with performance and also indicated the size of the cleaner. In a market where renewals were stable, the manufacturers had found it difficult to impose a second criterion, vacuum pressure, although it gave a better key to performance, i.e. suction power. During this period, the refrigerator market was stimulated by the introduction of environmental norms, but nothing of the sort existed for the vacuum cleaner market. The manufacturers increased suction power, worked on colours and industrial design, above all reduced prices and sometimes added air fresheners or extra accessories. There was a small amount of competition on noise levels, but it was several years before decibels (dB) were finally accepted as a criterion of choice.

The construction principles had not changed for several decades: an electrical motor (connected to the mains supply by a cord) drove a turbine which created a vacuum. A stream of air entered the cleaner through the intake port, sweeping the dust and debris along with it. It passed through a porous bag, which collected the dust and debris. It then went through a final filter, which collected the finest particles, before leaving by the exhaust port.

In this context, the firm studied in the following pages, the French market leader Rowenta, was nonetheless able to break away from the dominant design by proposing an ultra-compact cleaner. The innovation, which involved substantial efforts to redesign the internal workings and propose more compact, more powerful electric motors, was a huge commercial success.

There was a major upheaval in the vacuum cleaner market when Dyson launched its first bagless cleaner in the latter half of the 1990s. In just a few years, the company founded by the British industrial designer James Dyson became the market leader in the UK (in terms of turnover) and gained significant market share throughout Europe. The Dyson myth was doubtless an integral part of the firm's success (Dyson and Coren 1997). As an industrial designer, Dyson had already launched a number of inventions, including the Ballbarrow, a wheelbarrow whose spherical front wheel made it exceptionally stable. As the story goes, one day Dyson needed to change his vacuum cleaner bag. After the first obstacle – finding the reference for the bag to fit his cleaner – he noticed that the suction power had improved enormously once the bag had been changed, but then decreased again rapidly because the dust particles blocked up the pores, increasing power losses along the air stream. He had the idea of using another way to filter the dust in the stream of air: an old industrial principle for separating air and dust, frequently found in factories, i.e. the cyclone. The air stream is sent along a high-speed spiral path, thus separating out the dust particles due to their greater inertia.

Dyson had patented his invention at the end of the 1970s and had tried, like Marc Grégoire (*see* Chapter 4), to interest manufacturers in it, but with no success. In the end, again like Grégoire, he decided to produce the bagless vacuum cleaner himself and, after several attempts, met with extraordinary success. The vacuum cleaner's innovative design made it stand out from its competitors. It was sold for twice the price of traditional vacuum cleaners and in fact created a new market segment. James Dyson made his fortune and became a symbol of the revival of British industry.

7.3.2   Organizing the response to Dyson

After their initial scepticism, the other manufacturers soon began to worry. They knew that they had to respond to Dyson's success, but did not know how to go about it. Two student engineers from the Ecole des Mines, Geraldine Coppola and Laurent Kraif, were able to study how a major French vacuum cleaner manufacturer, Rowenta, managed its counterattack. Their work, which we summarize briefly below, underlines the great difficulties experienced by the firm's designers before they could market a product to respond to Dyson's move and shows how it involved a complete reorganization of the firm's design processes.

The first reaction was to turn to the research department. Weren't the large amounts of money regularly put into research supposed to be used to prepare for technological innovations? Had the researchers already worked on similar concepts, or alternative ones, and had they registered any patents? Unfortunately, the research department had nothing new to show them. So what had it been doing for all these years? The answer was that it had been responding – with the greatest possible rigour – to all the questions that people had asked it. The researchers had mastered issues such as aerodynamics in air streams and the Brownian motion of particles in carpets, but nobody had ever asked them to work on 'filter media'. In fact, it would have been difficult to do so as it was not clear which scientific discipline was involved. Was it an issue for an expert in materials or in fluid mechanics? What tests would be needed? From the client's point of view, what was a 'good' filter medium? Finally, was it really a good idea to work on such an ill-defined question as filter media and could anybody really commit themselves regarding the research programme?

The second reaction was therefore to turn to the marketing department to try to find out a little more about the needs that would have to be met by future products, as Dyson's success suggested that these needs had changed. What functional specifications was it looking for? The marketing department was extremely ill at ease because market studies had never given the slightest inkling that a bagless vacuum cleaner could be a success. Worse than that, bagless cleaners were noisy, cumbersome and extremely expensive, in fact far more expensive than anything that any serious market study had ever contemplated for a vacuum cleaner. In theory, there should be no demand for a vacuum cleaner of this sort.

Where could the firm go from there? It entered into a long, costly and painful process compared with the smooth-flowing product development processes the actors were used to. For example, the research department started to explore filter media, examining patent registers and existing industrial processes with a fine-tooth comb. They had to see whether the existing solutions were compatible with the needs of vacuum cleaners. For instance, could the techniques be adapted to deal with wood shavings or pieces of glass? The research department was confronted with completely new problems at each stage and had to develop new methods, new tools and new forms of organization.

However, it was not the only actor concerned. To see whether alternative techniques were suitable or not, the firm decided to check on the traditional functions of vacuum cleaner bags, but realized that there were no clear specifications on this point. The marketing department was therefore called on to rewrite a series of specifications: the media must be able to collect debris and separate flows of air and dust and must be hygienic.

A number of different paths were explored, often leading to design difficulties. In one case when the designers were unable to evaluate an innovative component using the usual specifications because the test related too specifically to the component used in the past, they had to introduce a completely new experiment plan. In another case, when it was hard to find

an economic balance, they used new marketing and design tools to find a
new product positioning, new aesthetics and new semiology. Finally, in
other cases, the product architectures had to be completely rethought due
to potential new techniques or simply due to size constraints relating to new
components.

In the years that followed, the design community's efforts gave birth to
innovative concepts – including a triangular suction head for vacuuming in
corners and a new bagless cleaner based on the concept of a worm screw – and
helped Rowenta maintain its position in a drastically changing market. But
in terms of the firm's strategy and growth (or at least its survival), the new
innovation capabilities acquired on this occasion were probably more
important than the new products as such. These efforts were vital because
the vacuum cleaner market had not recovered its stability since the shock
created by Dyson. The major manufacturers all gradually explored the newly
created top-of-the-range segment; they played with bagless techniques and
ended up proposing new concepts. The sector thus went into a system of
intensive innovation. Thanks to its initial efforts to counter Dyson, Rowenta
was better armed to face this new form of competition.

7.3.3   Lessons to be drawn from the response to bagless vacuum cleaners

In the above example, we are particularly interested in examining the
difficulties encountered by R&D-based firms when confronted with intensive innovation. The case of vacuum cleaners illustrates three main points:

The position of the research department: it was put in a very uncomfortable
position by the insistent demands for innovation, but was also
threatened by the economic constraints. Tight budgets tend to make
managers question the relevancy of research if innovations are not
immediately forthcoming. 'What's the point of research if it doesn't
innovate?' We will come back to this question later. In the meantime,
perhaps because they did not find a satisfactory answer, research
laboratories were hit by radical cutbacks in the 1990s. (Joël Birnbaum,
former Director of Hewlett-Packard Laboratories, spoke of a 'research
blood bath' (Buderi 2000).)

The position of the development department: intensive innovation forced it
to work on innovative concepts whilst at the same time rationalizing
product development processes in order to reduce costs and speed up
the rate of renewals. In these conditions, the development teams
tended to optimize performance, i.e. to develop products with

increasingly tight compromises in terms of quality, cost and time. But this left less and less space for exploring innovative concepts or new features. Project managers, who were already responsible for ambitious QCT targets, were loath to take the additional risk of launching new features when no one knew their market potential, or new components when no one could guarantee that they would work or at least that they would not be harmful to the overall project.

The position of the marketing department: intensive innovation made the traditional tools of strategic marketing obsolete. It is obviously a difficult task to study the market for a product that does not exist yet, but marketing managers have always had to face this problem. The difficulty stems above all from the fact that the techniques and concepts developed on this subject have reached their limits. Notions such as market positioning, niche and segment are becoming difficult to handle. It is no longer possible to carry out stratified surveys: the former stratifications based on socio-professional categories have long been out of date due to social evolutions and it is difficult to build pertinent new ones. Quite often, it is a question of reinventing the tools of prospect marketing. Increasing use is therefore made of new techniques such as ethnological studies, study of uses and user involvement in design. These are all symptoms of growing unease, if not of major changes in the profession.

7.3.4   What this second crisis tells us about the R&D-based model

This second crisis of R&D illustrates the limitations of the R&D model, particularly when compared with the model of the innovative firm found at Tefal. Let us go back to the four aspects seen in previous chapters – model of activity, means of action, performance and organization – to explain the differences:

Concerning the model of activity, the R&D-based firm builds its growth on stable object identities that fix the areas of competition.

Concerning the type of performance, there is a metabolism of knowledge in the R&D-based model, but it remains relatively limited. The case of vacuum cleaners shows that the model has difficulty in dealing with situations requiring the acquisition and extensive production of competencies. The R&D model is basically a model that *minimizes the excess knowledge produced.*

This can be done in several ways: for instance, the development team can seek to minimize the knowledge produced for each project, or it can ensure that knowledge is produced for well-identified goals, e.g. to provide a valuable plus point for a product, to improve calculation models in order to improve process controls, etc.

In such situations, it is possible to calculate the ratio between the expected benefit and the investments in design. Research itself, the R of R&D, in fact fits into this perspective: in the vacuum cleaner case, it was working on the questions that the firm asked it to work on, i.e. improving processes, mastering quality, etc.

It must be pointed out that minimizing knowledge produced is not the same thing as reusing excess knowledge produced. In the latter case, a great deal of knowledge can be produced and reused at a later date on another, completely unexpected project. This is obviously a vital difference in situations of innovative design where the question of building new competencies recurs constantly. The R&D-based model can launch into knowledge acquisition of this sort only if the return on the project is certain, whereas it is more frequent for the gradual mastering of competencies to make new opportunities emerge, as in the case of Tefal.

Concerning the means of action, the first crisis had already shown the limits of specific structuring, in which each lineage defines a set of functions, construction principles and processes so that the processes give body to the construction principles and the construction principles help fulfil the functions.

We have seen that the organizational techniques of project management and new CAD tools had helped to widen the notion of lineage to situations in which it was possible to add a function, construction principle or process to the initial set, but only on a marginal basis.

However, in the case of innovative design, designers are faced with situations that differ substantially from dominant designs. They may begin with a technical concept (a fuel cell, hydroforming, electroluminescence, etc.) or a space in which it is to be used (mobility, home cleaning, etc.); the embryo of the lineage has to be designed on a regular basis; and, for old lineages, competition consists in breaking away as far as possible from the dominant design, thus upsetting and surprising competitors.[3] Hence, the R&D model can work as long as there are

---

[3] Dyson was a typical example of this when he proposed an extremely expensive, bagless vacuum cleaner, which did not match the usual performance criteria (noise, power, size, etc.).

already vast areas of well-structured knowledge (inherited from products designed in the past or from a relatively old dominant industrial design) and as long as the product to be designed moves away from it only marginally, whereas innovative design takes place in circumstances where the outline of the lineage has not yet been determined: the functional space is not clearly identified, the construction principles are incomplete and the processes are unknown.

Finally, concerning the organization, there is clearly a fundamental difference between the R&D-based model and the model of the innovative firm such as Tefal. Admittedly, both cases involve the management of a lineage. In the case of the R&D model, this often takes the form of a matrix organization, with the major functional departments contributing to the projects launched by the product divisions. But the R&D model has no, or very little, conceptual core. In other words, the aim of the R&D organization is not to ensure that a new column or line emerges in the matrix, i.e. that a new product division or a new competency emerges. Its aim is to optimize the allocation of functional resources to the products to be designed.

7.4   Conclusion: the limits of R&D as a means of innovation

One important point highlighted by this study of the R&D-based firm is that, historically speaking, it was a model of the innovative firm. The R&D-based firm was capable of setting up metabolisms of knowledge, lineages and suitable forms of organization. This explains its exceptional capacity to domesticate innovation. The model was indeed so widely used and so successful that today it is difficult to imagine firms without R&D.

Nonetheless, we have also seen in this chapter that the model has its limits. It is restrictive compared with the more general model found at Tefal, as it is built on stable object identities and the metabolism is not directed to reusing excess knowledge but to minimizing the amount of knowledge produced; the lineages are developed only in cases where there are already three types of language (the language of functions, the language of concepts, or construction principles, and the physical-morphological language, i.e. the language of technologies and processes); the project/function organization manages the allocation of existing functional resources to the products to be designed in existing lineages, but not the emergence of new functions or new product lineages (*see* Table 7.1).

Table 7.1. The R&D firm, a limited model of the innovative firm

	Specifications for the innovative firm	Model of the innovative firm from the Tefal case	R&D-based firm
Models of activity and reasoning	A model of activity without stable product identities (flexibility for products and competencies)	The firm as a design function = coevolution of competencies and products	Product renewals within known dominant design
Objects to be managed – technical substratum	Structure innovation capabilities without basing them on 'functions' or 'performance'	Lineages and learning rents	Successive projects improving performance, using available resources
Type of performance	Growth by repeated innovation, in a context of unstable object identities (no one-off projects)	Prudent growth by reusing excess knowledge without stabilizing object identities	Regular improvement within cones of performance – minimize knowledge production
Forms of organization	At the firm level, including major R&D-based firms, without being limited to a project framework	Metabolism (ring-based, with conceptual core)	Project/function matrix

However, as we have seen in previous chapters, the current challenges of innovative design are to be found on the edges of the R&D model: firms must be highly responsive in terms of competencies and products, meaning that they must produce excess knowledge and use it as much as possible instead of minimizing it; and they must be capable of elaborating new lineages, by moving away from the dominant designs and inventing new forms of organization which give pride of place to the conceptual core responsible for generating new lineages.

We will address this point in the next chapter.

Questions for further study and discussion

What impact does a dominant design have on the activity of design? How are design activities organized when there is a dominant design?

For a few products, see what makes them cases of dominant design. See why recent changes can threaten these dominant designs (e.g. automobiles, food industry, telephones, clothing, etc.).

What are the causes of crises for dominant designs? What is intensive innovation? Compare intensive innovation and invention.

Key notions – Chapter 7

The R&D model as a model of the innovative firm. Its effectiveness for domesticating innovation

The dominant design as a specific lineage: known functional, conceptual and physical-morphological languages

The limitations of the R&D model in the face of innovative design

Specific context of the issue of innovation today

8 From R&D to RID: missions and organizations of innovative design

Should firms return to the 'wild' innovation model?
How can the R&D model be adapted to the contemporary challenges of innovation-intensive capitalism and become a model for innovative firms?

One solution is to return to 'wild' innovation, when firms set up small, unofficial teams of researchers working with limited resources, in the hope that by giving them more autonomy they will be able to explore new paths. In these rare forms of design organization, the firms count on serendipity, fortunate accidents and chance encounters in cross-functional teams, between wise experts who accept ideas from people throughout the firm as any suggestion can be worth investigating (Robinson and Stern 1997). The case of the Stephensons showed that wild innovation can be experimental and flexible; it can explore new ideas and create new values. However, wild innovation has its limits; it is in fact a poor model for the innovative firm, not least in comparison with the R&D model.

Although this type of organization can be interesting and can sometimes help new ideas emerge, it is never more than one element in a more general model, as we saw in our study of start-ups (*see* Avanti, Chapter 6), innovative firms (Chapter 4) and R&D-based firms (Chapter 7). Other issues must be dealt with, such as defining the functional spaces, launching the innovations and repeating them throughout lineages, and ensuring the gradual mastery of advanced technologies. If they fail to ensure a transition towards systematic design, firms based on wild innovation run the risk of being overtaken by competitors who do adopt systematic design strategies for new dominant designs. It is not so much ideas that are lacking as sound collective practices for exploring new value spaces and building up new competencies.

Faced with these challenges, the R&D firm can be an interesting starting point as it is capable of controlling lineages and making them work. What we are looking for is a comprehensive model of the innovative firm (as in the Tefal model, i.e. with a model of activity, a metabolism, lineages and a ring-based organization) that includes the R&D model and is in fact an extension of it. Unfortunately, the issue is complicated by the fact that R&D is currently undergoing a paradoxical crisis.

Innovative R&D?

On the one hand, R&D is very much in demand: in these times of intensive innovation, managers and development departments are constantly asking research departments to supply more knowledge and new concepts. Research work is carefully scrutinized, even by the financial markets. For instance, when Lucent announced in autumn 2000 that its new optoelectronic component was behind schedule and would not match performance expectations, the share price plunged immediately. On the other hand, there is strong criticism of the contribution research makes to innovation. Expectations are often disappointed: research does not innovate enough, its innovations are hard to manufacture, they are poorly targeted and are too oriented on technology and not enough on customer values, etc.

In these circumstances, research teams have of course been encouraged to work in close partnership with product development departments, with university researchers and with start-ups working in incubators, sometimes set up within large firms. They have also been asked to take into account firms' strategic plans.

These demands may seem relatively simple, but researchers find them extremely difficult to implement in practice. To illustrate this point, all research departments are criticized at one time or another for their mythical projects that were supposed to give them fame and fortune but never saw the light of day. They are accused of studying concepts for years on end and not taking into account the realities of product development. The results of research are often impossible to validate outside the confined world of the laboratory; research centres are teeming with high-tech enthusiasts accused of forgetting product uses and customer values. As Rosenbloom and Spencer (1996) pointed out, industrial research teams are confronted with the old dilemma of having 'two distinct and sometimes conflicting goals: the creation of new science and technology; and the facilitation of the process of innovation'.

The relationship between R&D and innovation is in fact more complex than it was thought and recent economic trends have confirmed this still further. Could the current problems be due to confusion between research, development and innovation? Are research departments being asked to satisfy demands which they are not capable of meeting? Should research centres be asked to design customer values, to choose which technologies should be investigated or to identify the constraints to be taken into account in laboratory experiments? Laboratories may have dealt with these issues in the past, but the nature of products has changed so much that it could be that research centres are no longer equipped to handle these tasks. Perhaps innovation is now so intense that research no longer has the resources to manage it.

This tension applies not only in research but also in development. However, the latter often hides behind a Maginot Line: the pressure of QCT compromises is such that innovation is too risky; innovation is fine, but only if it is not to the detriment of the reliability and quality of the existing processes.

In this context, can the R&D model be extended by making R or D innovative or, on the contrary, should a new function be imagined, which is different from R and from D and serves to irrigate them? To answer this question, we must begin by going back to R and D to see exactly what these activities entail. It is clear that they both contribute to the design process, with their actors, tools and methods of reasoning. But are these compatible with innovative design reasoning and, if not, how can innovative design reasoning be added to them? How can the R&D-based firm evolve to become an innovative firm? These are the challenging questions we address in this chapter.

We shall start by clarifying *the role played* by the former actors in the organization, research and development, with respect to *innovative design*. We shall go on to see how a new actor, the I function, can be a driving force for innovative design dynamics, joining R and D to establish a balanced capacity for repeated innovation. The notions will be illustrated by studying two cases of RID, one of R&D hidden by I (Tefal), the other of I hidden by R (nylon at Du Pont).

8.1   The origins: what is *R*, what is *D*?

What is the definition of R&D? A large number of studies have been carried out on the subject and we cannot cover them all here.[1] The main point that we would like to make is that the relationships between R&D and innovation are ambiguous in the literature, as the authors either speak of innovation but ignore R&D, or confuse innovation and R&D.

---

[1] *See* Chapter 1 and the bibliographical appendix. For a more comprehensive study of definitions of R&D *see* Le Masson (2001), in particular Part 3, pp. 279–300.

The *Frascati Manual*: an ambiguous definition of R&D

The notion of R&D is codified in the *Frascati Manual* to meet the econometric needs of OECD (Organisation for Economic Co-operation and Development) countries. Appendix 1 of the fourth edition (OECD 1981) details the history of the manual. A number of OECD member states began to collect data in the early 1960s, 'encouraged by the rapid growth of the amount of national resources devoted to research and experimental development (R&D)'. The national surveys were harmonized using 'the standard practice for surveys of research and development' proposed by Christopher Freeman in his report to the OECD in 1961, which was subsequently discussed in the Italian city of Frascati.

The 1993 edition of the *Frascati Manual* (OECD 1994) gave the following definition of R&D: 'Research and Experimental Development (R&D) comprise creative work undertaken on a systematic basis in order to increase the stock of knowledge of man, culture and society and the use of this stock of knowledge to devise new applications'. It is divided into three categories: basic research, which is 'undertaken primarily to acquire new knowledge without any particular application or use in view, and to formulate and test hypotheses, theories or laws'; applied research, which is 'undertaken in order to acquire new knowledge (. . .) directed primarily towards a specific practical aim or objective'; and experimental development, which draws on 'existing knowledge directed to producing new materials, products or devices, to installing new processes, systems and services, or to improving substantially those already produced or installed'.

Is there a link between R&D and innovation? The first chapter of the manual explains that 'it was written by and for the national experts in member countries who collect and issue national R&D data and submit responses to OECD R&D surveys', and that 'the Manual is not based on a single model of the scientific and technological system and how that system meshes with the economy and society;[2] its aim is to produce statistics that can be used to calculate indicators for use in various models'. In other words, the manual strives to be objective and completely independent from theories on innovation processes.

However, the definition of R&D given in the *Frascati Manual* cannot be separated from a view of innovation. Although it mentions the systematic production of knowledge, the criterion for classification is whether or not there is an application in view. The implicit representation is that *researchers produce knowledge, then look for what it can be used for*, before adding any knowledge required for the application.

The manual is even more explicit when it defines the boundaries of R&D. The basic criterion of R&D is the presence of 'an appreciable element of novelty and the resolution of scientific and/or technological uncertainty, i.e. when the solution to a problem is not readily apparent to someone familiar with the basic stock of common knowledge and techniques for the area concerned'. For example, as far as studies are concerned, prototypes and pilot plants come under R&D, but not work on standardization or catalogues. Similarly, education and training activities are considered to be R&D if they can be distinguished from routine teaching activities. Furthermore, 'an appreciable

---

[2] The 2002 version of the *Frascati Manual* contains all these definitions, apart from the latter part of this sentence, i.e. 'and how that system meshes with the economy and society'.

element of novelty or a resolution of scientific/technological uncertainty is again a useful criterion for defining the boundary between R&D and related (routine) scientific activities. Related activities of a routine nature can only be included in R&D if they are undertaken as an integral part of a specific research project'. As for development, it is important to find 'the cut-off point between experimental development and the related activities required to realize an innovation'. The manual refers to the rule laid down by the US National Science Foundation (NSF): 'If the primary objective is to make further technical improvements on the product or process, then the work comes within the definition of R&D. If, on the other hand, the product, process or approach is substantially set and the primary objective is to develop markets, to do pre-production planning or to get a production or control system working smoothly, the work is no longer R&D'.

R&D is therefore defined as an 'increase in the stock of knowledge' and 'the use of this stock of knowledge to devise new applications', but with a criterion of novelty in the production of knowledge or in the applications. This definition means that it is impossible to speak of R&D without speaking of innovation.

There is a close relationship between the two, but it is imprecise and simplistic:

- It is imprecise because the nature of the novelty is established only once the results of the activity are known. A rigorous decision as to whether or not an activity is R&D can be made only once a 'solution to a problem' has been found, as it is the nature of the solution that determines whether it was 'not readily apparent to someone familiar with the basic stock of common knowledge and techniques for the area concerned'. In other words, depending on the case, the result of a given piece of work may or may not lead to an innovation. This is another example of the traps of the term 'innovation' which we presented in the first part of this book.

- The relationship is also simplistic given that engineering and design departments are not systematically concerned with the innovative nature of their work, either in the production of knowledge or in the applications. In fact, they naturally tend to use existing knowledge and elements as far as this is possible. The implicit hypothesis is that innovation always includes new knowledge, but the relationship with innovation is not just a question of a 'novelty' in knowledge, as research can intervene in a far more subtle way. As we have seen, formulating knowledge, working on concepts and designing new measurement instruments or tests can be vital elements for innovation.

It is this vague, simplistic relationship which tends to cause discussions on R&D and whether or not it is profitable for firms. Either in favour or against it, the main criterion used to judge R&D is its success in terms of innovation. It is therefore important to take another look at R&D and its relationships with the design process.

In the following paragraphs, we define the notions of research and development from a management sciences perspective with a view to explaining the forms of collective action implied by these notions and the relationships between these forms of action and design activities. We give the genealogy of the two notions, in terms of their historical organizational forms (tools, organizations and actors) and also their doctrines, which often guided the emergence of new forms. We shall see that these design-oriented forms of collective action are extremely coherent. We examine their strengths and their weaknesses when faced with the current phenomenon of innovative design.

8.1.1 Development: a controlled specification process, based on known conceptual and generative models

8.1.1.1 The definition of development

There has been much debate on what exactly is meant by development. For example, in the 1980s, discussions were rife when successful Japanese firms drew attention to development, *D*, at a time when other manufacturers and above all the economic and management doctrines, in their quest for the engines of innovation, were more interested in research, *R*. However, if we start by linking development and innovation there is a risk of falling into the trap of innovation which we mentioned in Chapter 2. On the contrary, if we are to understand development from a management standpoint, we must start by *separating* development and innovation.

We propose the following definition: development is a controlled process which activates existing competencies and knowledge in order to specify a system (product, process, organization, etc.) which must meet well-defined criteria (quality, cost, time) and whose value has already been clearly conceptualized and sometimes evaluated.

This definition requires a number of explanations. It does not mean that all the knowledge required for the development has already been acquired at the start of the process, but that all the knowledge can be produced by the developers during the process. Problems can of course emerge during the development process that require research work to be done, in which case the research and development departments must work together to find solutions. Nonetheless, 'development' can be clearly identified by the fact that the values which guide the projects are clearly specified and that the approach consists of solving problems whilst having as little recourse as possible to 'research', or even avoiding going into areas where problems may arise. Development inherently seeks autonomy and linearity; it demands clear definitions of value, specifications and competencies as early in the process as possible.

This definition may appear somewhat arbitrary, but it nonetheless has
several advantages:

Contrary to the definition in the *Frascati Manual*, there is no need to
judge the products resulting from the process, particularly their degree
of innovation. It is therefore more operational because, confronted
with a design question, a manager can say whether or not it concerns
the firm's development process.

It corresponds to a historical model of design reasoning that was
developed to support product 'development' and was the foundation
stone of development and its performance, tools and techniques.

It helps clarify the position of development with respect to the model of
the innovative firm which emerged from the Tefal case. It also explains
the relationship between *D* and innovation.

Let us take a closer look at these last two points.

8.1.1.2 The foundations of consistent development reasoning: conceptual models and generative models

Development always seeks to meet two apparently contradictory imperatives,
i.e. the need for a *linear process* ensuring its completion – whether positive or
negative – in a set time and for *generative capacity to be maintained* despite the
constraints of convergence. Historically, development consisted of inventing a
specific 'design function' (with a model of reasoning, a technical substratum,
forms of organization and types of performance) to enable this performance.

What are the foundations of development? For example, can we say
that 'good' development simply involves bringing together experts or functions (experts in marketing, engineering sciences, in processes and procedures, etc.) and tying them to a schedule, as in a traditional stage-gate process
(customer needs, functional specifications, technical specifications, conceptual design, embodiment, detailed industrial design, etc.)? This representation is too limited and does not cover the performance of development in
terms of either convergence or generative power. However, functions
and schedules are indeed features of development, and the reasoning used
for development projects appears to fit in with a gradual specification process,
going from the functions to the conceptual models and then the embodiment
and the detailed design. The question has therefore evolved: what are the
foundations of development which guarantee the convergence and generative
power of the reasoning made during the development project?

The performance of development depends on the existence of what
we call a 'generative model' (Hatchuel, Le Masson and Weil 2005a),

which is itself based on conceptual models. We present these two notions briefly below. (*See* Le Masson and Weil (2004) for a more detailed presentation.)

8.1.1.2.1   *The notion of conceptual model*

A conceptual model specifies objects and their relationships with other elements by mobilizing a limited number of parameters which can either be 'acted on' or 'controlled' by the designer or be related to performance. Ohm's Law is a conceptual model: it defines the object 'conductor' (by its resistance and geometrical form) and the object 'current' (by tension and strength) and specifies the relationships between these parameters (in simplified form, V=RI, where V is the voltage, R the resistance and I the current). It limits the number of parameters as it does not mention forms of leakage, induced currents, the interactions between the different molecules present in the materials, radiating surfaces, etc. Depending on the circumstances, V, R and I can relate to performance, control or action (e.g. adding a resistor in a given, measurable circuit in order to obtain the required intensity). More generally speaking, some scientific knowledge and all engineering models in a wide range of disciplines take the form of a conceptual model.

Conceptual models have a number of advantages for developers: they fix the limits of a development by immediately showing whether or not an element of performance can be achieved; they help direct explorations within appropriate spaces; and in some cases, they speed up explorations by establishing clear relationships between the objects.

8.1.1.2.2   *The notion of generative model*

However, a conceptual model is not the only thing involved in a design process even if the latter is limited to a development project. The second foundation of the development activity is the generative model. This is a stock of knowledge (rules, but also technical and organizational devices), which can mobilize several conceptual models or heterogeneous knowledge blocks in an organized, targeted direction, in order to structure a repeated, convergent design process. The generative model serves to 'parametrize' design: the development project consists of instantiating parameters whose nature, and areas of validity, are set *ex ante* by the generative model.

The extent to which a generative model ensures that the processes converge towards a satisfactory product can vary, as can the model's generative capacities, i.e. its ability to explore new alternatives.

An example of a simple generative model is the design 'recipe': the recipe guarantees the result but does not strictly speaking allow for any alternatives to the initial specifications. Design 'recipes' were among the first generative models to be taught in engineering schools (in Germany in the 1840s). For example, their inventor, Ferdinand Redtenbacher, proposed recipes for designing hydraulic wheels using three parameters: the budget, the rate of flow of the watercourse (or the force exercised on the wheel's axle) and the height of the waterfall. The method used these three parameters to make a series of calculations based on empirical laws and existing models of wheel architectures.

Over the years, development departments learned to mobilize increasingly varied and heterogeneous conceptual models for which they devised more and more sophisticated generative models. We mentioned the basic generative model of systematic design in Chapter 7. It entails dividing the development process into four main structured phases: the functional phase, the conceptual phase, the physical-morphological phase (embodiment) and the detailed design phase. Each of these phases mobilizes conceptual models, but it is the generative model that ensures consistency from one language to another, i.e. it ensures that there is a conceptual language to match the functional language, that this conceptual language will lead to embodiment and that the resulting components can be given the correct dimensions.

It is important to stress that the distinction made at the end of the nineteenth century between the functional, conceptual and physical-morphological phases was not a natural evolution. Although it led to key successes and was widely adopted, suggesting that it was simply a question of common sense, this was not in fact the case. As we saw in the last chapter, the process was *discovered and organized into a generative model* which then became a success. It is the reference in terms of generative models in many development circles today. (It is the basic model used in Pahl and Beitz's manual of systematic design (Pahl and Beitz 1977), which continues to be used as a reference.)

8.1.1.3   Contemporary organizational models for development

Based on the two foundation stones – conceptual models and generative models – development departments set up efficient organizations, which took the form of engineering and design departments, marketing departments and methods departments in charge of industrialization.

The overall rationale of the development process (for a one-off project) is determined by managing targeted objectives. Only relatively limited adjustments or compromises can be made concerning these objectives during the development process because project management tools do not take into account changes in concepts or values. For instance, in the building industry, projects cannot be launched until the programmes and architects' plans are accepted.

The role of the project manager, whose task is to organize and plan the team's work, to control costs and take the project forward, often emerges from this process. The principles of project management stem from the traditional rules of Fayolism (Hatchuel and Weil 2000). Research has also shown that project management often involves political skills (Olilla, Norrgren and Schaller 1998), with the creation of legitimacy and the commitments of internal stakeholders, given that the support from general management or functional departments can change in the course of projects.

Apart from this managerial layer, we must remember the development capacities which it relies on for one-off projects: functions, capitalizing on competencies, standardized test and evaluation capabilities, rapid representation systems, object modelling (either real, in the form of prototypes, or virtual, with a digital model) and information systems to coordinate the different phases (division of work, synthesis, etc.). The efficiency of each of these forms of activity and organization depends on the conceptual and generative models: conceptual models at the heart of products' architectures; conceptual models for tests, evaluations and controls on performance; generative models for dividing out and scheduling tasks, etc.

8.1.1.4   *D* in the innovative firm model

Development is not just a set of functions with the competencies required to design new products. Above all, it is a relatively sophisticated, highly effective way of reasoning and of organizing the firm with a view to providing it with design capabilities. It is a paradox that, although it took approximately fifty years for this approach to emerge, it has gradually become so implicit that even those directly involved in the process find it difficult to express.

This takes us back to our initial question: what is the relationship between development and innovation?

Development is responsible for the repeated innovation capability that we highlighted in the R&D model. *D* is effective in domesticating innovation. *D* involves bureaucracy and demands well-organized, structured interventions from the different actors (functional, conceptual and physical-morphological), with sophisticated divisions of work carried out in a routine manner. However, the routinization of design does not mean that development is a classic example of administrative bureaucracy. The routines are based on complex languages and organize large spaces of expansion. Hence, development is an original example of *generative bureaucracy*.

This balance between 'routinized' and 'generative' is present at every level, from the overall architecture down to the detail of designing a single component. The figure of the 'reviser', who appeared in engineering and design departments at the end of the nineteenth century, is emblematic in this respect. Revisers were charged with checking that the designers had respected the department's norms and rules, but they did authorize 'new constructs' if they considered that the existing rules were not sufficient. They were therefore the guardians of areas of compromise, creation and novelty, which the engineering departments resorted to prudently despite their creative competencies.

Although development is capable of domesticating innovation, this applies only to certain forms, i.e. those in which the new product is based on existing conceptual and generative models. In cases when new value spaces and new business must be explored, when product architectures have to be revised or new systems of standardization set up, development departments no longer have the means to intervene. On the contrary, the techniques and forms of design reasoning found in development circles aim to make the most of value spaces which are already structured and existing conceptual models.

Development can be seen as a design function with its own model of activity, objects to be managed, types of performance and organization. It comprises the definition of appropriate values for the product/service parameters, with given specifications and competencies. It manages the convergence towards a quality, cost, time objective, on the basis of known conceptual and generative models; it is organized into project teams using cross-disciplinary competencies in the major functions of the R&D firm (*see* Table 8.1).

The key point here is that D is a coherent design activity and not just a combination of competencies or the ability to manage projects involving several different competencies. Development departments' real strength in domesticating innovation stems from their control of the objects involved, i.e. the conceptual and generative models. These fundamental points must be taken into account, otherwise D will be given design briefs that it is not capable of dealing with. If we take D as the engine of innovative design, we lose its main value (the generative models) and risk being disappointed by its abilities in terms of convergence and generation once it moves away from its models.

Table 8.1. The *D* function, a component of the model of the R&D-based firm with its own coherence

	The *D* function
Models of activity and reasoning	Controlled specifications, given requirements and competencies (given conceptual and generative models)
Objects to be managed – technical substratum	Convergence towards QCT target, on basis of known conceptual and generative models
Type of performance	Optimization of project's turnover/cost ratio
Forms of organization	Project teams (marketing, engineering and design, production methods, etc.)

8.1.2   Research, a controlled process of knowledge production

8.1.2.1   The definition of research

In the past, there have been heated discussions and even disputes about the relationship between innovation and research. However, seen from the perspective of the management sciences, the notion of research is not that hard to define.

Research can be defined as a controlled process of knowledge production. The key point is 'control'. All human actions produce knowledge, but only research can claim to produce it in such a way as to ensure that it is true, valid and robust and can inspire confidence. This is why research can be recognized only by its instruments and processes and not by its questions or its objects of investigation. This proposition is crucial as it means that research can be held responsible for its methods, but not for its objectives or for its areas of investigation. Even if we adopt a radical standpoint and claim that research is a completely random process for providing new knowledge, the above definition of research forces us to control the fact that the process is indeed random. Hence, there are only two possible sources of value from a research process:

Research studies questions formulated in advance and finds controlled answers to them. In this case, the 'value' of the research depends entirely on the value of the questions submitted to it.

Research can produce unexpected knowledge which creates value for the firm even though no demands were made in advance.

In the two cases, the research department is not directly involved in defining the value for the firm. It makes a contribution to the value but never defines it.

8.1.2.2 Integrating research into industrial design processes

Research has been integrated into firms due to two fundamental elements in its organization: first, its knowledge production techniques and, second, its relationship with production and design processes. We present these elements briefly below. For a more detailed presentation, *see* Le Masson (2001).

8.1.2.2.1 *The process of knowledge production*

Historically speaking, research management began by focusing on how to organize knowledge production processes. For instance, when Duisberg reorganized the research function at Bayer in 1890, he paid special attention to the researchers' 'workstations'. He designed a U-shaped work unit which enabled researchers to have their products and tools within easy reach and also facilitated exchanges between researchers (Beer 1958; Meyer-Thurow 1982).

There are three key aspects to managing a laboratory, i.e. to managing a system designed to produce knowledge:

the nature of the systems: having the right systems to deal with all the different types of measurements requested;

efficiency: carrying out measurements quickly, in a flexible manner, at any time. The laboratory tries to optimize production indicators such as the number of measurements made per operator;

the organization of long chains of experiments: organizing the laboratory so that it can make several successive analyses, each device representing a stage of the process in a networked workshop.

8.1.2.2.2 *Relationship to design process*

Development was defined as a specific design process, but research is independent from product design processes, even though its existence depends on them. A number of solutions have been found for organizing the connection between research and these design processes. *See* Table 8.2.

The first connection consists of *improving the existing processes*. In this case, the research laboratory serves the process industries in the same way that 'shop management functions' served the manufacturing industries.

The second connection is found in *the different phases of design*: in a stable architecture, development follows the phases of systematic design, each of these phases corresponding to a stock of knowledge (conceptual, functional and physical-morphological models). Each of these areas of knowledge

Table 8.2. The *R* function, a component of the model of the R&D-based firm with its own coherence

	The *R* function
Models of activity and reasoning	Controlled production of knowledge
Objects to be managed – technical substratum	Knowledge production systems, related to lineages
Type of performance	Optimization of quality of knowledge produced/resources consumed
Forms of organization	Cross-functional teams, activated by the firm

can be the subject of research, which facilitates the development work. Research provides new conceptual models or refines existing ones.

It is important to note that the position of research with respect to design processes is in fact very traditional. Engineering traditions have included research laboratories in their descriptions of the design process since the beginning of the twentieth century. Examples were found in German firms at the beginning of the nineteenth century (AEG, Siemens, MAN, etc.) and also in the machine construction manuals of the same period, showing clearly that the aim of research was to refine the manufacturers' conceptual models (Riedler 1916; König 1999).

Kline and Rosenberg's model: new for economics, but old for engineering

Kline and Rosenberg's (1985) model, which describes how research is activated by development, is in fact an adaptation of these very old forms of organization. Kline was professor of mechanical engineering and the article gave him the paternity of the model presented to the National Academy of Engineering in 1981. In fact, Kline and Rosenberg's main contribution was to take economic research away from its linear representations (*R* then *D*).

The third connection is simpler: the design process itself includes a phase of *systematic knowledge production*. This was the case in the chemical and later the pharmaceutical industries. In these domains, products' overall architecture was stabilized and a clear separation could therefore be made between a phase of systematic synthesis of new molecules and a phase for developing selected new molecules. The research activity could be carried out during the first phase. In the case of dyes, a screening phase was isolated when the industrial sectors became more stable and the actors gained a better understanding of dyes (chromophore and auxochrome groups).

This led to the development of the large research laboratories at Bayer, Hoechst and BASF. Today, the best examples of this model are to be found in the pharmaceutical industry (Ruffat 1996).

The fourth connection was frequently mentioned in the earlier literature: *research solves a certain number of recurrent problems regarding products and manufacturing processes.* A good example of this was described by Ayçoberry (1962). When Saint-Gobain created its first research laboratory in 1924, the head of the laboratory, Bernard Long, began by working on an unexplained problem: why did glass turn yellow in the sun? Another example was the General Electric Research Lab, whose initial work was on manufacturing and testing lightbulbs.

The fifth and final connection, which we shall return to later, is when different actors in the firm turn to research to find innovative design processes.

A historical curiosity: Fayol, research and innovation

Chevenard's laboratory in Imphy, France, was a particularly interesting case of a laboratory managed by an innovation programme. As Chevenard explained: 'In 1911, Fayol asked the Imphy laboratory to carry out a systematic study of steels and special alloys, setting two targets for the work: first, to shed light on the theory of these products in order to make practical studies easier and more fruitful, and second, to discover their exceptional properties with a view to finding applications' (Chevenard 1933).

The originality was not in the 'systematic study' itself, as systematic research was frequently carried out in the process industries at that time for 'mapping' materials (Schneider won several medals for this at the World Fairs held in that period). However, two points were particularly original. First, the programme focused on innovation and, second, it was launched by a manager outside the research laboratory, thus giving a glimpse of an innovative manager in research management. A manager named Fayol.

This shows the founder of administrative science in a different light. Whereas his most well-known works do not mention innovation, he was nonetheless a forerunner when he gave the 'administrator' the task of 'combining the efforts of learned men and practitioners' in order to satisfy 'the manufacturers' vital need to organize successful cooperation between Science and the world of business' (Fayol 1918). With Chevenard's laboratory, Fayol had equipped his company with a capacity for innovative design which consisted of systematically exploring the properties of metals and using 'research' in a very original manner for that period.

8.1.2.3   Contemporary organization models

Research management therefore comprises two parts:

the management of *resources used to produce knowledge,* i.e. capacities, expertise, tools, data banks, libraries, seminars, visits, etc.;

the management of *processing questions* stemming from the innovation process or coming from another part of the firm. As we have seen, these processes are initiated outside research, which can do nothing but try to adapt to them.

For both aspects, research management is similar to managing a department or to a consulting firm working for other departments in the firm. The quality of the service rendered depends on the accumulated resources, but the effectiveness of a research activity also depends to a great extent on the quality of its clients. In fact, instead of the expression 'good research leads to good innovations', it is perhaps more correct to say 'good innovative design processes activate good research'.

8.1.2.4   Research and innovation

As in the case of development, our definition of research highlights a consistent design function which is coherent with the overall process of the R&D firm, but not independent from it (*see* below).

Once again, there has been much debate about the relationship between research and innovation. The model helps clarify the situation: as in the case of development, research is an incomplete form of design function. It produces knowledge in a controlled manner, but does not carry out design reasoning except for its own experiments. Researchers are therefore no better equipped than others to carry out innovative design. In other words, *research is not designed to deal with innovation on its own; at best, it can contribute to it.*

If this is the case, why has there been so much confusion regarding the role of research for such a long time? Historically speaking, there were two distinct approaches to the relationships between research and innovative design. In the first, put forward by Le Châtelier (1850–1937), a 'discovery' was seen as the systematic consequence of the good application of a scientific method.[3] Le Châtelier believed that research should be entirely prescribed, should study objects in the world of industry and be capable of mobilizing its capacities to produce knowledge regarding these objects using experimental methods. He was convinced that the role of the inventor had become 'practically nil'. As he explained in 'La science et l'industrie': 'The most frequent error is to believe that the aim of research laboratories is to make sensational discoveries which can lead to profitable patents' (Le Châtelier 1930). In his view, sound application of method led to regular, continuous

---

[3] For further reading on Le Châtelier, *see* Letté (1998). For the two models in question, *see* Le Masson (2001) – see particularly p. 301 onwards.

progress. However, he also believed that major innovations could result from the knowledge accumulated, given that 'one often finds things one is not looking for'.

The relationship between research and innovation is somewhat paradoxical in Le Châtelier's reasoning: by advocating scientific method, by refusing the notion of invention and by seeking to rationalize scientific research, he opened the door to 'chance discoveries' and hence to an irrational use of science. Furthermore, a discovery systematically resulted from the sound application of method.

In the second, later approach, a discovery was seen as the probable consequence of the research, the probability depending on the extent to which the research was fundamental research. Whereas the first approach concerned industrial laboratories, close to factories, the second concerned central laboratories and the new research departments of the 1950s, and was put forward by C. E. Kenneth Mees, Research Director for Kodak Laboratories. Mees explained his theory in the first chapter of his manual (Mees and Leermakers 1950): there are several levels of research; each level always gives results; but when it is a more 'exploratory' level, the result is always more random. Mees' model is a probabilistic model, from which he deduced a mode of management: 'The chances of making discoveries (. . .) can be increased simply by having more men engaged in work in the field' (Chapter 1).

This probabilistic model was used for research management for several decades. For instance, Yvan Peychès, Research Director of Saint-Gobain from 1944 to 1966, considered that 'having in-house researchers engaged in fundamental research is like having an option on the unknown' (Peychès 1951). It is true that research management can be seen as a form of speculation in which the probability of success must be weighed up as carefully as possible for each of the investments.

Nonetheless, in both cases, the relationship between research and innovation is still relatively vague as the link between the knowledge produced and the design process is left unresolved. R is seen as a 'design function', focused on producing knowledge, but the new knowledge cannot replace an innovative design process. R produces knowledge activated by external design processes and this knowledge is used by the same external processes. If R is considered to be the source of innovation, there is the risk either of underestimating the importance of the innovative design reasoning or of asking researchers to employ a style of reasoning for which they are neither prepared nor equipped.

At the end of this first section, we have shown that R and D are both effective actors in design processes, but only for certain types of design. In the past, both developed techniques and conceptual tools to fulfil their objectives, but these objectives were also defined very precisely. D works on the basis of known specifications and existing knowledge; R must be activated by an external design process and provides scientifically controlled results. Neither R nor D is able to spark off design processes for objects with uncertain identities, with no known functional space, no reference architectures and no clear questions regarding identifiable experimental systems.

In view of these findings, our aim is no longer to extend R or D but to add a new function to the R&D model. Our work on R and on D will give us a better understanding of the relationships between this new function and R and D.

8.2   Innovation: the missing structures and processes

8.2.1   Definition of the *I* function

We can now describe the characteristics of a new design function which, when added to the R&D model, can meet the challenges of innovative design. We shall call it the *I* function. We could say that the *I* stands for innovation, but as this does not designate an activity, we prefer to give it the more scientific name of 'innovative design function'.

At this stage, having defined R and D, we must define I in such a way as to give an RID model the properties of a model of an innovative firm such as Tefal. In a way, we are writing the specifications for what an *I* function should be.

Assuming that research is a controlled process of knowledge production and is not responsible for the definition of value, and that development requires competencies and the specification of value to be given from the outset, we can define the innovative design function as being responsible for a dual design activity:

a process for defining value;

a process for identifying new competencies.

The role of the innovative design function is to carry out these two processes simultaneously, in a single *design* process, with a view to providing development with values and new competencies and to submitting new questions to research (*see* Figure 8.1).

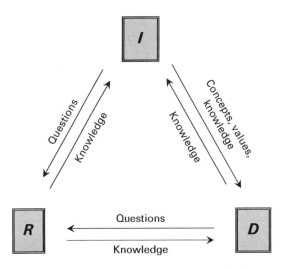

Figure 8.1   Relationships between *R*, *I* and *D*

We can illustrate this point by going back to the vacuum cleaner industry. Faced with the challenge of the bagless vacuum cleaner, a traditional firm wishing to counterattack by creating its own bagless cleaner soon came up against a number of difficulties. For its development and research departments, there were infinite numbers of solutions to meet the criterion of 'bagless'. For the other departments such as marketing, it was hard to propose surveys on customer needs before the new product had been defined. To avoid vicious circles and the tensions created by this sort of situation, a specific, structured approach was required, to explore in a symmetrical manner:

The creation of value: this could be value for the customer or for the manufacturers of the new product. The value could not be defined at the beginning of the process, but had to be reviewed as and when the internal and external competencies required for its implementation were established, e.g. a low-cost bagless vacuum cleaner, a hygienic bagless cleaner, a cleaner with visible performance, etc.

The concept and the knowledge: the concept had to be elaborated at the same time as the knowledge required to define it. For example, the notion of 'separating air and dust without using a bag' could be obtained in several ways, which were all worth rigorous study to assess their impact in terms of architecture and performance.

The innovative design function is dedicated to this specific, structured approach.

The *I* function in the management sciences literature

Several authors have implicitly referred to the *I* function without actually describing it as such.

Some authors noted the role of skunk works in innovation, but these were often considered as a loosely organized form (Peters and Waterman 1982). More recently, authors have shown more organized skunk works (Gwynne 1997). Studies of the historical Skunk Works at Lockheed underlined that they were well and self-consciously organized (Miller 1995). Skunk works are an interesting historical form of the *I* function.

Some authors noted the emergence of forms of intraprenariat (Basso 2004) or corporate entrepreneurship (Ahuja and Lampoert 2001) which, although apparently ill-structured, nonetheless have the advantage of targeting intensive innovation using original forms of organization (in terms of financing, work organization, time management, etc.).

Seeking to explain the inputs of research and development work, several authors put forward the notion of 'vision' (*see*, for example, Hamel and Prahalad 1994b; Jonash and Sommerlatte 1999; Krogh, Ichijo and Nonaka 2000). They defined it as the intellectual framework that gives birth to new architectures, to the identification of new values emerging in the market or, in fact, to new innovative products. Moore and Myers explained that Fairchild (Moore 1996) and Xerox (Myers and Rosenbloom 1996) had failed to use the knowledge produced by research whereas start-ups had been capable of taking advantage of it to design new innovative products. In their view, strategy could not be put in place without a 'vision', but at that stage they did not address the issue of how the vision emerged.

Tushman and Anderson (Tushman, Anderson and O'Reilly 1997) strongly criticized the notion of vision: 'Strategy, vision, and innovation are empty words – indeed the world is full of great visions, strategies, technologies, and innovations that were never implemented or were implemented well after the competition'. Their aim was to find ways of effectively managing innovation. They put forward the idea of 'ambidextrous' organizations, capable of managing both radical and incremental innovations. They began by observing that firms that were rich in terms of competencies – i.e. which satisfied the criteria of management by core competencies – were incapable of surviving in the turbulent technological environments that they had themselves helped to create. They put these failures down to the inability to 'proactively initiate streams of innovations', or in other words to elaborate new design strategies. The challenge for organizations was to make very different organizational units work together, whether they were dealing with incremental, 'discontinuous' or architectural innovation. In our view, the solution to the problem tended to forget that learning processes can provide continuity between incremental innovations and radical innovations, since the authors refer to exogenous 'technological cycles' which are therefore unmanageable. However, the authors at least had the merit of trying to move away from the vague notion of 'vision'.

In 'rethinking the role of industrial research' (1996), Myers and Rosenbloom started from the framework provided by Kline and Rosenberg (1985), which situated research in relation to product development processes and posed the question of innovation: for cases of radically new innovation, they proposed that research should elaborate 'technology platforms' to feed the 'development funnels' modelled by Wheelwright and Clark (1992). This consisted of mapping the full scope of technological frontiers, offering qualified technological alternatives at the entrance to the funnel and offering a set of industrial property rights in exchange for strategic partnerships. These explorations revealed a form of 'radical incrementalism' (Myers and Rosenbloom 1996) in the small successive steps that help learn about new markets and elaborate new ideas. This, too, was an effort to explain how research contributed to the elaboration of 'visions' or to firms' 'design strategies'. Several of the ideas put forward in the Tefal case were also found here, although the role of research was still relatively vague. Could researchers really map the full scope of technological frontiers at a reasonable cost? How could they know which technologies would really be needed by the development departments? In fact, very little was said about the front-end design process.

Taking studies on core competencies and dynamic capabilities applied to R&D as their starting point, Miller and Morris (1999) examined how 'vision' is essential to R&D work but is also built up by this work. They identified marketing$_1$ and R&D$_1$ as 'activities needed to maintain existing lines of business through continuous innovation', in which the marketing activity consists of asking customers what they want, and distinguished it from marketing$_2$ and R&D$_2$, 'activities more relevant to discontinuous innovation and the process of gathering and interpreting weak signals', in which the marketing activity is more exploratory. They pleaded in favour of organizational structures that clearly distinguished between the two activities:

- with a chief operating officer (COO) in charge of the existing organization, productivity, customers, R&D$_1$ and marketing$_1$ and product development in strategic business units;
- and a chief innovation officer (CINO) in charge of technology, long-term strategy, R&D$_2$ and marketing$_2$.

However, the example chosen by the authors to show how this structure works illustrates the limitations of approaches based essentially on organizational structures. The example describes the drastic changes in Hewlett-Packard's Test and Measurement Organization (TMO) in the mid-1990s when a visionary manager, seeing a drop in military contracts, decided to refocus the business on video servers for the audiovisual media industry. The description focuses mainly on the organizational aspects of the TMO project, but does not explain how these domains were identified, or the impact of the strategic changes on the organization's competencies. There is no mention either of how the relationships between short-term and long-term policies were organized, or those between the COO and the CINO. The authors pose the question of formulating new 'design strategies', but the proposed structural solution seems rather restricted.

The above-mentioned authors were all particularly interested in the management of innovation and the proposed solutions underline a major point: there is a need for a specific innovation process, which is not the same thing as traditional development or traditional research. The authors are therefore close to a proposal such as RID. The major contribution made by the notion of 'innovation function' is in fact the way in which it opens up new forms of action so that principles can be proposed for managing innovation structures.

More recently, O'Connor and de Martino studied the variety of forms of 'major innovation' structures in organizations (O'Connor and de Martino 2006). O'Connor proposed to study these major innovation structures as a specific activity, a dynamic capability analysed with a systems approach (O'Connor 2008). We follow this perspective of considering the *I* structure as specific (*see* Table 8.3). However, we depart from O'Connor's work in Chapter 10, when we are required to describe the activity in a more precise way. We will see that the systems approach has to be *embedded* in a design approach.

8.2.2   Principles of management for an innovation function

We can now define the principles of management for an innovation function, which are very different from those of the previous two functions. The role of the innovation function is to present suitable proposals to research and to development. As there is no evidence that innovation projects can be managed like *traditional projects*, traditional project management cannot be applied to innovation projects. We have defined innovation as an attempt to link concepts, values and competencies, therefore an innovation process has several aims. The results of an innovation process are:

- questions for research
- ideas of products ready to be developed
- emerging product concepts at different stages of maturation
- new emerging competencies for *R*, *I* and *D*.

Table 8.3. Comparison of the principles of management for research, innovative design (*I*) and development

	Research (*R*)	Innovative design (*I*)	Development (*D*) (rule-based design)
Mission	Response to independent or proposed scientific question	Innovation field	Functional specifications
Goals	Validated knowledge	Design strategies (lineages, platforms, etc.)	Project implementation
Resources	Laboratories, competency-based teams, universities, documentation	Coordinated exploration teams	Project teams and task/function teams
Horizon	Depends on investigation process	Contingent and strategic/ strategic milestones	Project lead times/ standard milestones
Economic value	Value of the question	Based on several products or transferred knowledge	Value of project

The target of an innovation process is not a well-defined objective but what we will call an 'innovation field' (IF), or a domain in which innovative design work is to be carried out. In the example of vacuum cleaners, the innovation field was clearly the principle of 'the bagless cleaner' as this was the only notion available to guide the managers concerned. In the following pages, we describe the main characteristics of the management of innovation fields, as distinct from traditional project management (*see* summary below).

> *Organizational divergence.* Instead of seeking the convergence of object-ives and lead times, managers in charge of innovation fields should quickly divide the fields into several competitive, independent (or inter-dependent) exploratory processes. Priorities and timetables should then be established and reviewed according to the results obtained by these explorations.
>
> *Contingent horizon.* There is no precise horizon for managing innovation fields. Some explorations reach the development phase quickly, others need a longer period before reaching maturity and some never lead to a product development.
>
> *Reusing excess knowledge produced.* The management of innovation fields must handle any 'excess knowledge' required to develop marketable products. The economic value of exploring an innovation field can be defined by the following relationship:

> *Economic value of innovation field = profitability of products actually developed + potential profits resulting from the reuse of excess knowledge produced and product ideas created.*

> *Formulating and adapting design strategies.* The notion of 'design strategy' takes its full meaning in relation to innovation fields. This strategy consists of setting the design rules for a product lineage and not just for a single product. These rules are aimed at creating a dominant design, specific to the firm. In the event of success, this leads to growth, through the constant renewal of innovation.

Hence, we can construct an *I* function with all the properties needed to 'connect' it to the R&D model, whilst at the same time building an RID model to serve as a model for an innovative firm such as Tefal (*see* Table 8.4).

At this stage, the *I* function is still in the form of a 'rational myth': it gives a new meaning to innovative design activities in R&D-based firms. Using a modelling process, we can already give some of its characteristics and write 'specifications' for what the *I* function should be. However, we are not yet

Table 8.4. The specifications of an *I* function for an RID model of the innovative firm

	Specifications for the *I* function
Models of activity and reasoning	Coevolution of competencies and products
Objects to be managed – technical substratum	Innovation fields
Type of performance	Reusing of excess knowledge without stabilizing object identities
Forms of organization	Conceptual core which activates *R* and *D* and is fed by their work

able to describe the detailed forms of an *I* function's activities, or the way in which this function emerges in firms. This issue is dealt with in the following chapters.

The *I* function and the actors involved in 'innovation'

The existence of an *I* function does not mean that innovation depends on a single actor. The first reason for this is simply that, although R&D innovates in a context of given object identities, it still innovates. It is a process of innovation through rule-based design.

The second reason is more complex: the notion of *I* function does not mean that the *innovative design* depends on a single actor. As we have seen, the *I* function does not work in isolation but 'activates' *R* and *D* (and, more generally speaking, the designers, the marketing department, etc. and other actors playing the role of designers, such as sales staff and manufacturers). The *I* function can be a way of organizing new cross-disciplinary relationships between a growing circle of actors who can potentially contribute to the innovation (cf. the new role of production function, for example).

As a result, the actors contributing to the *I* function can come from all the different design functions. Moreover, the *I* function makes it possible to extend design beyond the usual circle of people who were seen as 'designers' in the past (this is in line with the revision of object identities described in Chapters 2 and 3). Does this mean that the *I* function is simply an empty shell? On the contrary, these actors are often discouraged in their efforts, so *I* is responsible for making innovative design activities possible on all levels. It is not a question of adding a new body but of organizing a new metabolism.

8.3   *R, D* and *I* as a triadic system

Before studying various cases of the *I* function in the following part of the book, we shall begin by identifying some RID-type structures in a few simple cases. First, we will look for R&D in the innovative firms we have studied

in the previous chapters and for which we have already described an
I function, and second, we will look for the *I* structure in cases of
R&D-based firms.

8.3.1   R&D in the case of an innovative firm, Tefal

The *I* function was in a hypertrophic state in the case of Tefal. The firm's
conceptual core, the small team of expert managers who took part in the
product committee meetings, who generated new lineages (e.g. baby care),
thought up original hybrids and structured value in emerging lineages
(informal meals), was doubtless an exemplary case of the *I* function.

In terms of development, the process was rapid and controlled.
The design process fixed on a clear, stable target just a few weeks before a
product was launched on the market and it was only in this short period of
time that a development process took place (in particular for validation and
industrialization).

As for research, for many years Tefal in fact had no research department
and relied on results provided by public research studies. Tefal's CEO had
always been an assiduous reader of publications from the CNRS. When Tefal
finally decided to set up a research department, the firm charged Vincent
Chapel with the mission. He recommended a form of research department
which was coherent with the model and which he qualified as 'controlled'.
The term was to be taken in the mechanical sense of the term (rather than
the political), on the basis that the research department should deal with
questions arising from innovative design and should not be an independent
department defining its own subjects of research.

In the Tefal model, we can see an RID-type model in which the *I* function
played a key role: the innovative design function was in charge of specifications and value spaces which backed up the development work; the *I*
function asked the research department questions and then mobilized the
results.

8.3.2   Finding an *I* structure behind *R* or *D*

Can we identify *I* functions in traditional R&D-based firms? We have already
mentioned the very specific role played by Baldwin's partners when they
regularly redesigned families of locomotives, thus representing a form of
innovative design function. It is interesting to show that, behind the famous

stories of innovation attributed to research or to development, we can identify forms of *I* function. We will give two examples, the first concerning development, the second concerning research.

8.3.2.1 Dedicated teams

It has often been noted that, when confronted with the problem of designing innovative products, companies tend to create *ad hoc* teams, composed of dedicated designers working exclusively on a specific project (Tracy Kidder 1981). The central mission of these groups is to give birth to an innovative product, which is not clearly defined at the outset. A good example of this was the automobile manufacturer Citroën. In the 1950s and 1960s – the legendary period of the DS and SM models – it created a dedicated research department designed to study new concepts.

However, was this still development? For instance, could these dedicated teams be seen as traditional 'commando' or 'cheetah' teams, i.e. the inter-functional teams generally recommended for project development (Engwall and Svensson 2001)? In fact, the latter models are relevant only if the initial objective is clearly defined, whereas in the case of dedicated teams, the designers are working on product concepts or innovative technologies (e.g. a car that can go at 300 kph). In this case, the group has to define its own objectives and also justify its choices in terms of targets, timing and resources. In view of these fundamental differences, the innovative team must be clearly differentiated from the other work organizations in the engineering and design departments that deal with traditional 'development'. These teams are not simply organizations or networks set up to solve a well-defined problem; they carry out an innovative activity capable of having an impact on a firm's entire strategy, organization and production.

As a result, these groups often behave like in-house entrepreneurs in search of resources and legitimacy within the firm. The activities of these 'collateral organizations' (Zand 1974) are not limited exclusively to research or to development; they have had to organize a process in which certain research problems and elements of development are managed simultaneously, therefore showing precisely the characteristic features of an innovative design function.

Although most companies have not set up dedicated teams to deal with their innovative design projects, they do often leave some activities of this sort to the initiative of designers working in 'skunk work' teams (Peters and Waterman 1982). The *I* function is hidden (both in time and in resources) behind an official development activity. However, the increase of the constraints involved in *D* has made it more and more difficult to continue to work in this way.

8.3.2.2   The case of nylon

The story of nylon is one of the founding myths of 'innovative research'. When nylon stockings were first presented to the press in October 1938, Charles Stine, a member of the executive committee in charge of research at Du Pont, declared: 'Though wholly fabricated from such common raw materials as coal, water, and air, nylon can be fashioned into filaments as strong as steel, as fine as a spider's web, yet more elastic than any of the common natural fibres'. Women were immediately captivated by what they thought would be indestructible stockings and nylon became associated with the magic of science. This was not merely a marketing claim. According to the historians of R&D at Du Pont, Hounshell and Smith (1988), nylon was by far 'the biggest money-maker in the history of the Du Pont company' (p. 273), leading Du Pont's managers to think that 'further investment in high-calibre scientific research would lead to additional discoveries that Du Pont's legions of chemists, engineers, and salesmen could develop into successful products. This became known as the "nylon model" of innovation, which dominated Du Pont's research strategy for decades to come' (p. 274). The nylon model did indeed inspire a large number of research laboratories in the postwar years.

However, in the perspective of the RID model, was it not in fact a perfect example of confusion between research and innovation? Is there a trace of an 'innovative design function' distinct from research? Following Hounshell and Smith's account, the history of nylon can be reconstructed in three, sometimes overlapping, design phases.

8.3.2.2.1   *The Chemical Department and polymers*

Phase 1: at the beginning of the 1930s, Dr Wallace Carothers was in charge of a group of researchers working on a fundamental research programme on polymer chemistry in Du Pont's Chemical Department. Their aim was to resolve the controversy over whether polymers were held together by a kind of force peculiar to them, or whether ordinary chemical bonds were involved. Carothers proposed to test the latter hypothesis by synthesizing a polymer using initial components with well-understood chemical reactions (i.e. in a controlled process of knowledge production).

This explains why one of the researchers in Carothers' team, Julian W. Hill, tried to construct longer chains by extending simple chemical reactions to more active basic molecules such as diacids and dialcohols to form esters and perhaps polyesters. Given that the reaction [carboxylic acid +

alcohol → ester] could be produced only by removing the water as otherwise it hydrolyzed the chains, Carothers constructed a device called a molecular still, which enabled them to remove the water formed by the reactions and to prevent the molecules from being turned back into acid and alcohol. After several months' work, Hill obtained a polymer. He then observed that the polymer could be drawn into fibres which, when cooled, were very strong.

The result was very satisfactory in terms of research as they had obtained a polymer with twice the molecular weight of the longest chains obtained before then, thus validating the hypothesis they had made on the nature of the chemical bonds in polymers. At that stage, research had found a highly resistant fibre, but they were still a long way away from nylon stockings.

This fibre was then evaluated for applications in textiles and the Rayon Department was informed of the results.[4] The fibres proved to be unsuitable for textile applications because they melted below 100°C, were sensitive to water and soluble in dry-cleaning solvents.

An interesting point here is that the researchers who found the new molecule had mentioned a wide variety of potential applications such as boots and photographic films, so we might wonder why the fibre was evaluated as a textile. The most probable answer is the intervention of a key character, the assistant director of the Chemical Department, Elmer K. Bolton, whom we will mention again below. Another question concerns the tests: did they use the standard tests for the textile industry or for the chemistry of polymers? In fact neither, as we shall see in the next section.

In this phase, we can see the limits of the idea that research is responsible for innovative design. Left to its own devices, the research department would have published an article on polymers, kept a small sample and the story would have ended there. At the beginning of 1933, the subject had indeed been shelved.

8.3.2.2.2   *The Rayon Department asks the Chemical Department*
to design tests for a fibre
Phase 2: the Rayon Department's Pioneering Laboratory, headed by Hale Charch, was used to carrying out tests on factory samples. However, the trial protocol required a fabric sample, which meant that large quantities of a fibre had to be available before it could be tested. The system was

---

[4] Rayon, a textile fibre made of cellulose, was used widely for fabrics at that time. However, it did not have the same qualities of resistance and elasticity as silk, still less those of the future nylon.

appropriate for certifying new products proposed by suppliers, but at the end of the 1920s, the Rayon Department was looking for new products for the textile industry. In order to design a new fibre, they had to know rapidly whether or not it was suitable as a textile, but without having to produce it in large quantities. The test protocol was therefore inappropriate in these circumstances. This is why Church asked the Chemical Department (before Hill's work on polyesters) to draw up trial protocols for evaluating the qualities of a fibre as a textile on the basis of the fibre itself and without having to make a fabric sample. John B. Miles was charged with this work. He attempted to define fibre characteristics such as elasticity by specific laboratory tests. These were the tests that were used subsequently for Hill's polyester. Did this happen by chance?

The key player here was Bolton, as he was the one who actually managed the innovative design strategy. Bolton stressed the economic stakes behind 'synthetic silk' and asked the Chemical Department to make a 'new textile fibre'. Bolton worked on the question like a designer. He had two alternative solutions, cellulose and Carothers' synthetic polymers. He also had the means of evaluating the fibres. It was Bolton who held the essential keys to the design reasoning, far more than Carothers. Once again, in 1933, it was Bolton who asked Carothers to put at least one person to work on synthetic fibres. In May 1934, Coffman, who worked for Carothers, drew a fibre which was actually the future nylon. Bolton recognized the value of this fibre and already planned to use it in the textile industry.

8.3.2.2.3   *From polymers to 6–6 nylon*

Phase 3: the story did not end there – there was still quite a long way to go before the textile fibres obtained in the laboratory became nylon stockings. Once again, Bolton played a key role. The research department favoured products that were easily synthesized, but Bolton decided to redirect the work to products which were more complex to synthesize but which melted at higher temperatures and had cheaper basic components.

Whereas the researchers saw nylon as a universal product capable of replacing both textiles and photographic films, and development saw it as a simple substitute for rayon, another vital decision was to develop 'nylon' as a substitute for silk in the lingerie and hosiery market, whose value was indubitable. Once these two key decisions had been made, the development department was able to mobilize resources stemming from research, but also from the Rayon Department and the chemical engineering group that was emerging in the Chemical Department.

The example of nylon shows how the RID model helps us identify an innovative design function which, although it was not brought into the spotlight and was not represented in the structures or organizations, managed both research and development.[5] It was the *I* function, represented in particular by Bolton, which steered the research; it also enhanced the value of the results, revived the research when necessary and then entrusted the fibre to the development department, which could then work on a clearly identified value and with existing competencies.

8.4   Conclusion: organizing RID in large companies

In this chapter, we gave managerial definitions for *D* functions and *R* functions. These definitions explain the position of these functions in the design process, the tools that were invented in the past to help them fulfil their roles and the coherency of *D* and *R* as contributors to the design process.

We saw that, to help R&D-based firms face the challenges of competition through innovation, it is not enough to 'make research innovative' or to 'make development innovative', since it can result in the loss of the techniques, ways of reasoning and types of organization which these functions have developed over time.

The solution is to invent new forms of organization, new forms of collective reasoning and new techniques to build up a third function, which is neither *R* nor *D*, which we call the *I* function. We believe that the R&D model can become innovative by introducing a new function which fulfils roles played by neither *R* nor *D*. This *I* function can be defined 'implicitly' as a function which completes the R&D model, making it an innovative model in which neither *R* nor *D* loses its design capacities. These points are summarized in Table 8.5.

We tested the RID model in a few simple cases: in innovative firms, we identified a hypertrophic *I* function which activates research or development processes; in R&D-based firms, there are embryonic innovative design functions (these *I* functions are usually implicit and have not been described as such; they are hidden behind the names of *R* and *D*, which describe the existing organizations). In a famous historical case such as that of nylon, we saw that the discovery was not so much a question of hypothetical

---

[5] It should be noted that Du Pont's historians based their account on their own representation of the design process and that R&D was the only model available.

Table 8.5. From R&D to RID

	Specifications for the innovative firm	Model of the innovative firm from the Tefal case	R&D-based firm	The D function	The R function	Specifications for the I function
Models of activity and reasoning	A model of activity without stable product identities (flexibility for products and competencies)	The firm as a design function = coevolution of competencies and products	Product renewals within known dominant design	Controlled specifications, given requirements and competencies (given conceptual and generative models)	Controlled production of knowledge	Coevolution of competencies and products
Objects to be managed – technical substratum	Structure innovation capabilities without basing them on 'functions' or 'performance'	Lineages and learning rents	Successive projects improving performance, using available resources	Convergence towards QCT target, on basis of known conceptual and generative models	Knowledge production systems, related to lineages	Innovation fields
Type of performance	Growth by repeated innovation, in a context of unstable object identities (no one-off projects)	Prudent growth by reusing excess knowledge without stabilizing object identities	Regular improvement within cones of performance – minimize knowledge production	Optimization of project's turnover/cost ratio	Optimization of quality of knowledge produced/resources consumed	Reusing of excess knowledge without stabilizing object identities
Forms of organization	At the firm level, including major R&D-based firms, without being limited to a project framework	Metabolism (ring-based, with conceptual core)	Project/function matrix	Project teams (marketing, engineering and design, production methods, etc.)	Cross-functional teams, activated by the firm	Conceptual core which activates R and D and is fed by their work

'innovative research' as of innovative design reasoning made by an innovator, capable of activating the research and the development processes in a pertinent manner.

The notions of *I* function and RID firm are interesting but remain highly speculative. To test their viability, we must examine possible forms of organization and of collective reasoning, the tools and the instruments to be used for management and evaluation. We must also see which actors are capable of taking on these new forms of organization, which competencies they require, where they can be found and how they can be trained. At this stage, the *I* function is still a rational myth designed to help manage the transformations in R&D-based firms faced with the challenge of intensive innovation. How can the transformation take place? We shall examine this point in the following chapter, by studying a case of transformation from R&D to RID.

Questions for further study and discussion

What is a research department? How can it be managed and structured? What is the difference between research and development?

Compare the notion of innovation field with the more traditional notions of programme, market segment, target market and vision.

Exercise: find the *I* function in other famous cases of research (see in particular ductile tungsten, the birth of electronics and the chemistry of dyes in Le Masson (2001)).

Key notions – Chapter 8

Innovation as a structured process: the missing structure between *R* and *D*

The role of the research department from a historical standpoint. A few surprises from history: rediscovering *I* which had been too rapidly taken for *R*

Reinterpretation of recent trends in global R&D

9 Learning from experience: expansions from an innovative windscreen at Saint-Gobain Sekurit

Saint-Gobain Sekurit is one of the leading automotive glass manufacturers in the world. Each year, more than 12 million vehicles are equipped with Sekurit glass, representing nearly 20 per cent of the world market and 50 per cent of the European market. At the front end of the glazing supply chain, Saint-Gobain manufactures glass from raw materials, an activity which demands heavy investment and involves delicate techniques. Saint-Gobain Sekurit is recognized for its leading *savoir faire*; less than a dozen companies in the world are capable of producing such complex products.

In 1997, Saint-Gobain Sekurit was the archetype of the large R&D-based firm, with none of the characteristics of an industry where one would expect to find a system of intensive innovation. At the time, there was no newcomer competing through innovation, there was no contact with final users requiring innovation, there was no pressure for innovation, apart from costs and a clearly identified level of performance. So why, in the space of just a few years, did the firm switch to intensive innovation?

In the following pages, we study the birth, or rather the 'morphogenesis', of the new *I* function and see how Saint-Gobain Sekurit adopted RID.

In the first part, we explain why the R&D-based organization tended to prevent an *I* function from emerging. We focus on the scale of the transformation, which affected the firm's products (which became complex and multi-functional) and also its basic functions and technologies (in a few years, Saint-Gobain Sekurit switched from traditional thermomechanics to microelectronics). In the second part, we analyse the organizational transformations that made this change of design system possible, examining the stages in which the *I* function was structured to become more and more collective and increasingly effective.

9.1 The unexpected emergence of an innovative design function

9.1.1 R&D in automotive glass: a stable dominant design with little room for innovation

On 24 May 1699, Louis XIV's first architect, Mansart, ordered three panes of glass for his son's horse-drawn coach from the Manufacture des Glaces, the company that was to become Saint-Gobain. The order, which was probably one of the first orders of glass for a vehicle, was extremely simple: one pane measuring thirty-five inches high by twenty-nine inches wide and the other two, twenty-nine inches high by nineteen inches wide. The two dimensions were all that was needed to order the glass.

Since then, automotive glass has of course become more and more complex. It can be tinted, have different thicknesses, surface treatments and accessories, it can defrost, serve as an aerial or hold a rear-view mirror. It must also meet stringent norms in terms of shock resistance, optics, tolerance, durability, appearance and reflective qualities. And yet, until recently, orders for automotive glass were still quite similar to Mansart's letter. They were often simple CAD files with nothing more than the geometrical dimensions of the piece of glass to be produced. This relative simplicity for such a complex, multi-functional object can be explained by the fact that, for many decades, automotive glass manufacturers had optimized their performance to such an extent that the only thing that changed from one project to another was the shape that an imaginative designer had decided to give to this key element of the vehicle being designed.

This paradox illustrates the nature of competition in the automotive glass industry in the late 1990s: design was optimized and competition focused on a very small number of parameters. This form of competition corresponded to a stable industrial structure, insensitive to innovations in object identities, which practised co-development in a context of dominant design.

9.1.1.1 Glassmakers and car manufacturers: co-development over the very long term

9.1.1.1.1 Forty years of co-development

We can begin by studying the relationship between glassmakers and car manufacturers at that time.

Car manufacturers have almost never designed glass in-house. However, automotive glass is not found in an ordinary commodity market since every vehicle model has specific glazing. Relations between glassmakers and car manufacturers are characterized by the need to delegate design (due to the high levels of investment required to make glass, both in financial and cognitive terms) and the high stakes for the car manufacturer in terms of value (in particular since glazing has a strong visual impact). Under these conditions, glass and car manufacturers had worked with co-development agreements (Garel 1998; Midler 2000) for nearly forty years:

> The glassmakers worked in a coherent, well-defined *perimeter*: windscreens, windows and 'openings', rear quarter windows and sunroofs were all standard components of automobile projects, with well-defined functions. One of the key performance criteria was the ability to produce the shapes demanded by the car manufacturers' stylists, as these were often incompatible with the glassmakers' traditional expertise.

> The glassmakers were therefore involved very early on in the design process. They were consulted at the preliminary project stage and, when they were selected as developers, they then took part in the project as soon as the contract was signed.

> The glassmaker had *overall responsibility for quality, cost and time* and a large amount of leeway for finding the best compromises.

9.1.1.1.2   *Innovation stabilized by a dominant design*

In this context, there had been three main sources of innovation in automotive glass in the previous years: optics, security and complex shapes.

The question of the optical quality of glass had remained open, whilst there was competition between several production processes for flat glass, each with very different optical properties (glass for mirrors versus glass for windows). However, the float process introduced in the 1960s imposed a single optical quality for all flat glass. According to the specialists, this quality was actually not sufficient for certain special products, due to impurities and slight differences, but it was perfectly suitable for automotive glass.

As for security, there were heated debates until the beginning of the 1980s, mainly because two technologies had been available since the 1930s:

> tempering (patented in 1929): the glass is treated by a heating process. In the event of shocks, it breaks into small pieces without sharp edges;

> lamination: a core sheet of plastic is inserted between two sheets of glass in order to increase the resistance. In the event of shocks, the plastic absorbs part of the energy.

The supporters of the two technologies battled for more than twenty years on the strength of biomedical studies and technological progress. However,

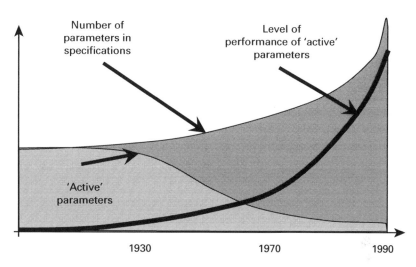

Figure 9.1   The stabilization of a dominant design

when compulsory seat belts were introduced for front-seat occupants in West Germany in 1976, this was the end of tempered glass windscreens. A dominant design was established, with laminated windscreens and tempered windows.

Innovation then concentrated on making increasingly complicated shapes to meet demands for new 'style'. Glass tended to be more and more curved (with 'bubbles' or flush glazing, i.e. windscreens which carry on from the roof) and the surface area of glass increased. However, the dominant design concerned the glass itself but left open the delicate question of the interface between the glass and the bodywork. It was therefore not surprising that, even in the context of co-development, several innovations were made in this domain. For example, new means of fixing the glass were devised, it became quite common for the transitions between glass/interior fittings/bodywork to be covered with enamel and a system was designed whereby extruded seals were added directly to windscreens, leaving the edges of the glass visible.

The dynamics of innovation were therefore concentrated on a very small number of parameters, whereas the other possible areas of innovation were constrained by a strong dominant design (Utterback 1994) – *see* Figure 9.1.

This did not mean that the product's specifications were reduced since, as for all the other vehicle components, in actuality the specifications increased. There were more and more regulations, norms, technical characteristics, tests and standards to be respected. However, the elements *discussed* between the car manufacturer and the glassmaker were limited to the

3-D shape, as all the other parameters were fixed and 'renewed by tacit agreement'.

Nonetheless, glass remained a strategic component of cars. There were major stakes involved in this focus on the shape of car glazing since some stylists believe that glass represents 80 per cent of a car's visual identity. If a glassmaker has difficulty producing the shape of glass demanded by a car designer, the car manufacturer's board of directors soon knows about it.

9.1.1.2   Difficult evolution of functional spaces

In this context of stable functions, the glassmakers and automobile manufacturers nonetheless studied a number of different paths for innovation at that time, although they were unable to challenge the product's functions or to use new expertise outside the world of automotive glass.

The first difficulty for potential innovations in the glazing was that they entailed changes to the cars themselves. For instance, a non-wired heated windscreen (which accelerated demisting and defrosting) needed a 42V battery instead of the usual 12V version; however, it was only when all the new demands in terms of electricity were added together that cars' electrical systems were actually changed. In other words, innovation was possible only if the car manufacturer agreed to invest in design projects that went beyond the traditional orders for glass to 'fill in gaps in the bodywork'.

Another difficulty was that the value of certain evolutions covered more than just the glazing itself and became apparent only if the car manufacturer took advantage of it in terms of the other components. For instance, by reducing the temperature in the passenger compartment, solar control glass meant that air-conditioning systems could be reduced in size. Also, with heated windscreens, dashboard architects no longer had to fit in the warm air supply ducts usually used for demisting and defrosting.

At that time, these new interactions between the glazing and the rest of the vehicle were often perceived as risky on the grounds that an innovation in the glasswork could jeopardize the car as a whole. The first heated windscreens in the 1970s illustrated this point. They had the defect of delaminating, i.e. the sheet of plastic split away from the glass and no longer retained the fragments in the event of shocks. A revelation of this sort, implying that windscreens no longer played their role in passenger security, would of course discredit the entire vehicle.

If innovation involved adding new properties to a product, it could also call into question the more traditional specifications of glazing. For instance, it might be necessary to revise durability tests, geometrical tolerances, optical constants, etc. However, these traditional specifications grouped together all sorts of different demands stemming from different designers (for reasons of design, security, geometrical tolerances for the body, wipeability, driving ergonomics, etc.). In fact, they were the result of fragile compromises, whose reasons were often long forgotten. There were fears that interfering with these compromises would be like opening Pandora's Box.

9.1.1.3   Obstacles to the emergence of new competencies in automotive glass

If innovation was not possible through new functions, could it come from new competencies and new technologies? Ongoing efforts were made to improve industrial facilities and enormous amounts of knowledge were produced to keep up with the competition on the subject of glass shaping. But despite all this, very few 'new technologies' actually emerged. How can this be explained?

9.1.1.3.1   *Ongoing improvements to industrial facilities*

Could the stability of industrial facilities be to blame, or the need to make them pay off before reinvesting? Not in the case of Sekurit, because the industrial facilities evolved constantly during this period. However, the investments did not necessarily lead to intensive innovation, quite the contrary. They were dictated by the question of glass shaping, as the tempering and bending furnaces became extremely sophisticated and required heavy investments and very high levels of expertise. Since the 1970s, new generations of furnaces had been introduced roughly every six or seven years. Each generation presented new refinements, whereas new types of glazing produced in existing furnaces meant that new tooling had to be designed, with all the difficulties inherent in bringing it into service.

Hence, new investments were not opportunities to innovate in anything but the dominant design. The successive investments were closely related and left little space for exploring new functional spaces.

9.1.1.3.2   *Specific knowledge in automotive glass*

Was it a case of new technologies not being adopted due to the conservatism of the stable competencies? On the contrary, the competencies made constant progress and were always being pushed to their limits. Paradoxically, it was the speed of change in the competencies and specific expertise which appeared to be the obstacle.

Glass is a specific, amorphous material whose molecules are not arranged in the same crystalline structure as metals; it represents a specific field of the science of materials and their configuration. For instance, the thermo-mechanical bending properties of glass demand specific simulation models and its optical properties are also a separate discipline. Consequently, knowledge must always be adapted or 'conditioned' before it can be used in the context of glassmaking. This is the case for furnaces, transport systems, cutting equipment, validation and test systems, etc. Technologies developed for a material other than glass (surface treatments, thin coatings, shaping, etc.) cannot be easily applied to glass.

Could automotive glass benefit from technologies developed for glass in other industrial sectors? Once again, great prudence was required because the automobile industry has specific demands in terms of quality, cost and uses. For instance, techniques for filtering infrared rays developed for glass in the construction industry had to be substantially reworked to obtain similar properties for automotive glass.

In addition, the design of automotive glass regularly pushes knowledge to its limits, as most new glazing systems pose fresh problems. Hence, the limits of glass shaping were constantly being pushed back. The knowledge was difficult to master as the slightest change could lead to significant challenges and require new explorations. This instability and the dynamics of the traditional competencies made it even more complicated to introduce new technologies.

Finally, knowledge was difficult to acquire: the processes took a long time to develop and often required full-scale pilot lines. Investments rapidly became significant because prototypes or mock-ups were not sufficient in such a complex domain. Only industrial applications could validate solutions, but the areas of validity were fragile and unstable as they depended on a large number of control factors; containment systems were uncertain and experiment plans often included highly interdependent variables.

9.1.1.4   No actors responsible for innovation

The cost of producing knowledge and the corresponding stability in object identities therefore had an enormous impact by limiting and orienting innovation. The system was all the more stable since none of the actors was in a position to design innovative proposals that would make the dominant design change.

The automobile manufacturers had lost a great deal of their ability to prescribe projects. The glassmakers were in contact with representatives who were *au fait* with only a small fraction of the product's many design parameters. Although they did sometimes make requests for new functions, for the reasons explained above (difficulty in controlling interactions with the rest of the car, the risks regarding the glazing, etc.) their role was mainly in simply renewing the previous specifications. There were of course a few experts in research departments working on innovative glass, but they were often isolated from the development departments and the glassmakers.

As for the glassmakers, the developers could have tried to add functions to the glass which had already been produced by other actors (defrosting, rain-repellents, etc.) or add new functions (sun filter, etc.), but in fact they concentrated on the existing specifications. They only explored design parameters that could potentially lead to the production of new shapes and neglected the exploration of new technologies. The glassmakers' research departments, as with those of the car manufacturers, explored innovative concepts but were often isolated from the development departments and from the client manufacturer.

The relations between car manufacturer and glassmaker can be summarized as follows:

First, the repeated, optimized matching of 'supply' and 'demand': the 'demand' for a stable functionality (the shape) matched the 'supply' of design parameters to meet this functionality. The exchanges took place between the developers.

Second, a 'demand' for new functionalities which was not matched by a 'supply' of design parameters. These were the explorations made by the researchers. The car manufacturer's researchers designed a demand for new functions which had not been expressed; and the supplier's researchers constructed new resources which were not used.

It was not easy to match this latent supply and demand. The problem was not only to facilitate exchanges between researchers but also to integrate the innovations into the general architecture of the vehicles and the glazing, when both were caught up in the dynamics of systematic design.

9.1.2   Ready for competition through intensive innovation

As we have seen, competition in a context of dominant design not only led to stable object identities but also made it difficult for new functions to be explored and for new competencies to emerge, as if the dynamics of systematic design were responsible for the stability. Given the context, who could have predicted in the mid-1990s that the nature of competition would change to become competition by intensive innovation and that this change would take place so quickly? Who would have thought that Saint-Gobain

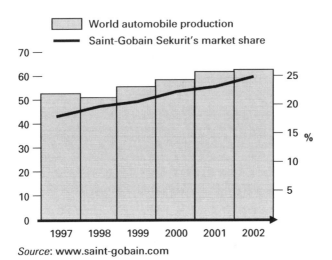

Source: www.saint-gobain.com

Figure 9.2 Growth rates for Saint-Gobain Sekurit

Sekurit would be the major player in this transformation? And yet, by 2001, there were three unmistakable symptoms of this radical change.

The first symptom was growth. The automotive glass industry was char-acterized by relatively stable market shares and fierce competition within a form of oligopoly. From 1995 onwards, Saint-Gobain Sekurit's market share increased with surprising regularity (one percentage point per year from 1997 to 2002) (*see* Figure 9.2). Although growth was slow in the automobile industry at that time, Saint-Gobain Sekurit's turnover rose regularly, approaching double-digit growth.

The second symptom was that glazing had become a multi-functional product. In 2002, Sekurit's product range still included 'larger, more complex' glazing products such as the wraparound windscreen for the Renault Espace and panoramic sunroofs. However, there were also solar control windscreens, noise-reducing acoustic glass windscreens, glazing with rain and light sensors, electrochromic roofs (to modulate the transmission of light) and even glazing in the form of plastic modules. Two years later, comprehensive functional ranges had appeared. Saint-Gobain Sekurit was not selling glazing so much as functions offered by the glass, such as thermocontrol® (thermal comfort), globalprotect® (safety and anti-theft), icecontrol® (demisting, defrosting), aquacontrol® (visual comfort in rainy weather, with sensors, hydrophobic and hydrophilic layers, etc.) and tennafit® (aerial system). Contrary to all expectations, the functional space had in fact opened up considerably.

The third symptom was the transformation in the competencies. In 2002, Saint-Gobain Sekurit mastered the technologies for magnetron sputtering (deposition of nanometric layers by high-energy plasma in an ultra high vacuum). These technologies were already used in microelectronics, but had had to be developed to obtain flawless coatings for glass products measuring several square metres – rather than just a few centimetres – which had to be resistant to cutting, washing and severe heat/cooling cycles. Saint-Gobain Sekurit factories offered clean room conditions, which guaranteed a particle-free environment for its high-tech products and processes.

9.2   Steering the transformation from R&D to RID

How did this come about and how can we explain the change? What impact did it have on the way the design process was organized at Sekurit?

The metamorphosis began when the firm's research was called into question. This led to a radical transformation in the research centre, which became an innovation centre capable of initiating a strategy of growth by repeated innovation, thus presenting us with an exceptional case of a large firm changing from R&D to RID. Our aim in the following pages is to examine the different stages in this transformation to find the keys to how the change took place.

9.2.1   Methodology

A number of hypotheses have been put forward to explain radical changes in organizations. For example, changes in environment can provoke 'adaptation' (Porter 1980), technologies are part of a process of natural change (Hannan and Freeman 1989), firms can take advantage of a charismatic leader or a providential entrepreneur (Peters and Waterman 1982), or an organization's routines are changed by a mechanism of mutation/selection (Nelson and Winter 1982). To a certain extent, these explanations apply to Saint-Gobain Sekurit, as the entrepreneurs who took part in the change were indeed talented and managed to make the most of a period when technologies and products were undergoing drastic changes and forms of competition were changing.

However, from a management sciences standpoint, these explanations are somewhat limited in terms of means of action. How many firms have gone bankrupt whilst waiting for their providential entrepreneur/designer? And even when they do find them, providential managers can remain isolated and be misunderstood. The director of the research centre whose actions we describe in the following pages therefore felt the need to make people understand the path he was following, to explain what he was managing, his reasoning regarding the objects and his targets. Hence, apart from the notion of the providential entrepreneur and favourable external factors, can an action model be derived from this case?

This raises an important question of methodology. What interpretative framework can we use to 'describe' the transformation and which aspects should we focus on? Similarly to the Tefal case, a framework based on 'technologies', leadership or transformations in the traditional organizational structures is not a satisfactory model, because some of the proposals are both true and false depending on ill-controlled external conditions. For example, a proposal such as 'the charismatic leader played a decisive role' was true only in certain phases and for certain objects, but which ones? If the object identities had been stable, it would have been possible to answer the question (cf. the role of the charismatic leader in the decision-making process), since competencies, techniques, organization and leader are clear notions when there are object identities to serve as a base and a common language. But what does a charismatic leader do without product concepts and without technical alternatives? In the Saint-Gobain Sekurit case, the competencies, organizations, processes and even the leaders emerged as and when the activities were extended, depending on the competencies, organizations, processes and leaders that had emerged before them. We therefore need a formal framework to explain this metabolism.

Our description of the transformations is based on the notions we have studied in the previous chapters, the main principle consisting of following the combined dynamics of competencies and products. We have seen that the borderline between systematic design and innovative design is a question of object identities. In Chapter 8 we saw that this identity can be stabilized in given high-level languages (functional, conceptual, embodiment) based on well-documented disciplinary knowledge. However, in a context of instability, there are no longer any 'references' for products and competencies and it is more a question of innovation fields combining value spaces and competencies in the process of being elaborated. In both cases, it is more important to follow the underlying concepts rather than one-off 'products', whether for a stable identity or an area of value; similarly, it is important to describe the emerging functions and competencies rather than simply to follow the disciplinary knowledge. We will therefore study the transformations in two spaces, the space of concepts (C) and the space of knowledge (K).

This is a simplified form of the formal framework for design reasoning, the C-K design theory, developed by Hatchuel and Weil (1996b, 2003). We will present the complete framework in Chapter 10.

9.2.2   The stages in the transformation

9.2.2.1   Fragmented, isolated research

In the mid-1990s, the Saint-Gobain Sekurit research centre in Germany was in the difficult position of research in a co-development system: the centre was isolated from the firm's other departments and in particular from product development. It was organized by major scientific discipline (organic and inorganic chemistry, physics, etc.).

The organization was mainly based on knowledge spaces: in each of the departments, researchers worked on one-off questions within the disciplines concerned. The questions were either devised by the researchers themselves or were the result of problems encountered on existing production lines. At the time, the subjects concerned recurrent defects in the glass, the certification of new plastic interlayers and the development of laser techniques for measuring edge stress. Researchers could be working on five or six questions at the same time. The director's role was to ensure that appropriate resources were available and that the questions were addressed in due time.

As for the product concepts, it should be noted that the questions were very 'concrete', i.e. the problems were formulated in long sentences and were extremely varied (a defect on line XXX with machines x,y,z for windscreen aaa, with parameters a,b,c, etc.). As we shall see later, they did not deal with abstract concepts.

As it was studying so many highly technical questions, research gave the impression of being fragmented (*see* Figure 9.3).

9.2.2.2   Focused research

9.2.2.2.1   *Organization by projects*

The balance was upset when the research centre was contacted for an urgent new product development, a solar control windscreen. Traditional glazing lets through the near infrared solar rays but blocks the re-emission in the far infrared range, thus heating the passenger compartment. The function of the solar control windscreen is to reflect the near infrared rays whilst,

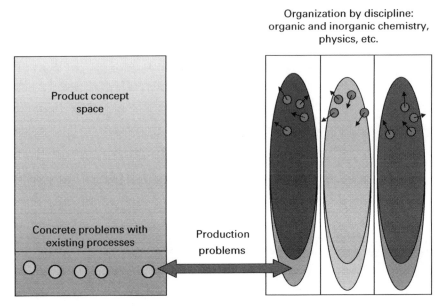

Figure 9.3   Initial stage, fragmented research

of course, remaining transparent in the visible range. This reduces the production of heat.

The automobile manufacturer Renault asked Saint-Gobain Sekurit to make a proposal for a product of this type, which was practically non-existent on the market at that time. Sekurit did not take this demand terribly seriously to begin with and replied that a product of this sort could possibly be produced in five or six years' time. Renault's reaction was to threaten to go to Sekurit's competitors, who claimed to be able to meet the demand immediately.

The solar control windscreen did not fit into the usual framework of co-development. It was no longer a question of producing glass with a sophisticated shape for the best possible price but of providing a completely new functionality as a result of new technology (a system of thin interference layers), even if it meant doubling the cost of the product. Sekurit's developers were not ready. As is often the case, they turned to the research department to see whether it had already studied thin layer technologies. The development project for the new glazing then suddenly mobilized all the centre's resources. Several disciplines were involved as well as the physics of thin layers, including optical analysis, the chemistry of polymers and lamination processes. A multi-disciplinary team was set up and a form of project management evolved.

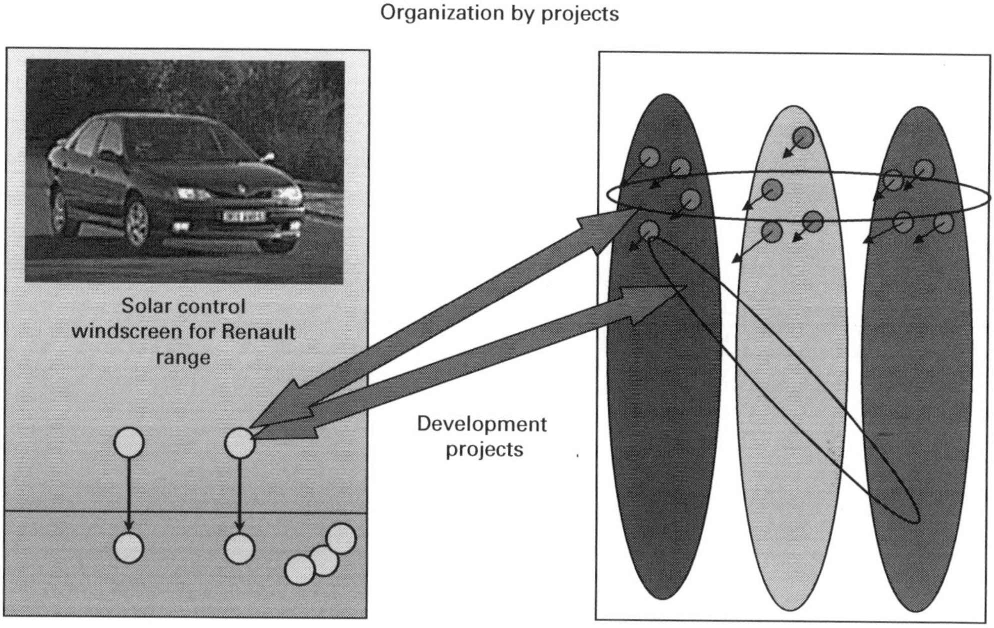

Organization by projects

Solar control
windscreen for Renault
range

Development
projects

Figure 9.4   Stage 1, focused research

Without describing all the different stages here, suffice to say that the project was a success since, within just a few months, Sekurit's designers were able to propose a reliable solution for the car manufacturer. And the project proved to be a forerunner for further demands from clients. The director of the centre rapidly reorganized the work to focus on a small number of projects, practically all of which related to client demands. The boundaries between the different departments became vaguer as the organization centred on projects.

A new style of organization emerged which, contrary to the previous situation, could not only be described in terms of knowledge but also depended on product concepts. However, these concepts were still described in lengthy phrases, such as 'designing a solar control windscreen for the Renault Laguna' (*see* Figure 9.4).

9.2.2.2.2   *Managing by concepts*

What were the keys to this change from fragmented research to project-oriented research? External factors obviously had an impact, as it was the car manufacturer's request for innovation in the glazing that led to the initial need for Sekurit to innovate outside the dominant design. However, Sekurit also responded well, by completely overhauling the portfolio of research concepts and grouping them around a limited number of projects which could be used directly for developing the glazing. Instead of working on a large number of small knowledge-oriented projects, researchers began to work on a small number of new product development projects. They had changed from 'personal research projects' to projects with direct product applications.

It was surprising to see how easily these radical changes were accepted. There were no organizational revolutions, no great campaigns to mobilize the troops and no staff changes. How was this profound transformation managed so smoothly?

How Renault acquired the knowledge needed to initiate an innovative design approach

It is worth asking why a car manufacturer decided to ask for an innovative function such as solar control, despite all the obstacles described in the previous part of the chapter.

For a long time, Sekurit had difficulty in interpreting Renault's demand. It was not so much the solar control windscreen as such that surprised them, as the research department had already explored various existing technologies that enabled windscreens to filter heat, but the designers had concluded that the market opportunities were insufficient. Whilst investing in one of the technologies, they could only imagine a gradual introduction, starting with the top-of-the-range models. But it was precisely this representation of the product's value that Renault called into question; Sekurit was extremely surprised that an 'ordinary' car manufacturer should be interested in a solar control windscreen. It was several months before it took Renault's demand seriously and several years later many people still failed to understand what they saw as an incomprehensible whim.

However, from Renault's point of view, the solar control windscreen was far from a caprice; it was, on the contrary, the result of a long process of gestation. It had taken far more than a vision from an audacious entrepreneur to come up with the concept of a 'filtering windscreen for all'. For several months teams of designers reworked the concept of automotive glass. They began by reappropriating the specifications and the fundamentals of the glass, which led to significant progress on the quality of glazing. From this point, there were more intense interactions with the glassmakers as, in order to understand defects in the glass, they had to understand the manufacturing processes and their advantages and disadvantages.

The designers were gradually able to renew the functional analyses, to study new technologies, to rebuild cost models, to reopen value spaces for the customers and to reinvent the relevant customer messages.

> This groundwork enabled them to bring a concept such as 'solar control glazing for all' to a successful conclusion. The work on value showed that a much higher price could be accepted for the glazing, whereas technical and commercial knowledge confirmed that it could be proposed for the entire product range; the marketing was backed by a clever communication strategy at the car dealers' premises (a small demonstration unit allowed the buyer to compare the temperatures behind reflective glass and normal glass). This strategy enabled them to reduce prices and to saturate the suppliers' production capacities, thus ensuring a *de facto* monopoly for several months. The strategy on value was backed by a 'technological' strategy. Renault studied the different technologies for producing solar control coatings and was therefore able to draft credible specifications and ask suppliers for proposals regarding these technological alternatives. It should be added that this work was brought to a successful conclusion for solar control glazing, but also concerned other interesting concepts for glazing.
>
> The changes at Renault were therefore the result of a vast amount of work on knowledge and concepts. It was a long, rigorous process that helped initiate the radical changes in the relationship of co-development, which had lasted for forty years. A similar process was then gradually undertaken by Sekurit.

Saint-Gobain Sekurit began to work in a different manner, focusing on concepts. This was a change from the previous period when work was focused on resources and the main aim was to provide researchers with satisfactory working conditions whilst limiting costs. There was little discussion about the concepts being studied: as they could not arbitrate between the different projects, the group's management bodies were content to renew the centre's budgets by appropriating the sums required for each project. The next phase, involving one-off innovation, was the start of management by concepts. The projects were based on clearly identified product concepts and budgets were quite often negotiated during the year, depending on the stakes involved. Certain 'strategic' projects were even launched even though they had not initially been budgeted for. This was a real revolution in the way the centre was managed.

However, to begin with, the transformation was not on the same scale as Renault's, as it did not lead to a redefining of competencies, knowledge, etc. and actually the challenge even seemed to be *to avoid producing new knowledge*.

If we take the case of the solar control windscreen, why was it successful in such a short time, although the researchers had said that the research would take several years? Quite simply because the technology developed for the short term was not the same as for the long term. The problem for solar control glazing is to insert into the glass a thin layer (a few hundred nanometres) with interferential properties (reflecting in the near infrared and transparent in the visible range). There was general agreement on the fact that it was impossible to develop a system of thin interference layers for glass and validate them for high production rates in just a few months, for the reasons mentioned in the previous section – although interferential layer systems already existed and certain layer systems had been developed for the construction industry, nothing existed for glass produced on a large scale. A whole new area of competency had to be built up, but in a very short period of time.

Nonetheless, other possibilities were open to them (see the box on p. 211). Instead of depositing a coating on the glass, the solution in fact consisted of buying a ready-made coating deposited on a thin plastic film. Saint-Gobain Sekurit found a supplier of PET (polyethylene terephtalate) plastic sheets covered with an interference layer with the required properties (initially developed for the construction industry). All that remained to be done was to validate it and to develop a system for inserting the additional plastic sheet into the laminated glass 'sandwich'. This time, the development process could be carried out using Sekurit's own expertise in the certification of optical systems and of plastic/glass interactions.

It was a specific design strategy to use thin layers of PET. Whereas Renault began its investigations with a detailed 'functional analysis' and explorations of new technologies and new user values, Saint-Gobain Sekurit began by studying a limited number of concepts whose value was certain. They had to be developed urgently if Sekurit was to stay in the contest. One vital obligation was that the exploration of these concepts should not require lengthy work to acquire knowledge. The firm used only existing knowledge or competencies that could be produced rapidly, at the lowest possible cost. This requirement was an example of an approach based on maximizing learning rents, but it greatly restricted conceptual explorations. This was why, in the initial stages of the process, only a small number of concepts were identified and the portfolio of products being developed remained limited.

This work on identifying the concepts appears to be the key to the successful transformation, but how did it happen? Whereas Renault had set up structured teams to do similar work (*see* the box on p. 206), at Sekurit it was still a question of relatively solitary work carried out by the director of the research centre. However, it was far from abstract. On the contrary, the reasoning was fed by knowledge coming from very different horizons.

The director had a network of relations and made the most of his regular contacts with the car manufacturer and with the group's marketing managers. His work was also enriched by his personal knowledge of glass and cars accumulated over the years, and by the competencies used in the research centre. He often suggested analyses or prototypes that could help the researchers explore certain ill-defined concepts.

Rather than a definitive 'stroke of genius', this process of managing by concepts was the result of ongoing work on formulating and elaborating the concepts. The concepts had to be sufficiently ripe for action, but they also matured by inventing new means of management.

The change was accepted so willingly by the Sekurit research centre because, although there were drastic changes in the number and type of projects it was working on, the knowledge corresponded to expertise that was mastered by the researchers. The apparent upheaval in fact maintained an essential element of continuity, the learning. This ability to change the product concepts whilst maintaining continuity in the learning trajectories was another key point to be attributed to the centre's director.

9.2.2.2.3   *The embryo of an I function*

In this first stage, the research centre had moved away from an R or D approach. We can analyse the transformation with the analytical framework for the I function (*see* Chapter 8):

The reasoning: the emergence of new functions corresponded to the destabilization of object identities. There was a form of coevolution of competencies and products because the new functions were developed with the existing competencies.

Performance: the strategy was above all responsive. To stand up to the pressure from demands for innovation, the researchers reused knowledge produced in the past (whether in excess or not) to explore new concepts requested by the clients.

The objects to be managed: these were vague innovation fields and in fact more like one-off projects. Although several technologies were rapidly listed in an innovation field such as solar control, explorations were restricted considerably by the concern to limit explorations in terms of knowledge. They focused on one technology.

Organization: a form of I function emerged, steered by the director of the centre. He was responsible for defining the development programmes which his researchers became involved in; he also managed the research projects that remained within the centre.

The story could have ended there, in that the centre had adapted to a new form of competition and was capable of responding quickly to demands from clients even if they were unexpected.

9.2.2.3   Intensive innovation: organization by lineage

9.2.2.3.1   Management by lineage

However, that was not the end of the story since the industrial context was changing rapidly. Once the idea of innovation in windscreens had been launched, other car manufacturers wanted to differentiate themselves from their competitors. A large number of projects rapidly surfaced, all stimulated by urgent client demands. For instance, more and more sophisticated connector technology (at the end of the 1990s, seven aerials had to be mounted in a rear quarter window of a BMW), heated windscreens, new sensors (rain, light, etc.), hydrophobic coatings, etc. There were also more and more functionalities and the combinations quickly became complex. Were the changes sustainable without the teams becoming worn out? Also, how efficient were these project management processes and were they profitable?

The study of a few projects shows that their individual success did not depend on the project leader so much as on the succession of previous projects, and that the design work on a given project also conditioned subsequent trajectories. In other words, the projects in portfolios were not independent one from the other. How could this be taken into account when managing portfolios? For example, how could they take into account the fact that the first solar control product with a simple shape and its nth multi-functional version (with a complex form, including a tinted filter band and an aerial) were the result of different approaches?

In order to make the best possible use of the knowledge produced from one project to the next, they gradually organized the work into lineages such as 'solar control' and 'connector technology'. In formal terms (*see* Tefal model), a lineage can be defined:

by a relatively abstract guiding concept: it no longer concerned only the 'solar control windscreen for the Laguna' but 'solar control' and all its different functional specifications. Progress consisted of exploring the functional space in question, e.g. performance levels for the solar filter, solar control and increasingly complex shapes, solar control and colouring, etc.;

by a knowledge base associated with or even closely linked with the guiding concept (specific new competency). Progress consisted of strengthening these competencies. In the case of solar control, a key element of knowledge concerned thin interference layers and in particular the associated bending techniques;

by a series of projects, which were all opportunities for learning, spaces for testing and sources of profit.

Managing lineages

Managing lineages entails more than:

appointing someone to do the job, as it is another matter to describe the mission. Managing by lineage implies reasoning in terms of innovative design strategy;

a project based on known competencies. The technologies are not given at the outset; the head of the lineage manages several projects, some of which target new learning processes (creation of new competencies);

a 'new competency' for a known function. Nor is it a question of developing a new technology for a well-identified area of performance; on the contrary, functional differentiation is one of the stakes of the exploration;

a project portfolio. The lineage manages interactions between projects, transferring the constraints and focusing learning on the appropriate design spaces.

Managing by lineage entails organizing functional exploration/technology in cases where neither element is stable. If the two elements become stable (or evolve relatively slowly), we return to the traditional situation in which the functional specifications and the design parameters are stable. However, lineages are precisely an original solution for managing situations in which the two spaces are expanding rapidly.

How did these lineages work in practice? One of the main reasons why the first 'lineages' emerged was that a group manager was appointed to develop a 'new business' with the following resources: a small project portfolio, specific tools for trials, tests and prototyping, a few experts in the laboratory, relations with a few external clients and with people in the marketing department and a strong presence in the production workshops related to the lineage's functions and technologies.

Managing the solar control lineage

There were at least three different alternatives for solar control layers (*see* Figure 9.6). The first involved depositing a thin layer on glass which had already been bent. Sekurit had already mastered this technology, but only for small series. The second alternative consisted of depositing a layer on flat glass, which then underwent the usual transformations (cutting, washing, bending and lamination). This technology involved developing a layer that could be bent once on the glass (*see* Figure 9.6). The third alternative consisted of using a film carrying the functional layer, inserting the film between two sheets of PVB (polyvinyl butyral), then laminating this sandwich between two sheets of normal glass. This third alternative was chosen for the solar control project for Renault.

When the latter project was successfully completed, the three technologies were in fact being used by Sekurit. A factory was still making small production runs of bent glass and even supplied glazing for certain Renault vehicles with particularly complex shapes; PET technology had gradually been introduced in all Sekurit's European factories; and the group's central research centre continued to experiment with different techniques for bendable layers on samples a few square centimetres large. It was tempting to bet on one of the technologies, on the basis of the usual technico-economic arguments (cost, performance, etc.). However, it was difficult to use cost criteria, since the technologies were at very different stages of maturity, or to determine the functional superiority of one of the options when the space of functions was, to a great extent, still to be discovered.

In the end, Sekurit decided to explore all three technologies at the same time. It began by setting up lineages to manage different types of projects:

Development projects corresponding to client demands, for which it used mature technologies, PET or layers on bent glass. As far as possible, these were managed like classic development projects (convergence, minimization of knowledge produced, technico-economic arbitration on a case-by-case basis, i.e. with some glazing by PET, some by layers on bent glass, etc.).

Exploratory projects on a given technology, with a view to gradually establishing the frontiers of what was possible for each alternative. They explored the very young PET technology in order to make more and more complex shapes, to integrate aerials and new types of PVB. There was even an exploratory project to appropriate the technology for depositing coatings on plastic, given the value provided by layering techniques. The firm registered patents in this domain. These projects explored new functional spaces, new value spaces and new design parameters.

Design projects for the new bendable layer technology, which explored a potential value/competency and also gradually built a new competency, i.e. bendable layer processes.

These projects had different approaches to the explorations, based on concepts at different levels of maturity. This is interesting for two reasons:

First, it made the project teams aware of the different nature of each mission, so that the types of learning could be carefully divided between the projects and individual learning processes could be of benefit to all.

Second, it helped manage sales relations in a context of intensive innovation, by spreading the risks over the different explorations. Management by lineage avoided distorting exploratory concepts because of sales imperatives: mature, validated, readily available solutions could be proposed to clients; exploratory concepts were thus free from market pressures and could gradually build up basic competencies. Conversely, to avoid going too far with a development solution – and taking major risks – management by portfolio helped manage the risks in a given exploratory project (the exploratory concepts prevented the mature concepts from taking too much risk in innovative projects, as audacious client demands could be treated like an exploratory partnership rather than co-development).

The technologies were gradually differentiated in this way. It was not so much a competition between them as a gradual exploration of the potential value of solar control.

Sekurit used two key tools to manage the lineages. The first was a table giving the values of the lineage. By listing the characteristics of the solar control 'species', the table gradually mapped the value. The characteristics were common, but could be used to differentiate between the technologies. For instance, the table showed the gradual building up of the solar control function (colour, levels of reflection, etc.) and the list of proven compatible (or incompatible) functions (aerials, complex shapes, heating, etc.), as well as criteria on cost and process (flexibility in terms of factory, logistics, etc.). The second key tool was regular monitoring of investments made and income generated for each of the technologies. Once again, it was not so much a question of comparing the technologies as of ensuring an overall balance in the lineage.

After a few years, the solar control lineage was characterized by three clearly differentiated technologies, the maximum value being obtained from bendable layer technology. The latter's design strategy would have been far less prudent had there not been the intermediate stage of PET technology. Researchers elaborated a rich functional and industrial language for the lineage, which led to efficient rule-based design, using standard, precise, detailed specifications, reliable conceptual models and robust competencies. It enabled them to explore alternatives effectively and to rapidly find QCT compromises.

Managing the lineages consisted not only of successfully completing projects but also of encouraging the creation of knowledge to help speed up all the projects, through charts, test procedures, routine trials, etc. Little by little, each lineage introduced forms of semi-designed products.[1] After observing that off-the-shelf glazing technologies were always ill-suited because each new vehicle had specific features, the designers decided to develop partially validated generic concepts, which could be adapted to the specific requirements of new development projects by modifying a certain number of well-identified parameters. For example, in the domain of solar control by PET, the designers fixed certain parameters concerning the layers (the latter being validated), but adapted other parameters for the lamination or bending processes for each development project.

The role of the lineage was not (only) to use semi-designed products but also to design them. In the long term, the lineage could even delegate development to the designers in the engineering and design departments

---

[1] This notion was devised by Benoît Weil (1999). A semi-designed product is a form of generative model, in the sense of the term given in Chapter 8.

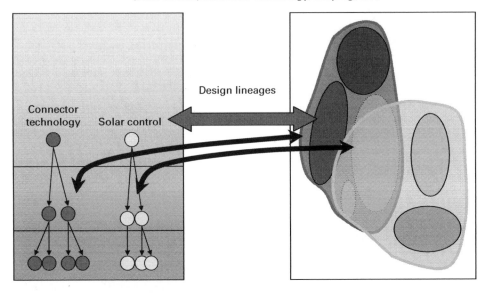

Figure 9.5   Stage 2, repeated innovation organized by lineages

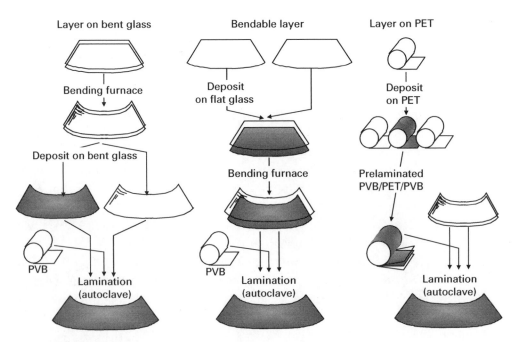

Figure 9.6   The alternatives for thin layers for windscreens

by providing them with suitable semi-designed products, and then focusing its activities on designing pertinent semi-designed products.

9.2.2.3.2 *Steering change by fostering learning*

What management processes were involved in setting up lineages? Similarly to the change to project-based management, the change to lineages was managed in terms of concepts. The challenge involved selecting what were believed to be suitable lineages and then providing the appropriate resources.

Whereas project management was based on minimizing learning, the aim of lineages was to form an embryo of competencies. The change to lineages therefore encouraged learning and the reuse of knowledge. The following points were essential in fostering learning:

ensuring that the knowledge was produced in relation to identified concepts;

ensuring transfer of expertise in development or in production (the experts, who often came originally from research, had access to increasingly formal, easily transmittable knowledge);

organizing the embryonic knowledge into competencies. The knowledge went from the 'embryonic' stage (of an imaginative designer's vague memories, or superficial explorations on the internet when a designer was confronted with a new problem) to an increasingly visible structuring process within the organization (with dedicated experts and the gradual building of competency relating to recurrent questions to do with development and production).

9.2.2.3.3 *A new I function*

Management by lineage was an original form of *I* function:

The coevolution of competencies and products was extended: in project-based management it was restricted by the limits on knowledge production, but with the lineages, expansions concerned both the knowledge and the concepts. Although the identity of the products was not stable, conceptual expansions were nonetheless guided by a form of 'dominant function', such as solar control or connector technology, which was the organizing principle of the lineage.

The performance consisted of responding, in a sustainable manner, to clients' demands.

Management was by lineage: these were forms of innovation field in which the conceptual notions and the knowledge bases expanded significantly but were nonetheless well structured from the start. The solar control lineage could be managed as such because there were already three well-identified technologies, at least two of which matured sufficiently to enable effective developments.

The organization no longer rested on a single person but included lineage managers, who discussed projects with the development department and called on the research department.

Once again, the story could have ended there as the centre had set up an organization capable of responding efficiently and cost-effectively to its clients' demands for innovation and was therefore equipped to deal with a system of repeated innovation.

9.2.2.4   Intensive innovation: structuring innovation fields

In practice, organization by lineages was only a stage in the process. Fairly quickly, the director of the centre realized that new means of organization were required to deal with two key issues, the coherency between lineages and the creation of new lineages. It was not only a question of sustainability but also of the ability to organize endogenous growth by creating new values.

A third phase then began, in which the centre moved from repeated innovation to intensive innovation. Repeated innovation was based on a list of functions; intensive innovation sought to anticipate possible functionalities. The first problem was to study the overall situation on a more general level than the existing lineages, in order to link them and open up new spaces to be explored.

The simplest of questions, such as how to present the research centre's activity to the branch or group management, posed difficulties. It was not enough to say that they made glazing, as this did not give enough information about the different sorts of glazing and their properties. The presentation exercise rapidly turned into an exercise on the theory of glazing. A few years previously, glazing could have been described as a piece of glass, shaped to fill in the holes in a car's bodywork; in a system of management by lineage, it had become a multi-functional glass medium, but the question of the functions themselves remained relatively vague. At that time, a new theoretical proposition was elaborated: automotive glazing was a protective/communicating membrane.

The formula includes some interesting concepts, in that a membrane is both a medium and an interface, thus reflecting the dual characteristic of glass as a physical support and the only component that is on the inside and the outside of the vehicle at the same time. The idea of associating protection and communication could easily lead to new ideas: glass to protect from shocks and intrusions, to hide passengers from other people's view; glass to communicate smells, or useful information to help the driver, etc.

The formula worked as *a generator of innovative concepts*, of future projects. However, it did not explain the transformation, as in fact it was relatively simplistic. The progress did not stem from the wording but from the way it was integrated into the collective system and how the abstract reasoning was used to gradually translate the concepts into innovative products.

Sekurit could not have used such an abstract notion a few years previously, but recent learning processes meant that the designers were able to use it to imagine new concepts, based on embryonic knowledge. We can take a few very simple examples: 'protecting the passenger compartment from people's view when the vehicle is empty' could concern electrochromic technologies or electric blinds; 'enhancing communication between the passengers and the outside environment' could concern wraparound windscreens, sunroofs or windows with filtering glass which lets some odours through.

In addition, the arrival of a few highly experienced lineage managers meant that work was better distributed between concepts concerning lineages in the process of being set up and concepts concerning embryonic innovation fields. A formula of this sort was therefore a way of making the existing functionalities more coherent and of generating new ones.

The notion of value when exploring innovation fields

The work on innovation fields obliged Sekurit to address the issue of value. Management by lineage had been based on relatively well-identified client demands, whereas innovation fields meant that they had to construct innovative proposals whose value could be appreciated only in a much wider perimeter than that of glazing.

The value of non-reflecting glass was a question not only of aesthetics but also of the fact that this property eliminated a number of design constraints for the passenger compartment and the dashboard. For example, lighter colours could be used; the visor which prevents the dashboard from being reflected in the windscreen or the side windows could be removed, etc.

More generally speaking, Sekurit studied whether value could be found by calling into question the traditional perimeters:

- Could the glazing become more independent and incorporate vital functions that had been provided by other suppliers until then (windscreen wipers and washers, defrosting devices, etc.)? For example, thermal comfort could be provided either by air-conditioning (which concerned the suppliers of such systems) or by improved filtering of the sun's rays (which concerned the glassmaker).

- Could they protect themselves from 'attacks' from new technologies (screens, helmet-mounted displays, curtains, blinds, etc.)?
- How could they design and incorporate more user value (driving aids, thermal comfort, style, etc.)? The value may have been presented earlier in another form (as was the case for aerials, which were incorporated in the glass but had for a long time been additions to the bodywork) or it could be a completely new function. In rainy weather, visual comfort can be obtained by windscreen wipers, but a hydrophobic layer on the glazing might provide a similar function and could be extended to all the vehicle's windows.

New systems of organization were needed to manage the introduction of innovation fields (*see* Figure 9.7). The centre's work no longer focused exclusively on well-defined projects or on well-established lineages, as its director also launched explorations to create new product lineages. This groundwork to explore innovation fields was sometimes carried out in the form of 'mini projects'. Limited in time and resources, these projects carried out rapid explorations, favoured exploratory trials and prototyping that revealed killer criteria and developed new expertise (in electronics, signal

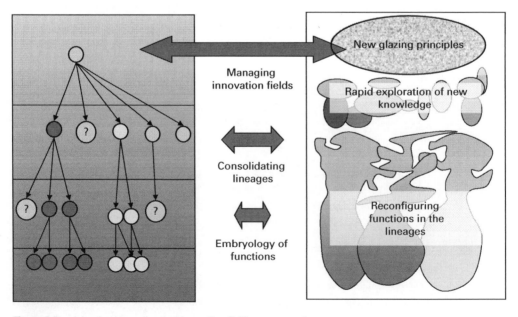

Figure 9.7   Intensive innovation and innovation field management

theory, IT, electroluminescent polymers, etc.) by contacting the appropriate research centres, manufacturers, innovative SMEs, etc.

Another area in which the organization changed was in interaction with car manufacturers in the very early stages of projects. The firm organized 'tech days', carefully prepared meetings when the top management of Saint-Gobain Sekurit's glazing branch and managers from its marketing and research departments met representatives from the car manufacturers. Rather than discussing portfolio projects in progress, they studied the innovation fields being explored at that time to see whether partnerships could be formed.

To quote the research director: 'This helped draw up strategies for objects which did not exist yet, for which there were neither specifications nor manufacturing procedures.' There is no better way of saying that the firm had adopted a system of intensive innovation.

At that stage, the system presented the features of an *I* function:

coevolution of competencies and products, with dual expansion on the most abstract concepts;

a type of performance consisting of adopting a system of supply and creation of value;

increasingly varied objects to be managed: projects, lineages and innovation fields;

organizations enriched with new roles: lineage managers, innovation field managers, etc.

9.3   Conclusion: a pioneer example?

Answers to a few classic questions on the Saint-Gobain Sekurit case help underline the key points.

Was innovation a passing 'crisis'?

Understanding the RID model and how it came into being helps us address the issue of its durability. It is quite legitimate to ask whether the changes at Saint-Gobain Sekurit were simply a temporary answer to a passing wave of innovation and whether once the wave had subsided the firm would return to the 'permanent system' of co-development. Without being able to give a definitive answer, we have nonetheless described organizations which were far from a simple accident or an *ad hoc* response, but which were in fact the result of robust, specific structuring.

> Was a single person, the director of the centre, responsible for the transformation?

The delicate transformation from traditional R&D to an original system of RID was indeed mainly managed by a single person, but he gradually organized a collective body. In the last phase, this body went far beyond the frontiers of the former laboratory. The tech days were a way of encouraging 'innovative marketing design'. Another important aspect of the management system was that the director of the centre had to constantly explain his own management approach to the firm's top management.

The size of the organization and the nature of the products and of the expertise most probably favoured management by a single person and we might wonder how the change could be managed in a collective environment where the innovative design reasoning has to be shared from the outset.

> Where did research stand in this sort of organization?

At the end of the 1990s, R and D were in a delicate situation, as research was accused of not having prepared for the future and development was incapable of responding to clients' demands. When the laboratory became a centre of innovation this did not mean that R and D disappeared: there is still a central research department and there are still development teams.

The emergence of the innovation laboratory led to significant changes in the relations with R and with D, and in fact made them far more peaceful. The innovation laboratory now prescribes the research centre's work, providing arguments for the value of the research programmes; it prepares for the transition to development by elaborating the languages and tools required for rule-based design in the lineages.

The example of Saint-Gobain Sekurit has helped show that a form of RID is possible in a large firm. At the beginning of 2001, Sekurit offered new product functionalities and developed new competencies (just as specialized as its former ones), and its turnover increased significantly, on a regular basis. A few key actors represented a new I function which activated research and development. The case of Sekurit helps understand how these actors' roles came into being. There was no great change of strategic plan, no evolutionary transition and no revolutions with a charismatic leader. The transition from R&D to RID presented three original features: management by concepts, organization of joint learning processes and a design strategy with an economical production of knowledge.

Questions for further study and discussion

What difficulties do large firms have in moving away from a dominant design?

What is the distinction between strategies based on lineages and intensive innovation strategies?

Is it enough to have good 'product theory' to organize innovative design? Why did it take several years before the 'protective/communicating membrane' concept was proposed?

What is meant by 'embryology of competencies'? Compare with the notion of knowledge enhancement.

PART IV

Innovative design: tools and organizations

10 The methodologies of innovative design: C-K theory, innovation fields and design spaces

Organizing the *I* function

As in previous chapters, we begin with a few practical comments and questions from the Innovation Manager. 'I agree with the idea that innovative design is a specific activity, different from activities in the engineering and design or research departments. This distinction clarifies the role of *D* and *R* and their interdependency with *I*. All too often, confusion between *I* and R&D has meant that *I*-type projects have been undertaken without having the right resources, with the result that they have been judged as bad research or bad development projects. I also agree that "innovation fields", which enable projects to be launched without necessarily thinking about the final product, favour exploratory approaches, both in terms of value and competencies, and help evaluate the work on the basis of new criteria.

'But *R* and *D* already have sophisticated management tools to organize and steer them, and we need to find similar management methods for innovative design. This raises a number of questions regarding evaluation criteria and organization, particularly with respect to interactions with R&D and with the other designers. Also, how can innovation fields be structured and how can any excess knowledge be reused? Do we already have any methods, tools, good practices or models?'

Models of activity and organization of the *I* function in large firms

In recent years there has been a massive increase in the number of 'innovation departments', in the form of business development units, innovation-oriented centres, departments for research, innovation and preliminary projects, etc. They are to be found in every sector, including the car industry, pharmaceuticals, chemicals, transport, insurance, agri-business, electrical equipment, metallurgy, glass and household electrical goods. Even the major retail chains have joined the trend. Whether upstream or downstream from the different sectors, B2B or B2C, in products or services, *I* functions are everywhere.

The place given to these *I* functions and the role they play can vary enormously depending on the context, ranging from simple support, event management or market intelligence to providing tools and methods, to full responsibility for identifying and managing the exploration of innovation fields. The challenge is therefore to find *a model of collective action for the I function itself*. This model must correspond to the specifications defined in Chapter 8 and cater for the variety of forms, whilst specifying the role of the existing players in *R*, *D*, marketing, industrial design, etc.

The usual approach in management is to start by looking for an organization model. But we need an adequate language to explain the activity, to describe the division of work, the groups of people concerned, the means of evaluation, the performance or the steering processes involved. In the case of innovation, we have already seen that the *I* function must manage innovation fields and activate R&D. This poses a difficult problem. On the one hand, *R* and *D* speak the language of disciplines and instruments (*R*) and that of product families, functions, components, technical principles and methods of validation (*D*), in short a language of activity based on stable object identities. On the other hand, an innovation field is built on the idea of revising these identities. What is being managed when we try to structure an innovation field? It is not the competencies, the components or the specifications, the engineering skills or the research disciplines (with their techniques, questions, models, etc.), given that it is their absence that makes the *I* function emerge. The idea is to organize a new metabolism designed precisely to regenerate products' functions and identities. This requires a new language of activity.

Our first step is therefore to propose a model for the *I* activity, built on the most recent formal frameworks of innovative design *reasoning*. This new language will serve as a base for a collective action model of *I*, specifying the objects to be managed, the performance and how the exploration of an innovation field can be organized. We will show how these elements enabled us to elaborate management tools to support explorations.

Before venturing further, we must point out that there is an important change of focus in the rest of the book. From this point forward, we are no longer at the level of the innovative firm as in the previous three parts of the book but move to the level of one of its functions. To be more precise, rather than looking at all the dimensions of the *I* function, we concentrate our work on the most specific objects to be managed, i.e. the innovation fields.

10.1   From creativity to innovative design reasoning

Tefal and Saint-Gobain Sekurit have served as emblematic examples of the *I* function. However, they are less helpful when it comes to the question of the model of activity. As we have seen, these companies had a remarkable talent for enabling competencies and products to evolve rapidly, at the same time. But whether as a collective, as with Tefal, or leaning towards more individualistic approaches, as with Saint-Gobain Sekurit, few explanations have been put forward for this talent. How can it be cultivated and how do we go about training the future players in innovative design? The challenge is to find a way of *thinking and reasoning collectively* on *the coevolution of competencies and products*. Can long periods of mentoring and costly trial and error processes be replaced by a formal framework describing the reasoning to be made in innovative design situations?

10.1.1   The paradoxical properties of innovative design reasoning

What properties should this formal framework have? The case studies on Tefal and Sekurit have clearly shown that it will be far removed from those seen for *R* or *D* (*see* Chapter 8). In fact, its properties are somewhat paradoxical. On the one hand, contrary to R&D, innovative design seeks to extend the areas of knowledge and revise the identity of objects. Innovative design reasoning must therefore enable a certain *power of expansion.* But on the other hand, not unlike R&D, innovative design aims to build sustainable trajectories for expansion, which appears to limit its power. Let us examine the two terms.

Creativity techniques – which are often experimented with *I* functions today, with varying degrees of success – help illustrate the notion of expansion. These techniques are precisely aimed at *improving the power of expansion.* For the founders of work on creativity (cf. the box below), it is a form of intelligence that comes into play when faced with open questions such as 'what can we do with a metre of cotton thread?'. Contrary, for instance, to IQ test questions there are obviously no set answers; they call for a series of answers. Assessing an individual's creativity involves characterizing *all* the answers he or she provides. Creativity can be evaluated on four criteria (the Guilford criteria; *see* box below):

fluency, evaluated by the number of answers;

flexibility, evaluated by the changes in the types of answers (variance);

originality, evaluated by the 'unique' nature of the answer (compared with a reference set);

elaboration, evaluated by the addition of details.

The origin of creativity techniques: to favour another form of intelligence in children, as opposed to IQ tests

Rather surprisingly, creativity techniques did not emerge in the world of industry to deal with questions of innovation but were developed as teaching tools to improve children's scoring in creativity tests.

To understand the history, we must go back to the origin of these tests, and particularly the most famous one, the Torrance Test of Creative Thinking (TTCT), thought up by E. Paul Torrance in the 1960s. E. Paul Torrance worked in the tradition of the American psychologist Guilford (Guilford 1959) on the criticism of IQ as a measurement of intelligence. IQ testing came in for much criticism in the 1950s, amongst other things for only highlighting the ability to solve well-formulated problems with known solutions. Against this form of 'intelligence', Guilford proposed the notion of 'divergent thinking', aimed at taking into account exploratory, imaginative and creative mental processes. It was this work that was the real starting point of research on 'creativity' seen as a natural, universal dimension of the human mind.

This rapid genealogy explains the limits of these techniques when they are applied to generating innovations in 'industrial' contexts, as they had their origin in psychology and teaching: do schools teach children 'intelligence' (IQ) or to be creative? Is creativity inborn and then inhibited? From the 1950s to the 1970s, a large number of initiatives were taken to set up creativity programmes in schools in the USA. Most creativity techniques were first developed in this particular context. This explains that they tend to be in the form of games, that they are democratic, open and stimulating and call very little on individual competencies. Creativity is an individual psychological matter and the main question is to find how to favour and develop as far as possible each person's 'creative personality' (defined by his or her motivation, perseverance, intellectual curiosity, strong commitment, independent mind and attitude, desire for personal fulfilment, strong sense of 'self', etc.).

Three main families of techniques were developed to improve scores in creativity tests:

To increase the variety of solutions (see Guilford's first and second criteria, flexibility and fluency), exercises encourage work on imagination, associations, comparisons, etc. They are based on the use of metaphors and more or less colourful narrative methods. They try to put things out of step, forcing people to take a fresh look at things, surprising them, even if this results in disorganized or even chaotic thought processes.

To encourage original answers (in a view to revising the identity of objects) (cf. originality, Guilford's third criterion), the idea is to force people to think in more or less paradoxical ways. Examples of this are to put the problem the other way round, or to use an 'ingenuous' person charged with asking the right questions. Another example is Bono's game, the 'six thinking hats', which looks at a problem from six radically different points of view, materialized by wearing different-coloured hats.

A third category, designed to encourage wider exploration (cf. elaboration, Guilford's fourth criterion), adopts a different perspective. Instead of thinking differently using their own natural resources, people are encouraged to observe the outside world. This can consist of increased awareness of meaning and forms by being put in real situations (do it!), as close contact can help lift certain inhibitions in thinking. These techniques are more or less the opposite of brainstorming: people are no longer asked to use their own capital of knowledge or feelings but to submit themselves to new, sometimes surprising learning processes in order to capture new ideas. Rather than organizing a workshop at a seminar and asking the participants to be creative, it is sometimes more effective to ask them to go and visit their clients or their competitors or any other place where discoveries are to be made.

Guilford's criteria and creativity techniques can be seen as a specific design strategy: *a strategy mainly based on expansion*. These properties of expansion are also to be found in the world of industrial design: the 'variety' can be found in the ability to propose a wide range of possible forms from a given conceptual brief. For example, 'hammering in a nail without hitting your fingers' has given birth to several concepts in the past (*see* Chapter 6). The challenge of innovative design is precisely to revise the identity of objects, as we saw with objects which aid mobility (Chapter 2). 'Exploring the world' can be found in the ability to explore the universe of new knowledge, whether through research, study of uses, through history or the exploration of other functions or other industrial worlds.

However, innovation managers are often baffled by creativity techniques.[1] Although they have the great advantage of proposing criteria to evaluate

---

[1] It was a request from one of these new innovation departments (at Renault) that led to the work on creativity (Hatchuel 2004a) that serves as a base here. On creativity and C-K design theory *see* Le Masson, Hatchuel and Weil (2007, 2008, 2009). For a short review on creativity, *see* the bibliographical appendix, Section 3.

expansion (variety, originality, exploring the world), these are usually not emphasized enough, meaning that this kind of approach meets with scepticism in the world of engineers, particularly in France. Creativity techniques are often used only in certain phases of the design process, especially the initial phases or for fire-fighting in difficult situations, whereas for an innovative design function, the power of expansion seems to be required throughout the process. Creativity techniques also run the risk of coming up with clichés and provoking reservations from the experts. For instance, a team working on a piece of electronic equipment is asked to think about the system as if it were a pencil or an elephant. The more the object chosen for comparison is disconcerting or eccentric, the more the exercise is likely to be successful, according to the method's promoters. It is easy to imagine the amused or ironical reaction of a top specialist faced with this sort of exercise, particularly when told that some of the people invited to take part know nothing whatsoever about electronics or the content of the project in question. Finally, this approach leaves no room for scientific research and often leaves designers perplexed by new ideas that may be very attractive but that can hardly be passed on as they stand to an engineering or R&D department.

This dilemma has nothing to do with an aversion to the expansion itself but stems from the fact that innovative design reasoning must also respect criteria other than those of the power of expansion, and vastly contradictory to it. In practice, the formal framework must also prepare the ground for all the dimensions of the *I* function, including the reuse of excess knowledge and the activation of both *R* and *D*. The expansion seems to be in conflict with the notions of coevolution, repetition, economizing resources and gradual building of trajectories, which could be seen at both Tefal and Saint-Gobain Sekurit.

The imperative of variety and divergence is faced with the necessary convergence regarding products; a prudent approach dictates that the latter should be put to the test of the market on a regular basis.

It seems difficult to reconcile originality and the incessant revision of the identity of objects, with the concern for continuity in exploring areas of values and building product lineages.

The need to explore the world seems to be in contradiction with the notion of reusing the excess knowledge produced.

From this point of view, creativity techniques seem very limited. Can we find a formal framework capable of solving these apparently insuperable contradictions (*see* Table 10.1)?

Table 10.1. The paradoxes of innovative design reasoning

Power of expansion (creativity)	Effective expansion
Variety: divergence	Convergence
Originality: revising the identity of objects	Design guided by a target value
Exploring the world	Reusing excess knowledge produced

10.1.2   C-K theory, a dual expansion theory

Armand Hatchuel (1996b) and later Armand Hatchuel and Benoît Weil (2003) developed an original formal framework of design reasoning called the C-K theory. We shall see that this formal framework enables a rigorous description of innovative design reasoning and solves the paradoxes mentioned above. Its fundamental principle involves separating two spaces:

The space of concepts, the 'starting point' for all designers. The notion will seem obvious for industrial designers: a 'women's car' is a concept. However, if an engineer is working on a 'fuel cell', for instance, this is a concept too. A concept does not represent reality but a potential for expansion. A concept cannot be judged straight away: it is not a question of being 'for' or 'against' the internet in the car, or 'believing' or 'not believing' in it. Working on a concept entails putting off judgement and specifying the concept by adding attributes to it. A concept is validated using knowledge that exists or that is created for the occasion.

The space of knowledge contains the validated propositions, which may be technical, commercial, social, regulatory, etc. All new knowledge produced by test, trial or measurement techniques (i.e. research in particular) consists of adding propositions to the knowledge space.

Design involves gradually specifying a concept in C by adding properties to it that come from K (possibly also producing new knowledge). This gives a series of movements backwards and forwards between the C space and the K space (*see* the box below for more details).

C-K theory: a formal theory of design reasoning

Below are some of the key notions of C-K formalism. For further details, readers are invited to consult the following publications: Hatchuel and Weil (2002, 2003, 2009) and Hatchuel, Le Masson and Weil (2004a). To understand the positioning of C-K theory with respect to other design theories *see* Hatchuel (2002) regarding Simon's approach to design; Kazakçi (2009) for the relationship to intuitionistic logic; Reich *et al.* (2008) for the relationship between design theory and maths; and Shai *et al.* (2009) for the relationship between infused design and C-K theory.

C-K theory aims to provide:

- a rigorous definition of design reasoning, at a level comparable to that used for decision-making theory;
- a better understanding of the organization and management of design in innovative projects. The theory is used in three different contexts: assistance for design teams in practical industrial situations (it is mainly this context that we explore in this book), the mathematical foundations of the theory (Hatchuel 2006) and software tools for assistance with innovative design (Doumas 2004; Kazakçi and Tsoukias 2005).

The space of concepts is a set of propositions without a logical status (neither true nor false). The K space contains propositions that have a logical status (true or false). This means that the design process is independent of the predicates of truth, although they need to exist. It should be noted that a concept is always K-relative: it must be comprehensible in K, otherwise the design process stops; it must not have a logical status; and it cannot be defined by extension or only by understanding, in other words C is defined solely by the Zermelo Fraenkel axiom system without the axiom of choice. It is impossible to 'pick out' an element of C.

Design then seeks to:

- extend the concepts (δC) with the existing knowledge (K);
- extend the knowledge (δK) with the existing concepts (C);
- using the operators: K→C and C→K but also K→K and C→C.

In formal terms, it is not possible to do anything but add a new proposition to C (or withdraw one). The most important thing is the nature of the attributes added: if they are considered to relate naturally to the concept, the partition is restrictive; if, on the contrary, they are original and change the identity of the concept, this is a creative process. In this case, the partition is referred to as *expansive*. After one or several partitions, the resulting concepts may have acquired a logical status (they become true or false in K), in which case they form a 'conjunction' and become propositions of K. However, propositions do not always acquire a logical status; associated concepts may remain disjunctions. It is generally necessary to produce new knowledge in K through exploration in order for these concepts to acquire a logical status.

Fundamental results in contemporary set theory prove the consistency of the design reasoning (Hatchuel 2006; Hatchuel and Weil 2007).

The process is illustrated in Figure 10.1. It shows the initial situation (a still barely specified concept and a few pieces of reference knowledge) and the situation after a few design stages (a better-specified concept and new knowledge). Each knot in the tree is in fact a sub-set of the unit above it and therefore a sub-set of the initial concept.

We can now show how the C-K theory solves the paradoxes of innovative design reasoning (*see* Table 10.2):

Table 10.2. How the C-K formal framework solves the paradoxes of innovative design

Power of expansion (creativity)	Effective expansion	Formal solution of paradoxes
Variety: divergence	Convergence	Tree-like structure
Originality: revising the identity of objects	Design guided by a target value	Expansive partition vs C_0 (root concept)
Exploring the world	Reusing excess knowledge produced	Creation of knowledge (K→K) vs. activation of knowledge (C→K)

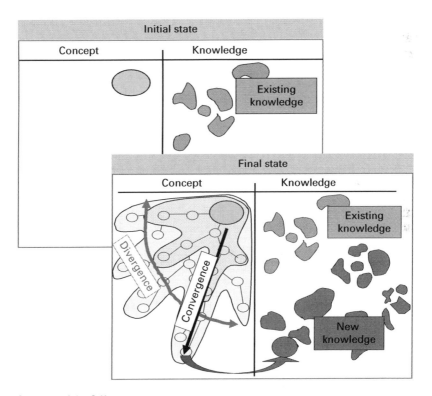

Figure 10.1 Summary of the C-K process

- The reasoning is *both convergent and divergent*: it is the tree-like structure of C that gives this dual property, as progress can be made either 'vertically' by adding successive properties ('convergence' towards a better-specified product) or 'horizontally' by finding different variations at a given level ('divergence').

- The reasoning *revises the identity of objects, whilst allowing for continuity in the exploration.* The area of value is the root concept. The revision of the identity comes from the contrast between a set of properties given to an object in K and the addition of a surprising property to this same object in the C space. A given general concept can enable the revision of several objects in the K base. The distinction between the root concept and the expansive partitions solves the contradiction. It should be noted that it is not necessary to start with a 'good idea' (an expansive partition) to 'begin' a design process. The expansive partition can appear during the reasoning process.
- Reasoning refers to both *exploration of the world* and to *expertise,* depending on whether it is an expansion of knowledge (K→K operator) or the activation of existing knowledge. The formal framework enables both 'reuse'-oriented and 'exploration'-oriented strategies for activating K.

10.1.3   Illustration: a new engine for missions to Mars

The properties can be illustrated with the following concrete example.

'How can we design an Mg-CO_2 engine for Mars explorations?' The CNRS laboratory for Combustion and Reactive Systems, which works for the European Space Agency (ESA), was studying this question at the beginning of the 2000s. The idea behind the concept was that, whereas a car engine burns fuel with an oxidizer provided by the surrounding air (oxygen), a space rocket has to take along both the fuel and the oxidizer. The initial mass for a sample return mission to Mars can be quite considerable: a 500kg mission has to leave Earth with more than 10 tons of fuel. Several people had had the idea of using a source of energy available on Mars, so that it would be necessary to take fuel for only one journey when going in each direction. As the atmosphere of Mars is composed of 95 per cent CO_2, could CO_2 be used as an oxidizer? Although CO_2 is a relatively stable molecule, it does enable the combustion of metals in certain specific conditions of temperature and pressure, but the metallic fuel was yet to be identified. One of the world specialists in combustion, Evgeni Shafirovich, worked in the CNRS laboratory. In the 1990s, he showed with other researchers that it was possible to generate a 'specific impulse' from the combustion of magnesium (Mg) particles in an atmosphere of CO_2. This result meant that magnesium, transported from Earth, was a serious candidate for an engine capable of bringing the mission safely back to Earth.

However, was this knowledge, which came from research, actually 'applicable'? There was one clear criterion for assessing this: the landed mass on Mars. Was the landed mass lower with $Mg-CO_2$ than that required for the same mission with a traditional propellant? Studies on this question gave a negative answer, suggesting that there was no advantage to be gained in using the new engine.

Could the project be continued? One solution was to look for all the possible scenarios in which an $Mg-CO_2$ engine would be better than one with the normal propellant. A special team was set up to systematically analyse all the scenarios of missions using $Mg-CO_2$ fuel. Each scenario was evaluated on the criterion of *landed mass on Mars*. Once again, the results were quite clear: in all the scenarios, $Mg-CO_2$ was less efficient than a traditional fuel.

The story could have ended there, with research once again the victim of development constraints or its inability to fully take them into account. But the head of the laboratory, Iskender Gökalp, asked a student studying engineering design and management at the Ecole des Mines de Paris, Mikael Salomon, to use the C-K framework to take another look at the results. The aim was to see whether the design reasoning had been sufficiently rigorous and whether it was possible to identify alternative paths that had been neglected and that might bring the project to life again. The study, carried out in 2003, led to the academic publication the same year of 'Mars Rover vs. Mars Hopper' (Shafirovich, Salomon and Gökalp 2003), which indicated new possibilities for $Mg-CO_2$ combustion for Mars missions.

First, the C-K formal framework helped explain the primary stages of the reasoning. The initial question was a concept in the theoretical sense, as the proposition 'an $Mg-CO_2$ motor for Mars exploration' had no logical status but could nonetheless be interpreted in the K base ('engine', '$Mg-CO_2$' and 'Mars mission' are known terms). This disjunction was written in C in the space of concepts. The two successive partitions resulting from the research (sufficient thrust, then whether or not it was a sample return mission) were then added to this space. The new knowledge produced by the research on this occasion was then written in K (*see* Figure 10.2).

We can now describe the stage consisting of finding missions. The concept became 'an $Mg-CO_2$ engine for a mission without sample return'; mission scenarios were generated in the K space. The concept was partitioned with each of the n scenarios generated and the scenarios were evaluated one after the other (in K). All the scenarios resulted in negative conjunctions.

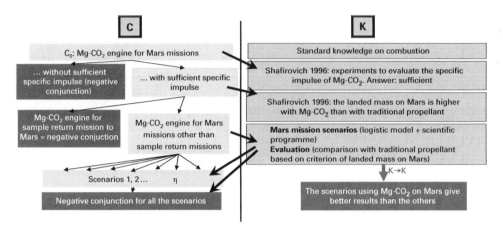

Figure 10.2 'Research' and 'development' reasoning

Guide to reading C-K graphs

Light grey background: restrictive partitions and existing knowledge.

Dark background, white characters: expansive partitions in C and creation of knowledge in K.

The arrows are C→K or K→C or even K→K operators. They schematize the main stages of the reasoning.

What was the next stage? The previous calculations were additional knowledge in K that had been used solely for purposes of evaluation until then. With an innovative design approach, this knowledge encouraged the idea of structuring the 'missions' differently, because the figures, although negative, seemed slightly better when $Mg\text{-}CO_2$ was used on Mars. This suggested a new partition of the missions: the initial concept was divided into 'used only on Mars' (versus used elsewhere) (*see* Figure 10.3). In this case, a new space had to be explored: *the possible uses of $Mg\text{-}CO_2$ technology on Mars*. This partition led to the acquisition of knowledge regarding mobility on Mars. The study revealed that mobility was not a question of just amplitude or speed but also of sensitivity to unexpected external conditions (storms, etc.) and the ability to make the most of opportunities, especially scientific ones. Hence, a partition had to be made between *planned mobility* and *unplanned mobility*. The concept of 'hopper' appeared at this point. In this way, successive expansions led to a drastic revision of the identity of the object, thus underlining the fact that the evaluation criterion was no longer the 'landed mass on Mars'.

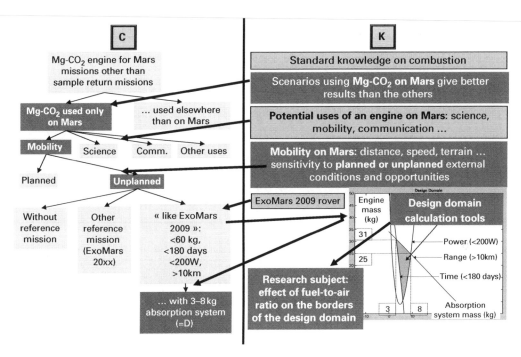

Figure 10.3 The object's identity is revised; the hopper concept appears; and reasoning continues until *R* and *D* are activated

The result of this design work was far from negligible. A real value space emerged for Mg-CO₂ and the ESA was again willing to finance the project.

However, it was difficult for the research laboratory specializing in combustion or the Mars mission's development teams to use the concept of 'unplanned mobility'. The design strategy therefore entailed adding properties to the initial concept to *enable learning processes in R or in D*. In this way, work was done on a hopper, capable of replacing the rover planned for the next ESA Mars mission, ExoMars 2009. At this point, the working hypothesis was a hopper weighing less than 60kg, capable of carrying out its mission in less than 180 days, consuming less than 200W (with energy from solar panels) and travelling at least 10km. This did not mean that all hoppers had to respect these constraints, but the assumption was that working on a hopper with these characteristics would create knowledge applicable in other situations.

Under the constraints of the space rocket's equations and knowledge on technology for absorbing CO₂, these new objectives immediately imposed quite precise dimensions for the mass of the Mg-CO₂ engine and of the absorption system, which represented the 'design domain'. *R* and *D* could work on this design domain: D was to develop an engine that met the 'specifications' in terms of mass; R was to look at the impact of changes to the combustion parameters (fuel-to-air ratio, for example) on the borders of the domain.

Does this example contain the properties expected from the formal framework?

Convergent and divergent: the Mg-CO$_2$ case showed the criterion of variety in the proposed paths but also showed a form of convergence by gradually identifying a design domain for the engine and questions that R and D could handle.

Revising the identity of objects and area of value: the concepts of a hopper (versus a rover) and of unplanned missions (versus scenarios) were revisions. All the same, there were without doubt many potential uses for Mg-CO$_2$.

Exploring the world and expertise: the traditional functions were present in the calculation of the design domain, for which the space rocket's equations were vital, but new pockets of knowledge appeared, such as knowledge on the conditions of mobility on Mars and data on CO$_2$ absorption systems.

The C-K theory provides a language for the activity and explains the general, and at first sight antagonistic, properties of innovative design reasoning. It represents vital progress towards a model of collective action.

10.2 The innovation function: organizing collective innovative design

As for the other dimensions of the collective action model, the technical substratum, the type of performance and the forms of organization, it can be observed that the formal framework presents an interesting property: it can describe the rule-based design reasoning of R&D as well as the innovative design reasoning concerning an innovation field. An innovation field can be formally described as a C_0 concept and an associated K base, which can in some cases be very limited. In the C-K formal framework, one of the reasonings made in development – presented in Chapter 8 – consists of adding properties to an initial concept in a predetermined order: first the functional properties, then the conceptual properties and finally the embodiment. For each 'level' of partitioning in C there is a unique, well-identified pocket of knowledge in K, i.e. respectively, functional language, conceptual language and the language of embodiment. C-K is therefore a general design theory that can be used in all types of design situations (*see also* Chapter 14 on this point).

10.2.1   Exploring an innovation field: design spaces and value management

However, a model for action cannot be deduced immediately as difficulties arise very quickly when an innovation field is designated:

Where is the value and what is to be designed? For example, for car designers, what does 'design a hybrid vehicle' mean, given that they are aware of the existence of the Toyota Prius, a worldwide success? In this case, the concept of an innovation field might be badly defined: a hybrid that is not the Prius is a concept, but are we sure of its value? Concepts based on exploring the potential of a new technology often pose this sort of problem (cf. 'the fuel cell' in Garel and Rosier (2006)).

How can the design process be started when the knowledge base is either non-existent or obsolete? For instance, how did a giant in silver film photography go about designing digital cameras?

What can be done to avoid an early end to an innovation field when there are so many obvious and apparently insurmountable obstacles surrounding it? How many innovative projects have been stopped simply because they could not prove from the start that they met a supposedly indispensable technical specification? In this case, the concept may be well defined and the K base already rich, but a strong negative conjunction seems inevitable due, for example, to the cost or draconian imperatives of certification (e.g. proving the airworthiness of an innovative UAV).

Once thought starts to be given to a project and the process begins, how can it be explored without going in too many directions at the same time or without limiting the explorations to arbitrarily chosen directions? It is easy to imagine that the reasoning will not take place in a single stage, but how can the different stages be defined, given that the definition of the stages results from successive learning processes?

The C-K theory helps to rapidly identify the major difficulty: it is neither the initial concept nor the initial K base that poses a problem but rather the operators.[2] The difficulties mentioned above are all linked to questions regarding the operators to be mobilized. The creation of knowledge (ΔK) and its mobilization in the reasoning in fact represent the management of exploration in an innovation field.

In formal terms, it is a question of managing the elementary design operators (C→K, K→K, K→C, C→C), sometimes in sophisticated combinations,

---

[2] It is tempting to 'select' the favourable C_0-K_0 configurations. But which selection criteria can be used, given that the value is precisely one of the results expected from the process? This is why the challenge is to focus on controlling the exploration.

corresponding to design actions such as simulating, modelling, testing, validating, discovering, prototyping, calculating, optimizing, selecting, organizing a focus group or observing uses. Managing the exploration process for an innovation field means making these elementary actions possible.

To describe this essential management object – the possibility of partitioning to explore innovation fields – we need a new notion, which we call a design space. It is a work space in which it is possible to initiate the learning processes required for design reasoning. In formal terms, it is a sub-set of the initial set $\{C_0, K_0\}$ in which the designers can learn things about what must be learned to explore the innovation field.

> ## Design spaces in the C-K formal framework (Hatchuel, Le Masson and Weil 2006b)
>
> The definition of a design space can be explained using the C-K formal framework. A design space can be defined as a C_0^*-K_0^* configuration with a clear link to the initial C_0-K_0 configuration:
>
> C_0^* *is related to C_0 by changing the attributes of the given entity: C_0 being of the form 'entity x with properties $P_1 . . . P_n(x)$', C_0^* can be 'entity x with the properties $P_i . . . P_j$. $P_1^* . . . P^*_m(x)$' where $P_i . . . P_j$ are properties chosen among $P_1 . . . P_n$ and $P^*_1 . . . P^*_m$ are new attributes, chosen to support the learning process.*
>
> K_0^* *is a set of knowledge that can be activated specifically in the design space (awaiting expansion). Therefore, $K_0 - K_0^*$ is a knowledge base that* cannot *be used by the designers working in the design space. It may seem strange that the design space restricts* the K space to be explored, but K_0^* can also force the return of knowledge that would not have been immediately activated in K_0.
>
> The design process in C_0^*-K_0^* is always a dual expansion δC_0^* (new attributes added to C_0^*) and δK_0^* (new propositions added to K_0^*).[3] In other words, the C-K formal framework is still appropriate in a design space.
>
> The relationship between the global C_0-K_0 and the design space is modelled with two types of transition operators. The first are operators going from C_0-K_0 to C_0^*-K_0^*, called *designation operators*; the second are *extractions* from δC_0^* and δK_0^* to bring them back to the context of C_0-K_0. The designation operators can consist of adding some attributes to C_0 or adding knowledge to K_0.
>
> The C-K formal framework can therefore serve to describe the expansion processes, both at a global level (space for managing the value working on C_0-K_0) and on the level of each of the specific design spaces (C_i^*-K_i^*).

---

[3] δC represents a small expansion in C, i.e. few partitions and a limited revision of the identity of objects. ΔC represents a large expansion. δK represents a small expansion in K (a small number of new propositions in K). ΔK represents a large expansion.

An example of a design space: designing an innovative UAV without studying flight certification

The initial concept was C_0: 'an innovative unmanned aircraft'. But the first design space was built on 'an automatic helicopter for traffic surveillance' and the research focused on artificial intelligence (AI) and image analysis:

C_0: 'x = a flying vehicle', P_1 = 'flight certified', P_2 = 'unmanned', P_3 = 'innovative'.

K_0: all the knowledge available or able to be produced.

C_0*: take away P_1 and add P_4 = 'being a helicopter' and P_5 = 'for a traffic surveillance mission'.

K_0*: all the knowledge on aircraft, military missions or automatic flights was deliberately put to one side. Why? Because UAVs are usually built around automatic flight, thus immediately determining the modes of reasoning. The design space explicitly excluded automatic systems to explicitly direct the learning process towards disciplines that were underestimated in the world of UAVs: AI (how can an object 'decide' when faced with an original situation?) and image analysis (which tools can be used to scan and analyse the environment?).

Validation in C_0*-K_0*: the validation related to the disciplines in question and flight certification was not considered.

We consider the design space as the minimum basis for describing an exploration process in an innovation field. Some additional notions can be deduced from it. The design space 'results from' a more global exploration process and feeds this process in return. The space that initiates the design spaces and synthesizes the learning processes can be called the 'value management' space. The relations between design spaces and value management are modelled using designation operators for building the design space, and extraction operators for integrating the learning from the design space into the overall reasoning. With these different notions, the exploration process for an innovation field can be summarized in Figure 10.4.

It should be noted that this modelling helps designate the actions to be carried out to deal with any difficulties encountered when exploring the innovation fields:

If the initial concept is badly defined, if it is difficult to make the disjunction or if the value appears to be very low, the exploration can be launched on a concept derived from the initial one. 'A hybrid car other than the Prius' could, for example, become 'a hybrid car with a French touch'.

If there is a lack of knowledge, the notion of design space helps create it and manage this creation. Conversely, the design space also helps manage cases where there is too much knowledge by arbitrarily limiting the exploration to a small number of K bases.

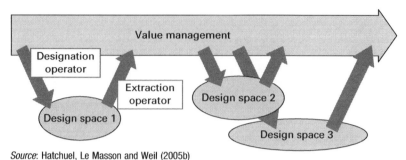

Source: Hatchuel, Le Masson and Weil (2005b)
Figure 10.4 Value management and design spaces

> If a killer criterion seems to be essential, it is possible to focus the exploration in such a way as to explicitly refuse the criterion in question. 'We can do the survey first without cost calculations'. For the UAVs: 'We can limit the exploration to simulated flight UAVs', or 'We can limit the exploration to a limited number of flights in a secured air space'.

As the process advances, the dual expansion takes place simultaneously: at the level of value management and at the level of each of the specific design spaces.

10.2.2   Innovative design management

At this stage, we can introduce a model of collective action for exploring innovation fields. Having described an acceptable model of reasoning for innovative design, we can move on to the other three dimensions.

The objects to be managed: the specifications stipulated that it was a question of managing innovation fields. Value management and design spaces appear to be the objects to be managed when exploring innovation fields. Actually, the notion of design space generalizes traditional notions, such as trials, focus groups and prototyping. The notion of value management gives visibility to things that are usually managed by a few innovation managers (design strategies and risk, project portfolios, etc.).

Performance: the specifications stipulated that excess knowledge was to be reused without stabilizing the identity of the objects. Several forms of indicators can now be considered. First, indicators on outputs. The C-K theory helps explain the value of design reasoning and therefore everything that can be 'reused'. Contrary to development, which retains only the new

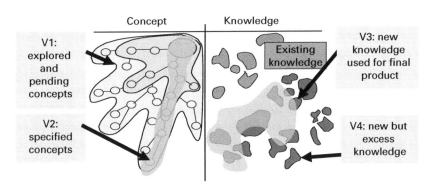

Figure 10.5 The value of an exploration in an *I* function

products, and contrary to research, which retains only the new knowledge, C-K reasoning produces four types of values, as shown in Figure 10.5:

V1: the concepts explored but put on hold due to lack of time or resources;

V2: the concepts explored, which become commercial products passed on to the development department (conjunction);

V3: new knowledge used, which can create value for another product;

V4: new knowledge not used in the design reasoning but which can create value for another product.

Different weights can be given to these four types of value, depending on the demands put on the innovative design. For example, if a firm favours strong expansions the focus will be on the criteria of variety, originality and exploring the world that we saw when discussing creativity. These criteria correspond to V1 and V4. If a firm prefers to move towards rule-based design, it will favour V2 (a product and its near neighbours) and the structuring of rule-based design languages (V3).

Another series of criteria refers to how the process of exploring the innovation field moves towards more systematic design (R&D). In order to return to systematic design reasoning, the K bases must be structured using development language. The 'move' towards rule-based design can therefore be analysed in terms of the structuring of the languages of functions, concepts and embodiment that appear, exploration after exploration, at the value management level.

Performance is also measured by the economical use of resources (not in the sense of minimizing them but in terms of effectiveness). An estimate of the costs of an exploration is obtained by adding the costs of each design space.

Organization: the specifications evoked a conceptual core that activates R&D and feeds from the results of this R&D work. The language of design spaces helps explain several elements of organization:

Within an innovation field, the exploration is organized in successive or parallel design spaces to divide out the exploration work (in a similar way to explorers in the desert who decide to send out scout teams). In fact, some of the design spaces can be placed under development (a design space with precise specifications and suitable, controlled functions) or under research (a design space limiting knowledge exploration to well-defined scientific questions).

During the exploration of an innovation field, the *I*-type exploration also prepares future R&D: the move from *I* to R&D is prepared by gradually structuring *D* to enable it to take over the variations and evolutions in a product family: new functions, handing over from one team to another, go-betweens, etc.

Finally, apart from individual innovation fields, the *I* function consists of organizing the interactions between innovation fields and the rebuilding of the portfolio of innovation fields. *I* seeks to pool resources for exploration. In particular, an *I* function can prepare specific design spaces (rapid prototyping capacities, spaces for interacting with uses, privileged relations with leading customers who help guide the exploration, etc.).

These results are summarized in Table 10.3.

To avoid the slightest ambiguity, two comments must be made concerning the model:

The model is not a 'one best way' to be followed to the letter. It serves to *generate different forms of the I function*. For instance, an *I* function can focus on certain forms of expansion (preference for C or preference for K; or on the contrary, restricting expansions in C or in K); the innovation fields can take a variety of forms, as can the design spaces that support the explorations. The notion of performance can exploit the four values V1 to V4 in different ways and can have varying relations to rule-based design (and to the dominant designs or stabilized identities that go with it). It can aim to destabilize an identity or on the contrary aim for expansion without destabilizing the dominant design; or it can aim for the emergence of a new dominant design following destabilization. We will study some of these alternatives in the following three chapters.

Not only must this model be clarified (instantiated) for individual cases, it is also *incomplete*. In a specific situation, the basic language of the

Table 10.3. C-K and design spaces: elements of an action model for an *I* function

	Specifications for the *I* function	The *I* function (model)	The *I* function: what remains to be defined
Models of activity and reasoning	Coevolution of competencies and products	C-K of design reasoning, dual expansion (of knowledge and concepts)	Standard reasoning in certain situations (head of lineage, regeneration of functions, SBPs, etc.)
Objects to be managed – technical substratum	Innovation fields	Innovation field = C-K configurations + design spaces to explore them	Agenda, committees, time pacing, type of reporting for teams, etc. (tools)
Type of performance	Reusing of excess knowledge without stabilizing object identities	Outputs (V1, V2, V3, V4); either expansion (variety, originality, exploring the world) or K bases for rule-based design; cost	Drafting and explaining value creation and risk management strategies
Forms of organization	Conceptual core which activates R and D and is fed by their work	Value management/ design spaces + handing over to R&D + maintaining specific design spaces	Building up resources (financial and human), exploratory partnerships, 'mixed' cooperation (State, users, labs, etc.)

organization would still need to be defined. As the Innovation Manager would say: 'I need to be able to organize agendas and steering committees, fix schedules for work and regular meetings and provide my teams with steering, reporting and evaluation tools'. The solutions depend on the industry, the company, its knowledge base and the concepts it is exploring. However, the model helps to show that it is the innovation fields (introduced in C and K) and the design spaces that serve as a basis for defining the agenda, the committees, the meetings and the management tools. The same applies to other questions such as the need to explain strategies regarding value creation and risk management to the firm's general management and to the teams. All the necessary arguments can be found by explaining the controlled expansion strategies, using values V1 to V4 and linked to rule-based design. Questions such as methods of financing, forms of budgeting and type of recruitment would also need to be addressed. In this respect, there is a host of solutions, from traditional budget lines to internal capital risk and from traditional hierarchies to go-betweens or 'sleeping agents' trained by regular, rapid visits to the innovation centre. Once again, these forms of management will depend on the nature of the design spaces and the way design spaces and value management involve the other partner designers.

It is amusing to note that in this respect the *I* function model works as a 'conceptual model'. It aims to help create innovation functions in firms, by enabling them to imagine various forms and by giving them the means, for each of these forms, to define the details of the everyday operation of a given function (i.e. embodiment).

However, some elements of embodiment occur quite frequently and we would like to study one of them in more detail here: the steering tools. In the following paragraphs, we give an example of a tool for mapping the exploration of an innovation field, before going on to present a range of tools for innovative design currently being developed in a large firm.

10.2.3   Tools for innovative design

10.2.3.1   An example of innovation field mapping

The WITAS research project was financed by the Swedish foundation Knut and Alice Wallenberg and run by Swedish universities and the aeronautics firm Saab Aerospace (subsidiary of the Saab AB Group). WITAS was a blue-sky project, designed to serve as a catalyst and to generate a series of interesting research paths. For Saab, this project was a means of learning about an extremely open innovation field, that of unmanned aerial vehicles. The initial brief, 'to study flying robots', seemed appropriate for a blue-sky project capable of stimulating fundamental research and leading to significant progress on future applications in the area of UAVs. However, the brief presented precisely the difficulties that we pointed out concerning the exploration of innovation fields. Where to start? Where was the value: for instance, wasn't an automatic pilot already a flying robot? What knowledge had to be mobilized? How could the obvious obstacles be avoided (airworthiness certification)?

WITAS is a good illustration of the new forms taken by research. The question was not confined, it did not fit neatly into a specific discipline and the objects in question were not specified from the start. How could this sort of project be steered and how could progress be evaluated? How could the work be organized and what types of coordination could be set up between teams? Retrospectively, WITAS also illustrated the difficulties inherent in blue-sky projects. The project perimeter evolved constantly – with research teams from all over the world joining and leaving all the time – there were several successive project managers, some of the objectives changed drastically as the exploration advanced, particularly on the impetus of the steering committee, and paths were abandoned along the way, whereas others that had been explicitly excluded were reintroduced. In short, the project could seem chaotic, or even incoherent.

If analysed using R&D evaluation criteria, the 'results' of the exploration give rise to scepticism. Relatively little research was published and the publications that did appear did not directly concern the usual questions in the disciplines concerned. In terms of 'development', none of the prototypes seemed suitable for product development. WITAS was therefore not really 'good research' – in the strictly academic sense – or 'good development'.

Should WITAS be criticized, or is the system of evaluation unsuitable? We shall now demonstrate how an analysis in terms of innovative design takes into account decisive results acquired through a controlled process. The method of analysis consists of following the exploration of the innovation field at the value management level using the C-K formal framework.

First of all, we can identify two main design spaces and a value management space linking them. The steering committee was responsible for value management. It worked on a concept C0, 'blue-sky project in the field of UAVs', with knowledge on competition in the UAV sector, and challenges regarding automation but also regarding artificial intelligence and image analysis.

The first design space made the following restrictions: the K_1^* base excluded criteria such as industrial, commercial or regulatory feasibility. It essentially consisted of 'computer' and 'image analysis' disciplines and excluded competencies in automation and control. Why did they exclude these competencies despite the fact that they are usually used to study UAVs? Precisely to preserve the blue-sky status, by directing the exploration to more unusual paths. The concept C_1^* restricted the initial concept of a flying robot to initiate learning processes: it became an 'autonomous traffic surveillance helicopter'. Knowing that a real flight required knowledge of automation and control and that he would not be able to count on this, the project manager pointed out that it would be a *simulated* autonomous traffic control helicopter (C_1^*). The work was divided between three teams, dealing respectively with computer systems, image analysis and simulation. Having defined the first design space, it was then possible to produce knowledge. For several months, the teams worked in these specific, predefined areas.

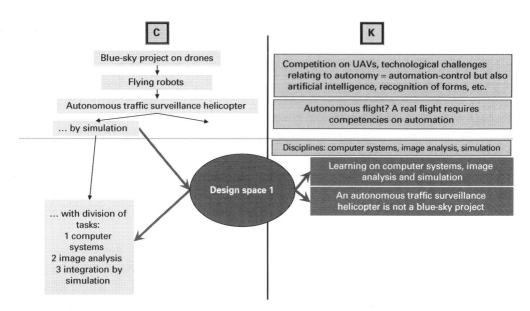

Figure 10.6   Initial configuration of the first design space

The results of this first design space were analysed by the steering committee, which evaluated both the expansions on the concept and the knowledge produced (*see* Figure 10.6). This evaluation highlighted an internal contradiction: an autonomous traffic surveillance helicopter made by simulation was no longer really a blue-sky project, given that it did not enable expansive partitions and that the learning processes concerned traditional disciplinary objects (as in a traditional research project). This resulted in a negative conjunction. The branch 'autonomous traffic surveillance helicopter by simulation' was impossible (it had a logical status: false). This was why the steering committee suggested exploring another alternative, an 'autonomous traffic surveillance helicopter with *a flying prototype*'. The existing knowledge showed that it was essential to acquire or to produce knowledge on automation (*see* Figure 10.7).

This new concept and new knowledge space defined a second design space, headed by a new project manager. But in terms of design reasoning, there were still several partitions to be made before they could organize the production of knowledge. A first path was explored concerning the architecture of the prototype and several possibilities were identified. This work (in K) showed that the choice of architecture depended on the mission in question. The design space became clearer: the aim was to work on scenarios for missions whilst using the knowledge acquired on architecture.

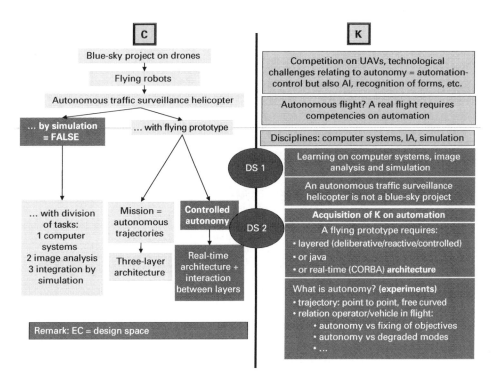

Figure 10.7 Summary of explorations

What were the results of this second design space? The experiments brought to light a major expansive partition based on the modelling of two important forms of autonomy, the autonomous trajectory versus 'controlled autonomy', i.e. the relation between the flying object and the pilot on the ground in different scenarios (degraded modes, change in vigilance level, alarms, etc.). Whereas the autonomous trajectory could be based on a layered architecture, controlled autonomy involved new real-time architectures in which objects could belong to different layers at different times depending on the events.

We have described the stages of the exploration using the notions of design space and value management. This analysis can be illustrated by a map of the innovation field, which summarizes the main results of the exploration and compares these results with the resources invested (*see* Figure 10.8).

In terms of resources: it consists of simply calculating the costs of each design space. The design spaces are represented as particularly sophisticated C-K operators (combining C→K, K→C, C→C and K→K). The design cost is the sum of these operators. It can be calculated in terms of the monetary

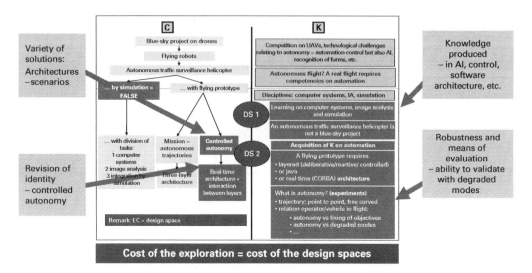

Figure 10.8 Evaluation of the exploration carried out on WITAS (the central section is a scaled-down version of Figure 10.7)

resources invested, the human resources or simply the time devoted to each design space.

In terms of results: the focus can be put, for instance, on the capacity of expansion in terms of reasoning. In this case, we use the evaluation criteria seen in work on creativity: variety (the variety of architectures explored), originality (revision of objects' identity, in this case the concept of controlled autonomy for a UAV), knowledge produced (in AI, computer vision, control, software architecture, etc.), elaboration or robustness (ability to validate with degraded modes, etc.) (*see* Figure 10.8). This work also prepared for rule-based design, particularly with respect to the exploration of original architectures, new methods of validation and the opening of functional spaces concerning controlled autonomy.

Other tools can be found in Elmquist and Le Masson (2009) on an evaluation framework for innovative projects; in Elmquist and Segrestin (2007) on the logic of technology acquisition through firm acquisition in the pharmaceuticals industry; and in Felk *et al.* (2009) on the evaluation of advanced R&D, based on the capacity to formulate relevant concepts.

10.2.2.3.2   Building a range of tools for innovative design

The question of management is at the heart of the range of tools for innovative design being developed by Renault. Renowned for its innovations, the car manufacturer is building this range in contrast to the existing range of tools for rule-based design, i.e. R&D:

A convergence plan fixes key project meetings and work packages for each person, based on the list of competencies and players.

The specifications for features, functions and technical aspects provide sequential definitions of the objectives and the contracts between the different players supplying defined components.

The value of features such as acoustics, thermal control, safety, etc. is an incentive for defining validation protocols and adopting the right solution as quickly as possible.

QCT reporting systems monitor progress in the overall project on a regular basis, with respect to the company's profitability and customer needs.

These tools are suitable for situations where there is a need to organize convergence towards a single good solution, when the objectives are known, the functions and interaction processes can be identified at the start of the project, knowledge is available and the validation protocols are known. But, as we have seen, innovative design works on new concepts, new knowledge and potential solutions for the projects. The objectives have to be built or revised, interactions between the functions have to be redefined, bricks of knowledge are missing and the validation protocol must also be built. In these conditions, the above tools are badly suited to innovative design and, worse still, can actually be harmful:

The convergence plan fixes *ex ante* the perimeter and the competencies involved, and any paths considered at a later stage must stay within these limits. This restricts explorations and makes it difficult to build new competencies.

Writing specifications for features implicitly imposes, from the start, a reference solution and set values. The project is managed by 'drifting', seeking to limit any loss of value from difficult technical compromises. The project is not aimed at designing new values.

The value of features and the validation define the validation criteria and the associated prototypes from the start, focusing on a specific technical solution with validation essentially concerning the risk of system non-performance. In innovative design, processes of this sort encourage costly prototyping with uncertain results; too often, the failure of makeshift technical solutions kills the root concept and the associated value; there can be no surprises concerning the features, as prototypes of this sort cannot be used to redirect exploration to more interesting areas of research.

QCT reporting mainly focuses on details of design; it does not take into account remaining uncertainties and considers that the objectives are clear. It does not help manage the benefits of features emerging from an innovative design and often leads to the brutal ending of innovation projects.

However, it is just as harmful if there are no tools for innovative design.

If objectives are not defined *ex ante*, without management tools the exploration is just as likely to wander about in the dark as it is to come up with a sophisticated, original solution.

The competencies and interactions between the functions need to be redefined, but if there are no tools to identify the new functions and how they are to be coordinated, the exploration will be limited to small teams who find it difficult to hand over to others and tend to limit themselves to solutions to be found locally.

Prototypes no longer play a role of validation. They are supposed to facilitate the exploration, but without tools to control the reasoning, the designers use prototypes to find design paths. In this case, prototypes are required to represent all the potential solutions; they rapidly become more costly and take longer to produce.

It is not possible for reporting systems for innovative design to be stabilized, along predefined lines. But without tools to make the work of innovative designers more visible and easy to evaluate, they are ill-recognized and have a limited ability to manage partners.

On the strength of these observations, a team at Renault in charge of promoting innovative design and its methods – the *Pôle Logique d'Innovation* – is currently working on a range of tools for innovative design. The range is being built up gradually and tested on internal projects. It is structured by questions that encourage the swing from rule-based design to innovative design.

If the objectives are clearly defined and fixed from the start, functional specifications can be written. If not, a tool asks for information concerning the potential value targeted (root concept C_0), the knowledge base to be used to generate it (K_0) and the initial explorations to be made (identification of the first design spaces).

If the perimeter of competencies and inter-functional operating is known at the start, division of work can be organized in a traditional manner. If not, the tool summarizes past explorations and identifies competencies in the process of being prepared (identification of past reasoning, of C and K generated at that time and the design spaces mobilized).

If there are validation protocols, the value of features and convergence plans can be used. If not, a tool helps identify appropriate design spaces and map the results of an exploration by prototyping.

If a set framework can be used for the reporting system, QCT reporting is used. If not, a tool gradually maps the explorations made in C and in K.

10.3   Conclusion: using the model to manage typical innovation fields

At the end of this chapter, we have a model for collective action that is coherent with the missions of an *I* function. We have given a few examples of tools to help this action, but we must emphasize the point that it is not a reference model or a 'master model' that can be simply duplicated. It is a conceptual model that should be used to help think up and organize the collective action of *ad hoc I* functions.

What forms can this model take when more specific innovation fields are explored? It is easy to imagine that they will be different if we are talking about front-end functions or creating new business, situations with intensive research or on the contrary where knowledge is produced easily. The forms depend on how much the identity of the objects is called into question and may require knowledge to be produced on original subjects such as uses or potential markets. In the following chapters, we study three main types of innovation fields:

The creation of product lineages, with restrictions to minimize the production of knowledge. This can be the task, for instance, for marketing or business development units seeking to exploit the value of existing technologies instead of multiplying costly R&D programmes. Creativity and the search for the 'good idea' are omnipresent. We shall see that, in this case, success is not so much the result of effective screening of a large number of ideas as of the ability to base a relatively long process of design reasoning on astute modelling in the knowledge space.

The regeneration of competencies, with an obligation to minimize product modifications, i.e. to avoid entirely redesigning an often well-established business. This is obviously in symmetry with the previous situation: knowledge production is required, and prototyping, trials, research and new technologies will be brought up, but conceptual expansion will be limited. We shall see that preparing off-the-shelf technology is a risky myth and that it is often a question of managing the acquisition of knowledge by thinking about the value, whilst constantly working on the relations with the established development process.

The emergence of new business demanding new knowledge (new technologies, new uses, new values, etc.). Uncertainty is at a maximum; expansion is required in terms of concepts and knowledge. We shall see that there are alternatives to high-risk approaches involving large initial investments and long research projects in the hope of high gains. It is quite possible to develop a system of repeated experiments that gradually structures the value and the competencies.

These three types of innovation field refer to different situations of innovation, with very different players, forms of relations and performance criteria. However, the distinction is also founded in theory. The three types correspond to three distinct design situations in C-K theory: the first case corresponds to a large expansion of design and a limited expansion of knowledge (ΔC-δK); the second, the opposite, corresponds to an expansion of knowledge and a limited conceptual expansion (δC-ΔK); and the third case corresponds to a large expansion of both dimensions (ΔC-ΔK). Cases where the expansion is limited in both dimensions are more like traditional rule-based design situations. It is these fundamental differences in reasoning that lead to different forms of organization.

For each of these situations, we will try to bring to light the key characteristics of innovation field management, using the same criteria as before:

The characteristics of the design reasoning.

The nature of the design spaces and the forms of value management. In particular, we will explain the cases in which it is possible to use design spaces coming from D or from R and the cases where, on the contrary, original design spaces are required.

The forms of performance: which outputs should be preferred out of V1, V2, V3 and V4? What is the relationship with rule-based design? Is the aim to destabilize the object's identity or is this to be avoided? Or should another identity be restored? In what forms can excess knowledge be reused?

How can the transition from innovative design to R&D be organized?

Questions for further study and discussion

Compare innovative design reasoning with research and with development reasoning.

Who manages innovation fields? Can they be called 'project managers'?

Compare a prototype for D and a prototype for I.

What is an idea in the context of innovative design?

Compare the notions of design space and of trial and error.

Key notions – Chapter 10

Objective of this part: agenda, resources and behaviour of *I* functions

The foundations of the *I* function: C-K theory of design reasoning

Managing innovation fields: what has to be managed and designed for a repeated innovation strategy

The new design approach for demonstrators and prototypes

11 Type 1 innovation fields: design in the search for new values – the innovative forms of user involvement

How can explorations be organized to ensure that they lead to high-value, profitable innovations such as the nail-holder, but without requiring costly learning processes? The sort of innovations which we think we could have invented ourselves. The first type of innovation field concerns this type of project. It aims to find a new value without having to make heavy investments in 'science' or conquer new technologies. There are many examples which fit into this category, such as customized mobile phone casings and 'plip' remote control car door locking systems. Projects of this sort can involve high technology, but only if its development can be planned – without surprises – or if it has already been developed. Such innovations rely heavily on user involvement, but user involvement is not a recipe in itself: it can be a solution, but it can also be a trap. In this chapter, we show how to deal with this type of apparently low-tech, high-user-value innovation.

11.1 Examples of creations of new product lineages in large firms

To illustrate the issues at stake in the context of different industries, we begin by examining the case of Telia, a Swedish telephone operator, which at the end of the 1990s was confronted with the problem of designing mobile telephone services for third generation (3G) technology. The technical norms for 3G were already well established at that time, but designers were wondering how to create value for customers. They knew that 3G increased bandwidth, but what was it going to be used for? What areas of business would be pertinent, for the users but also for the firms? Which services ought to be developed and who would the customers be, bearing in mind that 3G would be available only in five to ten years' time?

At Telia, the research laboratory's network services department was charged with studying the question. Typically for this sort of strategic marketing, there were too many ideas: everybody had ideas to put forward for the services of the future, but were they 'good' ideas? At that time, Telia's challenge was to find a system for organizing the generation of a large number of varied ideas and for selecting the 'good ideas'. From the innovation field perspective, two latent questions can be identified: (i) What *reasoning* was followed, in particular with respect to the screening process? (ii) What *design spaces* were involved and who took part? Was it just a question of organizing a suggestion box and then asking experts to select the best ideas, or was it more complicated than that? (The case is studied in detail below.)

Another interesting case comes from the tyre industry at the beginning of the 2000s, when all the manufacturers were studying the concept of 'intelligent tyres'. Michelin had a wealth of expertise in tyres and mobility which, together with technological developments in electronics, opened up great prospects for new business in this domain. The difficulty was in knowing how to turn a promising concept into high-growth business. There were an infinite number of potential solutions, which could concern all the actors in the automobile world. Should they focus on drivers, car manufacturers, distributors, insurance companies, infrastructure managers or the public authorities? There was potential value in many areas and there was no lack of ideas, although many seemed risky and/or costly. Michelin addressed the issue by experimenting with methods for enhancing its technical explorations with reasoning on how value is created and shared (we will come back to this case later in the chapter; for further information, *see* Barrois and Lindemann (2004)).

The third example comes from the pharmaceutical industry and the case of a firm which had traditionally focused on two types of pathologies but was anxious to diversify its portfolio. In this context, the 'ideas' space was extremely open, as new pathologies, modes of action, active principles, means of legal protection, partners, etc. could all be considered. 'High throughput screening' tools could generate several hundred thousand or even several million potential molecules (Thomke 2003a), but were not suitable in this case as they work only if the pathology is known and the methods of treatment are well identified, or if the molecular architecture is already well defined. An alternative exploration method involving another form of screening consisted of organizing a process for selecting biotechnology firms, with a view to finding an 'ideal case' which met all the conditions for a 'good' drug (pathology, method of treatment, active principle, identified, validated galenic form, intellectual property rights, etc.). However, it rapidly became clear that the ideal configuration did not exist. For instance, there were interesting molecules in certain portfolios, but the means of action were uncertain and the conditions of validation complex; or there was a new means of treatment but it had not yet led to the discovery of an effective active principle. This was typically a situation in which conceptual expansion was required, to move from screening molecules or firms to designing all the above-mentioned elements. The reasoning involved far more than just 'choice' or 'optimization'; the resulting organization activated new learning spaces (case not studied here – *see* Backman and Segrestin (2005)).

11.2   Innovation field exploration strategy: 'depth first'

The aim of this type of innovation field is to create or identify new business, new values and new uses without long 'technological' or 'scientific' explorations. Even extensive market studies are excluded for cost reasons and also because they are not really relevant in a context where markets are being explored. There are strong constraints on exploring for knowledge; the work must either be based on known technologies or it must be assumed that the technology is forthcoming.

As far as organization is concerned, these explorations are often run by small research, advanced marketing or business creation units, with limited resources and restricted access to research laboratories and engineering and design departments. They favour go-to-market strategies with minimum knowledge production. Among the four aspects of the value of design reasoning (presented in Chapter 10), they favour the value of pending concepts (V1) and conjunctive concepts (V2) and minimize the production of knowledge on conjunctive concepts (V3) and excess knowledge (V4). The unit's aim is to adopt a prudent economic approach as very little is known about the market potential; costly dK must be minimized. However, although there is a limited expansion of knowledge, it is nonetheless vital in this type of exploration. Even if the value is based on the conceptual expansion (ΔC), the exploration strategy is based on this minimum learning (δK).

To illustrate this point further, we can look at the classic traps in this sort of situation.

In terms of reasoning, there is a strong temptation to generate and then screen ideas. This involves taking a simple concept and adding a 'good idea' among n possible ideas, given that n is a large figure and that the list is apparently easy to generate. Telia, Michelin and pharmaceutical companies adopted this approach. Since the production of knowledge is constrained,

Table 11.1. The exploration of ΔC-δK innovation fields

ΔC-δK	Traps	Challenges
Reasoning	Screening, 'width first'	Target expansive partitions based on pertinent dK remodelling. 'Depth first'
Design spaces (DS) and value management	Brainstorming; no dedicated DS	New, dedicated DS, favouring the revision of object identities (use-oriented DS)
Organization – relations between *I* and R&D	Isolation then transfer	Reconfigure *D* and *R*. Identify new competencies
Performance	'Good idea'; no repetition	End dominant designs (V1&V2) with aim of identifying the conditions for creating new rule-based design (V3&V4). Favour reuse of knowledge by high-level modelling processes (see Sekurit's protective/communicating membrane; Telia's remote control system)

it is assumed that the solution is readily available as there cannot be a long process of conceptual development.

In terms of organizing the exploration of the innovation field, screening processes often lead to badly organized production of knowledge. It is often thought that a few brainstorming sessions will suffice, but as we shall see in our industrial cases, it was in fact the introduction of highly controlled processes that enabled them to elaborate clever conceptual proposals.

Finally, in terms of relations with the other actors, there is a temptation to work in temporary isolation, assuming that development (*D*) will follow later, once the market concept has been validated. However, we shall see that one of the properties of conceptual expansion is that knowledge explorations are launched along very precise but also very original paths, i.e. in directions which can sometimes be quite far removed from competencies existing in *D*.

We can begin to see the challenges of this type of exploration. For the reasoning, the value (in C) must be structured to obtain expansive partitions, based on minimum remodelling in K. It might be necessary to create new design spaces to enable rapid, cheap, use-oriented explorations, the exploration of potential markets, minimum economic modelling targeting expansive partitions or the end of a dominant design. Finally, concerning relations between *I* and R&D, the challenge is to reconfigure *R* and *D* as and when necessary (new research questions, new competencies, etc.). These elements are summarized in Table 11.1.

In the following sections, we give an example of reasoning (the nail-holder case), an example of a new design space (Telia's use-oriented design space) and an example of relations with R and with D (the Michelin case).

Examples of ΔC-δK reasoning

To illustrate this form of innovation field, we can look at a few cases where reasoning in terms of value had a strong impact on the technical reasoning. Kim and Mauborgne (1997) studied cases such as multiplex cinemas and the Formula 1 hotel chain, where value reasoning made a great difference. In the first case, it involved gambling on large, out-of-town cinema complexes, with easy access by car, offering a much wider selection of films and improved sound, image and seating facilities; the second involved a bottom-of-the-range hotel, which cut certain services but focused on providing high-quality bedding, hygiene and sound-proofing in the hotel rooms. Although knowledge production remained important, it appeared to be of secondary importance and did not condition the value reasoning. People carriers, mountain bikes and parabolic skis are other examples of manufactured products where the value reasoning predominated. They led to important changes in the dominant designs and introduced new ways of using cars, skiing or riding bikes.

We can also find examples in other spheres, such as architecture. In the fourteenth century, architects were faced with the problem of building the dome for the Basilica di Santa Maria del Fiore in Florence. The dome was very large for that period and also at a great height. A host of architects put forward proposals – from 1366 to 1418 – for solving the problem of making scaffolding for such large dimensions. The successful proposal by Brunelleschi was a major conceptual shift, as it involved building the dome without any scaffolding at all, using the techniques available at that time (King 2000). Several centuries later, Jorn Utzon was also confronted with difficulties for the construction of the sail-like shells of the roof of the Sydney Opera House. For several years, he tried in vain to make concrete shells using the most advanced technology of the time. He then proposed a conceptual shift, which was to make the shells from a single sphere (Fromonot 1998), meaning that pre-cast elements could be used and assembled without scaffolding (*see* Figure 11.1).

Certain mathematical problems can also be solved with this notion of conceptual expansion as opposed to calculative approaches. For example, take ten bags of gold coins each weighing 20g. One of the bags contains fake coins weighing 2g less than the real coins. How can this bag be identified in one weighing? The solution is based on indexing: the bags are numbered and one coin is taken from bag 1, two coins from bag 2, and so on. If all the coins were real, the total weight should be $20\times10\times11/2 = 1100$g. The difference compared with this sum equals $2\times$k, where k is the number of the bag containing the fake coins. Another example: how can you make five rows of four trees with ten trees? It is tempting to look for solutions using a grid whereas the solution is in fact a five-branch star.

Sydney Morning Herald, 30 January 1957

Project following call for tender (1957): sail-like concrete shells

The Opera House today

Solution adopted: spherical shells with identical curvature

All the shells were made from a single sphere

Figure 11.1   The sail-like shells of the Sydney Opera House

11.3   Example of ΔC-δK reasoning: the Avanti nail-holder

As we saw in Chapter 6, the nail-holder was the first product designed by Avanti. It is typical of the products to which consumers react by saying 'I could have designed that myself', as there was a limited expansion in knowledge. It is easy to find ideas for driving in nails without hitting one's fingers, but although a large number of solutions had indeed been proposed in the past (see below), none had met with the same success as Avanti's nail-holder. That product involved wide-ranging explorations in C (this section is based on work by Jean-Pierre Tetaz and Vincent Chapel, who now head Archilab).

The initial concept C_0 was 'to drive in a nail without hitting one's fingers'. It was a concept: the proposition could be interpreted in K but the means of driving in a nail (a hammer) could entail risks for people's fingers, particularly if they were amateurs. How could it be partitioned? One alternative was to try to find a solution by chance. This of course gave rise to a host of ideas (*see* Figure 11.2 and historical patents, Chapter 6).

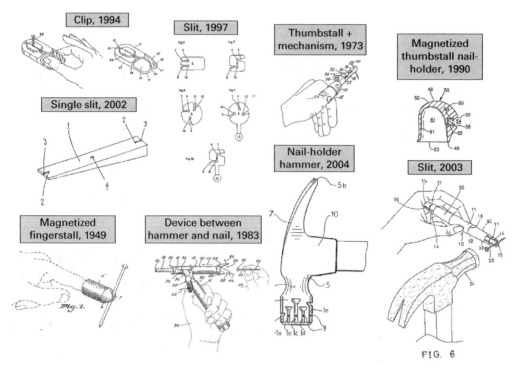

Figure 11.2 Examples of nail-holders

The C-K method served to structure this apparently simple exploration. The formal framework led to K in which the initial modelling concerned the action of driving in a nail. The hammer is held in the right hand (or left for left-handers), the nail in the left, and the energy for driving in the nail is provided by repeated hits (slow in the positioning phase, more rapid in the driving-in phase, then slow again in the final phase for a flush finish). This modelling rapidly led to two partitions: driving in a nail with or without a hammer (we do not explore the second option here), then with or without the left hand holding the nail. Figure 11.3 represents these initial partitions and the explorations of the branch 'C₀+hammer+left hand holding the nail'. In this branch, which may have seemed somewhat limited in scope, knowledge on the possible sources of injury compared with the different ways of hitting generated a number of more or less original solutions (cf. patents) and new alternatives.

A further modelling process explored the option where the left hand does not hold the nail, the aim being to model the role of the hand holding the nail (*see* Figure 11.4). The hand 'holds' the nail without immobilizing it

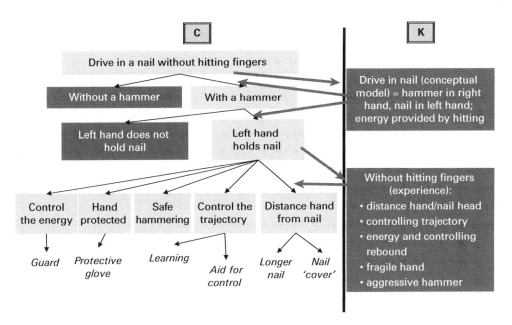

Figure 11.3 The initial partitions for nail-holders

completely. This was a major expansive partition: 'hold without holding'. The modelling helped study this partition. The aim was to find the means of 'holding' a shifting object on a fixed axis (there were several alternatives), of positioning it and, finally, of helping to guide it by finding the right support surfaces. These different levels gradually helped define the nail-holder: magnetized head, V-shaped, with support surfaces for the head and for the object's handle.

At the end of this exploration, there was an astonishingly large tree structure, with seven successive levels, based on *ad hoc* modelling processes that helped go from one to the other. It was the opposite of brainstorming as the idea was not to 'produce' ideas freely but to elaborate new solutions. The structure followed two paths: first, expansive partitions emerged – 'hold without holding' – and second, the modelling also helped elaborate complex solutions. In contrast, the past ideas were grouped into a small number of branches and were developed less than the nail-holder.

This example illustrates the reasoning. It should be noted that the modelling was based on work on trials and prototyping that was very different from a trial and error strategy. Trial and error is often seen like a lottery: coming up with an error means replaying. In the case of the nail-holder, the

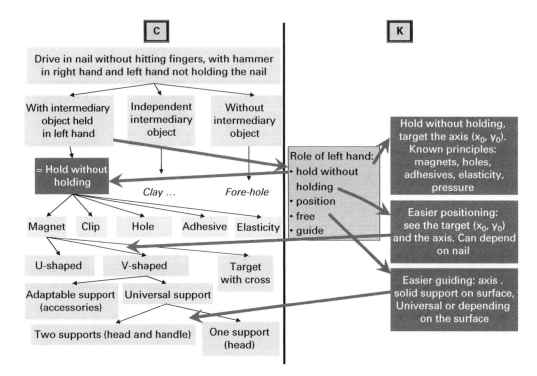

Figure 11.4 The nail-holder that 'holds without holding'

trials in fact supported learning processes – however simple – which helped restructure the space of alternatives and redirect the following trial. The process enabled Avanti to consider different ways of adding value, not only by selling a product but also by selling licences for other products, in particular an inexpensive nail-holder which is included in do-it-yourself furniture assembly kits.

11.4   Renewing design spaces by involving users – reverse engineering of users' ideas

In the case of the nail-holder, we saw some of the new design spaces mobilized, including 'uses'. Whilst minimizing δK, ΔC-δK explorations must often produce new knowledge. Traditional design spaces are often not sufficient. For instance, market studies produce a diagnosis on the dominant design but nothing about how to change it; R&D also works on the functions and disciplines of the dominant design. In the context of changes to object identities, new design spaces emerge to produce knowledge on what appeared to be the most stable elements. An interesting example of this is the case of studying uses, which are often partially configured by a dominant design. The identification of new uses should help move away from the uses inherent in the dominant design and also help identify pertinent value spaces for future customers.

It was this user-oriented design space that was mobilized by Telia's designers (this case is based on work by Peter Magnusson for his thesis at the Fenix Centre, Stockholm School of Economics (Magnusson 2003)). As we saw earlier in the chapter, a team in the network services department of Telia's research centre was charged with exploring future services to be proposed with 3G technology. This was clearly an issue involving innovative design. Mobile telephony had been available on the market since the mid-1980s, an operator's main service consisting of opening and maintaining a connection for verbal communications between two people. However, this role was changing due to digital convergence between telephony, television, GPS and the internet. Many different types of information could be combined and obtained through mobile phones, which had become a means of access to new services. New Universal Mobile Telecommunications Systems (UMTS), which were mainly designed to improve data communication, demanded far more of mobile telecommunication operators than a simple technological transition: it was the new services that would create the value. However, nobody really knew – particularly in 2000 when this work began – what values the users would find in the new services. Telia, Sweden's incumbent telephone operator, was confronted with this innovation field when it explored the new third-generation mobile phone services. One approach to the exploration was to involve users.

How was the design space organized? Telia selected a group of seventy-two students from the University of Karlstad (Sweden). They were asked to suggest one or more ideas for mobile telephone services that they would find useful as students. To give the participants a first impression of what 3G could be like and to stimulate their imaginations, they were given a device that simulated a 3G system: a clever system converted SMS messages (in GSM) and http queries (in IP) to give the students access to internet services on the ordinary mobile phones available at that time. The creative phase lasted twelve days, during which 374 ideas were produced (*see* Figure 11.5). Six experts from Telia, who were familiar with

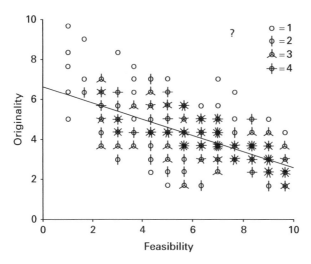

Figure 11.5   374 unfeasible or not very innovative ideas!

idea evaluation exercises of this sort in the context of mobile telecommunications services, assessed the originality and feasibility of the ideas, using
the CAT process (Consensual Assessment Technique), developed by
Amabile *et al.* (1996).

What were the results of this design space? The first observation concerned the ideas themselves: Telia's designers had been trying to find
feasible and original ideas, but were surprised and disappointed to find
that the ideas were either unfeasible or not very original. Was the method
to be blamed, or the user panel? In either case, the operation would have to
be repeated and a new design space created. However, in a bid to save time
and money, the designers tried to learn something from the initial findings.
They prepared a second series of results by taking another look at the ideas
that were both original and unfeasible. In one of the simplest and most
emblematic ideas, the user proposed the following service: 'For the third
time running, the delivery man made a mistake and gave me the wrong
newspaper. It would be good if the telephone could send a 10,000V electric
shock to teach him not to do it again'. Obviously, for technical, ethical
and legal reasons, the idea was not feasible. However, the experts wondered
whether it would be possible to propose a similar sort of service.
For example, if it was possible to warn the delivery man that he had made
a mistake so that he could correct it, that would be a feasible idea. This
was *a new output for the method,* consisting of identifying 'rough

diamonds', i.e. imperfect, badly worded ideas which became pertinent once they had been corrected, refined and simplified. When they went back to the original ideas, the experts identified a large number of 'rough diamonds'. However, these new ideas still posed problems as the designers were not sure whether they should be developed one at a time, or how they should select the best ones. Also, were they still talking about one service or a potential for *services*? Several new ideas sprang up in an ill-controlled manner from one rough diamond: when should they stop?

A third, even more important type of result appeared at this stage. During their work on the 'rough diamonds', the experts gradually realized why the delivery man idea had seemed so original. Until then, they had implicitly continued to model mobile telephone services as 'a connection for a verbal communication and data exchange', but in the case of the delivery man, the service was more like a remote control system. This notion created a knowledge space capable of designing new mobile telephone services which were more open than in the information exchange model. Several original ideas were gradually 'redesigned' (*see* the detailed example of the newspaper delivery man in Figure 11.6). The key point in this exercise was not so much that it generated new, feasible ideas as that it helped the designers change their initial perspective to a wider, more innovative modelling process for 3G telecommunications.

The idea was like a 'prototype' of a concept to be specified. The aim was not to 'develop' the idea but to find the underlying concept. By gradually de-partitioning (beginning at the bottom of the tree), a wider concept and new knowledge were generated. This is what we call the reverse engineering of an idea.

The remote control, the action (instead of information and data) and finally the interaction between action spaces were found in K. At the bottom of the tree, in C, were to be found the variations on the initial idea, which were possibly more feasible.

A major result was therefore found at the end of the experts' study: a remodelling of third-generation telecommunications. It was no longer just a system that 'opened and maintained a connection, with access to databases and query tools', but a system enabling the user to create new spaces of action at a distance (omnipresence).

The C-K formal framework can help us analyse the way this design space contributed to exploring the value (*see* Figure 11.7). In C_0 there was '3G services'. Without launching the design space, they activated knowledge

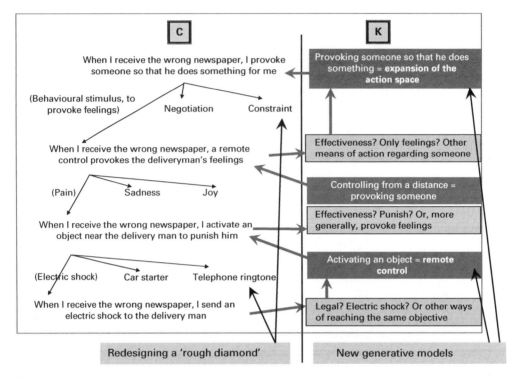

Figure 11.6 Redesigning from a user's idea – the reverse engineering of users' ideas

on 3G in K, i.e. model no. 1: '3G is a high bandwidth network for communication with internet databases, with systems for queries, access rights, etc.' With this knowledge, they generated a large number of services by instantiating each of the parameters in model no. 1 (Figure 11.7 shows the example of a road traffic information service).

The *design space* on uses helped create new knowledge about 3G: a large bandwidth network helps imagine communication as the interpenetration of two spaces of action (with a complex combination of sound, image, text, symbols, etc.). This model, i.e. model no. 2, contained the ideas of remote control and omnipresence. This knowledge produced a high-level expansive partition, which opened up numerous possibilities for future projects (e.g. services to help users configure their own action spaces for outside calls – 'do not disturb', etc.). The design space had therefore opened three different paths for Telia:

> To rethink configuration aids, due to evolutions in the action spaces of callers and called parties. The designers explored design spaces for designing *tool boxes* for users.

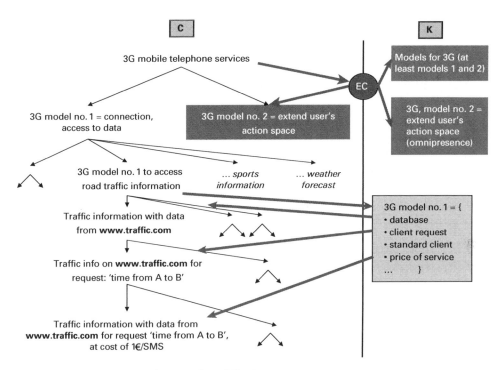

Figure 11.7 Structuring value from learning relating to uses

To rethink the location of the physical terminal (the telephone itself): it had become a key link between the system of information transfer and the action space. Telia made significant changes to its alliances with the terminal designers.

To work on new advertising slogans to appropriate the value space ('Telia's experience in mobile communications).

This case illustrates the three characteristic features of a ΔC-δK innovation field:

The reasoning: the temptation (and trap) of generating and screening ideas was constant and yet it was the efforts made to produce a small brick of new knowledge that led to the expansive partition.

Regarding the design space: a new design space (uses) led to new discussions on object identities. Even 3G had a fixed identity (as a telecommunications system). The use-oriented design space helped the transition from communications to the interpenetration of action spaces (omnipresence).

Regarding RID: the follow-up to these initial explorations did not only concern development but involved new design paths (designing tool boxes), new paths for communications and new alliances.

11.5 Value of the innovation: the impact on *R* and on *D* and the evaluation of *I*

Having focused on the reasoning and the specific design spaces, we can now study how *I* is linked to *R* and *D* in situations where a head of lineage is created (ΔC-δK).

As we have seen, there are traps involved in reasoning in terms of ideas and in organizations where 'good ideas' are supposed to go directly into the development phase. Admittedly, a low level of knowledge creation enables designers to use the existing functions and competencies, and in this respect the approach seems acceptable. However, organizations are just as sensitive to conceptual expansion as they are to changes in competencies, and they can be greatly upset by the slightest conceptual shift. Strictly speaking, development can take over from *I* only if the project still involves design in a dominant design context. If this is not the case, the major functions and their role in the design process have to be restructured. This can involve producing knowledge on a one-off basis (*R*); another solution is preparatory platforms, in charge of finding new compromises between the different functions for new concepts; and finally, in certain cases, the restrictions on in-firm explorations can lead to contacts with outside suppliers with competencies in the areas being explored. This raises the difficult issue of exploratory partnerships (Segrestin 2003) as the explorations must be managed and *ad hoc* contracts arranged. Hence, even in situations where dK is limited, it is vital to prepare for innovative concepts to be integrated into development projects.

The simplistic scenario of a unit charged with conceptual innovation which then hands over its 'good ideas' for development can therefore be replaced by an innovation unit with a large number of organic ties with the other actors in the design process. Michelin was a good example of this approach (Barrois and Lindemann 2004). The business development department worked on innovative concepts such as the 'intelligent tyre', but it did not work in isolation. The traditional product lines were involved in the process very early on, as soon as the explorations approached their work perimeter. The technical centre was also asked to investigate certain difficult scientific points, to help design prototypes and even to launch initial products. Partners were also contacted for the explorations, including future clients and future suppliers.

Complex martingales emerged in the innovation unit, which no longer simply carried out explorations to obtain new products. At that stage, its work consisted of carrying out projects ordered by other units and 'value management' activities linking several projects, with a view to studying new paths, lifting conceptual barriers and redirecting certain explorations. Rather than being grouped into project portfolios, the activity was organized into a complex tree structure of inter-related innovation paths. *I* was often highly fractal in nature: work on a given innovation field revealed its numerous variations, but also showed that it was itself one of the variations of a wider innovation field. Organizing learning rents involved taking advantage of extremely varied internal or external explorations, irrespective of the innovation field in which they initially emerged. One of the conditions for these rents to be effective was to constantly reorganize the tree structure, whilst retaining the minimum modelling (often on a very abstract level) to think up variations.

This echoes one of the aspects of the innovation function seen at Saint-Gobain Sekurit: a brick of knowledge on the theory of windscreens appeared in the high-level innovation system, and this brick helped organize the initial partitions and the innovation fields which followed. It was precisely this high level that guaranteed that learning rents were then possible between lineages.

The final key point in these situations is the evaluation of the quality of the exploratory work. Using the C-K formal framework, we can immediately say that ΔC-δK reasoning encourages conceptual explorations by maximizing two outputs: pending concepts (V1) and conjunctions (V2). On the contrary, it does not add value to the knowledge produced (V3 or V4) as one of the challenges of the reasoning is precisely to avoid dK. In positive terms, this means that it is possible to evaluate the ability to mobilize existing expertise and to build alliances. More generally speaking, an *I* function charged with ΔC will therefore be assessed on its capacity to work on new values (new business, drastic revision of existing business) in a federative manner (not redoing everything, making the most of explorations in progress).

It is clear that, if the assessment concerns V1 and V2, an effective exploration strategy entails careful management of learning (δK), however limited this may be, given that it is a key cost to be controlled and an essential lever for action to back up ΔC exploration.

Questions for further study and discussion

There are other areas in which original design spaces are emerging, particularly on the question of economic models. What are the specific features of a design space for economic models? Base the work on comparisons with traditional approaches.

Go back to the classical cases (Brunelleschi, the Sydney Opera House, Espace, parabolic skis, mathematics, etc.). See why they need in-depth reasoning, specific design spaces and organic ties to research and development.

Type 2 innovation fields: design by drastic technological change and by regenerating functions

The second type of innovation field involves regenerating functions. It covers a variety of relatively classic situations such as the use of promising technologies, reforms to functions, renewals in competencies, front-end functions or, more generally speaking, forms of 'innovative *D*'. It entails issues such as developing innovative technologies, solving recurrent problems, moving away from 'amateur' solutions, inventing 'creative compromises' (Weil 1999), launching technical 'monsters' and creating alliances and new interfaces between functions. In all these situations, the key focus is on knowledge production.

However, there are restrictions to such explorations as the aim is to *limit* the impact on the object to be designed, to avoid challenging neighbouring functions and to change the object's identity as little as possible. The context is similar to the design of complex systems, where one of the challenges is precisely to separate out, confine and reuse known solutions and avoid spreading constraints. The exercise entails renewing knowledge whilst changing only a minimum number of the object's attributes.

Examples of δC-ΔK

The predominant feature of δC-ΔK is an expansion in knowledge which has a significant impact but is mainly confined to value. This 'intuitive' situation has had wide coverage in economic literature and in the history of science and techniques. There are numerous examples of technical changes in an apparently stable functional perimeter, such as the change from cathode ray tubes to flat screens, from silver film to digital film photography, from steam to electric railways, from iodine lamps to transistors, from wind-up to quartz watches and from gas to electric lighting.

However, these examples are often questionable: was the expansion in C really so small and was it secondary compared with the expansion in knowledge? Is it really true, as a journalist said of silver film photography, that, 'although the technologies have changed, consumers' demands have been the same for over a century? Photography still has the same function, which is to keep a visual trace of loved ones, of places and events' (Leser 2004). Is it the case when mobile phones serve as cameras and there is a new function consisting of transmitting fleeting images in real time? Whatever the case may be, the expansion in C is of key importance: we are particularly interested in the way in which design organizations are able to control and manage this expansion.

Other examples relate to the most recent and most rapid forms of 'technical progress'. For instance, Henderson and Clark (1990) described how a rapid succession of new technologies produced the photolithographic processes required to manufacture electronic chips. More generally speaking, Moore's Law is an example of a situation in which the type of performance is unchanged (the processing speeds increase, but the notion still concerns processing speeds) whilst nonetheless producing a large amount of knowledge. For example, the latest microprocessors are capable of controlling the tunnel effect on an industrial scale whereas it used to be a mere scientific oddity or at best a sophisticated microscopic technique.

δC-ΔK situations can also be found when knowledge is a means of eliminating technical barriers. In the automobile industry at the end of the 1980s, cabling was beginning to pose serious problems. There were 3km of cables in a Peugeot 605 and the cable bundle for the Renault Clio dashboard weighed 6kg, took one and a half hours to mount and required weeks of training for the operators who had to master dozens of variations. Multiplexing simplified matters, but also led to the extension of electronics in cars. Another example is Michelin's radial tyre. Designed in 1946, the tyre's metal structure was very different from traditional tyres. Whereas with the traditional ply structure no distinction can be made between the tyre's various functions, the radial structure separates the radial carcass, designed to 'carry the weight', from the steel belt which reinforces the tread, designed to improve the grip. This separation helped improve the two functions and to explore compromises that had been impossible until then, but without changing the type of performance.

12.1   Taking advantage of new techniques: examples of δC-ΔK situations

The regeneration of functions takes place in engineering departments. A good example is the function of acoustics at Renault. For a long time, the job of the acoustics department mainly consisted of correcting defects during development, but in the 1990s certain vehicles attracted criticism and so a team was charged with working on reducing so-called 'harsh' noises. At that time, little was known about this sort of noise, so the team elaborated a typology of harsh noises, systems for measuring them, tools to quantify them and new models to understand the propagation of the vibrations that caused them. The modelling and the knowledge it produced helped to change the way certain components were designed and spectacular results were obtained in just a few years (e.g. the Vel Satis won the French government-sponsored Golden Decibel award).

Another example can be found in automotive glass. As we have seen, Saint-Gobain Sekurit had to gradually improve the performance of the function of shaping tempered glass (for side and rear windows) in order to keep pace with the functional trend for larger, increasingly complex glazing. How could the company maintain performance levels whilst also designing successive generations of processes? How should this be organized and what about testing? We shall come back to these questions later in the chapter.

A third case comes from the military aeronautics sector, where navigation is one of the key functions. The Swedish missile firm Saab Bofors Dynamic developed one of the world's leading navigation systems, based on original technological solutions, quite distinct from the traditional American systems. The story of how navigation systems were produced by Saab shows that the function was developed in an original manner: it did not involve a space for 'applying' knowledge found by research; nor was the research 'applied' by the functions; nor was it a case of incremental co-development, of updating an existing function. The project was carried out by an innovative design team, which had stable members over a period of twenty years. They seized on learning opportunities, particularly by taking part in most of the development projects, not only for missiles but also for certain fighter aircraft. They also made regular, successful use of internal and external research teams.

In this way, the team built up competencies enabling it to intervene effectively in highly constrained development projects. It was in a good position to discuss the products' features; it mastered high-level modelling processes which enabled it to intervene very early on in joint preliminary projects; it had tools for simulations, tests and certifications to control risk and optimize convergence; it knew the suppliers, their processes, the features to ask them for, the costs, etc. This third case is also particularly interesting because it did not only entail ΔK: in the context of major restructuring in the European defence industry, competency in navigation techniques became a form of service which could be marketed in its own right. The challenge for Saab was not to win contracts for complete missile systems but to obtain key positions in international consortiums, sometimes involving being 'designer of navigation systems'. In such cases, the aim was to master the language of the complex interactions between navigation features and the overall missile systems, in order to propose innovative features for missiles thanks to navigation. Although navigation features seemed relatively stable (navigation = 'increased precision'), the team gradually began to study conceptual expansions, including 'navigation and missile missions', 'typology of navigation for different missions' and 'how to enhance the value of navigation systems'.

12.2   Innovation field exploration strategy: 'width first'

Just as an innovation field whose main focus is to explore value (ΔC-δK) can be weakened through lack of attention to δK, explorations aimed at regenerating functions can run the risk of neglecting δC. Since the first thing to do in order to 'master a new technology' is to produce knowledge, there is a tendency to make simplistic hypotheses regarding C. For example, it is assumed that the concepts will emerge automatically once the technology has been validated and that the 'value will follow', or that the concept 'has to be as good as xx', meaning that the traditional specifications will serve to assess the new technology.

The risks are obvious. In the first case, there is the risk that no functionality will emerge, that no 'value' can be associated with the technology. In the second case, competition with existing technologies is harsh, so a single criterion may be enough to eliminate the potential technology. Worse still, the criteria used for the evaluation are so closely attached to the old technologies that it may not even be possible to evaluate the new ones (it is like assessing the power of an electric engine based on the size of its pistons).

Whatever the case may be, the first risk is to lose the investments made in the explorations. An even greater problem is that, if the project is not managed by value, the teams tend to be 'scattered in the knowledge space', carrying out trials and modelling in the hope of suddenly discovering unsuspected value, as if a decisive, well-formed concept will automatically emerge as a result of accumulating knowledge. The mythical features of nylon are a prime example of this situation (*see* Chapter 8).

Together with these traps in terms of reasoning, there are also traps in the organization of the exploration itself. There are two alternatives: either autonomous teams ask for more and more resources for demonstrators, prototypes, trials, etc. but are rapidly criticized for being isolated and for ignoring the needs and constraints, or the innovation process stays as near as possible to the development projects, to avoid fragmentation and to keep close to client demands, but this poses the problem of the spaces, time, resources and budgets devoted to explorations as such.

These ways of organizing the exploration process also correspond to archetypes in the relations with R&D. The great myth here is off-the-shelf technology or 'transfers' to development projects. The role of I is to ensure that 'everything' is ready and that the innovation can be integrated into the project without risks. The paradox is that development departments often consider things to be validated only once they have been subjected to the test of a project and a market launch.

These traps highlight the challenges of this type of exploration:

Concerning the reasoning, although the key activity is the expansion of knowledge, this must be managed by an expansion of the concept (i.e. managing by value). What do we mean by 'minimum δC'? It does not mean neglecting the value but making an effort to find minimum conceptual expansions, taking into account the objects' traditional constraints and attributes. There are several reasons for aiming to change the object identities as little as possible: to avoid upsetting other functions, to maintain the capacity for development, not to limit the innovative potential of other functions, not to upset market relations, to avoid forcing the customers to go through new learning processes, etc. Separation is often a good solution: either a new element of knowledge helps find a difficult compromise by separating the elements, or a new function can be separated from the other dimensions. A vital point here is that this is possible only with sound knowledge of the other functions, which often need to be reappropriated.

The value of the reasoning can be measured by the knowledge produced by the exploration, particularly in V3 and V4 (knowledge useful for the conjunctive concept, V3, or excess knowledge, V4). The value of this knowledge is all the greater if it is linked to the design process, particularly for rule-based design, and can be interpreted with the language of functions, conceptual models or embodiment.

In terms of design spaces, the aim is to control the relationship with the overall design reasoning (including the traditional D). As it is neither strictly separate from D nor completely assimilated with it, an innovation field focused on regenerating functions can, for example, use all the development projects as opportunities for marginal revisions to the design rules. If specific design spaces prove necessary, their relation to the design rules must therefore be controlled very

Table 12.1. The exploration of δC–ΔK innovation fields

δC–ΔK	Traps	Challenges
Reasoning	'The value will follow', at least respecting the existing criteria; finding value by chance	A small number of well-identified expansive partitions, which change object identities as little as possible. Dual effect of DK: not only a new function but also the reappropriation of existing functions
Design spaces and value management	Complete autonomy (costly and isolated); merging with D (exploration?)	Specific design spaces with regular project meetings with the development process ('catching up' with the pace of D), e.g. full-scale prototypes, market niches serving to validate
Organization – relations between I and R&D	Off-the-shelf technology, 'transfer'	Working on connections with D: ensuring both linking and separations from other aspects (confinement)
Performance	Temptation of V2 ('product'); repetition takes place in D; scarce, disruptive activity in I	V3 and V4 whilst maintaining links with the design process (i.e. on the condition that the generative model is respected). Continuous, fed by the experiences and difficulties in D. Capitalization by renewing the generative models and enriching the conceptual models (above all in D)

strictly. The challenge in this type of process is the value management, i.e. the ability to integrate these learning opportunities in order to build consistent functional languages.

As for the relations between I and R&D, the challenge is to find a balance between organizing project meetings throughout the systematic design process (being ready from the start or ensuring convergence during the projects) and the preservation of less restrictive learning spaces, to avoid 'makeshift' solutions during the project and head-on competition with validated technologies.

These points are summarized in Table 12.1.

In the following pages, we illustrate these points with a concrete example from industry.

12.3 Case study of the regeneration of a function: tempered automotive glass

12.3.1 Context

Once again, the case study concerns Saint-Gobain Sekurit. This time, it concerns the Industrial Development Centre (IDC) in Chantereine, near Compiègne, France, a few years before the case studied in Chapter 9. At that time, the challenge was to make larger, more complex glazing and the IDC's designers faced competition in inventing the best processes for shaping the glass. One of the most symbolic glazing projects in the mid-1990s was the rear windscreen of the Renault Clio 2 (*see* Figure 12.1). Saint-Gobain Sekurit won this key contract on the strength of a new process developed in the preceding years. Our study examines how this new technological generation was designed.

The high-speed tempering process (known as S4) is a perfect example of the regeneration of functions to improve existing performance. With a view to improving performance in terms of cycle times and edge quality, the project team totally revised the design of the tempering furnace and added new knowledge on automation and electronics – which had not been used before for this type of process – to the notion of 'horizontal, heat-treated glass'.

Figure 12.1 Rear windscreen of Clio 2

This regeneration of competencies took place in a difficult competitive context. Although its name gives no indication of this, the S4 process succeeded the ABS2 process, which was a disastrous failure for the IDC. In fact, the failure of ABS2 had nearly put an end to the design teams working on shaping processes, as they were in competition with an American furnace manufacturer, Glasstech, whose processes were just as good and cheaper. Founded by a group of American engineers who all had experience working with glass manufacturers, Glasstech began in the 1970s by designing a new shaping process which, at that time, was an innovative alternative to the Verlay process then in use at Saint-Gobain Sekurit, which had the drawback of leaving tong marks on the glass. The DB2 furnaces, which Glasstech sold to glassmakers throughout the world, were based on this process. Glasstech made constant improvements to the process, introducing the DB3 with a press system in the early 1980s, the DB4 allowing for more complex shaping in the late 1980s and the 'quick change' DB5 which reduced tool-change time. The ABS2 had in fact been the IDC's initial response to this competition. Before we look at the success of the S4 process, let us go back to the difficulties with the ABS2 as they are a good illustration of the traps involved in regenerating functions.

12.3.2   The ill-fated 'tempering with pressing ring' (ABS2) process

The process for manufacturing automotive tempered glass is as follows. The cut flat glass is heated until it becomes soft (visco-elastic) and can be bent. In this state, it is shaped and then rapidly cooled (tempering), at which point the tension moves to the core. After tempering, the surface is more resistant to minor impacts and, in the case of stronger shocks, the glass fractures into small fragments which are far less dangerous than the sharp edges of non-tempered glass.

Various methods were experimented with, such as moving the glass slowly along rollers, to shape it whilst cooling it (simultaneous shaping and tempering), and drawing the glass from the furnace to shape it against a mould before tempering it (shaping then tempering). The second procedure (horizontal heat shaping) was explored in the most detail, both by Saint-Gobain Sekurit and by Glasstech, the process involving 'retrieving hot glass from the furnace, shaping it with the mould and tempering it by rapid air quench' (see Figure 12.2).

The first ABS process (ABS1) entailed drawing the glass to shape it against a mould positioned above it. The glass was then deposited on a tempering

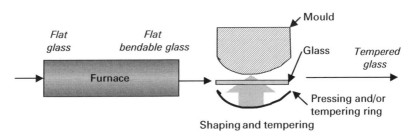

Figure 12.2 Horizontal heat-treated processes

ring. The drawback of this system was that it could not cater for high curvatures. However, at the end of the 1980s, Peugeot required glazing with sharp angles (high level of curvature at the edges) for its future 605 model. The engineers in the IDC came up with the solution of adding another ring (the so-called pressing ring) to compress the edges of the glass against the mould. This was the ABS2 project.

The project therefore mainly consisted of adding a feature. The pressing ring, which was in fact very much the same as the tempering ring, was used to compress the glass against the mould. Once the shape was given, the real tempering ring was positioned under the mould and from then on the process was identical to the ABS1 process. The industrial investment was scheduled immediately, without going through the stage of a prototype furnace. However, two years later, the process had still not been stabilized. The output for the 605 glazing was very low and, although the workshop technicians had made many adjustments to the shape of the mould and the ring, there was still too much variation from one unit to another, often exceeding tolerances.

12.3.3 Designing the 'high-speed, high-complexity' process (S3-S4)

The design of the high-speed tempering process (S3), which subsequently led to S4, started on a completely different footing. Rather than trying to improve the ABS1 or ABS2 processes by adding a feature, the designers decided not to automatically carry over any solutions at all. They set themselves two objectives: to keep the cycle times as low as possible and to produce high-quality edgings. There was no mention of complex shapes at this stage. The project was launched in February 1991.

The team consisted of about ten people from the different functions involved in the new process. There was a specialist in shaping technologies, another in engineering and setting up, a tooling expert, an ergonomist, etc.

Contrary to the tempering with a pressing ring process, they carried out a large amount of preparatory work. After several rapid explorations, the first observation was that they had to start from the most traditional process, i.e. horizontal, heat-treated glass. Although there were credible technological alternatives, these involved risky conceptual expansions. On the basis of a model of the horizontal, heat-treated process and a detailed study of the advantages and disadvantages of the existing processes, the second observation was that two vital parameters had been neglected in the ABS2 design process. One was the problem of transporting the glass (which had a strong impact on the cycle times) and the other was the problem of the relative positions of the glass, the mould and the pressing ring.

This design work (*see* C-K summary below) helped them ask the right questions and examine the skills in a relevant manner:

The traditional solutions for transporting the glass were the roller system (where the glass moves along a line of rotating rollers) and the 'pick-up' system (the glass is conveyed by a mould). The team explored a new solution involving air cushions, which had the advantage of preventing abrasion and enabling the glass to be repositioned under the moulds without leaving marks on the surface.

As far as positioning was concerned, the team members' experience in different fields of glazing helped find solutions for automatic correction of positioning in real time. Three design parameters were changed in order to upgrade the scale of precision:

Mechanically soldered tooling with a degree of precision to the millimetre was replaced by tooling designed by digital control with tolerances to one-tenth of a millimetre.

A new technique was developed to automatically adjust the settings, with a high degree of precision, by measuring the air-gap between the mould, the glass and the ring while hot.

The position of the mould was adjusted in real time by synchronizing four motors along four axes. This process implied the acquisition of new competencies.

Partnerships were set up to help explore new areas of knowledge. New suppliers were contacted worldwide for systems hitherto unknown to the group; test platforms were set up, each dealing with a new concept in the process (air cushions, sensors, digital controls, etc.). For each of the concepts, there were always two levels of development, consisting of an optimized solution and a simplified solution. If the first failed, the second allowed the project to continue without compromising it.

The results far exceeded the initial expectations. The prototype furnace was built by the summer of 1992, barely eighteen months after the start of the project. The series of tests carried out in 1993–1994 confirmed all the advantages of the process and the glazing for the Peugeot 605 was produced without difficulties. In the meantime, however, demands had changed in terms of shaping: it was no longer enough to have high production rates and to provide high-quality edgings; clients also required more complex shapes. The limitations of the S3 process soon became apparent simply because, during the shaping phase, when the glass was drawn against the mould, the centre of the glass was compressed and forced outwards towards the edges, which caused folds for deeper curvatures. The solution was the 'gravity sag' process: the glass is deposited on a ring, which immobilizes the edges, and takes its shape at the centre under its own weight. With this process, the position of the glass allows more curvature. The design of the S3 proved to be particularly flexible: as the pressing ring was controlled independently, it was possible to invert the sequence for compressing the glass against the mould and for pressing the edges with the tempering ring. Hence, the first stage became the gravity sag, followed by compression against the mould. This was the S4 cycle. The process achieved high production rates whilst nonetheless producing complex forms with high curvatures. A few months later, Saint-Gobain Sekurit was able to produce the most complex tempered glazing ever produced at high rates, the rear windscreen for the Renault Clio 2.

This achievement could be seen as a mere design fluke. However, the way the process was designed – defining precise conceptual models and separating out the issues of transport and positioning – led to a modular design structure that allowed the pressing phase to be freed from the constraints of positioning, thus meaning that it could be explored more freely.

12.3.4 The reasoning

The S4 case helps underline the challenges of reasoning in a context of the regeneration of a function (δC-ΔK; see Figure 12.3). It highlights the efforts made to structure effective minimum dC. If we take the counter example of the ABS2, it was a makeshift solution based on the previous process, but nonetheless involved a large amount of exploration in terms of knowledge (tests, trials, adjustments, etc.). No real work was done on concepts. On the contrary, the S4 project defined a relatively expansive concept, which was then partitioned in a restrictive manner. The designers started from far off – new concepts for glass shaping processes – but rapidly 'converged'

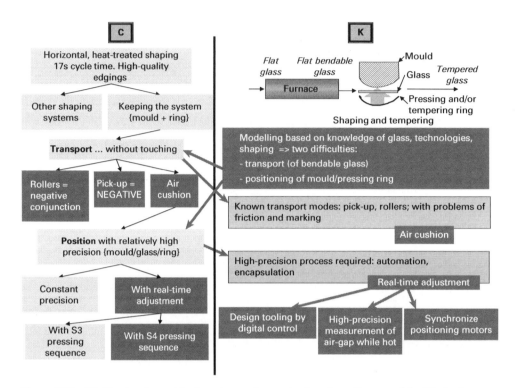

Figure 12.3   δC-ΔK reasoning and the importance of managing by value – the case of the S4 shaping process

and reused a large number of known attributes. The furnace and the production line were not called into question, as the process would still be 'horizontal, heat-treated glass', with a mould, a pressing ring, tempering by air quench, etc.

They could, of course, have carried out other explorations (tempering in the furnace, cold tempering without a furnace, etc.), but the project was to limit the expansion of C. Redesigning a furnace or a complete process would have involved highly risky explorations with no guarantee of added value. The aim was to *identify the technical constraints* that hampered performance, such as transport without contact and the precise positioning of the mould, glass and ring (δC). This identification phase did not involve too many risks as it was based on in-depth modelling of the existing processes. The first element of functional regenerations was therefore the reappropriation of knowledge and its relationship to the design process. This learning process is often neglected with a 'new function', but it is absolutely vital as it guarantees its success.

Second, the structuring of C guided the production of knowledge: the concepts of transport without contact and of precise positioning enabled them to launch explorations in K, whose value was already known.

The designers in fact launched a knowledge-oriented exploration that was both finely targeted and highly ambitious, thus resulting in a drastic renewal of the functions. The value of the exploration was guaranteed by its clear relation to the design process. Working on transport and positioning helped improve the overall performance without upsetting the other aspects of the process (furnace, tempering by air, type of mould and ring, etc.) and it was always possible to return to the previous solutions for transport and positioning (rollers, pick-up; constant precision for mould/ring) to find an acceptable process, i.e. a satisfactory conjunction.

Linking ΔK to design in cases of δC-ΔK

The new knowledge had to be linked to C by two operators:
- from C to K: it was clear when the new knowledge on transport and positioning had to be activated to design a version of the S4 process (i.e. for a specific glazing project);
- from K to C: activating this knowledge did not change the fundamental property of systematic design, i.e. the process's convergence in a finite time (it was clear in a finite time whether or not there was a solution). Maintaining this property implied that the acquired dK also had to include knowledge on the validation of a series of versions of the S4 process.

Finally, this case illustrates an increasingly frequent situation in the regeneration of functions, a feedback in terms of value. New organization models help speed up the exploration of new values. In the case of Sekurit, a new level of precision was obtained for high-speed production of complex glazing products. It was similar to the case of Saab Missiles, where the work on navigation led to new work on a set of properties for the missiles themselves (*see* Figure 12.4). This explains how δC-ΔK situations can lead to ΔC-ΔK situations.

12.3.5   The organization

The design of the ABS2 process suffered from a syndrome which involved keeping the exploration close to development, in the hope that it would converge more rapidly. S3-S4 did the opposite, although the processes were not completely disconnected from *D*. On the one hand, original explorations were made, in very new areas for engineering, such as electronics, digital

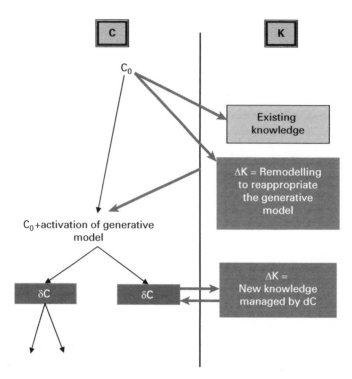

Figure 12.4   δC-ΔK reasoning pattern

control machining and automation, but, on the other, the process was punctuated with project meetings and facilitated by the production of a full-scale prototype. The prototype helped test and fine-tune processes, without having to deal with all the constraints of production but taking into account a growing number of them. Another advantage was that glazing that exploited the value of the processes could be fully developed (evaluation and certification procedures, initial deliveries for the car manufacturers' series of prototypes, etc.) before the industrial line was launched at full load. It was also this prototype that enabled the new glazing to be developed within the deadline set for the automobile project. Another key element of this process of 'transition' to development was the existence of back-up solutions which limited the risks and reassured the development department. The exploration strategy guaranteed that the S4 would be at least as good as a satisfactory Glasstech process, given that the back-up solutions enabled the manufacturer to return to solutions already recognized in the market.

The S4 case therefore illustrates an approach using design spaces which, through the project meetings, provided regular 'reckoning points' with traditional systematic design processes.

How was the activity evaluated and was it a success or a failure? It was undoubtedly a success, but not only due to the Clio 2 glazing, which could possibly have been made by 'promoting' an existing process. The design exercise must also be assessed on the basis of the new knowledge it produced, as revealed by the C-K formal framework. The outline of the firm's future functions emerges, as it is not so much the Clio or even the S4 that are important here but the shift from mechanically soldered processes to the age of automation and digital commands. Faced with the challenges of high production rates and complex shapes, new competencies were introduced, representing the genes of a new generation of systematic design (numerous variations of the S4: with quick change for tooling, optimized cycle times, high edge quality, maximum complexity, etc.). This implies that, in situations where competencies are regenerated, assessments of the first product based on the competency (V2) can be misleading, as there is far greater value in the potential created (V3 and V4).

Questions for further study and discussion

δC-ΔK and technology: show how the traps and specific features of δC-ΔK reasoning explain the paradoxes of 'new technologies'. Depending on their relationship to the generative models, they can either support a firm's growth or disrupt it.

Based on a few cases, find how success depends on conceptual management: in Henderson and Clark's (1990) architectural innovation, can it be said that the generative model is profoundly disrupted? Inspired by Gawer and Cusumano's (2002) work see two possible interpretations of Moore's Law: clever δC-ΔK or apparent δC-ΔK which in fact requires enormous efforts to redesign the value.

δC-ΔK and knowledge management: show that knowledge management concerning skills (and particularly concerning increase in competencies) must be based on design reasoning.

δC-ΔK and axiomatic design theory: show that Suh's (1990) axiomatic theory is a specific case of δC-ΔK, in which the generative model has been maintained (defined by a list of given functional requirements).

13 Type 3 innovation fields: combining scientific research and conceptual innovation

The third type of innovation field concerns projects for designing what we call science-based products (SBP). These products combine two difficulties: working on a functional definition whilst at the same time producing scientific knowledge on the main phenomena associated with the product. SBPs do not involve applied research, in which prior research results are applied to often well-identified functions; for SBPs, the functions are not specified and the phenomena to be investigated emerge during the process. Nor do SBPs involve fundamental research, which consists of working on a given phenomenon, with no target applications; SBPs have product development objectives with high (albeit ill-defined) stakes in terms of functions.

In this type of innovation field, there is a large expansion in both concepts and knowledge. It is not easy to make the distinction between 'techniques' and 'values'. Whereas the creation of new lineages (ΔC-δK) puts the priority on value (the techniques either being considered of secondary importance or already acquired) and the regeneration of functions (δC-ΔK) has to be content with minimum value explorations to produce knowledge, for SBPs, value and competencies must always be designed simultaneously. There are also some special cases when ΔC-δK and δC-ΔK follow on from each other.

Examples of ΔC-ΔK

WITAS and the Mg-CO$_2$ project studied in Chapter 10 both concerned SBPs.

There are also some famous cases of innovation which illustrate ΔC-ΔK, such as Edison's invention of incandescent lighting, a model of reasoning combining scientific production and value exploration (Hughes 1983). Hughes showed how reasoning on the value of electrical lighting systems for the home (ΔC) led to clever modelling of electrical systems (ΔK) which in turn led to further reflection on value and

---

competencies (work on different types of alternators, generators and, finally, a filament for an incandescent light bulb). We have already seen that nylon was not based on pure research reasoning (ΔK) but was developed by reasoning on value (a polymer with the properties of a textile fibre, to be used for nylon stockings), which had itself activated a great deal of research (particularly on 6–6 nylon, then for process engineering). *See* Chapter 8 and Hounshell and Smith (1988).

Another emblematic example is the Swatch watch. In the 1970s, the Swiss watch industry was confronted with the emergence of a new technique, quartz. Thanks to this technology, Japanese manufacturers had started to inundate world markets with watches which were not only cheap but also far more accurate than the best Swiss watches. Nicholas Hayek, the co-founder of Swatch, saved the Swiss watch-making industry by operating a dual expansion: first, in concepts, by turning watches into disposable fashion objects, and, second, in knowledge, since not only did the industry appropriate quartz technology but it also reinvented the architecture of watches by combining cases and supports to offer a wider variety of watch faces.

Innovative firms such as Boulton and Watt also illustrate ΔC-ΔK situations. The firm transformed a costly steam engine, used to pump water from mines, into a vital source of energy for the high-growth industries of the time (spinning, weaving, machine tools, etc.). In the process, it established the value of the steam engine for these businesses (ΔC) and the necessary competencies. From 1775 to 1800, it built and sold 325 engines, gradually introducing new developments such as the double-action engine, speed regulation, new materials and new methods of adjustment. The firm built up competencies and functions which almost consisted of systematic design. It set up a network of independent technical sales engineers (Roll 1930; Dickinson 1936) who helped manufacturers define their needs, prepared estimates using models and component catalogues, placed orders and installed the machines in the client establishments (ΔK); it mastered the competencies for machine architectures and for the key components (ΔK).

A number of major present-day innovation fields, such as nanotechnologies, biotechnologies and the reduction of CO_2 emissions, involve ΔC-ΔK. They cannot be reduced to a pure process of knowledge acquisition as reasoning is always required at the same time concerning the value. Although it could be said that 'nanotechnologies' are actually more concepts than technologies, there is often a search for uses and these potential uses require often deep investigations on value and competencies (*see also* the Mg-CO_2 project, Chapter 10, for the close interactions of value and competencies in SBP projects). The fight against CO_2 emissions can be seen as the need to master technology so that existing 'uses' can be maintained, but it seems unrealistic to think that emissions can be controlled without drastic changes in the current processes, whether for coal-fired power plants, car combustion engines, cement factories, etc. The issue is complicated by the fact that it involves situations with a host of actors and mutual interactions which constantly shift and redesign the spaces of exchange and competition.

13.1   Eventful innovation paths: examples of ΔC-ΔK situations in large firms

We can illustrate the difficulties encountered in this type of innovation field by describing some cases from industry. Take Schlumberger, a leading oilfield services provider with a strong reputation for innovation. One of the challenges for oil companies in the 1990s was to enhance oil recovery per oilfield; at that time, extraction rates were approximately 33 per cent. Schlumberger's CEO set the firm the goal of proposing services capable of increasing oil recovery rates to 50 per cent. This opened up a vast innovation field, but how could it be explored? It could not be a case of simply renewing functions, i.e. the sort of scientific explorations which Schlumberger was used to organizing (δC-ΔK), because the innovation field concerned a different area from the firm's traditional activities, which mainly focused on oil exploration. However, the exploration could not be limited to identifying a market potential (ΔC-δK) as the firm did not have the knowledge to back up the reasoning. The aim was therefore to combine the scientific stakes and the exploration of new business, an idea which was taken up by certain designers. One of the most promising solutions consisted of monitoring and controlling the flows of water injected to 'push' the mass of oil towards the extraction wells by equipping all the extraction wells with a permanent monitoring system. How could they design a system of this sort when the main phenomenon – water front advance – was not fully understood? Should they carry out laboratory tests or launch experiments with the clients? Furthermore, were the clients prepared to pay for such instruments? Was the solution a small 'commando' team?

Projects were launched and a number of trials were carried out, but several years later there were still reservations about the results and how they should be interpreted. A number of partnerships had been set up, but had not produced clients. In the end, it was difficult to say whether the project was a success or a failure, as there was no pertinent method of evaluation. One thing that was certain was that, judged by the criteria used by R and D, it was neither successful development, as no product had been developed, nor successful research, as it had produced little relevant academic knowledge. Should the project be rejected, or was it a good exploration of innovation fields? The case is studied later in the chapter.

The creation of the solar control branch at Saint-Gobain Sekurit (*see* Chapter 9) is also interesting in this respect. It was not only a case of acquiring new technology because new functionalities were explored, such as levels of heat filtering, defrosting and the compatibility of layer techniques and complex shapes. The problem was whether to start by specifying the functions and then finding the technology (ΔC-δK then δC-ΔK), or to develop the technology and then define its functional space. Functionalities were in fact revealed during the gradual exploration of several technologies, which began in competition with each other, until pertinent functionalities were found that showed that they were complementary. Other difficulties were when to start developing products and how to organize convergence towards rule-based design. In this case, certain technologies were elaborated during the development process whereas others followed the prudent, if somewhat fastidious, stages of more traditional design processes, i.e. small samples in the fundamental research department, then larger samples on a full-scale trial run in the 'applied' research centre, followed by prototype production line trials and finally the industrial production line. Was their approach simply based on opportunity or ignorance of concurrent engineering? In fact, their aim was to allow for rapid product launches with certain technologies whilst at the same time slowly designing processes to build the foundations of a new function. Better still, once a first technology had been developed, it served as a space for prototyping certain functionalities which were fully exploited with the following technology.

Another case of a ΔC-ΔK type innovation field was an automobile manufacturer's work on odours in vehicles. The work raised a number of questions, starting with the need to define 'odour' and 'olfaction'. Also, what were the underlying phenomena? What functions could provide value? Was it worth looking at signature scents for vehicles, in which case, what would be considered a 'good' smell? How should the exploration be organized? The project could not be based on ΔC-δK alone as it was vital to acquire knowledge on odours in order to explore the value; nor could it target a new function (δC-ΔK) as the link to the product was still too weak. It was clearly not a case for either research or development as the value had to be explored, but who should be charged with the exploration? How should the project be managed and what learning processes were involved? How could martingales (*see* Chapter 5) be found? We shall examine this example in more detail in Chapter 14.

13.2 Innovation field exploration strategy: dual expansion

In such situations, the innovation field is a strategic space. It can be promising for new business or a potential threat to existing business. There is a high level of uncertainty, as it involves new technologies, new uses, new business models, new competitors, new partners, etc.

The main trap in this type of situation is perhaps the term 'technology' itself as it hides two problems:

Either it is assumed that the technology must be developed, in which case the development of technology will have the effect of eliminating the value, to the benefit of a dominant function for example. This amounts to a form of δC-ΔK which *cannot be managed by C.*

Or it is assumed that the technology will be developed by others and that technological road maps will progress naturally, in which case it will be a case of studying possible uses. This amounts to a value-oriented exploration (ΔC-δK), but once again, it *cannot be managed by K.*

The notion of technology suggests that separation is possible, whereas in fact the challenge is precisely to maintain strong links between learning and conceptual explorations.

The challenges of the reasoning are therefore to preserve the link between expansions in C and in K and to map and steer learning. The highly complex explorations carried out by Schlumberger and in the automobile and the automotive glass industries all show the immense difficulties involved.

If we take the case where strong links are indeed maintained, how can the process be organized? There are two alternatives: trial and error, or the opposite, planning. As we know, one of the key phrases in innovation is 'fail often to succeed sooner'. Without taking this as an incentive to play more often on random lots, the real difficulty is the learning: is it all that easy to learn from one's errors in such situations? In ΔC-ΔK situations, the experimentations are often inconclusive, the projects often lead to uninterpretable results. Despite the injunctions to learn from failure, trial and error can lead to costly, pointless experiments if it is not based on structured reasoning. Does this mean that the solution is planning? Yes, if this is possible, but in this context it is often difficult to identify a future product, market or client base. Planning tends to be limited to areas such as 'proof-of-principle demonstrators' (often produced by a fundamental research laboratory), 'functional prototypes' (produced by an applied research laboratory), initial products (worked on with a development team), their distribution (with the marketing department) and the launching of a complete product range. This strategy in fact involves gambling on risky, one-off projects, with high investments.

There are two possible organizational approaches:

Either a series of transmissions from research, to development, to industrialization, for which the competencies are set *ex ante.*

Or skunk work teams, in the form of enthusiastic 'commandos' prepared to do anything to defend their ideas. However, the large expansions in the two dimensions imply that skunk teams have difficulty in doing all the work alone, as they are often confronted with long obstacle courses which compromise success. Sooner or later there is the risk that a development will rationalize the previous designs, thereby destroying the value.

Finally, the link between the organization of the exploration and the rest of the company is often neglected, on the grounds that, as the exploration involves new business, it should be given its independence and that it is better to wait for a few projects to be launched before evaluating success. And yet there is a vital challenge here: how should a business be structured? Without entering into considerations of business administration, a design perspective nonetheless provides a few indications: a structured business is based on systematic design, i.e. it has already identified the functional spaces, conceptual models and the foundations of embodiment and detailed design. Linking *I* to R&D involves establishing these systematic design languages for a new business project. The objective is not (only) to make profits but also to build the foundations of the functional, conceptual and physical-morphological languages for a product lineage.

These points are summarized in Table 13.1.

13.3   Value management: how Schlumberger managed complex design spaces

We shall now come back to the case of Schlumberger, to illustrate the complex reasoning and organizations found in ΔC-ΔK situations. The case is particularly interesting since Schlumberger has a worldwide reputation for innovation. In this project, the work practices were apparently interesting but the firm's management found it difficult to interpret them. The managers and designers all agreed that it was a strange case and, as we mentioned above, according to conventional criteria, it was bad research and bad

Table 13.1. The exploration of ∆C-∆K innovation fields

∆C-∆K	Traps	Challenges
Reasoning	Separating C and K through 'technology' ('the technology will follow', 'develop the technology')	To maintain the links Mapping
Design spaces and value management	Trial and error Planning: fundamental/applied research/development	Sequence of design spaces
Organization – relations between *I* and R&D	Transmissions; skunk work	To build the foundations of systematic design language; ensuring the exploitation of the most varied outputs
Performance	The first product. The business. No repetition. Isolated projects, launched using decisive initial concepts	V1 to V4 and ability to structure a rule-based design language. The initial concept is a simple vehicle for exploration and can be modified

development. However, by studying the exploration we shall understand its coherency and value in terms of innovative design.

The overall explorations relating to the 'reservoir monitoring and control' (RMC) project (*see* Figure 13.1) comprised nine design spaces. These explorations cost the firm a great deal of money, but the return on investment was far from clear: the electrode systems initially studied were not marketed and the research was not published. Another striking point was that the design spaces were very different in nature: the work at Flins (France) was aimed at validating different phenomena; the trials with oil companies (BP, Shell, Aramco) were opportunities to understand functional aspects; and experiments such as those in Indiana or for the Res 2000 project, carried out by the research department, aimed at improving understanding of the phenomena. How can all these very varied trials be interpreted? Was progress made? What was the value of the explorations?

The innovation field was structured in three successive phases.

1. The initial concept was 'services for recovering 50 per cent of the oil' (*see* Figure 13.2). The concept was immediately followed by attributes: the services would consist of monitoring the water front with a network of

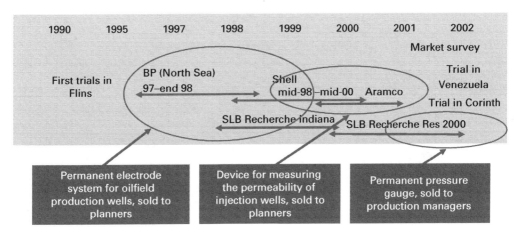

Figure 13.1   The design spaces in Schlumberger's 'reservoir monitoring and control' innovation field

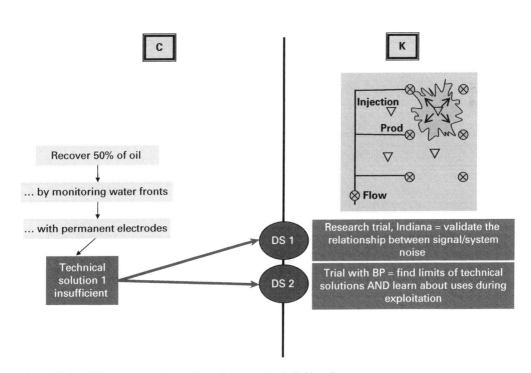

Figure 13.2   RMC phase 1, restricting the initial concept – initial learning

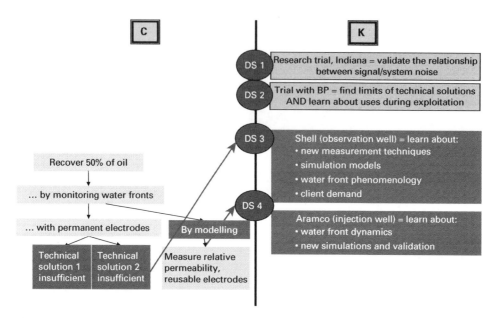

Figure 13.3 RMC phase 2, opening up alternatives

resistive electrodes designed to 'see' the advance of the water front underground.[1] The ability to 'see' the water front was partially validated by the work at Flins. With this proposition in C, an exploration was launched in K, i.e. the trial with BP. This trial was carried out by the French engineering and design departments and was very instructive concerning the possible technique and the functional dimensions. Whereas Schlumberger was more used to working on wells during the exploration phase, this trial was an opportunity to learn about the constraints involved for services in exploitation wells. The sensor was validated by a trial conducted by the research department in a well in Indiana. Until this point, the project appeared to be following traditional stages of research and development, albeit in a somewhat disorderly fashion.

2. A second trial, again carried out by the French engineering and design departments, was launched with Shell at an observation well (*see* Figure 13.3). Among other findings, this trial showed that rather than

---

[1] Reservoirs are exploited by boring a series of wells. There are two types of well: injection wells, in which water is injected at high pressure to 'push' the oil in front of it, and extraction wells, from which the oil is extracted. At that time, little was known about the behaviour of oil when it was pushed, or about the position of the water front.

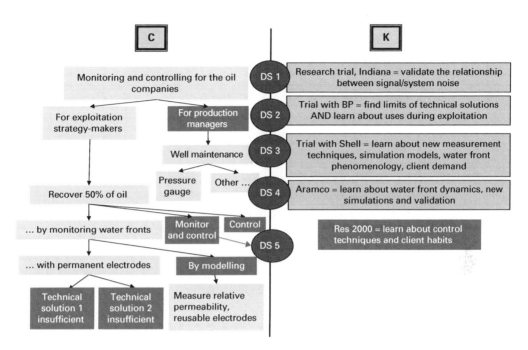

Figure 13.4 RMC phase 3, rewording the concept

monitoring a water front by 'seeing' it advance, it was possible to do so by improving predictive models using new knowledge on certain physical parameters. This new alternative was explored in partnership with Aramco and the approach was validated. As there was still the need to calibrate the physical parameters, the study encouraged them to consider very different services: instead of a permanent electrode system for exploitation wells, they studied activities concerning measurement systems, a domain which was more familiar to Schlumberger.

3. A further exploration opened up an alternative higher in the tree structure. Following the Res 2000 trials, it became clear that it was important to study not only 'monitoring' but also 'monitoring and control' or perhaps just 'control' alone. These two new possibilities were important, as they meant that the idea of simply providing information for operators, who would know how to put it to good use, was replaced by the idea of providing them with means of action. This led to a key question: who were the clients, strategy-makers or production/exploitation managers? On the basis of what they had learned so far, the '50 per cent recovery' concept was repositioned to become one of the branches of a far wider concept, 'monitoring and control for oil exploitation strategy-makers' (*see* Figure 13.4). This

concept was itself a branch of 'monitoring and control for oil companies', another branch of which was 'monitoring and control for on-site production managers'. A large number of new services and new concepts appeared on this new branch, in particular a pressure gauge for the preventive maintenance of wells.

The RMC case highlights all the traps in ΔC-ΔK situations, but also how the teams managed to deal with them.

First of all, there was the temptation of 'technological' solutions: the value space was considered as a given fact and its distribution into functions ('see the water front') was done independently from the technologies. Then, a potential technology was identified (among others which we have not shown here) and had to meet functional criteria ('see the water front, with a permanent electrode system') (dC-dK). There was also the temptation for planning or 'applied science': the proposition of a technical principle (measuring the water front with electrodes) followed by the validation of the principle (experiment at Flins), then its validation in a real well (Indiana) and putting into service with a client (trials with BP and Shell). Finally, there was the temptation of using a commando to push a 'good idea' at every possible opportunity (BP, Shell, Aramco).

However, the ΔC-ΔK exploration was also exemplary in the way that its teams managed to deal with these traps: despite the obstacles, knowledge was accumulated, new functions emerged, client value spaces were identified, novel alternatives were found to structure them and, finally, applications emerged, with V1, V2, V3 and V4. There were two key points:

The different teams' ability to build design spaces to learn from. In this respect, the '50 per cent recovery' concept had a vital quality, which was that it was 'lukewarm', i.e. not too cold to freeze the resources or too hot for the teams to rush into development, thereby interrupting the exploration. This work enabled the identity to be revised gradually (from monitoring to control) and fostered the emergence of a number of alternatives at varying timescales (short and medium term).

Continuity and coordination between the teams. Naturally, the stages indicated here were pieced together *a posteriori*, as there was no explicit project management. Nonetheless, the same people took part in several explorations, thus encouraging the transmission of learning from one design space to the next. The learning processes were essential for the subject of water fronts (models, techniques, tools, software, knowledge of geology, etc.) and for the value spaces of exploitation (strategy-makers versus production managers, conditions of exploitation, etc.).

Describing the process in terms of design spaces and design reasoning helps account for the successive learning processes and the original forms of collective action. It also explains why RMC may not have been successful development or successful research but was certainly an extremely rich exploration of an innovation field.

Questions for further study and discussion

What tools could be used for a ΔC-ΔK exploration? The focus should be put on tools for managing the general process, tools for economic management and tools for project milestones.

What are the relations between ΔC-ΔK and strategy? The focus should be on the new forms of action for managers. In systematic design, they managed the process on the basis of simple indicators. Do they now need to examine the reasoning in more detail with a view to stimulating the action, particularly by identifying new design spaces? What can be done to facilitate finely tuned strategic management?

ΔC-ΔK in a multi-institutional context: at present, there are numerous examples of ΔC-ΔK innovation fields which cover entire sectors of industry (*see* the box at the beginning of the chapter). How are explorations structured? What role can the public authorities play in this context? See in particular the case of sustainable development, with reference to Aggeri *et al.* (2005).

Historical case studies: Boulton and Watt, Wedgwood and Edison as innovative firms capable of exploring SBP innovation fields.

Key notions in Chapters 11, 12 and 13

Distinguishing between the three main types of innovation fields: ΔC-δK, δC-ΔK, ΔC-ΔK

Showing how the main dimension (ΔC or ΔK) is always controlled and managed by the secondary dimension (δC, δK)

With ΔC-δK: going from a 'good idea' to the ability to structure 'in-depth' reasoning

With δC-ΔK: going from 'technology' to the regeneration of skills and competencies relating to the existing generative models

With ΔC-ΔK: moving from the 'miracle product' to the structuring of systematic design

14 The inevitable return to rule-based design

'These theoretical frameworks and specific examples will be of great help in organizing innovative design and in finding effective instruments. I must say I was surprised by how technical the examples are. First, the objects have to be modelled very carefully and precisely, with a hands-on approach, but second, I was struck by how much knowledge is economized by the formal framework, as only knowledge that serves the reasoning comes into play. Nonetheless, the formal C-K framework illustrates the nature of the strategic reasoning needed for innovative design and makes the technical aspects easier to understand.'

'I now have a better idea of how to manage innovative design, but there is still one point which worries me. Can you explain the notion of "return to rule-based design", or the traditional system of R&D?'

Once again, the Innovation Manager's questions help us explain a vital point: there is no question of innovative design seeking to replace rule-based design. On the contrary, the greater the efforts made in rule-based design, the better the chances of being able to fully exploit the product lineages stemming from the innovation fields. Rule-based design is therefore vital in terms of return on investment. We shall now see how innovative design can prepare for rule-based design.

14.1 From the exploration of an innovation field to rule-based design

In formal terms, rule-based design reasoning can be explained by the C-K design theory (*see* Figure 14.1). It shows that rule-based design is based on (i) comprehensive knowledge bases on each of the languages (functional, conceptual, embodiment and detailed design; *see* Chapter 8) and (ii) mutually consistent bases, i.e. so that transition from one level to the next takes place without going backwards but with a gradual specification process. This is the *objective* of all innovative design projects seeking to change to

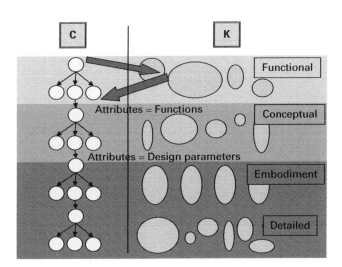

Figure 14.1 Rule-based design in the C-K formal framework

rule-based design. The K bases and their interdependent elements are *the things to be designed* in innovative design situations in order to return to rule-based design.

One of the main points in this chapter is that there is no obligation to follow the order of rule-based design when building up the K bases. In other words, there is no need to start by the functional language, then to elaborate the conceptual language and finally move to the embodiment stage. It can even be assumed that a linear process of this sort is not possible.

In formal terms, this proposition is obvious: the K bases of rule-based design can be built only by innovative design reasoning, but the different phases of language (functional, conceptual, embodiment, etc.) do not exist in innovative design. In practice, there are situations where designers try to build up the languages of rule-based design by restricting their explorations to certain types of language and by taking the others as given constraints. This can often be explained by the fact that, in the past, organizations were broken down in such a way as to designate specific actors for each of the phases, with no one in charge of revising all the languages at the same time or ensuring their coherency. This basically restricts the potential for exploration.

It results in the following organizational structure: successive design spaces elaborate interdependent elements of knowledge, but each design space only partially explores the languages, i.e. a few functions, accounted for by a few models and a few components. It is the succession of design spaces, whose contributions are combined at the value management level, which gradually builds up more comprehensive, more robust languages for functions, concepts and embodiment.

14.2   An extreme case: from a science-based product exploration to a rule-based design process

We have already mentioned situations of this sort in type-1 (head of lineage) and type-2 (regeneration of functions) innovation fields. For instance, Telia's use-based explorations regenerated a number of spaces for functions (e.g. limiting intrusions caused by telephone calls), concepts (architectures for 'information processing', 'accessories') and embodiment (type of terminal). Similarly, at Saint-Gobain Sekurit, explorations into the new tempering process (S4) led to a slight evolution in functions (not only to decrease cycle times but also to study complex shapes), the emergence of new design parameters (shaping by pressing, automatic repositioning, etc.) and new machine parts (pressing ring, calculators and positioning jigs).

We shall now study a more complex case, which we mentioned briefly in the previous chapter. The project aimed to design a signature scent for a vehicle (*see* Figure 14.2). It started with major uncertainties regarding both C and K. An innovation field then gradually emerged and was finally able to generate the basic languages of rule-based design. In this case of ΔC-ΔK exploration, we highlight the specific reasoning, the role played by the design spaces and their relationship to systematic design. This work was the subject of two projects by students at the Ecole des Mines de Paris, option Engineering and Design, working with French car manufacturer PSA (Champagnat and Lafrance 1999; Lapeyronnie and Macaire 2002).

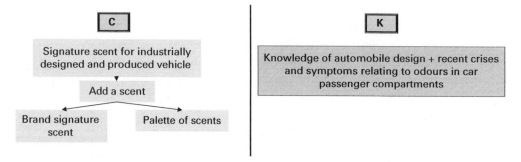

Figure 14.2   Initial configuration and launch of the first design space, 'adding a scent'

With this case, which concerned odours in car passenger compartments, we return to the automobile industry, a sector where product development is based on systematic design. First of all, it should be noted that the design project did not follow the usual phases of functions, concepts and then embodiment, but adopted a more roundabout, surprising approach. It started with an initial trial for a small function (adding a scent in the passenger compartment), then the formulation of a wide innovative concept (a microclimate), followed by a trial for a specific property (airtightness) and, at the same time, studies and work on a prototype (which was out-sourced) to define precise functionalities, as if the functions came at the end of the process. The same apparently chaotic features apply to the actors involved. Instead of using well-identified competencies, the exploration was initially carried out by a small, isolated team, working in an innovation and creation unit, before the concept federated a wider range of competencies, at which stage the type of organization changed and an external laboratory was asked to model, construct and test a prototype.

However, the explorations were managed very carefully. In the following pages, we examine the underlying reasoning and organizations by taking a closer look at the approach to design spaces.

14.2.1   First design space, 'adding a scent'

14.2.1.1   Transition from C_0-K_0 to C_1*-K_1*

The initial C-K configuration was characterized by knowledge of automobile design, a limited amount of knowledge of odours and of the recent crises that competitors' vehicles had experienced on the subject (*see* Figure 14.3). The C_0 concept is defined as 'a car's signature scent' (it is a concept, given that it does not have a logical status, but the proposition can be interpreted in K). The design process began by looking at two possibilities: adding an odour to obtain a signature scent for the brand or developing a palette of scents. However, lack of knowledge quickly halted work.

The project advanced when the innovation department suggested that a team of designers should explore a restriction to the initial concept (adding a scent). Instead of trying to find a solution, they should work on identifying the functions and main phenomena concerning odours in cars in general. This opened the first design space, defined by the following restrictions:

From C_0 to C_1*: many of the properties of 'cars' in the industrial sense were put to one side, although the notion of signature scent was not

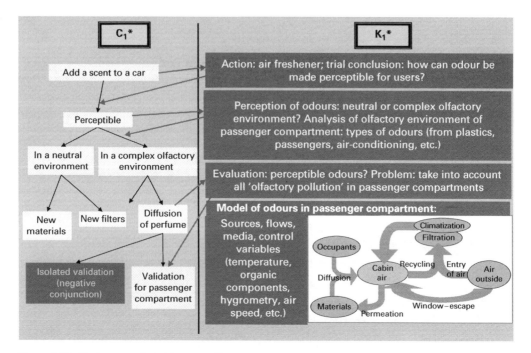

Figure 14.3 Design space 1, 'adding a scent'

examined as an isolated subject. The exploration focused on 'adding a scent to a car'.

From K_0 to K_1^*: the constraints of feasibility, relating to the factory, engineering or the market, were not taken into account.

14.2.1.2   Designing in C_1^*-K_1^*

In this initial design space, the study of existing air fresheners revealed one of the major difficulties in the field of olfaction, the notion of perception. Olfactory perception varies a great deal, depending on whether the passenger compartment is itself odourless or, on the contrary, is a complex olfactory environment. This observation led to a study on the sources of odours (desorption of plastic materials, air-conditioning, outside air, passengers, luggage, etc.) and how to control them to obtain a 'neutral olfactory environment' (filters, new materials, etc.). The designers developed a comprehensive model of odours in passenger compartments, identifying the sources, the flows and the control variables (especially temperature, air flow speed and hygrometry). They also showed that perfume was imperceptible if diffused in a complex environment.

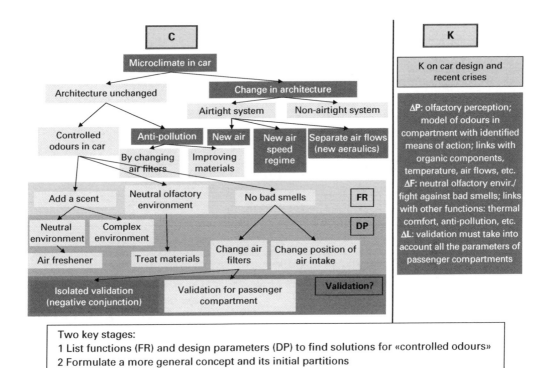

Figure 14.4 Return to main C-K (value management)

14.2.1.3 Transition from C_1*-K_1* to C_0-K_0: learning the languages of rule-based design and expansion of C_0-K_0

After working on the subject for five months, the designers reviewed the SBP in terms of value management. Were they ready for rule-based design? The knowledge base had been greatly increased and the learning could therefore be described in the basic languages of rule-based design. The knowledge acquired in the design space suggested several alternatives to the concept of 'controlled odours', each alternative structured as a partial rule-based design: first the *functions* and then the associated *design parameters*. However, the design was only partially systematic as it was impossible to validate the efficiency of the design parameters (*see* Figure 14.4) because not enough knowledge was available to organize a rule-based design process.

The knowledge acquired in the design space was also used to do more work on C_0-K_0. Knowledge of the phenomena suggested that the notion 'odours in cars' was a partition of a wider concept, i.e. a microclimate in cars. This concept involved controlling not only the temperature of car passenger compartments but also the odours, pollution, hygrometry, etc.

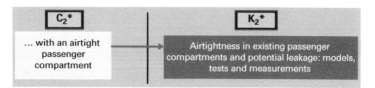

Figure 14.5   Design space 2, 'testing airtightness'

This is a good illustration of how *restricting an exploration* can result in *widening a concept*.

The concept of microclimate could be approached either by keeping the existing air flow architecture or by modifying it. The air flow model immediately suggested several alternatives: exploring new speeds for air flow systems (the existing air-conditioning systems worked at high air speeds, thus creating turbulence inside the vehicles), identifying, separating and differentiating several air flows in the compartment (e.g. for each passenger), and adding new and controlled sources of gas to air flows (*see* Figure 14.3).

Comments on the first exploration:

The exploration did not follow a systematic design process in the design space.

The design space was based on a strong restriction: it excluded vast areas of knowledge on issues such as costs, feasibility and the design of olfactory signatures.

The design space was not a fundamental research programme as the latter would have dealt only with the phenomenology of odours (independently from the question of vehicles). On the contrary, it simultaneously explored phenomena concerning odours in cars, the functions (perceptible odours) and the validation techniques.

14.2.2   Design spaces 2 and 3: testing and prototyping

14.2.2.1   Transition from value management to C_2^*-K_2^* and C_3^*-K_3^*

The main C-K tree suggested at least two paths (*see* Figure 14.5). First, as the flow models and the alternatives were very different depending on whether or not the passenger compartment was airtight, a rapid study was required on the subject of airtightness. Design space 2 therefore consisted of testing the proposition C_2^*, 'existing vehicle passenger compartments are airtight'. K_2^* knowledge concerned the airtightness tests in passenger compartments, which resulted in an expansion of knowledge on suitable measurement techniques.

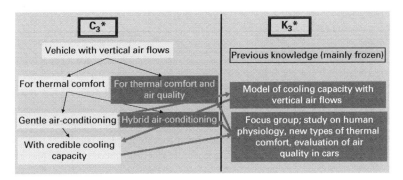

Figure 14.6   Design space 3, 'prototyping gentle air-conditioning'

The microclimate concept also opened up several architectural alternatives. To explore them rapidly, the designers proposed a prototype combining two paths, i.e. a new aeraulic system and separate air flows (design space 3). The concept was a 'vehicle with vertical air flows, for thermal comfort and gentle air-conditioning'. The previous knowledge on automobile engineering and odours was to a great extent frozen in the K_3^* knowledge space, which mainly dealt with modelling thermal phenomena. A focus group was also set up.

The design process was limited to a few months, after which time it had identified two new types of thermal comfort, i.e. gentle air-conditioning and hybrid air-conditioning combining a regime for short-term comfort and a regime for permanent comfort. It also modelled a system for cooling by vertical flows (*see* Figure 14.6).

14.2.2.2   Transition from C_2^*-K_2^* and $C_3^*K_3^*$ to value management. Learning the languages of rule-based design

At the value management level, the two design spaces resulted in improvements to the languages of functions, phenomena and validation – *see* Tables 14.1 and 14.2.

This provided a new structure of rule-based design for one of the alternatives for the microclimate ('airtight architecture with vertical air flows'). This is a key result: it represented the foundations of a rule-based design process for handling a concept which began as an SBP (*see* Figure 14.7).

We can now comment on the overall process (*see* Figure 14.8):

The C-K formal framework provides a clear picture of the different stages, the alternatives and the progress made by the exploration, on the local and global levels.

Table 14.1. The basic languages of rule-based design

Phenomena	Olfactory perception, models of odours in passenger compartments, with identified means of action, relationship with conditions such as temperature, air flows and hygrometry
Functions	Olfactory neutrality, fight against unpleasant smells, relationship with other functions such as thermal comfort and removing pollution
Validation	The notion could not be validated in isolation (e.g. diffusing air freshener) but had to include other phenomena relating to air flows in the passenger compartment

Table 14.2. The basic languages of rule-based design – application in the microclimate case

Phenomena	Models of air flows, cooling capacity, vertical flows, human physiology, air pollution
Functions	New types of thermal comfort (short-term/permanent); air quality
Validation	Validation by cooling models; focus group techniques

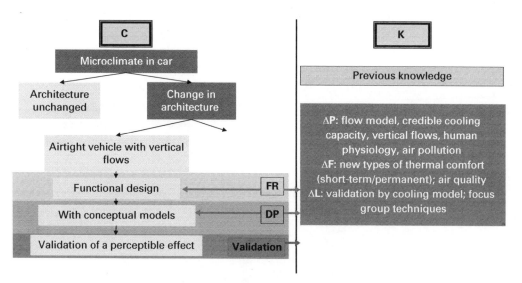

Figure 14.7   Return to value management – the embryo of rule-based design

The exploration was managed in three design spaces. Each was built with strong restrictions and was a source of decisive learning.

The variety of prototypes (conceptual exploration, tests, prototypes) shows that the design process was not a 'process of specification', in which the specifications became increasingly precise at each stage, with detailed design and tests being carried out at the end of the process. For example, design space 2 (testing airtightness) showed that an SBP can require an in-depth analysis of design details in the initial phases.

Each design space generated languages of rule-based design, thus building up the basis for future business projects on microclimates in cars.

Finally, the C-K language helped highlight the underlying organization. Far from a trial and error process, the exploration was organized and cumulative, and included two types of activities: first, learning in the design spaces and, second, value enhancement and management. This process was far removed from the linear processes which characterize systematic design, as shown in Figure 14.4.

To conclude this case on microclimates in car passenger compartments, we can underline the following key points:

The reasoning: the exploration was marked by a large number of expansions, in terms of both concepts and knowledge. The tree structures were far longer and more difficult to follow than in cases of δC-ΔK or ΔC-δK. The main reasoning by no means followed the linear process of systematic design (based on stable languages), or a two-phase model (research then systematic design), nor was it a simple process of 'improving precision'. The reasoning followed successive expansions and the operators involved.

The traps of the design spaces: in ΔC-ΔK situations, it is particularly difficult to interpret the design space, given that there can be ambiguity concerning the design regime (rule-based or innovative) in the design space itself. It is important to note a frequent trap, illustrated by the third design space, which is the validation with an exploratory prototype. During the prototyping stage, the teams were so enthusiastic about the initial results that they decided to validate the concept of vertical flows by subjecting the prototype to classic air-conditioning tests. As one of the criteria of these tests was the minimum flow to be provided by the air-conditioning (traditional air-conditioning works on a forced-air system), slow air flows were obviously not validated. The entire project was nearly stopped at this point. As the system had been declared non-valid, why continue? This highlights two problems: first, it is not certain that exploratory prototypes should also be used for validation, and second, the fact that a prototype was not valid should invalidate only one of the branches of the concept and not the entire tree structure.

The organization of the exploration of the innovation field: the case also highlights the effectiveness of managing by C-K reasoning, as it provides a clearer picture of the different stages, the alternatives and the status of the more or less detailed explorations. The formal nature of the reasoning also clarifies the underlying organization. Far from being a trial and error process, a paradoxically linear process appeared, with two types of activities: learning phases in the design spaces and value management phases at the main C-K level.

From I to R&D? The microclimate case illustrates how in these situations R&D manages to take advantage of the different values as they emerge in the innovation field (from V1 to V4). It also illustrates the gradual transformations in internal traditional functions and the way the innovation field stimulates research (external research in the case in point).

Evaluation: the exploration was marked by a wide variety of results, obtained throughout the process, including new filters, revised technical specifications for certain materials and new criteria for the functional specifications of 'comfort'. The results included V1, V2, V3 and V4 (new concepts, new products, knowledge produced for these products and excess knowledge). We must stress a specific aspect of these four outputs: the innovation field did not only aim to maximize V1–V4 but also sought to create a lineage. The innovation field can therefore be evaluated in terms of its capacity to generate languages for a new systematic design for microclimates. We can observe in this case that each design space made a contribution to the three languages – functions, phenomena and validation – which must be mastered before being able to progress to systematic design. Hence, one of the main results of this work was the gradual emergence of the knowledge bases required to move on to a systematic design process.

Questions for further study and discussion

Further discussion on the notion of ambidexterity using the microclimate case.

The microclimate case focuses very little on the organizational dimensions. Which organizations can cope with this sort of process?

Key notions – Chapter 14

Rule-based design/innovative design

What has to be designed to obtain rule-based design: functions, phenomenology, validation process

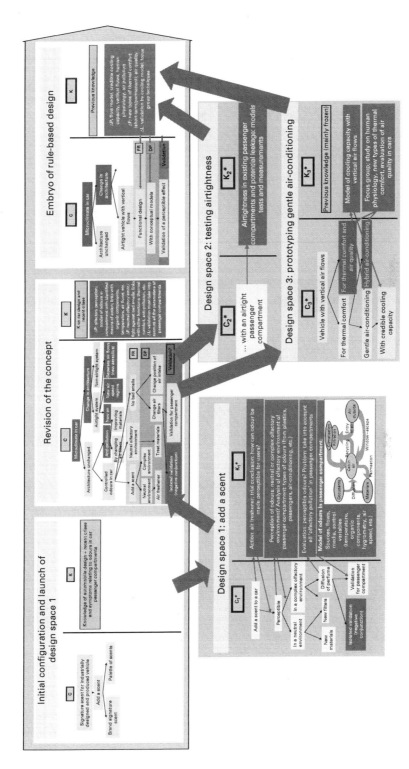

Figure 14.8 The SBP process in the language of design space and value management

15 Innovative design, platforms and open innovation: the management of exploratory partnerships

'All these elements will help me manage our innovative design projects and I am keen to put them into practice in our firm. But one last point is bothering me: I don't think we will be able to carry out all our explorations inside the firm. Quite a few of the innovation fields I have in mind will involve outside partners. Can you give me any advice on this matter?'

Our Innovation Manager is right, of course; this is a key point.

In previous chapters we have focused on exploring and structuring innovation fields, the main challenge being to understand the type of design reasoning involved. We showed that significant progress was possible in terms of constructing, sharing and evaluating this reasoning and also in organizing the collective action required to do so. In our view, it was crucial to begin by mastering the design reasoning even though it meant that the organizational perimeter of the explorations had to be put to one side. In practice, of course, it is relatively unusual for innovation fields to be explored within the strict perimeter of a single firm.

In most cases, innovative design requires outside resources. This explains the situation often described in the literature: open innovation (Chesbrough 2003). More fundamentally, the revision of object identities, inherent in innovative design, also revises firms' relationships to their environment. Stable identities enable dominant designs to emerge, industries to be structured, design work to be divided out and performance to be stabilized. Unstable identities challenge all these notions and can also lead to new forms of competition between a supplier and its clients. For instance, in the field of telecommunications, if a mobile telephone manufacturer installs voice-over IP software in its phones, it enters into competition with its operator clients. In the same sector, internet access providers (IAPs) and mobile telephone operators compete on the issue of fixed/mobile convergence. As far as IAPs are concerned, the stakes involve competing with other IAPs but also the option of joining forces with the latter to compete with the mobile telephone operators.

This issue of how people work together in innovative design situations was studied by Blanche Segrestin, who proposed a new theory and an analytical framework for what she calls 'exploratory partnerships' (Segrestin 2003, 2005). Her work is presented in this chapter. In the first part, we illustrate it with some of the cases mentioned earlier in the book and, in the second, we use it to draw some conclusions for innovation field managers working in partnerships.

15.1 What has to be managed in open innovation and platforms: coordination and cohesion in exploratory partnerships

A number of authors have noted the increase in partnerships in innovative design situations, despite persistent doubts as to their success and the high risks involved (Hagedoorn 2001). Part of the difficulty stems from the nature of the design reasoning and the enormous efforts required to elaborate it, as we have seen in previous chapters. However, partnerships pose additional problems relating to managing the interests and the risks, sharing the results and resolving disputes among partners.

Platforms and open innovation: brief literature overview

The literature provides us with several descriptions of 'openness' and collaborations in situations of strong innovation or, more generally speaking, innovative design. It underlines three main features:

1. The notion of 'open innovation' is today considered as a good description of the situations (firms have to be open) but does not provide formal models of innovative design (*see* the bibliographical appendix, Section 5).
2. The management of open innovation is currently a strong issue: what should be internalized/externalized (West 2003)? What are the resources for open innovation management and what is the role of R&D in terms of its absorptive capacity (Zahra and George 2002; Lane, Koka and Pathak 2006; Todorova and Durisin 2007)? Which industry structures favour distributed and open innovation (Baldwin and Clark 2000, 2006a, 2006b)? How can a firm influence the structure of its industry, either by internalizing complementary assets or by supporting asset mobility (Teece 1986; Jacobides, Knudsen and Augier 2006)?
3. New organizational forms for open innovation are emerging, such as platforms (Morris and Ferguson 1993; Gawer 2000, 2009; Gawer and Cusumano 2002, 2008; Gawer and Henderson 2007) and new market intermediaries such as InnoCentive (Lakhani and Panetta 2007; Sieg, Wallin and von Krogh 2009).

The works clarify the main issue: in cases of rule-based design, open innovation consists of organizing a modular architecture; in cases of innovative design, the whole sector becomes unstable; the issue is not to outsource one known resource but to work with new partners without knowing in advance what the common interests of the team will be.

They also help clarify what has to be managed: in rule-based design, it is a question of managing how the contract is respected; in innovative design, a wide variety of concepts, knowledge (existing or missing) and values (emerging interest by the partners and sometimes conflicting interests) must be managed.

The literature provides a clear picture of contemporary trends but gives few managerial insights and methods to deal with open innovation. What kinds of contracts are required? For which type of innovation? What are the possible steps in the partnership process? In this chapter we clarify:

1. The relationship between innovative design and open innovation.
2. The management issue: dealing simultaneously with cohesion and coordination.
3. A contingency approach to open innovation: the innovative process depends on the capacity of the firm to organize exploratory partnerships with its partners, i.e. its capacity to manage cohesion and coordination in the unknown.

For further information on this topic, *see* Segrestin (2005, 2009), Elmquist and Segrestin (2008) and Le Masson, Hatchuel and Weil (2009).

How can the innovative design reasoning described in this book stand up to the protagonists' specific, potentially contradictory or even conflicting approaches? Generally speaking, before working together, players agree on the objectives and their respective interests and then enter into a contract. However, in innovative design situations, traditional contracts can cover only part of the activities or the reasoning. Firms can, of course, sign contracts with research laboratories asking them to produce specific knowledge requiring a well-identified experimental system, or ask another manufacturer to design a sub-unit with well-defined specifications. However, there are a number of reasons why it is far more difficult to draw up contracts for joint explorations. For example, at the beginning of the adventure, none of the actors is capable of defining precise objectives or their interests in the project. Moreover, the objectives may change during the process. There are also cases where the partners differ in their evaluations of options opened up by the exploration, causing them to reassess their interests and sometimes put an end to the partnership. It is also difficult to decide in advance what resources will be required, to know whether one of the partners already has them, whether it would be wise to widen the circle of parties involved or whether one of the partners is willing to develop the required competencies. It is interesting to note that one of the main advantages of companies is precisely that there is no need to draw up contracts before their members can work together. This feature, which favours learning processes, was a key factor in the emergence of firms.

15.1.1   An analytical framework for exploratory partnerships

Blanche Segrestin (2003, 2005) explained the current difficulties of exploratory partnerships by the lack of a conceptual framework to help identify the different elements which have to be managed in such situations. In her view, two aspects must be managed at the same time: first, coordination, i.e. 'building the objects and the capacities for action', and second, what she calls cohesion, i.e. 'creating groups for collective action and the conditions for common interests'. She showed that one of the specific features of innovative design is that it is not possible to deal with one of the two aspects and assume that the other is stable. The interaction of the two elements has not been fully taken into account in the past due to the fact that, in most situations, organizations are able to handle them separately.

What exactly is covered by the terms 'cohesion' and 'coordination'? 'In traditional management literature, coordination concerns the object of the collective action: the concepts and the problems, and the associated management mechanisms, i.e. the efficiency criteria, the organizational means of dividing work and the collective learning processes. However, a second aspect needs to be addressed: how can individuals be encouraged to share a common purpose? It is this aspect that we have called "cohesion". It concerns the parties' interests and all the elements that make collective action possible. Among other things, it requires a legitimate framework and a means of handling any disputes, with rules for joining and leaving a partnership, for sharing the results and the risks, etc'. (Blanche Segrestin, conference at the Paris Institute of Technology thesis award ceremony).

Whereas coordination has mostly been mentioned in management literature, cohesion is more of a legal matter. Company law offers a number of solutions which enable actors to engage in collective action despite the uncertainties. Apart from contractual obligations, the different types of company (limited partnerships, joint stock companies, etc.) offer suitable protection in different situations. It should be noted that NPD and research projects are cases where cohesion is acquired from the beginning.

For exploratory projects, meanwhile, the actors prefer not to make mutual commitments and cohesion becomes an issue to be handled in the process.

In the context of innovative design, 'the situations are twice as risky, given that the partners are working on ill-defined objects [uncertainty regarding coordination] and are not sure that it is in their interests to cooperate [uncertainty concerning cohesion]: their collaboration should help them specify the actions to be carried out, the resources required, the risks and their respective interests'. The two notions are therefore highly inter-dependent, as any change in coordination has an impact on cohesion and vice versa. For example, interests can diverge when the partners learn more about the actions to be carried out and, conversely, there can be crises in terms of coordination when they learn more about what can be expected from the cooperation.

Segrestin (2003) shows that, in such situations, it is important to manage the interplay between cohesion and coordination: 'First, with conditional procedures for revising the two aspects and thereby readjusting the links between them; and second, with means of detecting problems and of evaluating how the interactions are working'. If this is not managed correctly, the actors tend to be reticent to commit themselves to exploratory partnerships. In this context, one of the paths proposed by Segrestin entails looking for different forms of 'special exploration contract' to provide the parties with the foundations of an agreement for entering into and managing exploratory partnerships in a strict legal framework.

15.1.2 Illustrating the analytical framework with previous case studies

As we mentioned in the introduction, we did not focus on the issue of exploratory partnerships in the different cases mentioned throughout this book as we believe that it is important to fully understand the innovative design reasoning required to carry out innovation field explorations before moving on to this question. However, many of the cases did involve this issue. For instance, Tefal and Avanti were specialists in co-development with their suppliers (Chapters 4 and 6). The partnerships between Schlumberger and its clients (BP, Shell and Aramco) illustrate a demanding situation in terms of coordination (experimental work on new phenomena and a new service) with a simplified contractual situation in terms of cohesion (sharing interests *ex ante*, no result-sharing – *see* Chapter 13). The microclimate case involved a partnership between an automobile manufacturer and a research laboratory (design space 3 – *see* Chapter 14), based on novel concepts (exploring coordination) and a minimum form of cohesion (service contract).

In this analytical framework, the relationship between Renault and Saint-Gobain Sekurit for the solar control windscreen project is particularly intriguing. The project was typical of innovative design reasoning as it changed the objects' identities, added a new multi-functional dimension and changed the perimeters of competition. (Did solar control in passenger compartments concern specialists in air-conditioning, the glassmaker, the car manufacturer or other potential players?) However, from the 1970s, the relationships between glassmakers and automobile manufacturers seemed to prevent drastic changes of this sort, given that the functional language was implicit and linked to the latter and the design parameters were limited and linked to the former. Hence, the glassmaker could not see the value of radical new design parameters, whereas the car manufacturer could not see the feasibility of new functionalities. How did the firms manage to change things? Was it a purely random or a truly exploratory process?

The two firms could have used an exploratory partnership to upset this balance, but Renault, and more specifically the head of glass purchasing, Jacques Civilise, decided not to set up sophisticated forms of collaboration with the glassmaker for the solar control windscreen concept, but to use the strict framework of the company's usual commercial contracts (stable cohesion for the coordination of innovative objects). Renault's designers justified their choice by their fears of difficulties in an exploratory partnership with a supplier which was far more competent than its client and had the reputation of not wanting to share its expertise and being against any innovations that questioned its processes. Moreover, the oligopolistic context (finally condemned by the European Commission in 2008) was not in favour of co-innovation partnerships. How did Jacques Civilise and his designers at Renault manage this deliberately minimalist design strategy?

The initial concept was not 'a solar control windscreen' – the notion of solar control did not exist at the beginning – but was more general: 'glazing with innovative properties perceived by the customer (taking into account probable resistance from the glassmaker)'. Initially, the knowledge space was limited: the specifications for glazing were usually renewed implicitly and the idea of 'functions' for a windscreen no longer seemed to have any meaning. The designers used the ongoing commercial contracts to reappropriate the specifications by asking questions about glass defects in the glazing being produced at the time. Whilst improving the quality of the glazing, this work also helped them understand more about the glassmaker's design parameters.

At the same time, but independently, Renault's designers studied possible innovative functionalities for glazing. They identified a number of options, including solar control properties, and explored several of these paths, the aim being to study customer value, to see how this could be appropriated by Renault – at least in terms of image and for a limited period of time – and, above all, to assess the possibility of obliging the glassmaker to design and produce the product in question. During this study, the designers visited a number of glass factories, including suppliers and non-suppliers. Once again, the visits did not entail any sort of partnership framework other than normal commercial relations. Renault thus built up knowledge for its own purposes, using contracts already in progress. At the end of the explorations, the solar control windscreen had been identified as an interesting solution for two reasons: first, it offered value for customers ('coloured', blue-tinted windscreen; perceptible heat absorption), and second, there was a way of obliging the glassmaker to produce it. On this second point, an American glassmaker had confirmed that it could supply solar control windscreens, so competition became a plausible way of putting pressure on the French glassmaker.

A final problem concerned the appropriation of the value. How could the designers be sure that the image of innovation in windscreens would be attributed to Renault? They rapidly excluded the possibility of registering a patent as a number of patents already existed for solar control windscreens. It seemed impossible to negotiate exclusive rights. They opted for the solution of saturating all existing production capacities worldwide by immediately equipping their entire range of vehicles with solar control windscreens. As we saw earlier, the result was that Saint-Gobain Sekurit embarked on designing a solar control windscreen – and was commended by all the parties for its efficiency – and Renault became the recognized leader for this new feature of car comfort, keeping a near monopoly for several years.

This case illustrates minimal cooperation: Renault avoided setting up an exploratory partnership and carried out the exploration on its own. In doing so, it gave priority to certain methods of exploration and certain concepts. In other words, the choice (or the obligation) of certain forms of collaboration has an impact on the exploration as such. Renault was aware of the need to start by finding a common purpose with its supplier. Hence, it began by reducing the pressure on cohesion, in favour of clear, transparent coordination.

15.2 How collaborative devices shape the exploration of innovation fields

We shall now illustrate how different forms of collaboration shape the exploration of innovation fields with a view to identifying ways of managing such explorations in various situations.

15.2.1 General model

The situation can be modelled as follows. An innovation field manager carries out explorations, which are organized on a value management/design space basis. As it is a case of innovative design, the initial concept always has attributes relating to an environment outside the firm or outside its traditional space of competition. It will take a form such as 'a product concept P taking into account the interests of x,y,z'. We have just seen an example of this with the case of Renault. It should be noted that this implies that the role of the 'client' or the 'supplier' can be radically changed during the exploration (e.g. Renault could have entered into a joint venture with one of Saint-Gobain Sekurit's competitors, in which case it would have become its competitor rather than its client). In other words, the roles of 'client' and 'supplier' are not enough to determine the respective interests *ex ante.*

Innovation field managers can, of course, launch explorations in independent design spaces, but it can sometimes be wise, or necessary, to launch design spaces involving partners. These design spaces can be linked to the partner's own value management concerning a similar or even a different innovation field (*see* Figure 15.1).

With partnerships, the difficulty for innovation field managers is to know what sort of collaborative design spaces are available. What conditions have to be met before setting up a partnership? What can be learned from them? What can the innovation field gain from them? How will they improve value management? Also, depending on the 'tools', i.e. the possible types of exploratory partnerships, how should the project be organized?

We can characterize the types of 'resources' available to an innovation field manager by going back to the two concepts proposed by Segrestin, cohesion and coordination:

> *The capacity to manage cohesion.* This involves defining a legitimate framework, which makes the action possible despite uncertainties as

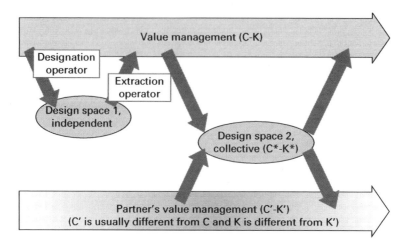

Figure 15.1   Partnerships in a context of 'value management and design spaces'

to the parties' respective interests; it also involves jointly managing the parties' interests as they emerge *during* the collaboration. The cooperation can be launched despite shared uncertainties concerning the interests, or the terms of cohesion can be set in advance by making assumptions as to the parties' interests.

In formal C-K terms, the C^*-K^* configuration of the collaborative design space must define the interests initially and the expansion does not make common (converging or conflicting) interests emerge.

The capacity to manage coordination. This involves managing more or less uncertain, abstract concepts during the collaboration. If this capacity is weak, the objects mobilized by the partnership must be better defined at the start and cannot be revised during the project.

In formal C-K terms, the C^* concept in the design space has a large number of attributes.

There are four possible cases: co-innovation without a partnership, partnership for new objects without creating shared interests, joint elaboration of shared interests for known objects and joint elaboration of shared interests for new objects (*see* Table 15.1).

Innovation field managers are obviously confronted with different types of partnerships depending on the actors concerned; different alternatives can also emerge during the explorations, and partnerships that seemed impossible at the start of the project may become feasible later on in the process. Detailed examples of the different possibilities can be found in Segrestin's

Table 15.1. Four families of collaborative partnerships

		Capacity to manage *cohesion*, i.e. capacity to start the action despite uncertainties regarding interests (e.g. settling disputes other than by *ex ante* result and risk-sharing)	
		Weak	Strong
Capacity to manage *coordination*, i.e. capacity for handling abstract/ill-determined concepts during the collaboration	Strong	Partnership for unknown objects without creating shared interests Example: research partnerships, co-development	Joint elaboration of shared interests for unknown objects
		Real case: Schlumberger and its clients in the RMC case; the car manufacturer and the research centre in the microclimate case	Real case: Intel and its relations with 'complementors', organized by Intel Architecture Lab
	Weak	Innovative design without partnerships Example: commercial contracts Real case: Renault and Saint-Gobain Sekurit for the solar control windscreen	Joint elaboration of shared interests for known objects Real case: Renault–Nissan; user involvement in design

work. Our aim here is to show how each of these situations restricts innovation field managers in their explorations. In fact, these restrictions justify their efforts to set up wide-reaching types of collaboration as and when necessary.

15.2.2 Examples of the four cases

We shall now illustrate each of the four situations.

In the first case – co-innovation without a partnership – cohesion and coordination are unable to deal with the uncertainties (the interests at stake and the objects must therefore be delimited *a priori*) and the innovation field manager must study the interests of all the parties concerned. The initial concept states that the final product should be in the interests of the parties, but the nature of these interests remains to be specified, *outside the collaborative framework*. This explains why it is essential in these cases to organize design spaces to analyse the competition (clients, suppliers, neighbouring industrial sectors, etc.) to understand and build up the interests in question. The ways of regulating these new interests are not studied collectively, but the firm can either try to separate them (i.e. to create value independently from the clients, suppliers and other neighbouring firms) or handle the value collectively in a strict framework in which the interests and the objects are known. This often takes the form of a negotiation late on in the exploration process. Renault and Saint-Gobain Sekurit were a typical example of this situation (*see* above).

The second case – partnership for new objects without creating shared interests – is similar as far as cohesion is concerned, but the firm also has the capacity to organize collaborations concerning more uncertain objects. The most common example is a *research contract* between a firm and an outside laboratory. There is an opportunity for obtaining known converging interests which make the cooperation possible in the short term, but the framework of cohesion does not enable the parties to discuss the interests which may arise during the cooperation. The relationship between the car manufacturer and the energy research laboratory in the microclimate case is an example of this situation. Another example is Schlumberger's relations with its clients in the RMC case: the partnership was organized to deal with a specific research issue – predict the arrival of an injected water front in a working context – but the collaboration covered only interests that were defined *ex ante*. This implies that it is not possible for common interests to be the subject of the collaboration. In other words, paradoxically, trials carried out with clients do not enable firms to learn very much about needs and particularly any new needs which may be discovered during the collaboration, because the risk of disputes is too high. Any learning can take place only indirectly, at the risk of causing budgetary problems in operational partnerships.

Co-development also fits into this category: it covers concepts, but the question of interests must be separated from the overall development budget fixed *ex ante*. The co-development is restricted by the limited exploration of each of the partner's interests: a discovery made by X but interesting for Y has little chance of survival in this sort of situation.

Although partnerships of this sort prevent common interests from emerging and do not encourage the partners to study their interests together, they do have some advantages. They offer the innovation field manager more scope for experiments, particularly in environments or with resources which would be difficult to access otherwise. For instance, the car manufacturer took advantage of the research laboratory's capacities in prototyping and rapid modelling; Schlumberger had access to the exploitation wells in a working context, i.e. access to unique phenomena which were hard to simulate.

The third case – joint elaboration of shared interests for known objects – is symmetrical to the previous one. The framework of cohesion enables the parties to start exploring the common interests *during the collaboration,* as long as *the objects of the collaboration are well delimited.* The symmetry can be illustrated by the formal analysis of the relationship between C-K and C*-K* in the collaborative design space: as we saw, C_0 takes the form 'a product concept P taking into account the interests of x,y,z'. In the previous case, C* concerns the product concept and restricts the uncertainties concerning the interests before the exploration begins. In the present case, C* concerns the question of the interests but cannot treat it directly with the product concept P, but with a more precise concept P*. The exploration is limited in terms of coordination in order to improve the exploration of the interests. Segrestin refers to this as a 'cohesion-oriented' exploration.

She studied an exemplary case of such partnerships, the development of a common platform in the Renault–Nissan alliance (Segrestin 2004). The alliance was seen by the two car manufacturers' designers as a special design space for their projects, whose purpose was not initially to work on particularly innovative projects but to identify their common/conflicting interests by working on relatively mature concepts. The alliance offered a framework of cohesion suited to managing the *discovery* of their mutual interests whilst designing a future common platform for replacing the existing vehicles. It worked well when the objects of their work enabled the partners to discover the interests during their collaboration, but innovative concepts tended to be excluded from these exchanges as each of the partners took them over separately, outside the alliance. However, design spaces of this sort have the advantage of making one partner's designers aware of the other partner's interests.

Let us take an imaginary example of such a design space. A designer from Renault working on innovative air-conditioning systems decided to enhance the exploration by taking part in a feasibility study for a common air-conditioning system for a middle-of-the-range platform (well-specified object but uncertainty concerning mutual interests). On this occasion, he found out that Nissan was particularly interested in compact air-conditioning blocks whereas Renault gave priority to power, for instance. The information could influence him the wrong way when it came to the vehicle being developed for the platform (if traditional air-conditioning was chosen), but the compact system could be introduced in the design of an innovative system for another vehicle developed in common. Hence, differences in interests were discovered, leading to the redefinition of possible common interactions.

In general terms, these tools should help innovation field managers explore the other actors' interests, with the prospect of innovative design, but *using existing objects or at least highly specified concepts*. To a certain extent, Telia's collaboration with its users (Chapter 11) is an example of this paradox: the idea was to identify interests shared by the users and the firm for third-generation mobile phone services, but this exploration could be carried out only using specific prototypes ('consult bus timetable on the internet') or 'ideas' (which are restrictive concepts because they have many attributes which can be useless or even misleading). As we saw, the risk is to lose sight of the initial general concept and to use specific 'ideas' which have the advantage of being of interest to outside partners: people expect to find an idea which is both feasible and with original user value. But this way of reasoning was a failure. The challenge was to distinguish between the object of the shared interest (the concept of remote control) and a one-off idea which 'reflected' this interest in a limited and incomplete way.

The fourth case – joint elaboration of shared interests for new objects – concerns exploratory partnerships as such. The innovation field manager has the resources to set up design spaces in which the mutual interests can emerge and in which the designers can work on abstract concepts. A famous example of this situation is the Intel Architecture Lab (IAL), described by Gawer and Cusumano (2002). The authors showed how Intel's innovation dynamics and growth were based on its ability to explore and create value with 'complementors', i.e. developers of complementary products. Until the mid-2000s, Intel's innovation strategy consisted of increasing the processing speeds of its microprocessors, but this could create value only if the increased speeds provided new uses for the final users. IAL's aim was precisely to explore these new uses with the players concerned, i.e. PC designers and suppliers of accessories and software.

One of IAL's first results was the peripheral component interconnect (PCI) bus standard. The bus is a PC's 'nervous system', which connects the microprocessor to the different internal and external peripherals. In the 1990s, the PCI bus standard replaced all the previous proprietary buses which were unable to keep up with the high-speed performance of the new generations of Intel chips. Intel's partners were also interested in the

PCI bus as it provided them with a simpler interface for their own innovations. The interesting point here is that the bus was designed collectively. There were several alternatives and the designers had to explore all the parties' interests (first, the level of integration of the microprocessors and, second, the level of innovation offered to complementors). The PCI bus can be seen as the result of a design exercise on an abstract product concept (design the 'nervous system' of a computer) also aiming to build up collective interests. The authors described similar exercises carried out by IAL, including the USB port, the FireWire port and the AGP graphic interface. They stressed the importance of IAL's methods, in particular the Intel Developer Forums and PlugFest events, the latter involving hiring a venue where complementors can meet Intel and other complementors and test the interoperability of their future products with Intel's platform.

A key point here is that the PCI bus (like the USB port) is not a proprietary standard and can be used freely without being subject to royalties. The aim is to encourage market growth and to ensure that this growth is due to Intel's products, and more precisely to their increased performance. Once again, from a formal standpoint, IAL is not an independent designer; its activity depends on Intel's innovative concepts: $C_0 = $ 'high-speed microprocessors with an interest for end-users'. The IAL enables the manager of this innovation field to work on certain attributes of the proposition ('interest for the end-users'); for the others ('high-speed performance'), Intel uses its traditional in-house design capacities.

The situation can seem attractive, but partnerships of this sort are rare and demanding. Segrestin has shown how, by nature, such situations evolve and suffer crises if cohesion and coordination mechanisms are not mutually adjusted to take into account the knowledge acquired during the projects. However, without going into these difficulties, it is interesting to note that the first risk is for the innovation field managers: as the design spaces have the capacity to explore common interests and innovative concepts, they may tend to neglect other means of learning (i.e. other non-collective design spaces), although these could be vital to a successful partnership. In practice, it can be useful to anticipate some of the partners' interests to maintain cohesion and to anticipate conceptual variations to facilitate coordination. To go back to the notions of value management and design spaces, although it may seem as if the partners' value management processes have merged in this fourth case, this is not true in formal terms. On the contrary, they are quite distinct. For instance, at Intel there were fierce discussions regarding the direction the partnerships should take and, more generally, the evolutions in innovative concepts: there was independent, distinct value management; it was the design space which managed to operate with abstract concepts and to integrate the explorations of the parties' interests, in what can be seen as a third process of value management, shared by the parties. It can be assumed that this third value management process will be all the more successful if it is fed with explorations stemming from the independent value management processes.

15.3 Conclusion: towards new spaces for exploratory partnerships?

There can also be dynamic changes in the different situations described above. For instance, an innovation field can start as a restricted partnership (type 1) but gradual learning processes can help it move on (to type 2 or 3). Renault's explorations on the solar control windscreen began with simple commercial contracts (type 1) but finally led to a co-development partnership (type 2) for the first solar control windscreen with Saint-Gobain Sekurit.

The typology also suggests potential new forms of partnership. For instance, some firms and research laboratories try to change their partnerships from type 2 to type 4, i.e. to encourage them to build up common interests, based on new phenomena and properties, which emerge during the explorations. Classic research partnerships are based on the prior identification of an object which, although still abstract, is often partly defined, leading to one-off projects of academic and industrial interest (which can be covered by a work contract). On the contrary, spaces for innovative research and design are geared to setting up joint explorations of ill-identified phenomena and ill-formulated questions. The Linklab laboratory founded by Saab Aerospace following the WITAS project (see Chapter 10) seeks to be a meeting place for innovative design teams – from Saab or from research laboratories – looking for partners for innovative explorations. It offers innovation field managers different types of relationships, from type 1 to type 4 partnerships. Schlumberger's decision to create an innovation hub at Clamart, in the Paris region, also stems from the same approach, i.e. to encourage exploratory partnerships. In the same vein, laboratories and universities are increasingly keen to host exploratory partnerships. The challenge is to deal with new scientific objects with the greatest possible agility, both in intellectual and experimental terms, and to be capable of controlling joint value-oriented explorations, requiring extremely varied expertise.

'There are still a number of pending questions', concludes our Innovation Manager, 'but I have some very useful elements to be going on with, which should help me and my teams design the tools we need. For instance, I'm convinced of the importance of using the right economic tools. The model suggests that a Real Option framework could be appropriate'.

The field of innovative design tools is indeed beginning to open up, suggesting that many new approaches and new tools will be developed in the near future.

It is clear that the organization of innovative design and innovation field management are still in the early stages. There is a host of questions still to be explored and approaches and tools still to be invented or perfected. In short, there are plenty of key discoveries in store for innovative firms and researchers. Our aim in this part of the book was not to provide an exhaustive list of all the problems and all the tools for managing innovation fields but to show through a few concrete examples the nature of the issues involved in innovative design and in innovation field explorations. Our aim was also to show the type of instruments and approaches that can be used to manage the principles explained in the previous parts of the book, bearing in mind that these developments must also be based on a new modelling process, in terms of both the design reasoning (the C-K theory) and the design organization (value management and design spaces).

Questions for further study and discussion

Give present-day examples of entire sectors confronted with innovative design issues. Identify cases where no actors are able to meet the challenges of innovative design on their own in their sector.

Analyse cases of open innovation or platforms by examining the nature of the questions raised in terms of coordination and cohesion and the nature of the expansions produced with respect to concepts and knowledge.

Key notions – Chapter 15

Exploratory partnerships

Cohesion and coordination

Conclusion: the governance of innovative design, a third era of modern management?

Throughout this book we have described the key tools and organizing principles for innovative design. In this conclusion, we would like to bring the central themes into focus with a rapid overview of the main stages in our research itinerary. A few questions will serve as a thread and help understand the overall implications of our findings. How can we explain the emergence of RID in the long history of management? What does it tell us about how companies will be organized in the future? What impact does the development of innovative design tools and theories have on the major paradigms of the management sciences? Have new avenues of research been opened?

Each of these questions merits long developments, but here we will simply give a few indications for further reflection without going into detail or coming to any firm conclusions. In fact, our main aim here is to emphasize that the current progress in innovative design opens a wide debate on the evolution of contemporary management. The debate cannot be limited to a discussion on management techniques and, although we must discuss the impact of the tools used for innovative design, it is also important to carry out a wider analysis of the issue of innovation in management today. Management research is sufficiently mature to recognize that the current progress in terms of instruments and theories is ambivalent. Techniques and organization may have improved, but the emergence of RID is not a panacea and can have adverse effects that must be carefully weighed against its advantages.

1 Research itinerary: key stages

The key stages in our research itinerary, each conditioned by scientific choices, are summarized below.

From innovation to innovative design

The first stage entailed distancing ourselves from *the notion of innovation* to study *the innovative action* as such. 'Innovation' belongs to the family of terms that designates both an action and its result. It is in good company: 'organization', 'coordination', 'judgement' and 'evaluation' also have this double meaning. It may be a useful way of economizing on words, but there is a risk of forgetting that the action of innovating is not its own result and can be analysed separately. Innovation as a 'result' depends on a judgement made by an actor, designer, user, public body, etc. However, with the 'action of innovating', the designers of the innovation must *objectively* mobilize – i.e. think up, express, defend and promote – operations, reasoning, risk-taking and resources that can have complex links with later market success.

The second stage of our research consisted of studying the design activities developed in firms since the industrial revolution. These activities gave birth to new techniques, organizations and functions, but surprisingly, these have been practically ignored in the classic management treatises. This is an important historical gap in academic management research, which we will come back to later. However, it did not have serious consequences until we entered into a socio-economic system that demanded major transformations in design activities.

R&D: a confusing concept

It is not only researchers who have tended to overlook design activities – firms must take their share of responsibility too, as they were too eager to accept the all-encompassing notion of R&D. The latter was a practical tool for economic statisticians who, for lack of more appropriate notions, over-hastily grouped together complex activities that differ greatly from one company to the next. The notion of R&D covered a whole wealth of design activities in the same way that 'manufacturing' covered a great variety of productive systems in the nineteenth century. From the engineering departments invented by the machine manufacturers in the nineteenth century to the 'machines for innovation' epitomized by Edison and Bell's laboratories at the turn of the twentieth century, to the present-day R&D departments, *diverse entities have built the most dynamic engine in business history.* And yet, we know far less about the history of their principles of management and different practices than we do about the history of factories. In our research, we had to fill this gap and put a new focus on the vital role played by design work as an instrument for innovation.

Back to pioneer firms: repeated innovation and innovative design

However enlightening it may be, historical research was not enough. We discovered that new ways of organizing design activities were emerging, which seemed to increase firms' capacities to innovate. These new practices were the 'playing field', where research could make progress and perhaps find new organizations. At that stage, we decided to look beyond the current management icons and to study a series of less well-known firms. Whatever their sector or size, they were selected on the one condition that a detailed study had shown that they had a significant capacity for innovation. We had to be careful to avoid the well-known trap of radical or naïve empiricism where the reasoning goes round in a circle: they are the best because we have chosen them and what they do is interesting because they are the best. Fortunately, we had the advantage of being able to use an original theoretical framework to closely analyse the design activities and to detect original practices. Our position was similar to that of a biologist who discovers a new living species with unique physiological characteristics that enhance its capacity for survival. The scientific value of a discovery does not simply stem from the observation itself but also from the researcher's ability to rigorously describe the properties of the new model. Our study consisted of this work on modelling.

The next stages in the project followed on logically because, once the general direction had been decided, we were able to advance along two paths. On the one hand, we carried out a detailed study of several particularly innovative firms, including Tefal, Avanti and Sekurit, building an original model for innovative design activities. On the other, we developed a theoretical framework for the design activity that validates the model as an original system and is adapted to the challenge of innovation-based capitalism. The system adds to the more traditional forms of 'rule-based' design and 'wild' design.

The new front-end phase: key notions

Step by step, we discovered a new front-end phase and developed our theories. Front-end activities are at the heart of the capacity to innovate but do not follow firms' traditional functions and structures. At the innovative design stage, a financial or sociological concept, or a marketing approach, can generate leading-edge technical or scientific research, and vice versa. Similarly, a product concept can give birth to a new industrial strategy or to a change in a company's identity. In fact, an innovative design process is *an activity that regenerates firms and their value potential* and which cannot be reduced to just research or development. We had found the content and the identity of the 'innovation function' that many authors have referred to since Schumpeter, but without being able to explain its underlying reasoning, i.e. the tools, organizations and rules required for collective work. We can now summarize some of the key notions in our study.

Rule-based design/innovative design. This vital distinction helps explain why innovation always results from design work, but why all design work is not necessarily innovative. The distinction is not to be found in a judgement on the results but in the reasoning and competencies mobilized. For rule-based design, the object to be designed has a known identity, stable functional groups, suppliers and competencies. Rule-based design enables linear project planning with precise specifications that serve to control the results. Innovative design is defined by contrast: it does away with all the assumptions made for rule-based design.

From R&D to RID. The formula indicates that the I function must be at least as important and as well organized as the function R or D. But in practice, it is the notion of 'innovation field' that has the most positive impact as it helps combat a number of received ideas. For example, it shows that taking action to innovate is not simply a question of managing a project, developing a product or targeting a market. All these things are necessary, but only after the most difficult and the most rewarding part has been accomplished.

Exploring and structuring innovation fields. It is this activity that puts a new focus on the reality and the value of innovative design work. We saw that an innovation field gives birth to a number of rival or complementary projects, each with differing horizons. At the same time, a string of competencies and knowledge is mobilized, acquired or discovered. It is the sound management of this *potential for expansion* that makes an innovation field meaningful. This does not simply consist of sorting ideas and there is nothing mechanical about it. The 'same' innovation field will take very different forms from one company to another. It is rather like a garden: the show of flowers can be very different depending on how competent the gardeners are and how well they care for their flower beds. Similarly to agronomic research, management research cannot do away with the variations, but it now offers a means of validating the reasoning and modes of collective action that make it possible to have a beautiful show of flowers. Without research, this is just a stroke of luck.

Building innovation fields, structuring them collectively, memorizing acquired knowledge and concepts, reusing knowledge from one field to another and ensuring good coordination between innovative design and rule-based design: these are the pillars of the innovation function. After our theoretical and practical work, our claim is that they are just as easy *to formalize* and *to manage* as any other function in the firm.

2   Management history: the eclipse of design?

Looking back on this research project, we might wonder why all this had not been observed far earlier. There is the problem of the compartmentalization and the rigidity of research, and we described the different interpretations that weighed on the question of innovation in the social sciences. But if we confine our discussion to management history, it must be said that the fundamental management theories of modern times, those of Fayol and Taylor, were not terribly forthcoming about the place of innovation. This is worth examining more closely as it sheds light on the eclipse of design in the management doctrines.

Fayol and Taylor: thinkers on innovation?

Both Fayol and Taylor are considered to be the founders of modern manage-ment and leading innovators. They therefore had remarkable potential for thinking up innovation processes in firms. Nonetheless, this notion does not have a key place in their doctrines. Moreover, the little they did say about it was not taken up by academic and practical management tradition. This issue is far from anachronistic as the current emergence of RID will inevitably come up against the problem. We must therefore take a brief look at how innovation has been represented in the history of management doctrines.

Why didn't Frederick Winslow Taylor, who was a great inventor before turning to the theory of industrial organization, feel the need to deal with innovative design even though his books describe the introduction of new work or production processes? Why did Fayol, who gave scientific and technical progress such an important place, deal with innovation in only a very allusive fashion in his *Principles of General and Industrial Management?* Yet the same Fayol gave his constant support to the creation of the famous metallurgical laboratory in the factory at Imphy in France, where so many original, even revolutionary alloys were produced.[1]

There is no single explanation for these observations, but one key point is worth considering here because it sheds light on how innovation was represented at that time. Not enough emphasis has been put on the fact that the revolution sparked off by Taylor and Fayol came after another management revolution that had less impact on doctrine, i.e. the invention of large engineering departments. Around 1870, these departments reached an impressive scale, with several hundred technicians designing locomotives (Hatchuel, Le Masson and Weil 2005a). These engineering departments had no secrets for Taylor: he even designated them as the model for creating the production planning departments he invented. But the American engineer remained, through his training and his practical experience, a specialist in factory processes and work methods. In all the experiences he described, the design activity comes down to a well-conducted experiment. This was sufficient for improving and optimizing processes, and indeed led to scientific investigations and major discoveries, such as the high-speed steel processes that Taylor developed with White. However, it is not sufficient to describe and organize design work for new machines that must cater for multiple, changing functions. Taylor therefore remained a follower of the experimental approach to science and not one of innovative design, although the latter had already made progress in industry at that time, in the automobile and aircraft sectors.

The explanation is more complicated for Fayol because it is clear that he had conceived what we call innovation fields and innovative design approaches and had put them into practice. He fully understood and anticipated the place of innovation in sectors such as new military armoured vehicles, naval construction, the automobile and the new electrical industry. He even accelerated the pace by asking the laboratory at Imphy to explore new alloys in a systematic way, in preparation for these emerging industries. He went still further and stated that one of a manager's essential tasks is to organize cooperation between industry and scientists.[2] Unquestionably, *Fayol thought out and implemented a real innovation policy.* It can even be

---

[1] For further information on this point, *see* the notes on scientific works written by Henri Fayol (French National Library) (Fayol 1918).
[2] *Ibid.*

said that the notions of product lineage and the reuse of knowledge are to be found in his work. So why did he not make this a systematic doctrine? We can only dream of what Fayol could have written in a treatise on the management of innovation, but it would doubtless have helped to interpret his famous management principles: planning, organization, commanding people, coordination, control, etc. But once again, the explanation is to be found in the representations of that time. In our view, for Fayol, innovation policy was simply the same thing as introducing a scientific approach in firms and part of an overall movement, the progress of science in society. He believed in a collective *acquis* that did not need defending because the real challenge of his management doctrine was elsewhere: to demonstrate that new management practices were emerging that were nothing like those used by managers and foremen in the past. Hence, Fayol, like Taylor, did not separate the traditional scientific approach, or technical progress, from the design process.

Science and industrial design overlooked design processes

Their view became increasingly widespread despite the fact that the modern economies were at a radical turning point and were adopting a host of new objects, tools and machines. People's everyday lives were being drastically changed, at home and in the workplace, by a multitude of devices. At that time, industrial aesthetics – the forerunner of industrial design – worked in almost virgin territory, abandoned by the engineers. It needed Raymond Loewy, one of the founders of industrial design, to introduce the technique of clay models to engineering departments, so that the forms of objects could be designed rapidly without having to represent their technical properties. Industrial designers retained certain features of design reasoning and paved the way for a major economic and cultural revolution by merging artistic design systems and engineering systems. However, although everything points to the fact that contemporary civilizations were *design-based civilizations*, the design processes were confused with scientific approaches, which largely explains the difficulties encountered in developing scientific thinking on innovation. The irony is that the explosion of design activities in modern societies went hand in hand with their intellectual eclipse. For the general public and politicians, design activities were increasingly thought to be the same thing as scientific research, or they were simply assimilated with 'creations' based on individual talent, despite the fact that they are always collective activities.

The expression 'R&D', which dates from the 1960s, marked the peak of the eclipse. The work carried out by engineers and commercial staff was frequently described as 'putting research into practice', with a relationship of logical deduction between the knowledge produced by scientific research and the innovation, which was seen as a simple development. Of course, we must not forget the key contribution made by Herbert Simon (1969) to make people aware of the specific nature of design activities. But Simon tended to bury design in the general theories on problem-solving (Hatchuel 2002) and limited his arguments to a debate between classic and constructivist epistemology (Le Moigne 1995). Our aim was to add to these two positions by proposing a rigorous, formal design theory (Hatchuel and Weil 2003), the only theory to date that sets the traditional operations of science (experiments, axiomatization, etc.) in the wider family of the operators required for design reasoning. In this way, the C-K design theory shows that *traditional science does not describe the space of concepts*, or wrongly confuses it with the space of hypotheses or axioms. The specific nature of hypotheses or axioms is that they are always put forward, even temporarily, as truths, whereas a concept is, by definition, *a proposition that is neither true nor false*, i.e. a proposition that cannot be decided with the knowledge available (in K).

For historical and theoretical reasons, the design activity was obscured by an over-simplification of the notions of research and science. This meant that the question of innovations, or inventions, became an inextricable mystery. This had important inhibitory effects in the philosophical field, as shown by the widely misunderstood work by Boirel in his general theory of invention (Boirel 1961), or Simondon, whose work has only recently received any real recognition (Simondon 1958, 2005). We will develop this argument further in a separate book devoted exclusively to design theories.

Returning to the world of management, we will now briefly mention the question of public incentives for innovation before concluding with a discussion on the impact of the theories and principles for organizing innovative design presented in this book.

3   Public incentives for innovation: can government measures spark off industrial revolutions?

In this book, we have concentrated on innovative processes in firms and have not studied government intervention mechanisms. There are two reasons why we decided to confine our discussion of the issue to this conclusion.

The first reason is obvious: the literature is overflowing with studies on public incentives for innovation. The research has mainly been carried out by economists, with numerous international comparisons concerning a host of different government interventions. These range from corporate taxes, to university and research institute budgets, various forms of support such as aids for innovative projects, start-ups, etc., and, more recently, new mechanisms such as competitive clusters and laws on companies set up by public sector researchers. The stakes involved in the research are easy to set out in theory but more difficult in practice, the problem being to assess the effectiveness of such interventions. A more detailed account of this literature would have made this book considerably longer but without adding anything to the specific subject of our research. As we mention elsewhere (Chapters 1 and 2; the bibliographical appendix), all the policies and supporting studies tend to reduce the firm to a 'black box' or to a simple behavioural approach, a stance that is perfectly justified in the case of governments seeking measures to develop the performances of a given population of companies.

The second reason for putting to one side the issue of public incentives for innovation stems from our own results. All our research shows that, if there is one economic analogy that must not be made, it is *to confuse investment and innovation*. Of course, in absolute terms, investments are expenditures made to ensure future revenues and this concerns innovative design activities, too. However, innovative design introduces vital aspects that are not usually taken into account when thinking of investments.

Take, for example, a company manager who buys a machine to manufacture a product. Generally speaking, we can assume that 'he knows what he's doing', i.e. that he knows the machine and the product he is going to make with it, but that there remains, for example, a commercial risk. These assumptions no longer apply in the case of innovative design. Imagine that the company manager would like to design a machine himself and focus on innovative solutions that have not been fully explored in the past. This increases the risks, but the potential profits, too. Designing a new machine will involve structuring several innovation fields, changes in functions, research work, building of partnership(s), etc., i.e. all the innovative design processes described in this book. The company is then faced with a far more global risk depending on *its ability to successfully manage the innovative design*. This risk was not apparent in the case of the investment, because the representation of the act of investment implied that the company manager 'knew what he was doing'. We have moved from an investment situation with risks relating to certain parameters (e.g. sales) to an innovative design situation where the risks relate to every aspect of the company's operations.

This distinction helps explain our point of view on public actions in favour of innovation. The many different types of public incentives can be divided into three main categories:

1. Financial incentives designed to limit the risks of economic losses for firms.
2. Financial support for training or public research that can be used by companies to develop resources and competencies.
3. Incentives to take part in collective projects (competitive clusters).

Which measures correspond best to our research findings? Certainly not the first category: except for staunch believers in economic Darwinism, it is absurd to encourage a company to innovate if it does not have the ability to do so. As for the third category, competitive clusters can help certain firms acquire capacities to innovate through exchanges with partners. However, this mechanism is not very probable and, whatever the case may be, we must wait and see how these clusters work before counting on them in this respect.

There remains the second category of interventions, i.e. government support for developing research and training designed to help companies acquire innovation capacities. Our research therefore leads us to a revised interpretation of public aid for innovation: either we assume that companies 'know how to innovate', in which case we should keep the current range of interventions as the most difficult part has already been accomplished, or we consider that, on the whole, this is not the case and that most interventions will therefore be ineffective, not to mention the 'windfall effect' from the financial incentives.

Research is nonetheless required before support can be offered to firms to enhance their capacity to innovate and so we are pleading our own cause. Basically, this discussion is not really new. Governments are capable of offering financial incentives for known behaviour or for available competencies, but do not find it easy to set industrial or managerial revolutions in motion. At the most, they can favour research, help with consulting or with setting up specialized centres, and hope that the best practices will be disseminated in the firms. However, all our work points to the fact that innovation-related aid policies can be effective only if one precondition is met, i.e. that firms change to RID.

4   Innovative design and innovation policies: a third period of management?

What impact does our work have on the major paradigms of the management sciences? As we know, neither design nor innovation is a major stream of academic research and, depending on the circumstances, they tend to be put under strategy, organizational theory or industrial management. However, in the past few years, specialized disciplines such as innovation management, engineering design and design management have begun to appear. This excellent move is convenient for research institutes and universities, but on a scientific level, it is also important to examine the more general impact of the knowledge acquired on design and innovation for the management sciences as a whole. In our view, there are three key topics that must be addressed in future research on fundamental management concepts: first, a new approach to the notion of strategy, second, a new approach to work organization and, third, a new form of management.

A new approach to strategy

Although strategy is one of the most important notions in the management sciences, it is also one of the most difficult to define, as witnessed by the numerous arguments it has given rise to in the past fifty years. There is general agreement on the basic idea that strategy is the sum of all the actions used by managers (or groups of managers) to give content and direction to the various teams they manage. But different 'conceptions' of strategy confront each other when it comes to describing, characterizing and assessing the managers' actions: top-down or bottom-up, centralized or decentralized, planned or 'formed', intentional or emergent, reactive or proactive, technocratic or participatory, procedural or culture-based, rationalist or political, concrete or symbolic, structuralist or personalist, etc. It is very difficult to cover all the different arguments studied in the host of literature on the subject. Why are so many different meanings given to the notion of strategy? Is it badly defined or does it not have a clear status?

The work on innovative design sheds light on both these questions at the same time. On reflection, the management sciences have no reason to give a more precise or stable definition for the notion of strategy than they do for the notion of 'chair'. To understand the notion, or even to observe it as a practical phenomenon, suffice to say that strategy helps manage a company, in the same way that a chair enables people to sit down. There are as many types of chair as it is possible to design, and designers will go on designing new ones in the future. This *property of expansion* is not a congenital defect in the notion of strategy: on the contrary, the notion has been capable of harnessing such a wide spectrum of different meanings that it offers strategy designers vast innovation fields. But what object is being studied in the discipline of strategy? It cannot be the word itself because, like a fractal object, its meaning is extended each time someone focuses on it. The object of the scientific analysis must therefore be found in the methods used to design the strategy and not in the strategy itself. This idea was found, at least implicitly, in a movement in Anglo-Saxon management literature that attempted to describe the transition from object to action. It was expressed in a shift from 'organization' to 'organizing', from 'knowledge' to 'knowing', from 'strategic' to 'strategizing', etc. This goes in the right direction but lacks solid theoretical foundations, as an action cannot be captured simply by replacing a noun with a verb. For the notion to be fully described, understood and universal, we must remember that the action itself requires design work.

The classic antagonisms of strategy disappear with this approach, or are no longer intrinsic properties of the object 'strategy'. They become characteristics of the design reasoning. For example, from the angle of innovative design, the opposition between intentional and emerging strategy no longer exists: emerging phenomena can be the result of intentional aims, and this is clearly the case when open or exploratory prototypes are built. Similarly, participatory and technocratic strategies are no longer incompatible and can easily be combined in innovative design. For instance, an event organizer can 'technocratically' plan the intervention of players in charge of creating 'surprises' without deciding what the surprises will be. Apart from these examples that show that prescription and autonomy are perfectly compatible in design, similar demonstrations can be made to show that all the traditional antagonisms concerning strategy are the direct results of the design methods used.

Consequently, the universality of scientific projects no longer consists of finding a fixed, absolute definition of strategy, and strategy can no longer be studied as if it were independent from design capacity. The object of research moves naturally towards the study of the design methods themselves. In this case, it seems that we are not free to invent as many design theories as we like, or at least this is the hypothesis put forward here. The obvious scarcity of design theories in the past few centuries appears to back our position, as does the limited number of principles on scientific approaches. However, our work supports the point of view that management sciences are not so much sciences of strategy as sciences studying the methods used to design strategy (Tranfield and Starkey 1998).

A new approach to the division of work: cohesion coordination

Another key notion in the management sciences is the organization of the division of work, an issue at the heart of debates on the structures of firms. Traditionally speaking, the division of work is based on principles and knowledge *that precede* the act of dividing. For example, work can be divided once tasks, types of qualifications or skills and fields of intervention (market, territory, etc.) have been defined. However, this assumes that there is sufficient knowledge in each case to carry out the division of work and stabilize it. Yet, as we have seen, in innovative design situations concepts and knowledge undergo a dual expansion, which usually destabilizes the points of reference used to divide work. It can no longer be an outcome in itself, but takes a transitory form that generates its own revision or obsolescence. The division of work hence becomes *a dynamic variable of collective action* and can no longer represent its 'structure', if we take this to mean the invariants of an organization.

If we accept this analysis, we must then find the ingredients for stability and invariance. Following Mintzberg (1981), we can draw up a list of the design parameters for the division of work or for coordination, which comes to the same thing. Mintzberg made a distinction between direct supervision, qualification, mutual adjustment, work standards and objectives. In innovative design, the category of mutual adjustment is tempting for its openness, but it is not explicit enough. We must bear in mind that innovative design features all the forms of division of work based on explorations.

Take two industrial designers working on a project for a new vehicle. They can choose to look at the same question but from two different angles. For example, one can base his work on how cars are represented in society, the other on recent trends. This example shows that there are as many ways of dividing work as there are ways of forging an opinion about an object. In innovative design situations, it is impossible to imagine a set list of principles for dividing work, because this would mean that there was already a major design rule encompassing innovative design. However, if our two industrial designers are to choose their paths of investigation freely, they need a principle of intelligibility based on their common understanding of the exploratory approach to be used. In this case the invariant is not in the procedure, as too often believed since Simon, but *in the reasoning that gives the procedure an intelligible meaning.* It is the innovative design reasoning that justifies the fact that the division of work is both necessary and contingent to the exploratory approach. At the same time, it is accepted that the division is temporary and that the results of the exploration will almost certainly change it.

We must insist on a fundamental point: innovative design is not simply a case of 'the path is made by walking', as the constructivist thinkers like to say, as this does not take into account the great complexity of the approach and forgets the most important issues. Innovative design requires several conditions: a) that the players are convinced that the path cannot be made in any other way; b) that they are certain that any changes in the initial direction are based on reasoning that takes into account their own investigations; c) that the different changes that take place over the period are memorized so that it is possible to come back to the previous crossroads if the wrong path is taken; d) that the destination can be rediscussed with the option of abandoning the path altogether. These conditions are in fact the basic operations of an innovative design process. Despite the attractive metaphor, the process cannot be summed up by a path made by walking.

However, there is nothing to say that the process, however intelligible it may be, will be accepted or will seem reasonable. This comes back to the question of the social legitimacy of innovative design (Laufer 1993): in what circumstances can the innovative design approach be considered a legitimate principle if it upsets the principles of the division of work, which guarantee, to a greater or lesser extent, a certain degree of social stability? This important question obliges us to take a critical look at the conditions of implementation and the impact of innovation policies in firms, which appear to result in the instability of roles, jobs and relations of prescription (Hatchuel 2001b). Without going into more detail here, we would like to point out that Segrestin (2006) opened a fruitful path for exploring this question in her study of inter-firm cooperation in innovative design situations (*see* Chapter 15 on innovative partnerships). She demonstrates that two models of collective action must constantly be brought together, i.e. a *coordination model* that follows the innovative design system and a *cohesion model* aimed at maintaining the coherency of the different interests, expectations and aspirations. An innovative design system also obliges the parties to revise the cohesion model in an intelligible, acceptable way. The coordination model and the cohesion model form a single unit of analysis and any transformations to them must be addressed without disassociating them.

Hence, innovative design opens up the principles for dividing work and the principles of cohesion. Once again, the object of the scientific research must be revised. It can no longer be defined by one or other of the models, but by *a combination of the two*. Although this observation was made by management research, it leads to questions about the relationships between the separate disciplines of economics and sociology. In innovative design contexts, which models or theories can economists or sociologists use for the inevitable mutual adjustment of cohesion and coordination, and does this mean that the paradigms that organize disciplinary divisions in the social sciences should be revised? The debate is open.

Innovation policies: the third era of modern management?

With the notion of RID, it is clear that the *I* function – the innovative design activities – should make a vital contribution to the value created by the firm and thus be a determining element in its future. As a result, a good manager cannot escape from the major responsibility of ensuring that the *I* function works as smoothly as possible. However, it is not so much the responsibility as such that matters but the way it is exercised. In other words, the *I* function poses a unique management problem for managers today: on which factors can they, and must they, act?

Rather than listing all the models and tools that have been explained in this book, we can focus on six propositions which make up a form of brief for designing an innovation management system, based on the knowledge acquired through our research project.[3]

P1. Generalized innovation. Innovation is not confined to any one department in particular. Every function or work unit must, to a certain extent, have its share in innovative design and in anticipating the future. Everybody must be prepared to take part, with others, in work on designing the future. No department acts as the exclusive specialist in innovation on behalf of all the others and each department explores the future from its own particular standpoint.[4]

P2. Support units for innovative design. However, units must be created – that can be called innovation divisions or innovative design divisions – which

---

[3] 'Brief' generally describes a mission. In industrial design, it is used to describe the initial indications given to designers without too many restrictions on their freedom to create.

[4] This is in line with the notion of generalized ambidexterity explored by Kamila Kohn (2005) in her thesis at the Fenix Centre of the Chalmers Institute in Gothenburg.

are capable of proposing, structuring and managing the major innovation fields that carry the firm's potential transformations. These units require all the players in the firm to imagine 'desirable futures' and to be able to take part in the innovation process. But they will also be required to help transform this potential into innovative design.

P3. A front-end metabolism. Where should these support units be placed in the organization chart? Conflicts tend to arise when too much emphasis is put on this point. It is not so much the place that is important as the work methods used by these support units in order to cooperate with the other units. Due to their activities, the units will have close relationships with all the front-end departments working on company policy: the research department exploring changes in knowledge, the marketing department exploring the markets and competition, the product divisions examining habits and possible opportunities, the industrial design department imagining new trends, etc. The innovation function is an activity whose object is to organize a *collective metabolism* (Chapel 1997), as the study on Tefal illustrated so well. The aim of this metabolism is to regenerate the firm's products/ services, competencies and resources.

P4. C-K-inspired steering tools. Developing innovation fields must not be confused with participatory creative exercises or with new product development projects. Several chapters in this book focus on this point and we will simply emphasize here that managing innovation fields requires the right tools and forms of collective work, and that this is where all the tools relating to the C-K design theory take their full meaning.

P5. Memory and delegation. The function of memory and accumulation also plays an important role. Innovative design constantly creates possibilities that are then abandoned and knowledge that is not used. It must try to conserve if not a complete trace at least some rules of accessibility. As this task rapidly becomes too demanding, it can be delegated by sector, branch or division, in the same way as R&D at present. The only difference is that, contrary to research programmes, there is nothing to prevent an innovation field from being studied in several different places, because each player's contribution is enhanced when the work is put together.

P6. Management by value. The entire process must be *monitored by a managing body to oversee the global value* created by the process. Although the composition of the body will vary from one firm to another, it must not be managed exclusively on meaningless quantitative criteria. The value of the innovation fields cannot be separated from the work of this managing body, which, among other things, will give its opinion on the maturity of projects coming from the innovation fields, identify new fields and new competencies, monitor and manage risks, make choices and allocate resources. It will have to build its points of reference to deal with all these issues. This work will give legitimacy to the overall process, as the managing body gradually builds up precious skills consisting of the ability to give collective thought to the major notions of value in a company. If the innovation process is properly managed, this will doubtless result in direct improvements to the firm's overall governance.

Are there firms where all these propositions have been put into practice? If we take the firms we studied, these propositions did not necessarily cover the same practices.[5] It seems likely that each firm will develop different practices, even if they take inspiration from the models and approaches explained in this book. However, it may be that we are still in a preparatory phase and that best practices will emerge later that can be generalized. Nonetheless, it usually takes training and consultants to build up and disseminate references and best practices throughout firms before they become routine. It may be that the transition to RID that we defend here will be widely adopted. This was, after all, one of the aims of this book. But we are well aware that this sort of change can lead to dangerous routinization and that 'recipes' are sometimes disseminated that do not have the same spirit or meaning. The only real way to avoid the problem is to raise the level of knowledge and critical thinking.

We shall conclude by examining the place of innovative design policies in business history, with a particular focus on the history of the major management models. To do so, we follow the interpretation proposed at a recent seminar by two managers from the Paris Transport Authority (RATP), one of our main research partners.[6] They remarked that, basically, the development of innovative design can be interpreted as *a third era of modern management.*

The first era of management focused on building good relations between the management system and the operational units. This form of management, essential in large groups, was built up gradually from the 1960s to the 1980s with the emergence of business units, the clarification of relationships

---

[5] The KCP (Knowledge, Concept, Proposition) workshops that we have developed in several companies have acquired a certain form of repeatability. The workshops, held over a period of several weeks or months and directly inspired by the C-K theory, will be the subject of future scientific publications.

[6] Georges Amar (foresight studies and innovative development) and Yo Kaminagai (design management).

between client units and supplier units, the introduction of standard rules for human resources management, etc.

The second era of management, *project management*, emerged at the beginning of the 1990s. It consisted of organizing the development of processes (especially computerization) and products, changes in manufacturing, outsourcing and acquisition and transfer transactions. Project management underwent unprecedented growth during this period, sometimes to the detriment of quality control. Above all, this second era of management helped simplify corporate management for firms confronted with increasingly strong, rapid changes. Project management was used as a sandbag to protect against the flood of change, in the hope of channelling it and limiting the all too frequent excesses in terms of costs and lead times.

Project management was obviously necessary, but it is no longer sufficient. When projects relied on existing competencies and rules, and did not call into question the identity of the firms, the products or the clients, companies could be content with an effective, planned system. But this is no longer the case. Competition through intensive innovation, new regulations, new social values and emerging powers are all pushing in the same direction: the growing need for collective work designed to regenerate firms' products and competencies in a sustained, repeated and organized manner. This work, inside and outside the firm, involves the clients and the suppliers, but also research and academic partners. It must be devised as a collective innovative design activity and as an innovation policy. All this points to a third era of management: *innovation management.*

This brief description of the three eras of modern management illustrates the challenges that are still facing us today. It also allows us to pay a modest tribute to all our research partners by letting two of them have the last word in this book.

Bibliographical appendix. Innovation viewed by the different disciplines: an extended survey of the literature

Our study of innovation would not be complete without mentioning the economic, marketing, cognitive, organizational and managerial dimensions that come into play. The aim of this appendix is to summarize the extensive literature on each of these aspects. We will look at the five disciplines in turn: economics, sociology, the cognitive sciences, organization and management. For each discipline, we will focus on three characteristics:

The genealogy of the research questions. A number of concepts have been proposed in each of the five disciplines, but to understand how they came into being and their impact, they have to be placed in the genealogical context of the different streams of research. For each concept, we will look at the type of question it dealt with and the context that led the different disciplines to address the issue and to produce the different models and theories. By studying when and why the new concepts emerged, we will have a clearer picture of the different questions which researchers were confronted with over the years.

The key notions and their links with action. In the past, research was very much affected by the discipline it belonged to. In many cases, innovation as such was not the subject of the research but reflected a tactical stance: the authors used a description of phenomena relating to innovation to challenge their disciplines' established theories. This perspective led to progress in studying the *phenomena* involved in innovation but, contrary to a management approach, did not focus on *the generation of new forms of collective action.* This is why the concepts sometimes appear inadequate compared with the challenges involved in managing the economic, marketing, organizational or cognitive aspects of activities designed to encourage innovation.

The recent trends. This study of past research also helps highlight the most recent trends, which can be as much the result of the disciplinary approaches themselves as of the emergence of new phenomena relating to innovation. The most recent research suggests that some of the traditional actors in innovation (research, marketing, etc.) have entered a period of crisis and that new practices are emerging (design by users, etc.).

1 Economic policy and innovation

1.1 Genealogy of research questions and key notions

The first tools for economic policy on innovation:
from Colbert to the New Deal

The links between innovation and economic policy go back a long way. For example, the rise of new industries played an enormous role in the economic policies of Colbert, French Minister of Finance from 1665 to 1683. More generally speaking, the policies of patents and privileges practised in both France and England in the seventeenth and eighteenth centuries favoured inventors, entrepreneurs and the growth of new economic sectors (Hilaire-Pérez 2000). With the arrival of the railways, which required concessions and different forms of State intervention, each new project gave rise to debates on whether the new techniques were really 'progress', as Booth described when one of the first railways, the Manchester–Liverpool line, was opened in 1831 (Booth 1831). The first 'technical economists' demanded State intervention to support science in the name of industrial progress. For example, Charles Babbage questioned the British authorities on their scientific policies and on the 'decline of science in England' (Babbage 1830), speaking of the threat for the 'future development of industry' and proposing 'compensations' for people carrying out scientific investigations.

At that time, economic policy addressed innovation in many different ways: training programmes, financing for research, laws covering inventions and protecting inventors, regulations on monopolies (concessions, privileges, competition laws, etc.), the creation of factories and major infrastructure programmes. In some cases, public policies also sought to assess the impact of innovation. For instance, when the US government introduced planned public policies such as the New Deal after the 1929 crisis, it began to wonder about the consequences of scientific discoveries for the nation, in terms of new products, new risks such as unemployment, infrastructure planning, etc. (Susskind and Inouye 1983). Innovations and inventions – the distinction was not clearly made at this stage – were analysed as given entities and studies were made on the impact of their dissemination.

The introduction of innovation in the discipline
of economics: Schumpeter and growth

In the period between the two world wars, economists proposed a series of concepts designed to introduce the question of innovation to the discipline of economics. For example, Joseph Schumpeter, an Austrian who had been teaching at Harvard University since 1932, looked beyond Walras's economic equilibrium and chose to study economic dynamics, i.e. growth, a question that was particularly pertinent in the midst of the 1929 crisis.

In Schumpeter's view, innovation was a concept that covered any change in the supply of products or services: 'Technological change in the production of commodities already in use, the opening up of new markets or of new sources of supply, Taylorization of work, improved handling of material, the setting up of new business organizations such as department stores – in short, any "doing things differently" in the realm of economic life – all these are instances of what we shall refer to by the term Innovation' (Schumpeter 1964, p. 59). More precisely, Schumpeter defined innovation as the 'setting up of a new production function'. At this point, Schumpeter specifically distinguished between innovations and inventions on the grounds that the latter had no economic impact (he referred to the sociologist Sean C. Gilfillan for an analysis of the social causes of invention (Gilfillan 1970)). He often simplified the distinction after that, saying that an innovation was an invention that had found a mode of production and a market, but, as in the above quotations, he was always careful to explain that innovations were not necessarily inventions. As for the determinants of innovation, Schumpeter began by highlighting the essential role of entrepreneurs and later, as a shrewd observer of the transformations in capitalism, insisted on the role played by the large firms in the renewal of 'production functions' (Schumpeter 1942).

This analysis enabled him to conduct an important economic policy debate on the question of the regulation of monopolies. He showed that routine innovation in large groups created situations of monopolistic competition (Chamberlin 1953) in which the dynamics stemmed from technological evolutions and product renewals (Schumpeter 1942). Schumpeter described a process of 'creative destruction' when former products, means of transport, markets, organizations and processes were made obsolete by new ones. Baumol (2002) returned to this question and showed that the fixed costs relating to research and development can be covered only by a situation of monopoly, but that there can be competition even in this situation insofar as innovations make the markets 'contestable'.[1]

Measuring the determinants of innovation: emergence of a typology of innovation

After the Second World War, research played an essential role in developing not only new technologies but also a new society, as Vannevar Bush pointed out in his report to the President of the United States, with its evocative title 'Science, the endless frontier' (Bush 1945). Bush used the same argument as Babbage a century earlier: scientific progress was the key to industrial development in a context of international competition (and also the arms race in the Cold War period). Western States were financing science on a massive scale.

Politicians were anxious to get a clearer picture of the different flows of resources. Sophisticated statistical systems were introduced, coded by the OECD in the *Frascati Manual*, to measure the investments made by the different nations in what was to be called R&D.[2] (*See* history of the *Frascati Manual* in Appendix 1 (OECD 1981).) The definition of R&D is discussed in Section 8.1 of this book.

In the face of these changes and following Schumpeter's intuitions, economists such as Maclaurin (1953) sought to identify the determinants of investment by using various indicators of economic and scientific activity. Maclaurin called for a scientific device capable of measuring investments in 'pure science' and 'applied science' and of counting patent applications, thus prefiguring the statistical tools introduced twenty years later by the OECD. For other economic indicators, he introduced what became classic distinctions:

Innovation versus invention: only 'inventions' that have been introduced commercially should be counted.

Radical versus incremental: when counting innovations, minor improvements (he referred to those made in automobiles since 1927) should not be given the same value as radical innovations (such as nylon).

Product, process, service: innovations in these three domains cannot be studied in the same way. Analyses should be based on sales volumes in

---

[1] According to Baumol, innovation requires fairly low initial sunk costs and relatively high recurring costs to keep up with continuous innovation. As a result, in his view an innovative market is usually contestable.

[2] There was no specific statistical work on outputs until the 1980s (fourth version of the *Frascati Manual*, 1981).

the first case, productivity figures in the second and data from the Census of Business or other equivalent bodies in the third.

The 1973 oil crisis led to renewed interest in Schumpeter's work on economic cycles. Mensch used the notion of 'cluster of innovations' (the innovation is not isolated as, according to Schumpeter, an innovation calls for other innovations and interdependencies are created) and introduced the notion of 'fundamental innovations', defined as a series of social and technical innovations adopted in a given society (Mensch 1975).

Introducing technical progress in microeconomic models: endogenous growth

In the years following the war, many economists were interested in the question of growth. For Keynesians such as Harrod and Domar, the market was not effective in regulating capital accumulation so that 'long-term evolutions are likely to be subject to a chronic excess of savings, resulting in a latent threat of depression' (Malinvaud 1993, p. 173). The famous Solow (1956) model opposed these pessimistic views by trying to demonstrate that it was possible to attain regular growth.

The Solow model

For a detailed presentation of the model *see* Solow (1970) or Guellec and Ralle (1995). A brief summary follows.

The Harrod–Domar model had concluded that growth was possible only if s = vn, with s = the savings rate, v = capital output ratio (K/Q) and n = the population's growth rate. This took into account three major stylized facts: real production per capita grows at a constant rate over long periods, the stock of real capital grows at a constant rate and the capital output ratio is more or less constant. According to these authors, this equilibrium could only be a matter of chance or the result of *public intervention* (e.g. regulating the savings rate).

In his model, Solow showed on the contrary that the economy returns *naturally* to this state of continued balanced growth: 'It is possible to treat the capital output rate as a variable and to combine it subsequently with an endogenous savings rate' (Guellec 1999), i.e. to consider that when the savings rate or the population's growth rate vary (e.g. a rise in the savings rate) there is a move from a 'low-capital' economy to a 'high-capital' economy (the capital output ratio, v, increases).

As Malinvaud (1993) pointed out, all the research on growth carried out in the 1950s and 1960s – of which Solow is just one example – was set in a planning perspective. The problems to be solved were logical or even mathematical. What was optimal growth and how could it be calculated using the new dynamic programming techniques? He noted that, in France, the problem was posed simultaneously in an academic article (by Dutch economist Jan Tinbergen) and by a senior civil servant, Marcel Boiteux, in a memo for the State Planning Commission (Malinvaud 1993). In the end, it was also a question of defining frameworks for economic policies to favour continued, balanced growth. How should they estimate the respective shares to be attributed to the accumulation of productive capital, to the raising of levels of education in the active population or to the transfer of labour from the traditional branches such as agriculture to other, apparently more productive branches, etc.? But what about innovation in all this?

Macroeconomic approaches were gradually used to treat the question of innovation through the issue of *technical progress*. In the Solow model, technical progress was an exogenous variable. The future Nobel Prize winner did not link technical progress and growth but described the way in which the major economic variables (capital, production, savings) adjust to a growth path that is already fixed by an exogenous rate of technical progress which, according to the economists of the time, could not be considered as an action variable.

The crisis in the United States in the 1980s questioned the Solow model as it showed that the savings rate could have an impact on countries' growth trajectories. Japan had a high savings rate and the country was in a period of growth, whereas the United States had low savings rates and was stagnating. If savings could play this sort of role, then the Solow model was invalidated (as in theory the long-term growth path did not depend on the savings rate).

To avoid having to regulate the savings rate, economists began to look at how to reintegrate the variable of technical progress that they had always considered exogenous and uncontrollable. They began to explore the relationship between growth and technology. In 1985, a collective work edited by Landau and Rosenberg listed the different paths that would be followed a few years later by the endogenous growth theorists (Landau and Rosenberg 1985).[3] It was precisely the question of the exogenous nature of technical progress that endogenous growth economists sought to clarify by examining the different sources of technical progress to measure their impact on growth. Most of these sources had already been identified long before then, of course (as Guellec and Ralle (1995) pointed out, most had been

---

[3] The book is in fact a compendium of the conferences on economic growth and technology held at Stanford in March 1985 and co-directed by Rosenberg and Landau.

mentioned by Adam Smith), but the idea was to understand the impact of these variables and to find a model to refine the concepts involved.

Authors in the endogenous growth 'school' then sought to reintroduce parameters such as human capital, learning by doing, public capital and technological research and innovation. Romer (1986) modelled growth with positive externalities, then with an increase in the list of intermediate goods (1990). Guellec and Ralle (1993) completed this model by adding an obsolescence hypothesis, whereas Aghion and Howitt (1992) modelled Schumpeterian growth in which innovations follow one another at a Poisson rate and replace one another at the intermediate good level. Recently, Aghion and Howitt (2006) showed that their Schumpeterian growth model can be considered as a unifying framework that explains how growth-maximizing policies (e.g. competition and entry policies, the allocation of education funding, the design of macroeconomic policies) should vary with a country's or sector's distance to the technological frontier, and/or with the country's level of financial development. Jones (1995a) strongly criticized the basic hypothesis of these models, namely the link between the amount of R&D and the growth rate.

Evolutionary theories: routines, technological trajectories, innovation as an interactive process, National Systems of Innovation

Another major stream of research was created in the 1970s: 'evolutionary' theory was at the crossroads between microeconomic research inspired by Schumpeter and macroeconomic work, inspired by US economist Kenneth J. Arrow in particular (Nelson and Winter 1973, 1982). Its proponents started with the observation that firms have trajectories and 'innovation paths', that they can be differentiated and that the differentiations can be irreversible. They considered that the phenomenon of irreversibility could not be analysed using assumptions on the rationality of players but, on the contrary, believed that it illustrated the idea of bounded rationality (Simon 1969). In their belief, organizations' routines guide their decisions and can lead to apparently sub-optimal decisions. The evolutionists therefore tried to model company growth dynamics by addressing the question of production and the dissemination of knowledge in the form of routines.

One of the important notions was path dependence. Authors such as Paul David (1985) showed how technologies that subsequently proved sub-optimal – such as the QWERTY keyboard – imposed themselves because of the players (firms, institutions, customers, etc.) and their routines. When applied to technological choices, this phenomenon of path-dependence led to what were called 'technological trajectories' or technical regimes, defined as a set of rules for how to produce, use and regulate specific technologies. As summarized by Schot and Geels (2007): 'Technical regime can be considered the genetic make-up (the genotype) of a technology expressing itself in products and processes (the phenotype) championed by different firms and sold on the market'. The first definitions, by Nelson and Winter, focused on engineers' minds, firms and other technological actors, while more recent definitions (Rip and Kemp 1998; Geels 2004) also include regulatory structures, demand and broader social and cultural aspects and hence favour a notion of 'sociotechnical regime'. Recently the interest shifted to the question of the transition between regimes, through path creation and niches (Schot and Geels 2007).

Another stream of research focuses on industrial dynamics. Based on Abernathy and Utterback's (1978) work on the emergence of dominant design in an industry (*see also* the follow-up to this work in organization, in Section 4 of this appendix) and the marketing analyses of innovation diffusion (*see* Section 2 of this appendix on the S-curve in marketing), authors have tried to explain a classical pattern for an industry's lifecycle: a three-phase cycle where innovation goes from product to process, where the outputs follow an S-shaped curve (slow growth at a low level, followed by high growth and then slow growth at high output) and where, over time, the entry–exit rate decreases, the market shares of the remaining players increase and the firms are increasingly functionally organized (Klepper 1997). Several models of industry lifecycles (ILCs) have been proposed to account for dominant design phenomena: Utterback underlined reduction of uncertainty on the supply-side, Klepper (1996) favoured an explanation based on the appropriation of returns and Adner and Levinthal (2001) modelled the role of demand heterogeneity and technology evolution. However, recent works underlined that new knowledge-intensive industrial sectors (biotech, telecoms) show different features from classical dominant design (Grebel, Krafft and Saviotti 2006), with new entrants cohabiting with large diversified incumbent firms and strong networks.

The evolutionary theories were a useful input to the study of innovation as an economic phenomenon. The econometric studies of the 1970s had tended to caricature the innovation process: scientific research, the development of technologies and new products seemed to follow on from one another in a linear process. The evolutionary approach, meanwhile, described innovation as an interactive process. It was based on the representation proposed by Kline and Rosenberg (1986) of a 'chain-linked' model in which the innovation process is a circular movement between market demand, development and new product supply, whereas research lies alongside and irrigates the process with the knowledge it produces.

Several economic studies then addressed the interactions between private and public research laboratories, between laboratories and production systems and between universities and industry. They also looked at education systems and training programmes, and the financial markets and their links to the innovation process. As Lundvall (1999) pointed out, the notion of National System of Innovation (NSI) was proposed for the first time in 1985 (Lundvall 1985) to characterize the relationship between R&D laboratories and institutes of technology on the one hand and production systems on the other. It was adopted by Freeman (1988) for his study on Japan and then used by the evolutionary economists. Public policies in favour of innovation were at stake: the NSIs showed that there was no single solution, given that incentive policies depend on the institutional, economic, social, political and scientific context at the national and sometimes regional level (Encaoua *et al.* 2001). The notion of the triple helix generalized NSIs by modelling the different forms of interactions between State, university and industry. The authors underlined the limits of NSIs when the impetus for innovation is still given by the firms, and insisted on the recent emergence of hybrid organizations overlapping academia, State and industry (Etzkowitz and Leydesdorff 2000; Etzkowitz 2002; Shinn 2002).

1.2   Recent trends

When viewed in terms of economics and the stakes of economic policy, we have seen that, to begin with, innovation was regarded as a challenge or at least a powerful means of questioning the traditional economic theories. First, innovation finds fault in the general equilibrium theory as it is a dynamic force whereas general equilibrium describes a static equilibrium. Second, it calls into question the theory of pure, perfect competition. Third, it means that forms of knowledge production and exchanges of skills, and not just products and services, must be taken into account. Work on these questions led to a series of now widely used concepts: innovation typologies (product/process, radical/incremental, invention/innovation), the notion of R&D and investment in R&D, notions of technological trajectory, of national systems of innovation, etc. These notions cannot be separated from the economic contexts in which they came to life, whether it be the Great Depression of 1929, planning and massive State intervention in scientific research after the Second World War, the rise of Japan in the 1980s, etc.

Are these concepts appropriate for present-day issues? Dynamic streams of research on economic policies and innovation seem to infer that new questions have appeared which also result from changes in the economic context. There are three main trends: the question of knowledge, the need for new models for the actors in the innovation process and an emerging new challenge of how to endogenize Schumpeterian 'development':

The question of knowledge: the use of the term 'knowledge-based economy' underlines the importance attached to the production and exchange of knowledge. This is not an easy question from a theoretical standpoint. What is a knowledge market? What are the advantages and disadvantages of barter or of contractual exchange? What are the different forms of appropriation: public goods, patents, etc. (Foray 2000, 2003)? From the point of view of economic policy, these questions reflect the major challenges of legislative changes to contract and intellectual property laws in the face of new forms of partnership and collective production of knowledge (Segrestin 2003). In addition, although knowledge is an essential variable, the relationship between knowledge production and innovation is far from deterministic (Jones 1995a), implying that there are other variables which have still not been correctly modelled (Hatchuel and Le Masson 2006).

The question of the actors: all the above-mentioned research was inevitably based on certain representations of the innovation process and of the actors involved. The authors were often obliged to discuss these representations, as illustrated by the success of Kline and Rosenberg's (1986) article, which proposed a new representation of the innovation process for economists. Today, there seems to be a need to reassess these representations. On the one hand, evolutionary works have come to a point where authors claim that 'research has to reach a much finer analysis at both the empirical and the theoretical levels, and to move from the statement that everything is changing with everything else' (Malerba 2006). On the other hand, micro-economists, whose theories of endogenous growth were based on a traditional representation of the firm as a production function, are rediscussing the status that firms should hold in a theory of endogenous growth designed to take into account the characteristics of 'innovative firms' (Pakes and Ericson 1998; Klette and Griliches 2000). More heterodox works, which had discussed the modelling of firms very early on (Cohendet 1998), are observing an apparently growing number of actors involved in the innovation process. Does this mean that new models are required for firms? How can the different actors' collaboration be modelled (Foray 2003)?

The question of the nature of innovation itself: new phenomenologies on industry lifecycles (Grebel, Krafft and Saviotti 2006) and on socio-technical regime transition echo recently discovered works on novelty by Schumpeter (1932 [2005]). Schumpeter defined development as 'a transition from one norm of the economic system to another norm in such a way that this transition cannot be decomposed into infinitesimal steps', wherein the norm represents 'all the concrete relationships of the concrete data that correspond to the Walrasian system'. Hence development is the renewal of both production functions and utility functions in the whole economy. This goes much further than the classical Schumpeterian growth models. Contemporary works on growth and innovation are now studying how to endogenize Schumpeterian 'development'.

2   Social networks, market and innovation

2.1   Genealogy of research questions and key notions

Merchants in the Middle Ages were probably the first to think about the relationships between new products, markets and society, one of their primary concerns naturally being to supply customers with products they wanted to buy (Renouard 1949). Later, the arrival of mass consumer goods led to the invention of new ways of interacting with the market. For instance, at the end of the eighteenth century, Wedgwood pottery was sold to the burgeoning urban middle classes in showrooms and in illustrated catalogues (Forty 1986, Chapter 1); at the end of the nineteenth century, Lever used a brand strategy combining packaging and advertising and targeting low-income households to sell its soap products (Forty 1986, Chapter 3). When the food processing industry launched its first products, it used famous scientists to vouch for their quality and reassure customers that there were no health risks. For example, in 1865, George Giebert, founder of the Liebig Extract of Meat Company (LEMCO), a world leader in meat extracts, appointed a famous organic chemist, Justus von Liebig, as director. With great media coverage and for a comfortable salary, the company used Liebig's name – on the products, calendars, recipe books, etc. – and entrusted him with the task of controlling the products (Brock 1997).

At the beginning of the twentieth century, new market relations developed as production became more concentrated, major centres of production emerged and transport capacities grew. The need arose for scientific tools capable of targeting advertising campaigns, improving the organization of sales forces and adapting products to the specific needs of local markets (Freeland 1920, 1926; Cochoy 1999). A series of concepts was gradually developed to describe the relationships between social networks, markets and innovation.

Diffusion and adoption of innovations: the S-curve

At the risk of anachronism, the first models that emerged could be qualified as 'behaviourist', in that they contended that there was a cause and effect relationship between levels of stimulation and repetition (quantity of advertising messages) and levels of purchases. However, at the end of the 1960s, Maslow argued against the simplistic mechanics of behaviourism and put forward the idea of a 'hierarchy of needs', with the pyramid which has since been used in marketing classes the world over (Maslow 1987). He argued that people function at five different levels, each with specific needs: first physiological/bodily needs, then safety needs, social needs, the need for self-esteem and, finally, the need for self-actualization. He believed that individuals should not be represented in a way that limited them to their subconscious instincts.

Other works in the 1960s and 1970s moved away from the issue of consumers' personalities to study the notions of the adoption and diffusion of innovation in society. They considered Gabriel de Tarde, a French lawyer and sociologist from the end of the nineteenth century, as their founding father. de Tarde (1903) had studied the laws of imitation and considered that 'invention and imitation represent the chief forces in society'.[4] Rogers (1983) defined diffusion as the process by which an innovation is communicated through certain channels, over time, among the members of a social system. A key point for Rogers was that the message that was communicated contained new ideas. Rogers was interested in all the factors that influence the diffusion of an innovation, such as opinion leaders, the profile of 'early adopters', social systems, market segments, the impact of marketing activities

---

[4] Gabriel de Tarde's school of sociology saw imitation as a fundamental social relationship. However, if everything was a question of imitation, this automatically posed the question of inventions. In de Tarde's view, there was no need to introduce the notion of a specific creative act because invention itself was simply a series of imitations: it was the combination of imitated ideas through a system of relationships that was also imitated (Karsenti 1993). The system, based purely on relationships, was therefore somewhat similar to contemporary information theories.

and of competition. Rogers introduced the notion of 'innovativeness', defined as the speed at which an individual or other 'unit of adoption' adopts a new idea, measured in comparison with that of the other members of the system. It is important to note that, in these works, the 'innovators' are in fact the 'pioneers' who adopt the new product, thus becoming social innovators. They go against the general rule of 'resisting change'.

This research tried to explain the mechanisms behind the diffusion of a product in the market. It was observed that, over time, both market share and product turnover follow an S-shaped curve: a slow start at a low level, then fast diffusion and finally a third phase of high-level output and slow growth. Communication models (Bass 1969) explained that the S-curve resulted from two mechanisms that affect adoption decisions: to begin with, communications from mass media get the process moving; then, at a later stage, word of mouth, which is even more important, causes a quick rise in diffusion. Rogers, however, contended that the form of the curve was more the result of five different categories of adopters: venturesome innovators, early 'respectable' adopters, early deliberate majority, late sceptical majority and laggards, attached to tradition. Rogers also defined five attributes for innovations which he considered vital to its diffusion: relative advantage, compatibility, complexity, 'trialability' and observability.

The customer's influence on innovation: notion of lead-user

In the 1970s, the 'technology assessment' movement focused on the fact that citizens could have an active role to play in technological innovations. Things had changed drastically since the Vannevar Bush report, 'Science, the endless frontier', and the time when no one doubted the contributions that science made to people's lives. There were protests against the Vietnam war, new concerns for ecology and great criticism of the 'military-industrial complex', all of which led the American government to set up an Office of Technology Assessment in 1972, whose role was to demand that technology and scientific research 'proved their innocence' (Salomon 1992).

Several authors examined the active role played by customers in developing new products. von Hippel, who pioneered work in this domain (1977, 1978, 1982), showed that in certain industries the majority of the products had been invented by customers with specific characteristics, whom he called 'lead-users'. 'Lead users face needs that will be general in a marketplace, but they face them months or years before the bulk of that marketplace encounters them, and lead users are positioned to benefit significantly by obtaining a solution to those needs' (von Hippel 1988).

Another stream of research focuses on the social acceptance of innovation. Based on experiments in public forums on highly controversial topics such as genetically modified organisms (GMOs), researchers have proposed models for governing innovation and risks at the interface between science and the public (Joly 2001).

Innovation as a whirlwind process in an emerging sociotechnical network

Sociologists then became more and more interested in what they saw as double conditioning: on the one hand, techniques influence their environment (the diffusion theory), but on the other, the environment shapes the techniques (the role of customers). Inspired by research carried out at the end of the 1960s by historians of technology (Layton 1971) in academic publications such as *Technology and Culture*, these authors believed that it was not possible to account for complex processes using a simple theory of supply and demand; they were also wary of what they called 'simplistic biological metaphors that talk about the selection of innovations by their environment without seeing that the environment is being fashioned at the same time as the innovation it will be judging' (Akrich, Callon and Latour 1988). They suggested that the diffusion model should be replaced by a model of *intéressement*, or aligned interests, in which successful innovations are those which have the greatest number of allies and which are transformed by sociotechnical networks that take part in their elaboration.[5] The notion of sociotechnical network generalizes the mutual conditioning between techniques and environments. The researchers sought to analyse sociotechnical systems to find 'the precise location of innovation, the hard to define point at which the technique and the social milieu that adopts it take shape simultaneously'.

This research into sociotechnical networks led to a definition of innovation as a whirlwind process involving the initial anticipation of constraints, successive experiments and sociotechnical transformations, in a search for 'human or non-human' allies, with a combination of enrolment processes (to bring in new allies) and 'translation' (i.e. a new language designed to describe the innovation to the new allies).

This research was widely disseminated and put into practice in a number of very different domains. These included work on the role of research laboratories; work on new therapies to combat muscular dystrophy, which highlighted the role played by the patients in the research activities

---

[5] In actor network theory, *intéressement* is defined as the action of interesting, enrolling or translating.

sponsored by the *Association Française contre les Myopathies* (Rabeharisoa and Callon 1998); work on product packaging and consumer mediators (Cochoy 2002); and work on 'the economy of qualities', which explained the conditions required for a market to be established, referring to qualification processes and the role of 'market professionals' capable of 'shaping both demand and the consumer' (Callon, Méadel and Rabeharisoa 2000).

Communities of practice: a social consequence of innovation

Another angle on the research consisted of going beyond the generic notion of 'network' and studying the way in which new forms of social relations are established when an innovation is developed and diffused. The authors showed how new questions and common problems can spark off innovative responses and stronger social links, which can then create 'communities of practice'. The concept was proposed for the first time by Orr (1990), who studied how newly hired, low-skilled photocopier repair technicians managed to face problems in their new jobs. His findings underlined the importance of the technicians' informal discussions, when they told each other stories of their successes and failures, rather than their use of the expert systems available to them. Lave and Wenger (1991) undertook further research following on from Orr's work. They proposed new thinking on learning processes in communities of practice, showing that learning is more than just a question of receiving facts and information: people engage in activities and in doing so interact with each other and with the world, tuning their relationships accordingly. They put forward the notion of 'legitimate peripheral participation': when people join a community of practice, their participation is at first legitimately peripheral but then gradually increases in engagement and complexity, in terms of both knowledge and social relationships. The process gradually creates shared, validated knowledge and a close community of practice.

This work followed on from studies on the way work communities invented new ways of doing things in the face of recurrent difficulties. Starting with studies on work communities, the research was then extended to users. For example, Franke and Shah (2002) studied sports communities (for sailplaning, canyoning, boardercross and handicapped cycling) to see how lead-users received support from communities in developing their new products.

Apart from studying the role of communities of practice, Brown and Duguid (1998) also brought to light the role played by other actors who take part in spreading innovations but also propagating the knowledge that shapes future innovations. They describe these actors as 'translators' and 'knowledge brokers' who are capable of linking two communities of practice and facilitating relations between them.

Innovators in organizations: deviation from the norm and resistance to change

It is important to note that the question of organization was never very far away in any of the above research; all the points made about social relationships were also valid for organizations. This accounts for the strange situation whereby, in all the research on diffusion, the 'innovator' is a pioneering consumer who deviates from the usual patterns of consumption, rather than a designer working for a firm. If this situation is applied to firms – seen as a specific form of society – the innovator is still not the designer but a manager or an operator who adopts new practices in the firm. Rogers (1983) described the different stages of innovation in organizations as the way in which an organization adopts, in response to its problems, an innovation observed in its environment. The same representation was then found in the case of 'ordinary innovation', where everybody innovates (Alter 2000), and in communities of practice. The latter refer to any production of knowledge, with no distinction between good practices shared in sales networks and the design functions with their specific means of producing knowledge.

For instance, Alter (2003) looked at what he called 'organizational innovation', which is 'different from product innovation. It takes place in a hierarchical, regulated context, in which innovation always, in the end, goes against the established order'. He described a process in which 'everyday innovators' begin with an 'intention to innovate' favoured by the firm's management, then elaborate new practices and uses. The latter are diffused until they come up against the established order, which will institutionalize some new uses while refusing others. Alter (2002) described the processes involved in setting up sociotechnical networks within communities of innovators: it is not a question of cooperation by people who belong to the same social group but of relationships where information etc. is exchanged on a win-win basis.

Radical innovation through research technologies

Classical sociology of science barely addresses innovation, whether in the classical Mertonian approach, in *The New Production of Knowledge* (Gibbons *et al.* 1994), or in works on the sociology of knowledge (*see* Barley (1996) on technicians in research laboratories). Recent works are now bridging the gap between the sociology of science and innovation: for example, Joerges and Shinn (2001) showed that instrumentation is a 'research technology' defined by generic devices, interstitial arenas and improved metrologies. A research technology is a particular class of general-purpose technology (Bresnahan and Trajtenberg 1995), which at the same time defies classical divisions of labour (scientific disciplines, organizational departments, technological spheres) and supports their integration through a new lingua franca (formulating generic concepts) (Shinn 2006).

2.2   Recent trends

As we saw in the previous section, innovation raises some fundamental questions in the field of economic policy. The same applies to markets and social networks. As Norbert Alter pointed out, it is a paradox to talk about sociology applied to innovation as the aim of sociology is to analyse the stable systems of rules on which social relations are built, whereas innovation poses the question of the dynamics of these systems of rules. For markets, innovation raises the question of how markets can be established when there is no obvious demand or when the customers do not yet know the products being offered. For society, innovation brings up the question of the plasticity of social groups and systems of rules.

Several key notions were developed as a result of these questions, including needs, adoption and diffusion, lead-user, sociotechnical network and community of practice.

This research on the impact of innovation on social networks also sparked off new representations of the innovation process itself: the question of needs led to the idea that they should be analysed before finding an answer to them; the lead-user theory encouraged von Hippel to recommend an innovation process consisting of identifying the lead-users' inventions and marketing them; the notions of actor and sociotechnical network represent innovation as a whirlwind process that is hard to manage, in which points of convergence are difficult to find; and communities of practice develop innovation through an emerging process consisting of providing and sharing solutions to new problems. *It is the social analyses that result in the different representations of the innovation process,* often confusing the way in which the innovation is diffused with the design process itself.

This research also highlighted three key trends:

A marker for the nature of new products and new services. Behaviourism ignored the products, apparently assuming that they could be sold to anyone; needs analysis used simple vocabulary to describe products; and niche analysis, product differentiation and the analysis of sociostyles have provided an enriched vision of products (defined by their utility value but also their hedonic and symbolic values) (Holbrook and Hirschman 1982; Laurent and Kapferer 1985). Today, research on the difficult problem of describing product quality and diversity, on the need for mediators and on the personalization of products through customer service relations, underlines a current trend in new products and services: products are not only diverse but also pose a problem of 'qualification' (Callon, Méadel and Rabeharisoa 2000).

The growing presence of organizational issues. When the authors renewed their interest in organizations, they treated them as if they were societies with specific properties (hierarchy, established order). New 'figures' were introduced, as inventors were joined by deviators, communities of practice, functions, instrument makers, etc. In adding these descriptions, the authors also explained the specific features of the 'organizations', with a special emphasis on firms' ability to create links between different communities of practice. More recent works have also analysed the social phenomena relating to companies' organizations for intensive innovation (Minguet and Osty 2008).

Growing use of the notions by firms. Most of the research referred to above concerned innovation, but without establishing an explicit relationship to firms. However, more and more firms today are using research of this sort in their innovation processes. For instance, Brown (1991) described how Xerox used anthropological studies on users of photocopiers, practices in accounting departments and repair technicians' work to help them develop new products and services. Questions such as analysing current uses, exploring new uses, for instance through virtual communities on the internet (Kozinets 2002), and even customers' involvement in design processes (Magnusson 2003; Piller *et al.* 2003) have become highly strategic issues in many companies.

3 Cognitive processes and innovation

3.1 Genealogy of research questions and key notions

Knowledge and reasoning are major challenges in all innovation processes, as shown by the wealth of architects' manuals, encyclopaedias, engineering science treatises, theories on machine construction, etc. that has been penned over the years. During the nineteenth century, doctrine was gradually built up on experimental methods and their relations to scientific discovery and there were great debates on how to train engineers, especially regarding theoretical versus practical training. (*See* the remarkable study by Anne-Françoise Garçon (2004) on the history of Ecole des Mines in Saint-Etienne.) Issues such as how new knowledge is produced and transmitted and how methods for innovation are passed on became almost national debates.

However, in the past few decades, progress in research into individual and collective decision-making processes and the new concepts proposed by the theory of information have brought innovation to the foreground once again, but from a different perspective. On the one hand, progress in modelling decision-making processes encouraged researchers to look at the process of invention and individual discoveries and the question of collective decisions in the face of unusual, new situations. On the other, the success of information theories opened a new field of research on the transfer and accumulation of knowledge. More recently, this research converged on questions of knowledge production in action.

Innovation: creative thinking?

In the tradition of nineteenth-century historical works regarding the engineers of the first industrial revolution (Smiles 1874; Thurston 1878; Dickinson 1936), a number of researchers focused their work on the psychology of inventors. Between the two world wars, this led to the *psychological* study of inventive genius. The aim of this work was to highlight a form of intelligence that could not be measured by IQ tests (Guilford 1959), described as 'divergent thinking' or the ability to generate a number of alternative answers to a simple question such as 'what can we do with a metre of cotton thread?'. The authors developed a series of tests for this specific form of intelligence (*see* the Torrance Test of Creative Thinking, thought up by E. Paul Torrance in the 1970s). As the research originally aimed to improve children's creativity, the techniques tended to call very little on individual competencies. More recently, several authors have focused on creativity techniques in product development: recent versions of the reference book by Pahl and Beitz (2006) refer to creativity techniques either for the initial phases or for solving technical problems emerging during the development process. In the context of engineering design, authors insist on the role of creativity templates (Goldenberg and Mazursky 2002), the critical place of knowledge (Cropley 2006), the interaction between convergent thinking and divergent thinking (Eris 2004), the dual risk of pseudo creativity (Cattell and Butcher 1968; Weisberg 1992) and 'bounded' creativity (Le Masson, Hatchuel and Weil 2007).

The studies were conducted in cognitive psychology. Studying the creative mind, Boden (1990) characterized a 'creative idea' as an idea that breaks the 'generative rules'. ('A merely novel idea is one which can be described and/or produced by the same set of generative rules as other, familiar ideas. A genuinely original, or creative, idea is one which cannot.') Authors also studied biases in creative cognition, characterized as fixation effects: people follow a 'path of least resistance' in creative exercise, reusing existing models of objects (Ward 1994); they tend to reuse recently activated knowledge (Jansson and Smith 1991; Smith, Ward and Schumacher 1993); and they are trapped by preinventive structures contaminated by knowledge of the specific goal and task (Finke 1990). More recently, works by Nagai and Taura (2006; Nagai, Taura and Mukai 2008) focused on the different forms of concept synthesis that lead to creative concepts, underlining the key role of concept blending (Fauconnier and Turner 1996).

Creativity has also been studied in groups. The technique of brainstorming was invented by Alex F. Osborn, general manager of the advertising company BBDO, at the end of the 1930s, to foster collective creativity by delaying judgement on ideas (Osborn 1957). Laboratory experiments on brainstorming have given two main results: 1) groups that follow Osborn's rules do indeed generate more ideas than those that do not (Parnes and Meadow 1959); 2) groups appear to generate half as many ideas as the combined total of ideas generated by the same number of individuals working separately (referred to as the nominal group) (Diehl and Stroebe 1987; Mullen, Johnson and Salas 1991; Paulus and Dzindolet 1993).

Factors explaining the loss of production are social (perceived expertness, lack of recognition, conflicts, etc.) and cognitive (knowledge base restricted to common knowledge (Stewart and Stasser 1995; Paulus 2000); similarity in association of ideas (Paulus, Brown and Ortega 1999; Stasser and Birchmeier 2003)).

These works were also used in creativity management to analyse creativity killers (Amabile *et al.* 1996) and creative organizations (Sutton and Hargadon 1996; Sundgren and Styhre 2003).

Innovation as 'problem-solving'

The study of invention also led to a stream of research on the sociology of invention and the model of the inventor's mind (for a summary of this research, *see* McGee (1995)). In the 1920s, authors such as Bernard,

Kaempffert, Usher and Gilfillan put forward the idea that invention did not need heroic genius but consisted of the 'continuous activity of common mental processes' (Usher 1929). Usher proposed a four-stage model of the inventive process: 1) 'recognition of a new or an incompletely gratified want'; 2) 'setting the stage', i.e. a review of any elements obtained from past experience that can be reused; 3) 'act of insight', i.e. the rearrangement of all the elements of experience into a new configuration capable of satisfying the non-gratified wants; 4) 'critical revision'. However, at this stage, the 'act of insight' remained a mystery.

Simon went back to the problem of this 'sudden flash of insight' in 1962, qualifying it as a characteristic of creativity (Simon, Newell and Shaw 1979). Simon's aim was to build a program (in the sense of a computer program) for mechanisms that could think creatively. The main idea was that tree-structure research processes with the 'branch and bound'-style heuristics used in problem-solving theory gave a good idea of the creativity process. According to Simon, problem-solving consists of finding, in a set P, an element or a sub-set with specific properties that represent a 'satisficing' solution to the problem. The difficulty of a problem stems from the size of the initial set P to be searched and from knowing whether a given solution is a good answer to the specific problem. Sound heuristic techniques should have an 'efficient generator' for exploring P and simple selection methods, to avoid exploring unpromising sub-sets of P.

More generally speaking, Simon drew up a research programme for a design theory (1969). He insisted on the fact that a great majority of design problems can be solved by heuristics based on decision-making in a state of bounded rationality, thus coming back to 'problem-solving' situations. Simon also examined the process of scientific discovery (Simon and Kulkarni 1989) to show that tree-structured research procedures were also relevant in this case. Alexander discussed and refined Simon's 'problem-solving' approach for cases where there is no 'general symbolic way of generating new alternatives' (or rather, they are not radical enough) and of evaluating them. He proposed a 'diagram' or 'pattern' approach to abstract, model and decompose a complex problem into sub-sets where 'internal interactions are very rich' whilst the variables in the different sub-sets of the partition exercise as few informational constraints on one another as possible (Alexander 1964, pp. 124–125). Rittel underlined that these kinds of 'planning' processes for solving problems were suitable for 'tame' problems but not for 'wicked' ones, i.e. problems with no definitive formulation, no stopping rule, for which solutions are neither true nor false, where there is no exhaustive, enumerable list of permissible operations (Rittel 1972). Schön underlined that Simon's and Alexander's approaches cannot be applied in cases of figural complexity, i.e. situations (particularly in arts) where a very small change in one design parameter radically changes the whole, impeding 'search processes' based on design parameter combinations and incremental changes. He hence insisted on the role of generative metaphors to 'provide a schema for exploring problematic situations' (Schön 1990).

As Armand Hatchuel pointed out (Hatchuel 2002), Simon started with the question of decisions, then built a 'conceptual arm' – the notion of bounded rationality – to fight against the 'optimizing' decision-making theory and to introduce subjectivity and heuristic decision-making processes that obtained not optimal solutions but 'satisficing' ones. He then analysed decision-making processes by computer simulation, empirical analysis and laboratory experiments, going on to show that they were tree-structured exploratory processes. He looked at the most extreme situations (discovery, design and creativity) to show that these processes did not require new theories but could be dealt with by problem-solving theory. Nonetheless, Hatchuel also underlined the reservations made by Simon himself about these findings: in the case of ill-defined problems, he had to resort to imagery, in order to draw up an initial list of possible choices to start off the problem-solving process.

Organizational change, organizational learning: adaptive processes

Research on decision-making theory was also applied to organizations. If optimization is no longer the sole aim of firms, how do they make collective decisions and how do they learn to adapt to changing environments? In this context, there is a close relationship between innovation and knowledge, but one that works in a very special way, in that it is external innovations, i.e. changes in the environment, that force organizations to learn so that they too can change. This area of research did not study innovation as much as the forms of learning employed by firms to face up to new situations. There were two main streams of research:

A behavioural school, which considered firms and organizations to be adaptive systems (Cyert and March 1963; March and Olsen 1975; Levitt and March 1988). The authors came to the conclusion that learning was essentially low-key, based on incremental adjustments to change, and that radical changes were rare. This conclusion was contested by Argyris and Schön (1978, 1996). Among the key contributions of the behavioural school was that it pointed out certain biases in interpretations of experience and memorization, and explained negative forms of learning that arise when fundamentally ill-adapted routines are reused in a new environment, resulting in what Levitt and March called 'competency traps'. This stream of research was mainly critical of the notion of learning, explaining its limitations rather than describing its potential forms and mechanisms. However, it enabled the authors to return to the issue of organizational innovation and define it as the result of a balance between the exploitation of existing procedures and the exploration of new ways of doing things (March 1991).[6] The balance depends on internal processes (rapid socialization of individuals and slow turnover, favouring exploitation) and it is more or less pertinent depending on the competitive context (survival in a highly competitive environment imposes high standard deviations in the results of actions, thus implying that exploration should be favoured).

A cognitive school, which studied small communities rather than firms in general. The researchers believed that human conduct can be explained for the greater part by individuals' state of mind and their representations. According to Argyris and Schön (1978, 1996), individuals faced with changing circumstances can either adapt to them using their initial representations (single-loop learning) or challenge their 'espoused theory', i.e. their theoretical representations, by adopting new 'theories in use', i.e. new, previously implicit representations that actually govern their actions (double-loop learning). Fiol and Lyles (1985) added to this research by making a distinction between adaptation and learning. This work was also in a critical vein as it can be said that single-loop learning is similar to Levitt and March's cognitive traps. Although double-loop learning concerns knowledge creation, from an organizational point of view the authors nonetheless considered that it takes place in very particular, if not exceptional, circumstances and not as part of firms' usual practices. Indeed, it should preferably be undertaken with outside consultants in situations that the authors called 'action research' processes.

---

[6] March (1991) defined the two notions in an allusive fashion: 'Exploration includes things captured by terms such as search, variation, risk taking, experimentation, play, flexibility, discovery, innovation. Exploitation includes such things as refinement, choice, production, efficiency, selection, implementation, execution.'

Knowledge transfer: tacit and explicit knowledge

Cognitive processes relating to innovation were studied in another stream of research: knowledge transfers. This research was markedly different from the previous work on decision-making processes. It was initially inspired by questions on the diffusion of innovation, with authors such as Gruber and Marquis searching for the factors that favour the diffusion of new technologies (Gruber and Marquis 1969). This literature on transfers was based to a great extent on the paradigm of the theory of information: the actors processed information, their relations consisted of exchanges of information and learning was done through feedback loops. Successes or failures in transferring knowledge or in developing new technologies could therefore be interpreted by the configurations of communications networks used by the teams in charge of the said transfers or developments (Allen 1977).

Research later made the distinction between information and knowledge, with the authors postulating about how sophisticated knowledge, such as that required to master a technology, can transit via information networks. For instance, Cohen and Levinthal (1990) modelled absorptive capacity, i.e. all the information available to actors (which may also be organizations) to enable them to assimilate new information. The absorptive capacity was the conceptual link between information and knowledge: whereas the former can be assimilated by anyone, the latter requires the ability to translate or interpret, which the authors assimilate with a set of information required to absorb a flow of relatively complex information.

The work of Nonaka, who did a great deal of research into product development in Japanese firms in the 1980s, also comes under this paradigm of technological transfer (Imai, Nonaka and Takeuchi 1985; Takeuchi and Nonaka 1986). At that time, Japan was extremely successful and western companies were eager to find out why. In Nonaka's view, it could be explained by the fact that cognitive processes in Japanese firms took into account types of knowledge that had been abandoned by western 'information processors'. In Japanese firms, innovation was not just a question of solving problems with predetermined algorithms after searching for items in a long-term memory but consisted of creating new order through redundancy and chaos (Nonaka 1990). Nonaka believed that it was important to take into account both explicit and tacit exchanges of knowledge, following the well-known distinction in sociology put forward by Polanyi (1969). He defined the two categories as follows: 'Explicit or codified knowledge refers to knowledge that is transmittable in formal, systematic language. On the other hand tacit knowledge has a personal quality, which makes it hard to formalize and communicate. Tacit knowledge is deeply rooted in action, commitment, and involvement in a specific context' (1994, p. 16).

Nonaka's work had enormous repercussions because the notion of tacit knowledge goes against the notion of information, given that it is precisely 'hard to communicate'. Nonaka identified a body of knowledge that could not be managed using traditional methods of information transfer. In fact, his work was very similar to that of ergonomists and sociologists when they analyse employees' skills and ability to react to unexpected situations. By introducing the distinction between real work and prescribed work, they too pointed to knowledge and practices for which traditional management methods were unsuited. Nonaka also explained to western managers that cryptic slogans could be highly effective tools for creating new knowledge, giving examples such as 'optoelectronics', used by Sharp in 1973, for a new branch of technology combining electronics and optics; the Theory of Automobile Evolution, used as a design concept for the Honda City, an innovative urban car, which led to a 'man-maximum, machine minimum' trend that challenged the methods used by car manufacturers in Detroit; and allusive analogies such as that between a personal copier and a beer can, used by Canon to design a revolutionary mini-copier (Nonaka and Takeuchi 1995).

However, the paradigm remained the same, as Nonaka's work was on exchanges of information rather than on creation. Once he had identified the category of knowledge, his position consisted of looking for the types of relationships between actors that would be suitable to manage these competencies. As Blackler (1995) underlined, by maintaining the separation between knowledge production and circulation and being essentially interested in the latter, Nonaka stayed with the paradigm of information transfer, even if that 'information' was sometimes tacit. The forms of transformation he described (socialization, internalization, externalization, combination) are forms of transmission of knowledge between the actors, and the new figures of actors he focused on (middle-top-down management) serve to translate tacit knowledge (between the managers' visionary ideals and the chaotic reality experienced by actors in the field). Nonaka was not really interested in how things happened or in explaining tacit knowledge, he simply observed transfers of a new sort of knowledge.

Expert systems and knowledge in action

Continuing on the subject of knowledge transfer, research on expert systems – which was initially less interested in innovation than in preserving and spreading experts' knowledge – provided key information about the nature of the knowledge used in innovation processes.

Expert systems were first developed in the mid-1980s, as part of research into artificial intelligence. This new form of computer program was designed to capitalize on individual specialists' skills that had become rare or difficult to apprehend, by making them available to a wider public. The advocates of these systems were not pleading for radical change; they simply wanted to 'listen to' human experts and record what they knew. This was a move from information storage tools to systems capable of clarifying how forms of knowledge could be put to work (Leonard-Barton and Sviokla 1988). In their detailed analysis of several industrial expert systems projects, Hatchuel and Weil showed that the representation of knowledge was highly restrictive and that the problems encountered by expert systems revealed the variety of learning types and their current crises (Hatchuel and Weil 1992, 1995). Their contribution can be summarized in three main points:

The expert systems of the 1980s made a distinction between knowledge (a set of facts and rules) and reasoning about such knowledge (inference engines). However, this hypothesis holds only for certain very particular forms of knowledge, such as that of skilled craftsmen who follow the same unchanging method, step by step. For more dynamic knowledge, used for instance for 'reparative' work (e.g. maintenance technicians) and 'strategy/design' (systems designer, planner, etc.), the initial hypothesis is too strong, in the sense that knowledge and reasoning are very closely related in these cases. Very different collective learning processes are required for each of these forms of knowledge. As we move from skilled craftsmen to strategists, the knowledge dynamics are more and more closely linked to the actors' involvement in what is taking place. In situations of innovation, it can be said that the actors are directly concerned by the 'reparative' and 'strategy/design' aspects of their work.

The metaphors of knowledge 'collection' and 'transfer' are often misleading: expert systems neither imitate reasoning nor collect knowledge and can function only by transforming knowledge. More generally speaking, we never really 'collect' other people's knowledge but in fact transform our own knowledge through interactions with other people's knowledge. The exchange of knowledge cannot be treated in the same way as the circulation of currency. A more accurate view would be that during the exchange 'what each of us knows' changes, and also we all have our own ideas of what has been given and received. This in fact confirms the view that 'teaching' is a difficult task requiring special mechanisms to ensure interaction and, in particular, to control the knowledge 'acquired'.

Who, then, were the experts whose knowledge was to be collected? Hatchuel and Weil showed that the focus of attention was no longer on skilled workers but on white-collar workers. The latter, who were created by recent company history, are themselves 'knowledge workers'. This observation points to a particularly striking change: the major industrial transformations of the late 1970s hit white-collar workers badly and led in most firms to what the authors call 'the hidden crises of industrial knowledge or the crises of design' (Hatchuel and Weil 1995). What were the likely consequences of these crises? When the people who regulate a firm's activity – by defining its products, procedures and organizational rules – find it difficult to stabilize and reconstruct their knowledge, the firm's entire system of governance is under threat.

The production of knowledge for innovation: evolution of core competencies, experiments, intuition and interpretations

During the same period, other research on transfers of technology looked at producing knowledge in and for action, particularly for the purposes of innovation.

For instance, Leonard-Barton (1995) looked at the core competencies that give firms a competitive advantage. To be more precise, she examined the possibilities for 'managing the interaction between activities pursued in the course of developing new products and processes, and the organization's core capabilities'. She began by asking which activities an organization uses to change and improve its core capabilities to avoid them becoming 'core rigidities' (Leonard-Barton 1992). She posited that four activities were involved and must be managed in such a way as to guarantee growth in core competencies:

product development, which she merged with problem-solving;

implementation and integration of new processes to encourage the co-development of tools (e.g. expert systems) with the users (other experts or non-experts);

experimentation, where new skills, new information channels and new methods can emerge;

importing new knowledge (new techniques or learning about the market).

Leonard-Barton therefore considered that product development and innovation are essentially prime opportunities for observing processes of learning by experimentation.

However, another part of her research looked at the issue from the opposite angle, i.e. how experimental dynamics can help develop more or less innovative processes. In her view, the innovation process, or the product development process, is always the same, but the degree of innovation will depend on the development team's ability to be creative at all times: in phases of divergence, the differences between the people and their experiences provides 'creative abrasion'; in phases of convergence, the empathic understanding of the customer's desires and the development of communities of practice contribute to innovation. The latter share implicit, common ways of working and learning and above all of understanding objectives that go way beyond the explicitly named objectives, of which there are usually so few in the case of innovations (Leonard and Sensiper 1998). This implies that the innovation will be based on experiential learning that takes original forms, which are difficult to implement. What the authors call tacit knowledge is hard to explain and appears to be incomplete or surprising when compared with traditional *reasoning*. The authors use the notion of intuition to clarify the issue. Intuition can help get round a problem; the solution to a problem can also be intuitive; and 'flashes of insight' help predict and anticipate solutions.

Daft and Weick (1984) also examined the question of experiential learning in organizations, proposing a model for organizations as interpretive systems. They distinguished between two elements that characterize practices in organizations.

1. Assumptions about the environment: an organization can consider that the environment is fixed and tangible and can be easily identified by explorations; or it can assume that it is impossible to make an objective analysis of the environment (because it is changing too rapidly, is uncertain, etc.), in which case it has to construct the environment through interpretation.
2. The organizational intrusiveness, i.e. the extent to which the organization intrudes when examining its environment. This can take the form of active scanning (trial and error processes, tests, etc.) or passive scanning (events are simply recorded).

A combination of these two dimensions led to four modes of interpretation, the most famous being the 'enacting' mode. In this mode (i) the interpretation is based on the assumption that the environment cannot be analysed and that it is constructed by the interpretation and (ii) data collection takes place actively. The enacting organization is shown to be the most 'forward-looking' and therefore the most capable of innovation.

Brown and Duguid (1991) developed this point: 'Innovation in this view is not only a response to empirical observations of the environment. (. . .) The process of innovating involves actively constructing a conceptual framework, imposing it on the environment, and reflecting on their interaction.' They went on to ask how this new interpretation is brought about by organizations that seem inescapably trapped in their own views of the world. Their answer was that interstitial communities were continually developing new interpretations of the world within organizations, because these communities have a practical rather than formal connection to the world. Once again, it is a question of experiential learning that enables an organization such as the enacting organization to be capable of 'reconceiving not only its environment but also its own identity, for in a significant sense the two are mutually constitutive'. However, it should be noted that the notion of interstitial community does not answer the question of how such communities develop the new interpretations that are the foundation of innovation.

3.2   Recent trends

Similarly to economic policy and to markets and social networks, the question of innovation poses a problem for research into cognitive processes, but it is also the source of progress.

The main problem is that very little work has been done to date on one of the most vital issues for the cognitive sciences, i.e. how to describe creative reasoning. The question of innovation has led to progress as work on knowledge in action has gone beyond the paradigm of information to concentrate on new fields: first, the nature of knowledge (the distinction between tacit and explicit) and, second, the production of knowledge (typology of knowledge in action: 'doing know-how', 'understanding know-how', 'combining know-how' and experiential learning).

Two key trends are currently emerging:

A change in context. The main reason why current work on modelling is interested not only in communication channels but also in the nature of experts' knowledge and how it is produced is that the knowledge and its production are presently undergoing a major crisis. Although it is not always clearly stated, what is really being studied in this research is the way the work of engineers, researchers, designers, strategists and marketing specialists is changing in firms today.

Merging of work on reasoning and knowledge. In the work reviewed above, we can distinguish between two main streams of research: first, work on individual and collective reasoning (Simon, March, Argyris and Schön, etc.) and, second, work on knowledge (its nature, relation to action, etc. – see authors above: Nonaka, Blackler, Cohen, etc.). The authors in the first stream came up against ill-defined problems, where imagery must be used and the production of knowledge is hard to control.[7] The second stream went through several stages. The authors began by looking at the nature of the knowledge used (tacit/explicit), then at the way in which knowledge production was influenced by innovation (dynamic evolution of core competencies, analysis of forms of activities: experiential learning, trial and error, etc.) and finally how a form of knowledge production could be more or less innovative, more or less 'enacting'. How can a knowledge production process be organized in such a way as to lead to innovation? At this stage, the authors came back to the question of reasoning. And it is therefore not surprising that, precisely on this issue of innovation reasoning, they were obliged, once again, to raise the question of intuition and 'flashes of insight'. We should point out that the question is also raised in the more technical field of knowledge engineering, the descendant of artificial intelligence and expert systems: how to move from static to dynamic representations of ontologies.

There seems to be a vital gap concerning cognitive processes in the context of innovation, i.e. how can reasoning and knowledge be combined, or more precisely, how can innovative reasoning and knowledge production be combined? Which forms of reasoning should be used and how can they be implemented collectively, that is without being limited to creative contributions, or flashes of insight, from individuals?

4   Organizational theory and innovation

4.1   Genealogy of research questions and key notions

In the past, organizations have been continually modelled by innovation, which often acted as a stimulus but sometimes upset and disorganized their

---

[7] However, it is important to note that the work on organizational learning looked chiefly at situations of adaptation rather than of 'creation' and that, in double loop learning situations when a theory in use is reformulated, knowledge can be provided by outside contributors.

activities. At the end of the nineteenth century, innovation-related issues played a key role in the creation of research laboratories, whether in terms of providing support for new product design, controlling innovations made by independent inventors and even blocking the competitive environment by means of patents. When planning departments appeared in Taylor's time, one of their main aims was to match the levels of innovation achieved with Taylor's high-speed steel processes. Engineering departments came into being because they distinguished between new work and routine work; and manufacturing units were developed to enable joint innovations (Lefebvre 1998), i.e. innovations at the interface between two trades, made possible by their physical closeness and the opportunities for making mutual adjustments.

However, literature on organizational theory was less interested in these historical issues than in more general questions. Can innovation be organized? What is the place of innovation in organizational theory? What are the characteristic features of innovative organizations? Which organizational forms suit which systems of innovation?

Does innovation have a place in organizational theory?

Since the seminal works of Fayol (1917), administrative science has given relatively little place to innovation in organization manuals. Organization theorists have mainly concentrated on the division of work and coordination for inter-related tasks (Mintzberg 1982). In this context, innovation emerged in two different ways: first, outside the theory – can innovation be organized? – and, second, inside the theory – is the theory robust in situations of innovation?

From a historical standpoint, the first point was discussed by Jewkes *et al.*, who criticized the traditional idea that science had replaced inventors as the driving force of inventions in the twentieth century. In their view, there was no real break given that science already existed at the beginning of the nineteenth century and also that inventors went on playing an essential role in contemporary inventions. No 'infallible methods of invention' had been discovered, although the search for new ideas and techniques was carried out in a more systematic manner, more economically and with greater resources, and 'chance remains an important factor in invention and the intuition, will and obstinacy of individuals spurred on by the desire of knowledge, renown or personal gain [remain] the great driving force in technical progress' (Jewkes, Sawers and Stillerman 1958). The authors did not consider that organizations were more effective than individual inventors and pleaded in favour of systems such as intellectual property rights that assisted inventions.

The question of innovation was also seen from the standpoint of organizational theory itself: if there is a general theory of organization, is it able to describe innovation? Innovation was a means of testing the theories. This research was part of contingency theory (Woodward 1965), whereby an organization's efficiency results from a good fit between its situation and structure, and where the better performing companies have a stronger model than the others. The authors then tried to identify the characteristic structural features of innovative organizations.

For instance, Burns and Stalker tried to show that there is no 'single set of rules for good organization', but that these rules depend on the environment's predictability. Their study on innovative electronics firms in post-war Britain showed that management should be attentive to evolutions in the market and to technologies. In mechanistic systems, each individual's behaviour is well organized, the tasks well prescribed and the organizational boundaries clearly established. They are well suited to situations where the environment is predictable. In rapidly changing situations, as was the case in the electronics industry, these mechanistic organizations were not as good as so-called organic systems in which individuals cannot hide behind organizational boundaries that limit the demands that can be made of them, but must feel personally concerned by any problems that may arise and constantly involved in the firm's success (Burns and Stalker 1961).

The authors went on to consider why firms did not change more easily from a mechanistic to an organic-style organization as and when necessary, and concluded that the rigidity came from political game-playing and career plans within organizations. Shortly after that, work by Lorsch and Lawrence, again in the contingency stream of research, compared the organizational methods of two innovative firms in the plastics industry, a sector which demands regular product renewals and also the ability to frequently propose major new products. They focused on the importance of cross-functional teams that provide a good balance between firms' marketing, production and R&D departments (Lorsch and Lawrence 1965).

At the end of the 1970s, Mintzberg proposed a conceptual description of the organization, based on a vast synthesis of the literature on the subject. He identified five fundamental coordination mechanisms (mutual adjustment, direct supervision, standardization of work processes, results and qualifications), five basic components (an operating core, a strategic apex, the middle line, a technostructure and support staff) and five types of organization structure (a simple structure, a machine bureaucracy, a professional bureaucracy, a divisionalized form and an adhocracy).

Although he did not specifically deal with the question of innovation, the issue was present throughout Mintzberg's work, in which he referred, amongst others, to research by Lorsch and Lawrence and Burns and Stalker. Mintzberg stressed the importance of forms of mutual adjustment in small but also in certain large organizations, on the grounds that it was the only thing that works in extremely difficult conditions such as going to the moon. 'At the outset, no one can be sure exactly what needs to be done. That knowledge develops as work unfolds. So in the first final analysis, despite the use of other coordinating mechanisms, the success of the undertaking depends primarily on the ability of the specialists to adapt to each other along their uncharted route' (Mintzberg 1979, p. 3).

Mintzberg classified 'analysts' (the specialists who help standardize the work of others and adapt the organization to meet environmental change) in the 'technostructure' category, but put research and development in the 'support staff' category, together with cafeteria staff and the legal, payroll, public relations and mail departments. However, this does not mean that he considered R&D unimportant. In fact, he stressed the fact that there had been a dramatic growth in support functions in organizations at that time and that their activities should be studied more closely.

As for the different configurations, Mintzberg insisted on a preferable form of organization for innovation: adhocracy. In this type of organization, the prime coordination mechanism is mutual adjustment and the support staff are the most important organizational entity. Adhocracy is designed to face up to complex, dynamic environments, favouring frequent product changes (single-piece production, high tech, etc.). He underlined that adhocracy was 'fashionable' and 'tomorrow's structure', but he also showed that it is highly unstable and therefore ephemeral, attracted by forms of stability found in bureaucracy.

In this widely used conceptual description, innovation can be seen as the focal point of a series of contemporary questions that had not been studied in any depth in the past: the specific form of coordination, the new actors in organizations and the specific configuration of the firm.

The specific structural features that favour innovation

Several research projects then sought to find the 'organizational determinants of innovation'. The notion of innovation had a precise definition:

'Organizational innovation has been constantly defined as the adoption of an idea or behaviour that is new to the organization. The innovation can either be a new product, a new service, a new technology, or a new administrative practice' (Hage 1999). As for the determinants, they all fitted into a generic description of the structures of an organization, i.e. centralization, functional divisions, levels of expertise, etc. This research aimed to bring together past work on the subject and draw up a general model: 'Organizational change is one instance where consistent findings have accumulated across more than thirty years of research' (Hage 1999).

In a meta-analysis involving twenty-three studies from the literature, Damanpour found a significant positive correlation between innovation and traditional characteristics found in different works: specialization (number of occupations), functional differentiation (number of departments), professionalism (level of education and training), centralization, positive managerial attitudes towards change, technical knowledge resources, administrative intensity, excess resources (slack) and internal and external communication (Damanpour 1991). The author considered that this confirmed Burns and Stalker's idea that innovation is easier in organizations with an organic rather than a mechanistic organizational form. To be more precise, it also confirmed the idea that administrative innovations are favoured by mechanistic structures, whereas technical innovations are favoured by organic structures, as in the dual-core model (administrative core, technical core) proposed by Daft (1978).

Referring in particular to Damanpour's work, Hage put forward three essential characteristics of organizational innovation: organic structure, complex division of labour and high-risk strategy, the second point being the most important in his view and also the one that had the least coverage in the literature. As he explained: 'Neither the organic structure nor the pro-change or high-risk strategy refer to the intellectual or problem-solving capacities or learning capacities of the organization, to say nothing about the creative capacities (. . .). Organic structures help mobilize this (diverse) knowledge and strategies provide goals and motivation, but ultimately one has to have the knowledge base represented by complexity and its various indicators' (Hage 1999).

Hage himself underlined the limitations of these works and gave some suggestions for further research: to control for the amount of investment in research and development (particularly as it had risen dramatically in certain sectors), to take into account prior innovations (signs of an organization's specific culture) and take into account micro analyses of the innovation process. He also focused on the need to carry out research in certain domains such as the radical innovations occurring in the components of assembled products (automobiles, aeroplanes, trains, etc.) and in large-scale technical systems (telephone, railways, electricity, etc.).

Organizations and rates of innovation: punctuated equilibrium and ambidextrous organizations or organizations for continuous change?

Other research concentrated on the dynamics of techniques, i.e. changes in processes and new product launches, to find the different forms of organization that are the best suited to the different phases of these dynamics. Two issues were treated at the same time: first, finding which structures are suited to certain forms of innovation, and second, seeing how the structures adapt to a changing environment, i.e. how organizations can undergo drastic changes to follow technical trends.

In the 1970s, Abernathy studied the history of Ford and observed the difficulties the firm experienced in moving from a strategy based on the mass production of a single product (the Ford T) to a strategy of variety (the Ford A). This work led first to highlight *repetitive characteristics in product and process development*: dominant designs are established over time and shared by the industries. In the first, 'fluid' stage, product innovations are multiplied; the products' functional characteristics then gradually become fixed, thereby setting the main lines of competition between firms. In the second, 'transition' phase, innovations take place in the processes. Finally, in the 'specific' phase, the processes are in turn rationalized (Abernathy and Townsend 1975).

Abernathy and Utterback deduced different forms of organization that were more or less pertinent depending on the technical context. For instance, in the initial fluid phase, the uncertainties concerning both the product and the processes rule out investments in R&D; later, in the transition phase when there is less uncertainty concerning the products, it becomes possible to invest in R&D; finally, in the specific phase, there is no more uncertainty concerning the products or the processes and competition tends to shift to the optimization of production directly inside the factory (Abernathy and Utterback 1978).

More generally speaking, the authors identified four main types of technological context and the four corresponding forms of organization. First, 'architectural innovation', which is a new technology that creates new relations with the market and requires an organic structure; second, 'innovation in the market niche', which uses existing technologies to find new markets and requires minute planning in terms of timing and very quick responses to competitors' initiatives; third, 'regular innovation', which consists of improving the technology and productivity and is based on methodical, coherent planning; and fourth, 'revolutionary innovation', which is a 'technology push' although it is still applied to the same markets and customers (Abernathy and Clark 1985).

The authors presented what they called a 'transilience map', the combination of transient and resilience illustrating the idea of following a path and overcoming obstacles along the way. They explained how innovation systems can change, with phases where there is an established dominant design, but also the phenomenon of 'dematurity', i.e. the re-emergence of an architectural innovation within an established dominant design, due to the introduction of new technical options and changes in customer demands and/or in regulations.

The authors also underlined *the difficulties experienced by firms* in following these different phases before establishing a dominant design. For instance, the initial research looked at the limits of strategies based on the learning curve alone, finding that, although such strategies help optimize existing processes, they also gradually increase the fixed costs, introduce narrower specializations and limit innovation capabilities (Abernathy and Wayne 1974). As for the transilience map, the authors provided few indications as to its possible implications for changes in firms.

The above research underlined the need for management to take into account technological change and proposed models for technical trends to serve as a reference for 'technology managers'. The research was continued by Tushman and his colleagues. Starting with the idea that organizations are sensitive to their environment, they began by examining the forces that make this environment change. Tushman and Anderson (1986) then proposed a punctuated equilibrium model for technical change: 'Technological change within a product class will be characterized by long periods of incremental change punctuated by discontinuities' and the latter can either destroy previous competencies or on the contrary enhance existing competencies. If competencies are destroyed, there can be new market entrants; if competencies are enhanced, the number of firms present in the market tends to fall. In terms of dynamics, each stage provides new opportunities, overall market growth and greater uncertainty. The propositions were based on surveys of firms in the cement, domestic air transport and minicomputer industries.

With data on two very different systems of innovation – with or without equilibrium – a second avenue of research involved finding which type of firm could survive in the two environments. Tushman and O'Reilly III (1996) proposed the notion of the ambidextrous organization. The ambidextrous organization must first of all escape the congruence trap, i.e. the inertia of simply adapting to the current innovation system; in the same way that the learning curve prevented the firm from getting ready for future innovation, in the equilibrium phase there is a tendency to adapt and align to the structures, strategies and culture within the firm, and this tendency is increased by structural inertia due to the size, complexity and interdependency in the organization's structures, systems, procedures and processes. However, ambidextrous organizations host multiple cultures and small, autonomous units whilst at the same time having a common overall culture; they must sometimes destroy the previous alignment of structure, strategy and culture. For instance, incremental innovation is carried out by older, experienced work teams, whereas for radical innovation, the teams are younger and more heterogeneous and skunk work is more frequent (Tushman, Anderson and O'Reilly 1997).

Finally, more recent work has focused on the processes themselves: Benner and Tushman showed that process management can be extremely effective for new product development but that success is sometimes at the expense of the exploratory processes found in radical innovation (Benner and Tushman 2002).

Eisenhardt and her colleagues argued against the theories on punctuated equilibrium and ambidextrous organizations. In their view, the rate of innovation has increased, with shorter product lifecycles and a rapidly evolving competitive environment (d'Aveni and Gunther 1994), to such an extent that it is no longer a question of adapting to 'rare, episodic and risky' change, but to 'frequent, relentless and even endemic change' (Eisenhardt 1989; Brown and Eisenhardt 1997). What are these 'relentlessly shifting organizations'? The authors described three characteristics: they are semi-structured, without too much structure that would prevent change, but with enough to avoid chaos; they are linked in time, i.e. they prepare for the future without planning or simply reacting to events, but by managing to organize a wide variety of low-cost trials; finally, they are based on 'sequenced steps', with regular product replacements, which serve as a reference for organizing the team's work, as periods of intensive project work can be alternated with more prospective periods of front-end development (Brown and Eisenhardt 1997).

They also explained that the best way of observing these new organizations that are capable of constantly adapting to the market was to look at product innovation rather than organizational or technological innovation: 'Product innovation is a primary way in which this alternative form of adaptation can happen (. . .) for many organizations, creating new products is a central path by which they adapt and sometimes even transform themselves in changing environments' (Eisenhardt and Tabrizi 1995). It is interesting to note that, by concentrating on product innovation, Eisenhardt combined the previously separate issues of the structures best suited to certain forms of innovation and the adaptations made to the structures to enable them to follow external trends. In her view, rather than corresponding to a system of innovation, the product is a way of adapting to a changing environment and sometimes even a way of transforming that environment.

This focus on new products led Brown and Eisenhardt to a closer examination of certain functions in firms and, in particular, product development processes (Brown and Eisenhardt 1995). The authors developed models for different types of products: they compared forms of product design based on planning and cross-functional teams, which are suited to stable products in a mature environment (automobile industry for Clark and Fujimoto 1991; mainframe computers for Iansiti 1993), with more experimental forms of product design, with frequent iterations, extensive testing and short milestones, which are better suited to less predictable products in more unstable environments (such as all IT products, with far shorter lifecycles than automobiles and mainframe computers, for Eisenhardt and Tabrizi 1995).

Revising techniques and descriptive language for organizations: innovation journey and complexity theory

Another major contribution to organizational theory was made by a group of researchers from the Minnesota Innovation Research Program (MIRP). To find out 'how and why innovations develop over time from concept to implementation', they studied the development of fourteen innovations 'in real time and in their natural field settings', for more than ten years. They explained that after an initial phase where they concluded that 'no overarching process theory of innovation has yet emerged from the research program, nor are prospects bright in the near future' (Van de Ven, Angle and Poole 1989), they developed a new process theory and new analytic tools for long series of events which, using work on the 'innovation journey', enabled them to obtain interesting results concerning several traditional questions posed by the management sciences: change and development processes, learning, innovation leadership, business and start-up development, inter-organizational relations, infrastructures for innovation at the industrial branch level, etc.

More specifically in the area of organization and processes, Van de Ven *et al.* (1989) stressed that their discoveries challenged two canonical models of innovation processes. The development of innovations did not follow a stable, stagewise model in which learning simply served to reduce uncertainty between the action and its result; nor did it follow a random process model in which the source of the innovation is external and the high number of factors involved prevents any control. In the authors' view, there are forms of repetition in an innovation process, but the right tools are required *to observe and identify them.* This raised a problem: as the MIRP study was carried out using observations over a long period of time, and as the innovation process is defined as 'new ideas that are developed and implemented to achieve desired outcomes by people who engage in transactions (relationships) with others in changing organizational and institutional contexts', any change in one of the parameters (i.e. those outlined here) is an event. How could they interpret the series of events resulting from observing innovations over several years?

The authors believed that the theory of complexity was the best tool to observe and explain complex organizational dynamics (Dooley and Van de Ven 1999). The theory of complexity is used to identify specific forms in event time series. When the series is periodic, a pattern can be observed. When it is not, the causal system is complex, in varying degrees. A time series is characterized by a limited number of causal factors that act independently, or in a linear fashion; when even a small number of causal factors act in a non-linear way this can provoke a form of chaos. Finally, there are situations where a large number of causal factors present non-periodic, non-chaotic forms of repetition. These are described as 'white noise' (a large number of factors acting in an independent or simple linear fashion) or 'pink noise' (a large number of factors with possible non-linear relations). The authors explained that 'each of these different temporal patterns tells the organizational research different things about the inner workings of the observed process'.

Applied to the MIRP study data, the complexity theory helps identify different phases in the innovation process. In the first stage, forms of white noise can be observed, characterizing upstream phases 'where multiple organizations pursue multiple innovation searches in a divergent fashion' (with numerous independent factors). In the next phase there are forms of pink noise when 'innovators take advantage of knowledge present within their personal social network', thus creating local feedback loops, i.e. forms of non-linear relations between causal factors. Finally, forms of chaos are observed. This does not indicate a large number of variables (as put forward in theories that see innovation as a chaotic process) but, on the contrary, a small number of strongly inter-related variables. In other words, in complexity theory, chaotic forms in fact indicate 'a significant control and/or cooperative mechanism' (Dooley and Van de Ven 1999). The researchers' general conclusion was that 'the innovation journey is a nonlinear cycle of divergent and convergent activities that may repeat over time and at different organizational levels if resources are obtained to renew the cycle' (Van de Ven *et al.* 1999).

Competence-based theories of the innovative firm

Following on from economic studies on resource-based theories (Penrose 1959), several research projects examined the question of the links between organizations and innovation. To explain growth in firms, Penrose had introduced the question of resources – considered as means that have not yet been appropriated to products or services, i.e. which are not yet production factors – and had then had to address the problem of firms' organizational capacities to explain how they managed these resources. 'A firm is essentially a pool of resources the utilization of which is organized in an administrative framework (. . .). Within the limits set by the rate at which the administrative structure of the firm can be adopted and adjusted to larger and larger scales of operation, there's nothing inherent in the nature of the firm or of its economic function to prevent the infinite expansion of its activities' (Penrose 1959).

However, this question of the administration of resources was covered in very general terms, with relatively little relation to the resources themselves: the management's aim is to distribute clear responsibilities for existing activities, whereas new business springs from new opportunities emerging from the firm's competencies. For the same competencies, it is not the administration that makes the difference but the entrepreneurial spirit that helps seize opportunities. In this way, small enterprises are able to seize new opportunities whereas large enterprises will tend to invest in fields that they know well. However, in doing so, large firms mechanically create knowledge, and hence new opportunities, although they do not seize them, so that small firms survive and develop in the interstices created and abandoned by the large firms. This so-called interstitial growth mechanism explains how there can be growth in small firms at the same time as in large ones.

In the 1980s, the notion of 'specific competencies' emerged as a path for elaborating a theory of the firm. The aim was to account for organization in a better way than production function modelling and to identify specific organizational features that went beyond the notion of 'nexus of contracts' and purely transactional analyses. As they are both 'sticky' and costly to copy, specific competencies help identify the firm and explain longevity beyond one-off products; they explain both the diversity of product portfolios and their non-random nature, as a competency can be mobilized for several products (Conner 1991; Coriat and Weinstein 1995). The difficulty resided in explaining changes. The most radical evolutionary theories were based on mechanisms where the market selects 'good routines', but some research addressed the problem of how organizations favour this adaptation and change. In strategic management, Barney (1991) proposed a resource-based view (RBV) of the firm and its competitive advantage: as resources are heterogeneously distributed across firms and these differences persist over time, this could explain constant differences between companies. He proposed four features to characterize resources in the RBV: value, rareness, inimitability and non-substitutability (VRIN).

Hamel and Prahalad went back to the notion of competency in a management and innovation perspective: to prepare for the future, firms have to manage what they called 'core competencies' (Hamel and Prahalad 1994b). The authors were anxious to find ways of avoiding the trap of downsizing, which was threatening western economies, observing that optimizing resources from an existing activity did not enable firms to think about the future and therefore to create the markets of tomorrow. How can firms organize themselves in such a way as to prepare for the future? In their view, the first step is to find a shared vision of the future, a task that is one of the essential functions of senior management (Hamel and Prahalad 1994a).

In this context, what is a core competency? Hamel and Prahalad explain that it is neither an asset, an infrastructure, a competitive advantage nor a critical success factor, but a value for the customer that distinguishes it from the competitors. It is not related to the products as it can be used for several product ranges. For Hamel and Prahalad, competency is not simply specific knowledge, but rather a form of 'base line' that characterizes new business for a firm, as in the case of 'quality' for Japanese companies, for example. The difficulty is to identify core competencies and to ensure that they last over time, since they are more of a concept than actual knowledge. This work led to a theory of the firm that was not based on certain specific competencies but on *the ability to combine competencies in business activity*. On the one hand, the firm – through a work contract – can direct employees to use their knowledge in a way that they would not otherwise do; on the other hand, the firm can benefit from the knowledge and opportunities produced during the action without having to renegotiate and sign new contracts (Conner and Prahalad 1996).

Dynamic capabilities and innovation capabilities as a dynamic capability

Teece *et al.* (Teece, Pisano and Shuen 1997) looked at the question of competencies from a slightly different angle. In their view, whereas resource-based theory considered knowledge as difficult for competitors to copy, but also as 'sticky' and therefore hard to redeploy, the real issue in rapidly changing environments is to analyse firms' capacity to adapt. They therefore introduced the notion of dynamic capabilities, defined as 'the firm's ability to integrate, and reconfigure internal and external competencies to address rapidly changing environment'. The dynamic capabilities are 'dynamic' due to their capacity to renew competencies so as to achieve congruence with the changing environment and are 'capabilities' as they reflect the aptitude of management to adapt, integrate and reconfigure organization and functional competencies. Whereas Penrose's resources can be seen as firm-specific knowledge and Hamel and Prahalad's core competencies as firm-specific concepts, Teece *et al.*'s dynamic capabilities can be seen as an organization's capacity to mobilize the right knowledge to deal with the most pertinent business issues.

The notion was then developed further, in particular to analyse the capacity for innovation. Helfat and Raubitschek (2000) showed that the building of core competencies and dynamic capabilities has to be related to the dynamics of products. They modelled a learning system in interaction with the sequence of products: 'The sequence of products is supported by an underlying system of knowledge and systems of learning. At any given point, an organization's portfolio of products serves as a platform for future product sequences' (p. 961). This analysis echoes Penrose's (1960) descriptions of the evolution of competencies. Eisenhardt and Martin (2000) put forward that an 'expanded view of routines' was sufficient to analyse firms' competitive advantage in moderately dynamic markets, whereas the notion of dynamic capability was extremely useful to analyse firms in dynamic markets. O'Connor (2008) refined this analysis by underlining that market dynamics are only a symptom; in her view, the decisive contingency factor is rather the uncertainty about links between action and outcome. She then analysed so-called 'major innovation dynamic capability' in a systems approach: an MI dynamic capability is characterized by a clearly identified structure, internal and external interface mechanisms, exploratory processes, requisite skills, appropriate governance and decision-making mechanisms and criteria, appropriate metrics and cultural and leadership context.

4.2 Progress and recent trends

Similarly to questions of economic policy, social networks and cognitive processes, it is clear that innovation has had an incredibly corrosive effect on organizational theories. The latter now seem extremely fragile, with their boundaries being disputed by the sociology of networks, by economics (especially by evolutionary theorists), by work on organizational learning and by all sorts of managerial currents, each trying to find a definition for the innovative organization. Nonetheless, a large number of concepts have emerged from this conjunction of innovation and organizational theory: the distinction between product innovation and organizational innovation, notions such as organic organizations, ambidextrous organizations and continuously changing organizations, the use of complexity theory to analyse 'pink noise' or 'white noise' phenomena, core competencies, dynamic capabilities, etc.

Two major trends can be found in this abundant, complex body of research, the first concerning the nature of innovation and the second, the languages that describe organizations.

Over the years, the term 'innovation' was used to refer to different forms of innovation. From the 1960s to the 1980s, the authors were mainly interested in *organizational innovation,* or how organizations managed to take on new forms. They addressed organizational change and changes in structures and processes. Product innovation was touched on only to underline that different types of product renewals required different organizational structures.

There was an important change of course at the beginning of the 1990s, following Brown and Eisenhardt's work. The authors no longer looked at *product design* as one situation involving change among others (product innovation, organizational innovation, market innovation, etc.) but as *the means of adapting to change par excellence.* We can take this idea as a general working hypothesis: could it be that product innovation – and even product design, whether for new products or not – is the best context for inventing new methods of organization?

The authors who studied innovation challenged the notions of universal organization theory on the grounds that it failed to take organizational change into account. They therefore proposed a new language to describe organizations. One of the best examples was organic organization (together with adhocracy and mutual adjustment in large organizations). However, this solution was in fact more problematic than initially thought: instead of proposing a new structure, organic organizations in fact opened up a new dimension, that of the actors' *behaviour*. This element was then implicit in all the work on ambidextrous organizations and organizations undergoing continuous change.

Other research projects then sought more radical means of avoiding the traditional language of structure and process. In particular, the Innovation Journey and work on strategic competencies proposed *new languages to describe the inner workings of innovation*: the first identified the natural laws of organizations using statistical data on 'events'; the second identified hybrid objects (dynamic capabilities and core competencies) that combine elements of structure, process and behaviour (dynamic capabilities are both organizational routines and hypotheses on the actors' behaviour; core competencies are both specific entities in the structure and the inner secret of its metabolism).

Other research concentrated on organizational behaviour and, instead of trying to reduce it to structural forms, tried to *deduce its specific mechanisms*. For instance, Weick (1998) suggested that jazz improvisation was an excellent metaphor for organizing creativity, while Starkey *et al.* showed that the UK television industry was based on organizations that were in the form of neither networks nor hierarchies but could be considered as latent organizations (Starkey, Barnatt and Tempest 2000).

5   Innovation and management

Heads of laboratories, engineering departments, marketing departments and design studios have been developing management techniques in one way or another for a long time now. For example, engineering departments invented most of their management techniques in the period from 1880 to 1900; planning departments, industrial research and marketing developed theirs in the period from 1900 to 1920. Taylor made an important contribution not only to the doctrine of shop floor management but also to the techniques that were used (the famous time and motion studies and, more generally speaking, the scientific analysis of production activities). The same techniques were sometimes used to organize industrial research laboratories (*see* Charpy 1919; Chevenard 1933), often considered to be the planning and management departments for the process industries (*see* Le Châtelier 1930). Scientific organization also had a major impact on sales and, later, marketing departments (*see* Freeland 1920, 1926). Until the 1970s, these management techniques remained relatively stable, to such an extent that they were even considered 'natural'.

In the context of stable functions, management tended to focus on processes, with two contrasting approaches: first, managing product development processes, i.e. coordinating and integrating the different functional experts mentioned above, and second, managing the innovation process, i.e. going beyond product development as such by recognizing opportunities for innovation and acquiring new knowledge. It is only very recently that there has been renewed interest in management techniques for the different functions themselves, i.e. research, marketing, engineering, etc.

5.1   Genealogy of research questions and key notions

Managing product development processes

Product development issues were first raised in the 1950s in the United States with a view to coordinating the key functions of development, research, engineering, marketing, industrialization and planning in the rapidly expanding consumer goods industry. An article in the *Harvard Business Review* by Johnson and Jones, respectively New Products Director at S.C. Johnson & Son Inc. and Vice President of a major consulting firm, Booz Allen Hamilton, became the reference at that time (Johnson and Jones 1957). The authors described Johnson & Son's newly founded 'new products' department. They stressed the importance of distinguishing between types of development depending on their degree of innovation (market newness and technological newness) and also of setting up effective coordination mechanisms between the firm's different functional departments. The new products department was in charge of organizing interactions between the different departments for each new product development. Each potential product development was treated as a unique proposal requiring a unique inter-departmental organization to deal with it. Each development was divided into well-defined phases: exploration, screening, proposal, development, testing and commercialization. This contained the seeds of 'stage-gate' models, integration and project management and the relations between these types of organization and product lifecycles (depending on the degree of innovation).

The above article was inspired by a study made by Booz Allen Hamilton in 1956. The firm's studies continued to punctuate waves of new product management doctrine in the following years. In 1967 a study pointed out that five out of six hours of engineers' and scientists' work was on products that would be commercial failures. This observation inspired Cooper's first work on the subject (Cooper 1976). He put forward the idea of product development in well-identified stages, each stage comprising all the market and technical activities undertaken by people from different functional areas in the firm, including information gathering, evaluation and decision. It was the first step towards what became the Stage-Gate™ model (copyrighted by Cooper) (Cooper 1990; for a study of the different forms of the Stage-Gate model *see* Varnes 2005).

In the early 1980s, a further report (Booz, Allen and Hamilton 1982) again underlined the high failure rates in product development, in a context where development lead times were increasing, non-quality was rising and project costs were seldom under control. During the 1980s, new concerns to quicken the pace and to improve cost-effectiveness, quality and strategic vision made it more and more difficult to keep to the traditional stages of product development. A seminal article by Henderson and Clark (1990) showed that 'architectural innovation' could not be handled in this way. In a study on photolithography equipment (used to produce integrated circuits) they had observed that, from one generation of instruments to another, the market leader always changed. They had also noted that the change in generation was not so much a question of evolving technologies or markets as of changes in the product's architecture. They concluded that structured development processes are based on implicit product architecture. A firm that never calls into question the different stages in its product development is never able to innovate in terms of architecture. This explained why firms remained leaders for only a short time in this market where the speed of change in required performance left no choice but to constantly use new architectures for the precision instruments in question.

In this context, project management emerged as a means of integrating upstream and downstream stages, through concurrent engineering, product-process integration, etc. (Clark and Fujimoto 1991). The project management unit was responsible for the overall strategy, if not for elaborating it.

The figure of the 'heavyweight product manager' was observed in many industries at that time (Wheelwright and Clark 1992; Midler 1993).

In these 'unique' projects, industry was in fact adopting the project management tradition used, precisely in specific circumstances, outside the strict context of firms, for major public-sector initiatives such as the Hoover Dam (1930s), the Manhattan Project (1940s), Polaris Missiles (1958) and NASA (1950s–1960s) and all the other projects launched by the US government in the 1960s. Industry also used the tools developed for these projects: budget management, work breakdown structure (WBS) and PERT/COST planning (Program Evaluation and Review Technique), which built on the famous Gantt diagrams (1917; Henry Gantt (1861–1919) was a disciple of Taylor) (on project management, *see* Garel 2003). More recently, Loch focused on managing so-called 'unk unks', i.e. unknown unknowns (Wideman 1992), or risks that are not identified at the beginning of projects (Loch, De Meyer and Pich 2006). The initial studies were then extended to entrepreneurship (Loch, Solt and Bailey 2008).

Set-based design, flexible product development and modular design

However, other approaches contrasted with this notion of unique projects. For example, in the mid-1990s, a study on product development at Toyota showed its ability to standardize and to capitalize on developments. In particular, Toyota studied sets of alternatives for a project, knowing that seemingly superfluous studies would be reused for other projects (Ward *et al.* 1995; Sobek, Liker and Ward 1998). In this way, Toyota had developed a system of set-based design which involved exploring a number of solutions for a relatively long time during the process of developing a vehicle.

In the software industry, other authors (MacCormack, Verganti and Iansiti 2001) studied how flexible development – as opposed to rigid stage-gate development – was in fact based on closely studied product architectures, highly experienced development teams and flexible product adaptations through the rapid, continuous integration of market information. According to the authors, these three characteristics – architectural design effort, generational experience from the development team and earlier feedback from the market – were the key conditions for flexible product development.

Fuzzy front-end

Other authors addressed the issue of innovation in product development by coming back to the notion of unique projects, this time focusing in particular on the initial stages of a project, referred to as the 'fuzzy front-end' (FFE). In their view, this phase had an enormous impact on the future of a project, in particular in terms of innovation.

Initially seen as a means of reducing time to market (in Reinertsen's words (1994): 'to beat an Olympic runner in the 100-metre dash, start running a minute before he does', fuzzy front-end management was then seen as a means of honing the business concept stage by stage with successive studies (assessment, detailed market studies, competitive analysis, concept tests) and technical analyses (Cooper 1997), designed to anticipate future technical problems (with the notion of 'front loading', developed by Thomke and Fujimoto (2000)). Khurana and Rosenthal (1998) saw the FFE as a process combining 'product strategy formulation and communication, opportunity identification and assessment, idea generation, product definition, project planning and executive reviews'. Koen *et al.* (2001) preferred the notion of front-end innovation (FEI) rather than FFE.

Innovative projects

Work on managing innovation as an 'innovative project' began with a completely different perspective, that of discipline on the part of the manager or the innovator. The authors worked on the idea that, instead of waiting for genius or the 'kiss of the muses' (Drucker 1985), it was more productive to apply good principles of management. Taking the example of the hamburger chain McDonald's, Drucker explained that it was a 'systematic entrepreneurship'. By asking what is 'value' to the customer, by standardizing the product, and designing process and tools, it had created a new market and new customers. More recently, consultants such as Gaynor (2002) have continued in this vein, insisting that firms should focus on optimizing people's involvement, guiding management practices and encouraging professional attitudes. The same theme was taken up in Storey and Salaman's book *Managers of Innovation*, which recommends that managers should have 'clarity of purpose' and should be challenging, ambitious and heroic in change-focused organizations (Storey and Salaman 2005). This is an example of the effect that Taylor's and Fayol's work has had on how companies are run, with a swing from the idea of a moral authority at the head of the firm to the idea of theoretical and practical 'education' (*see* Hatchuel 2001b).

This discipline was seen from the perspective of 'good collective routines' in work by Tidd *et al.* (Tidd, Bessant and Pavitt 1997), in which they proposed a four-phase model of the innovation process. First, scan and search the environment to find signals about potential innovations; second, select those that offer the best chance of success; third, find the resources to develop the options, in the firm (R&D) or, more frequently, outside it (through technology transfer); finally, implement and develop the innovation, from the idea through to the final launch. These phases involve four main types of routines: those involving strategy (competitive environment, market, technological trajectories, strategic learning in the organization), the capacity to build effective external relations (management by alliances), the capacity to organize the implementation and those concerning the innovative organization (leadership, shared vision, creative climate, etc.).

Other authors made in-depth studies of forms of innovative projects in different sectors of industry that had built innovative supply-based strategies (Lenfle 1997; Lenfle and Midler 2000; Ben Mahmoud-Jouini 2004). The studies showed that the projects had involved drawing up business models and creating new competencies. Lenfle showed recently that historical references of project management, such as the Manhattan Project, were actually strongly innovative and used organizational tools and methods that went far beyond traditional PERT, leadership principles and cost management. It was as if the doctrine had only retained the non-innovative aspects of project management (Lenfle 2008). In another perspective, Varnes and Christianson (Christianson *et al.* 2005; Varnes 2005; Varnes and Christianson 2006) also showed that firms do not actually use the stage-gate processes they maintain they rely on. Finally, Seidel particularly focused on a critical issue in innovative project management: the capacity to organize concept shifts (2006, 2007).

A specific function for innovation?

Leifer and his colleagues carried out a series of empirical studies of twelve radical innovation projects in ten large, mature companies over a period of six years. The studies identified certain good management practices and showed that radical innovation projects were very different from incremental projects. They put forward the idea of a 'hub of innovation' with the following key roles: to protect innovators from bureaucracy; to deploy 'hunters and gatherers' capable of looking for and pointing out new ideas emerging in departments and business units; to monitor and direct projects, rather than control their convergence, by avoiding skunk work and favouring work in the mainstream organization; to develop resource acquisition (financial and human); to accelerate and facilitate project transition to become solid business; and to attract talents and entrepreneurs (Leifer *et al.* 2000; Leifer, O'Connor and Rice 2001). More recently, O'Connor and de Martino (2006) studied several organizational structures linking innovation actors in large firms: beyond the stereotypes of the incubator and central R&D, they found complex configurations combining R&D and incubators at the central level and in business units.

This idea of an organization in charge of innovative projects was also the solution proposed by Christenson to solve his 'innovator's dilemma'. In his view, major firms fail because they use traditional product development methods (listening responsively to customers, following the competition, investing massively in new technologies and the most profitable, most sought-after products), and in doing so fail to work on 'disruptive technologies'. This work can be carried out only by small teams, content with small profits, targeting technologies where there is demand without betting on a 'breakthrough' product as this is always risky, always alert to market responses and able to consider that the initial product launch is an opportunity to learn (Christenson 1997; Christenson and Raynor 2003).

Evolutions in functions

The above research described different forms of coordination between the major design functions and specific organizations in charge of managing innovative projects. Some research also looked at evolutions in the departments themselves, asking how the R&D or the marketing departments had changed.

For R&D, a book published in the early 1990s by consultants at Arthur D. Little, *Third Generation R&D* (Roussel, Saad and Erickson 1991), stood as a reference for many heads of research laboratories. The authors argued that whereas first-generation R&D, from the 1930s to the 1960s, had been able to do as it pleased, and the second generation, in the 1970s and 1980s, had been controlled by project structuring and immediate customer demands, third-generation R&D was obliged to integrate the firm's overall strategy. The authors insisted on the importance of good project portfolio management, where each project is identified in terms of its risk, attractiveness, technological maturity, cost and probability of success. This technique must be accompanied by sound management practices: stable, shared vocabulary, clear targets and priorities, good use of suggestion boxes, the ability to go straight to the point, a 'killer attitude' to projects and constant resource optimization.

Miller and Morris, who put forward the idea of fourth-generation R&D, considered that the third generation was based on the hypothesis that research would provide technology for a well-expressed, identified demand.

The authors suggested that fourth-generation R&D organized the exploration of markets and techniques at the same time. They proposed that more exploratory marketing$_2$ and R&D$_2$ activities should be added respectively to traditional marketing$_1$ (which simply asks customers what they want) and R&D$_1$ (which ensures incremental innovation on existing product lines) (Miller and Morris 1999).

A journalist, Buderi, studied the transformations taking place in research in American firms (Buderi 2000). After describing the 'research blood bath' of the 1990s, he pointed out new practices in research that were closer to the market, had closer links to marketing and paid more attention to the evaluation of research projects. More generally speaking, he considered that research laboratories were no longer a source of innovation but rather a filter for external innovation and a link with external research laboratories (which is reminiscent of the absorptive capacity described by Cohen and Levinthal (1990)).

More recently, several authors have focused on the importance of industrial design for innovation (von Stamm 2003; Best 2006; Utterback *et al.* 2006; Verganti 2008; Dell'Era and Verganti 2009), underlining that designers are more sensitive to users, emotions, symbols, creativity and the arts, and fashion. This helped identify a new type of innovation, 'design-driven innovation' (Verganti 2008), which radically changes the emotional and symbolic content of a product.

Managing platforms and industry architectures

As we have described in the previous sections on the economics, sociology and organization of innovation, several authors have underlined that industry structures strongly influence the type of innovation. More recently, several authors have pointed out that some firms not only take these constraints into account but also manage to influence the structure of their sector for their own growth and for the growth of the sector itself. This notion appeared by analysing technologies: following Henderson and Clark (1990), works by Morris and Ferguson (1993) and Baldwin and Clark (2000, 2006b) developed the idea that the traditional approach to technology, considered as a stable asset providing a clear output, was not relevant since several architectures and technology strategies could unfold for the same type of product. In particular, Baldwin and Clark underlined that design rules and modularity account better for competition through innovation. Design rules are a 'minimum language' required in each module to ensure that the overall system functions; these rules leave vast areas of freedom for integrating innovative modules, for introducing additional modules in a system at a later stage or for exploring several paths for the same product. The authors described the power of modularity for encouraging innovation in a whole sector and showed how modular architecture can be reworked, improved and (marginally) changed by actors.

Following the same path, Jacobides, Knudsen and Augier (2006) studied how firms were able to 'influence the structure of their sector in ways that would eventually fit their own capabilities'. They defined 'industry architecture' as two templates: '1. a template defining value creation and the division of labor (who can do what) and 2. a template defining value appropriation and the division of surplus or revenue, i.e. who gets what.' Using Teece's (1986) notion of 'complementary asset', whereby profits from innovation accrue to the owners of complementary assets rather than to the developers of the intellectual property, Jacobides *et al.* showed that besides the traditional strategy of buying or building complementary assets, which tends to 'shrink the pie', firms can also try to increase complementary asset mobility, by encouraging competition on complementary assets they do not own, on the assumption that this will make the pie grow.

This framework was inspired by the emerging practices observed and analysed by Annabelle Gawer at Intel. Gawer *et al.* described the Intel Architecture Lab (IAL), designed to help partners invent new products using Intel microprocessors (Gawer and Cusumano 2002). The organization is in charge of third-party innovations; its work helps Intel keep its platform leadership by ensuring that the microprocessor remains at the heart of the computer system. Gawer and Cusumano (2008) focused on two principles for becoming a platform leader: 1) coring, i.e. building a strong core, that 'performs at least one essential function or solves an essential problem within an industry' and is easy to connect to or to build upon to expand the system of use as well as to allow new and even unintended end-uses; and 2) tipping, i.e. implementing actions designed to win platform wars.

Methods for innovation management: experimentation, creativity, user involvement, open innovation, real options

Several researchers have underlined the importance of specific techniques and methods for innovation such as experimentation, creativity, user involvement, open innovation and real options. We shall give a brief overview of these techniques, some of which are more broadly discussed in the book. For instance, Thomke worked on modes of experimentation and their renewal via new analytical tools and models (high throughput screening, virtual reality, etc.) and via new needs (emergence of forms of experimentation in designing consumer services such as banking services) (Thomke, von Hippel and Franke 1998; Thomke 2003a, 2003b).

Another increasingly popular domain is the analysis of uses and design by users. Inspired by von Hippel's work on users' ability to design products (notion of lead-users; *see* the section on innovation and society in this appendix), firms tried to set up processes that involved users in their design activities. For instance, the researchers and practitioners in the Swedish laboratory Fenix have accompanied or even sometimes steered such practices, in varied industrial environments (mobile telephone services (Magnusson 2003); automobile design (Dahlsten 2004); trade unions (Björkman 2005)). Work by Piller *et al.* also described these new forms of innovation management with intensive customer involvement, asking questions such as what the firm should design to enable the user to customize the product and ensure mass customization, and also how the process should be managed (Tseng and Piller 2003), beyond the classical contradiction between strong and weak ties with the customers (Fredberg and Piller 2008).

In a more general approach, several studies have underlined that contemporary companies are relying on external resources for innovation. They are able to use external knowledge and ideas and are not necessarily obliged to source them internally. The authors focus on the capacity of some firms to use and organize platforms, user communities, crowd sourcing, etc. (Chesbrough 2003; West 2003; West and Gallagher 2006). In this respect, some companies have developed the capacity to organize open innovation at the interface between large companies and research laboratories. Researchers studying these organizations (Lakhani and Panetta 2007; Sieg, Wallin and von Krogh 2009) have shown that managing open innovation requires real know-how, 1) to enrol in-house scientists to work with innovation intermediaries; 2) to select the right problems; and 3) to formulate problems so as to enable novel solutions (Sieg, Wallin and von Krogh 2009).

Some authors have underlined the importance of creativity techniques for performing innovation. Creativity can be found in marketing manuals and techniques (Goldenberg and Mazursky 2002; Kotler *et al.* 2006; Rosier 2007), in work on creative organizations (Amabile 1996; Amabile *et al.* 2005) and in user involvement (Kristensson, Magnusson and Matthing 2002). Creativity plays a key role in all these approaches, as the resource, the process that generates the innovation and the original idea. However, in all these cases, creativity is treated as a known, available resource, which may simply need to be protected from the harmful influence of the organization. Most of the authors underline that organizations have great difficulties in allowing this creativity to survive, with the exception of a few particularly successful cases (Sutton and Hargadon 1996).

Another technique often advocated for managing innovation is that of real options. In fact, options are the only techniques mentioned by O'Connor in her ground-breaking article on major innovation as a dynamic capability. Real option approaches aim to evaluate R&D projects by introducing flexible decision-making to R&D projects. The method was initially developed to overcome the limits of traditional net present value (NPV) evaluation. Whereas NPV is an *ex ante* evaluation for Go/No Go decisions in early stages, real option aims to introduce flexibility in decision-making throughout projects (Trigeorgis 1993; Herath and Park 1999), taking into account the uncertainty of the target (in terms of market and technology). However, the method is not easy to apply, which could explain its limited use in practice (Hartmann and Hassan 2006), and careful attention must be paid to the way it is implemented (Perlitz, Peske and Schrank 1999).

The theoretical background of real options (Trigeorgis 1996) and the most generic models (Schneider *et al.* 2008) underline that real option evaluation requires good knowledge of the potential of the project (to be able to draw on underlying assets) and also that all the potential alternatives and all the possible actions to be taken in the future are well known, the list of actions being limited to 'defer, expand, switch and default' and all the related combinations.

In a context of discontinuous innovation, several authors have underlined that these conditions might be difficult to fulfil since the design process involved in such projects can lead to unexpected expansions and require unexpected actions (Adner and Levinthal 2004b; Fredberg 2007). In such cases, real options reasoning is suggested as a managerial tool (Lander and Pinches 1998; Lint and Pennings 2001; McGrath 2001; Adner and Levinthal 2004a; Fredberg 2007). This leads to propositions such as evaluating projects as parts of continuous development, taking into account the options created, seeking projects with a high variance in the value of the product, etc. These recommendations do enable companies to take into account a project's contribution to the innovation capabilities of the firm. But this stream of literature does not propose an integrated framework for using real options as an evaluation framework in such cases. Moreover, some authors have argued that real options reasoning is a restrictive way of evaluating projects with flexible target markets and flexible technical agendas (Adner and Levinthal 2004a, 2004b).

5.2   Recent trends

In recent managerial literature, there is often less sense of being attached to a specific discipline. The authors tend to come from very different backgrounds (consulting firms, academic research and practitioners); either an author plays on two different fronts or different authors group together to publish their work. They often seem to take their inspiration from other disciplines (cf. radical versus incremental innovation, tacit knowledge, routines, etc.) and use these theoretical devices to analyse 'phenomenology' that is new to firms. In fact, it is this phenomenology that is then used in turn in the disciplines in question (*see*, for example, Eisenhardt's work using Clark's research on project management). One point that characterizes all this work is that the approaches are very fragmented (processes, strategy, functions, activities, etc.) due to a lack of a unified framework.

However, these phenomena should not be taken for solutions. User involvement, open innovation, real options, etc. are seen as new imperatives for firms to innovate, but they are not recipes. As described in this book, platform management (Chapter 15), open innovation, user involvement (Chapter 11) and creativity (Chapter 10) require specific management methods to be managed efficiently.

The second remark is a paradox: putting these authors into a wide category of innovation management is not really controversial, yet it is surprising to note that many of them do not mention innovation at all. They either prefer the new product development perspective or the traditional organizational breakdown (R&D, marketing). This is more important than it may seem. The management perspective adopted by most of these authors led them to abandon the term 'innovation' which, in its classic sense, is not an actionable notion (*see* Chapter 2).

These works were written following consultants' and analysts' reports on trends in firms or the emergence of original practices in specific firms. The authors therefore seem to be explaining transformations in firms. Two major trends can be noted:

Managerial approaches have changed drastically in the past few years. We have moved from the coordination of major functions – stage-gate organization, project management – to a transformation of the activities themselves (new research, new marketing and the appearance of new activities).

As we have said, innovation is not really mentioned as a result, but it has emerged as a specific activity, which must apparently be distinguished from traditional activities, involving not only a form of 'discipline' but also tools, missions and special forms of interaction with other partners.

Afterword

We were very pleased to accept the authors' request to focus on the key prospects opened up by this book. Renault, which has a fruitful research partnership with the Ecole des Mines de Paris (CGS), was directly involved in the issues covered here.

For Renault, this research has already encouraged us to set up an Innovation Centre and to develop experimental innovative design tools; today it helps build more effective 'front-end' functions for the firm, in terms of innovation capability and value creation. We were also very pleased to find that the experience provided by Renault for this research contributed to the results described in this book. The research partnership was even the subject of a joint communication by Renault and the Ecole des Mines de Paris in 2005, by special invitation from the Annual Conference of the European Academy of Management.

The distinction between innovative design and rule-based design is doubtless the latest idea and the one which will have the most impact on the way design systems operate in the future. It helps build innovative design teams more effectively. They will, of course, be composed of designers, engineers, product managers, researchers, partner suppliers, etc. But above all, these teams will have a wider scope for exploration and research, whilst also being better organized and more involved in our sales projects. The major contribution of the C-K design theory developed by the Ecole des Mines is doubtless to reconcile these two notions. There is a common belief that innovation and creativeness are contrary to the principles of structuring and organization. And yet it is often true that the most successfully completed innovations combine audacious concepts, wide-ranging expertise and methodical work processes. It is therefore interesting to see that theory meets practice here and corrects the first intuitions.

If we give the innovative design teams more suitable principles, resources and targets, this can only be to the benefit of good rule-based design, i.e. our sales projects. The latter are bound to be more attractive and more innovative, without this being detrimental to their targets, which are often vital to the company. Other advantages can be expected from well-organized innovative design. We have a better understanding of scientific research and how it should be used; we will become more efficient in setting up our major strategies in conceptual or technical 'innovation fields'. Renault is keen to maintain its partnership with the researchers, as progress in these areas stems from the interactions between theoretical research and practical industrial implementation.

Many other prospects for change are opened up by this extremely rich book, which studies a vital issue for firms. It is most appropriate that, through what we hope will be a widely read book, research should provide the people involved – manufacturers, consultants, teachers and students – with tools to help face this major challenge in the most effective way possible.

Jacques Lacambre
Former Director of DARP, Renault
Dominique Levent
Head of the Innovation Centre, DREAM, Renault

Innovative design glossary

---

1 Repeated innovation, intensive innovation and identity of objects

---

Definitions: Introduction and Chapter 2; example of growth by intensive innovation: Chapters 4 and 5; models and methods of organization for intensive innovation: Chapters 8, 10 and following.

Definitions: the term 'repeated innovation' focuses on the fact that the innovation is not a natural, random (Poissonian) phenomenon but the result of the activity of communities that determine its form and conditions of acceptability. These communities are therefore organized to repeat the innovation, at varying rates and on a greater or lesser scale.

Innovation is intensive when all the visible or invisible attributes of a product or service are potential areas of innovation. The process involves introducing new functionalities or new value spaces, which stimulate new techniques, which in turn give birth to new aesthetics, new functions, etc.

The most visible and striking effect of intensive innovation is that the actual identity of the objects or values is called into question and renewed (renewal of technologies, functions, aesthetics, uses, business model, etc.).

To be distinguished from:
* *Radical, discontinued, disruptive, major innovations* (see the bibliographical appendix for these terms). These terms reflect, per discipline, the perception that certain types of innovation break a form of continuity. The notions all refer to the implicit idea of a crisis in a permanent system and the idea of one-off innovation rather than a normal, more 'continual', rate of innovation.
  * Radical versus incremental = innovations which the firm cannot finance or finds it difficult to finance on its own (cf. innovation economics, the bibliographical appendix, Section 1).

- Discontinuous versus continuous = innovation which cannot be achieved by traditional R&D processes (Tidd, Bessant and Pavitt 1997).
- Disruptive versus sustaining = innovation which does not correspond to a market and a well-identified, dominant client demand (Christenson 1997).
- Major = really new, radical innovation, when 'reliance on experience, current knowledge assets and loyal customers is not an advantage' (O'Connor 2008).

The notion of intensive innovation (change in the object's identity) provides a better description of the nature of the innovation (change of one or several of an object's attributes which had usually remained unchanged in design processes undergone in the past: new functional space, new competencies, new business models, etc.). The notion does not make assumptions concerning possible 'crises' or about the nature of the permanent system; intensive innovation can be a permanent system of innovation. In some respects, intensive innovation can therefore be 'continuous', 'incremental' and 'sustaining' (*see* the Tefal and Saint-Gobain Sekurit models; also the notion of radical incrementalism, Chapter 4).

2 Design, design activities, rule-based design and innovative design

Definitions: Chapters 1, 3 and 10; detailed examples described using C-K design theory: Chapters 10 to 15.

Definitions: in a C-K formal framework, design consists of making undecidable propositions decidable, through a dual expansion of knowledge and concepts.

Design activities are the activities used to conceive and formulate innovations. Traditionally divided into R&D, engineering, industrial design and marketing, in the rare cases when these activities have been studied it was, until recently, often without an adequate theoretical framework.

To be distinguished from:
- Planning, optimization and modelling. It also differs from the theory of decision-making under uncertainty and from problem-solving (for these points, *see* Rittel (1972); Schön (1990); Hatchuel (2002)) .
- Design is also different from creativity (*see* Chapter 10 and also Le Masson, Hatchuel and Weil (2007); Hatchuel, Le Masson and Weil (2008)).

- Systematic design is a specific class of design in which the designers use existing design rules whenever possible (*see* discussion on systematic design according to an AFNOR norm, Chapter 3).
- More generally, there are two classes of design:
  - rule-based design, which aims to minimize expansions and to reuse established design rules whenever possible; for example, it focuses on modularity (Baldwin and Clark 2000). Systematic design is a form of rule-based design;
  - innovative design, which tries to revise the identity of objects, break away from the existing design rules and generate new rules.
- Recent works have studied the rise of industrial design in organizations (von Stamm 2003; Best 2006; Utterback *et al.* 2006; Verganti 2008; Dell'Era and Verganti 2009). The emergence of what we call innovative design cannot be assimilated with the rise of industrial design, even though the latter may be a symptom of the former. Innovative design refers to a new form of design which concerns all the traditional design functions (R&D, marketing, industrial design) and even new actors (in particular users).

3   Innovation-oriented metabolism

Definition and application in the Tefal case: Introduction and Chapter 4; modelling: Chapter 5; implementation in the Avanti case: Chapter 6; analysis of metabolisms in R&D-based firms: Chapter 7; I function and metabolisms: Chapters 8 and 10.

Definition: a collective capacity to continually and simultaneously recreate *sources of value* (products, concepts, patents, environmental and social values, etc.) and new *competencies* (knowledge, expertise, rules, functions, etc.).

A metabolism can be described as a series of metabolic pathways. A metabolic pathway corresponds to a transformation process, a regulation process, a conditioning process or an interaction between regulation, transformation and conditioning. Metabolisms are studied in terms of organs and functions. For firms, the organs are, for example, the major activities such as the marketing department, engineering department, research laboratories and production plants; the functions are, for example, strengthening product and price competitiveness, industrial property positioning, brand awareness and attractiveness as an employer.

To be distinguished from:
- *Evolutionary generation and selection of routines*: this process of routine generation and selection is one metabolism among others, which can be more complex (*see*, for example, the ability of certain metabolisms to play on the interaction between generation and selection processes; or the way in which certain metabolisms go beyond the notion of routine (i.e. the process of stimulus-response) and use algebras for dealing with unknowns, i.e. structures in the space of concepts). See Chapters 4, 5, 9 and 11 to 15 (case studies).
- *Organic/mechanistic firms*: there are metabolisms for mechanistic firms and metabolisms for organic firms. We show that the term 'organic' as used by Burns and Stalker (1961) is mainly based on individual behaviours. Burns and Stalker identified metabolic pathways, which are based on individual behaviours and are often neutralized in mechanistic firms (*see* the bibliographical appendix, Section 4, organizational theory and innovation). It should be noted that innovative firms implement highly innovative metabolisms (intensive innovation) by introducing processes which go way beyond the issue of the actors' behaviour (*see* case studies, Chapters 4, 5, 9 and 11 to 15).

4   Learning rents from the market/from design

Definition and examples from the Tefal case: Chapter 5; the Avanti case: Chapter 6.

Definition: investments in new product design produce two sources of rents, the first coming directly from the product sales and the second, which we call 'learning rents', from all the knowledge that is acquired during the design process for product n *and that will be used for products developed at a later stage* (n+1, n+2, etc.). It is a rent in the sense that the project n helps make the following projects more successful. It should be noted that learning processes are not intrinsically rents: knowledge can be lost (e.g. turnover in teams) or unusable (very specialized knowledge concerning a technical path or niche market which proves unsuitable): the rent occurs when the learning is reused.

We can distinguish between two different types of rents: those from marketing, referred to as learning rents from the market, and those from the design activity itself, learning rents from design (*see* Section 5.2 and following).

To be distinguished from:
- *Learning by doing*. The notion of 'learning by doing' (in economics, *see* Arrow (1962)) gives the illusion of a gain in productivity by simply repeating an action. The action in itself creates an infinite number of possible learning processes. If the action is to teach people how to 'do things better' or to produce 'new ideas', it must include selective practices for questioning the effects, sorting the causes and formulating new knowledge. This means that feedback from experience must be organized and above all that the knowledge must be used. In fact, it is more a case of *learning from doing*. Active measures must therefore be taken to identify and encourage learning rents (*see* Section 5.5).

5 Lineage

Definition: Chapter 5; examples of applications: Chapters 6 and 9; examples of methods: Chapter 10 and following.

Definition: a sustainable regime for the coevolution of competencies and products as and when the design activities take place. It consists of stabilizing (but not stopping) the expansions of the products and competencies by adopting a stable guiding concept.

The notion of lineage therefore describes all the associated (expanding) competencies, an (expanding) product family and a stable guiding concept.

To be distinguished from:
- *Product families, dominant design, platforms*: a product family is defined by products with a series of common traits, which helps stabilize user values for the customers and stabilize the design principles for the firm (architecture, validation techniques, etc.). The stabilizing of design principles and user values corresponds to a dominant design. Product families are lineages with very limited coevolution (*see* Section 5.3).
- *Core competency, technological trajectory*: these notions describe certain stable elements of competency-based lineages. However, in some cases, a lineage's core competencies can change drastically (*see* Section 5.3).
- *Business unit*: a business unit is defined by the space occupied by the products and competencies it is charged with exploiting. A lineage is built on the basis of the expansion and the evolution of the 'territory' taken up by the competency and the product. Business units are based on the idea of separating territories whereas lineages can adopt a hybridization process (*see* Section 5.4).

6 Prudent model

Chapter 4

Definition: the notion of 'prudence' is used in bankruptcy law to assess a firm's risk of failure. In innovative design, a model is prudent when (i) it is prudence itself that imposes innovation, in terms of the firm's survival, and (ii) it minimizes the risks inherent in innovation (in particular the financial risks).

These two aspects led Tefal to regularly launch new products *and* to adopt a 'low break-even point' strategy, by minimizing investments in each project so that no individual project could threaten the firm's ability to launch other projects.

To be distinguished from:
- *Risk management*: Risk management models tend to reduce uncertainties, including those relating to innovative projects (*see* work by Loch, for example). In the context of intensive innovation, a prudent approach, on the contrary, consists of increasing, with rigour and control, the number of unknowns (by modifying the object's identity and hence its functions, competencies, business models, etc.) in order to survive.

7 Martingale

Chapter 5

Definition: the term relates to probabilities and games of chance. In innovative design, a martingale describes a succession of design efforts aimed at taking advantage of learning from design (*see* learning rents), not only by reusing the knowledge produced in the earlier moves but, above all, by playing the next move depending on the learning that it will produce and which will help define the following ones.

In games of chance, martingales do not have an influence on the expected profit; similarly, in innovative design, martingales do not allow for a determinist, planned process. Nonetheless, contrary to martingales in games of chance, martingales in innovation change the probability space and uncertainties are reduced by knowledge gained at each step (learning rents from the market/from design).

To be distinguished from:
- *Innovations and discoveries at a Poisson rate* (*see* endogenous growth, the bibliographical appendix, Section 1): classical economic modelling of

innovation is generally based on the hypothesis of a 'discovery' (new patents, new technologies, new products, etc.) with the Poisson rate parameter depending on R&D efforts. Such models assume that there are no design martingales; with a design martingale, the efforts made at step n have an impact on the success of the following steps.

8 *I* function (innovative design function) and RID

Definition: Chapter 8; action model for the I *function: Chapter 10; the* I *function in management literature: Section 8.2; the principles of management for an* I *function and the* I *function and the other functions of the firm: Section 8.2.*

Definition: transition from R&D to RID. The *I* (for innovative design) between research and development refers to the functions and competencies of innovative design. This is neither another structure or body nor a simple coordinating function, but an innovative design function, responsible for two activities: the designing of new sources of value (products, concepts, patents, environmental and social values) and the identification and construction of new competencies.

It should be noted that:
- This definition assumes that the relationships between research and development and innovation have been clarified (Section 8.1). Based on the genealogy and the modelling of research and development activities, we propose the following definitions:
  - Development is a controlled process which activates existing competencies and knowledge in order to specify a system (product, process, organization, etc.) which must meet well-defined criteria (quality, cost, time) and whose value has already been clearly conceptualized and sometimes evaluated (*see* Section 8.1.1).
  - Research is a controlled process of knowledge production (*see* Section 8.1.2).
- *Ambidextrous organizations:* The innovative design function serves to enrich and model the notion of ambidextrous organization, which is often ambiguous in the literature (*see* Section 8.2).

9 Concept (C) and knowledge (K) in C-K design theory

Definition: Chapter 10. See reference publications on the subject (Hatchuel and Weil 2003, 2007, 2009).

Definition: given a set of propositions with a logical status (true or false) (propositions in the knowledge space K), a concept is a proposition that can be interpreted with the propositions in K but is undecidable with respect to all the propositions in the space K. A concept is a proposition that is neither true nor false with respect to the space K. A concept C is a set in the space C.

It should be noted that:
- By 'knowledge' we mean all propositions with a logical status. Such knowledge can be technical, aesthetical, symbolic, managerial, economic, etc.
- Concepts can take the form of briefs for industrial designers ('a women's car') or for engineers ('a fuel cell for mobility').
- As a concept is neither true nor false, no judgement can be made as to its truth. In particular, it is not possible to say immediately whether it is 'sellable' or 'feasible'. Adding attributes to a concept can consist of enriching (and diversifying) the criteria of judgement applied to it (and gradually enable evaluations of the feasibility or the market for the product or products resulting from the concept).

10   Innovation fields and design strategy

Definitions: Section 8.2; typology of innovation fields: Chapter 10 and following; evaluation criteria for managing innovation fields: Section 10.2.

Definitions: an innovation field is an area in which a firm wishes to carry out work on innovative design. This apparently simple definition implies that the *intention* is to revise the identity of the objects, i.e. the intention is to break the design rules. C-K design theory gives a more precise formal definition: an innovation field is defined as a concept C_0, an associated K base, which may be very limited, and the mission to carry out one or several expansive partitions using the initial concept.

Exploring an innovation field helps elaborate a design strategy, characterized by a set of interdependent design paths, a set of revisions to the identity of objects (revisions to the design rules of certain of the firm's objects) and the identification of competencies to be acquired.

To be distinguished from:
- *Project*: in the traditional engineering sense of the term, a project is defined by specifications which define the future product (or service, or process), the associated design resources and a QCT objective. The project corresponds to a 'development' activity. Nonetheless, a project can be innovative

within this framework, when its actors are confronted with surprises (*see* Wideman and Loch's 'unknown unknowns' – Wideman (1992); Loch, De Meyer and Pich (2006)). Contrary to a project, the management of innovation fields is characterized by organizational divergence (i.e. the fields are divided into several parallel exploratory processes), a contingent horizon, the gradual reusing of the knowledge produced and the gradual formulating of a design strategy. In this way, an innovation field can generate several more or less innovative projects (*see* Section 8.2).

- *Project portfolio*: an innovation field is not defined as a set of projects but it generates a set of projects. These projects are not independent and in competition for resources; they are interdependent and can gradually generate resources for each other.
- *Strategic vision, insight*: a vision is an intellectual framework. It identifies emerging values and helps give birth to new products. In classical models, the vision is provided by top management and then implemented by the rest of the firm. However, this representation implies that the terms of the vision are sufficiently clear to solve all the innovative design issues, i.e. that the innovative design work has already been carried out by the 'visionary' top management. In general, top management in fact tends to identify innovation fields which still require a large amount of work in terms of innovative design before a design strategy can be defined. The latter consists of drawing up a structured set of alternatives and identifying design rules to be revised and competencies to be acquired. It is this work which leads to a 'shared vision'.

11   Value management and design space

Definition: Chapter 10; examples: Chapters 11 to 15.

Definition: a design space is a work space in which it is possible to implement the learning processes required for the design reasoning. In formal terms, it is a sub-set of the initial $\{C_0, K_0\}$ set in which the designers can learn things about what must be learned to explore the innovation field. The design space 'results from' a more global exploration process and feeds this process in return. The space that initiates the design spaces and synthesizes the learning processes is called the 'value management' space. The relations between design spaces and value management are modelled using designation operators for building the design space, and extraction operators for integrating the learning from the design space into the overall reasoning.

To be distinguished from:

- *Project management steering committees.* A project steering committee is a limited form of value management as the project generally works with a clearly identified value target. In innovative design, a steering committee is in charge of value management and is hence responsible for gradually elaborating the design strategy, coordinating the actions and integrating the contributions of several parallel explorations (*see* Chapter 10).
- *Prototypes, demonstrators, experiments, trials, etc.* A design space can include devices of this sort. The notion of design space serves to clarify what is to be managed by using such devices: What is the initial concept? What competencies are available? What learning can be expected? (*See* Chapter 14 in particular.)
- *Experiments and value space* (Thomke 1998) and *NK model and fitness landscape* (Levinthal 1997). Recent models represent innovation as a process which explores a value space and studies the appropriate means of experimentation depending on the topology of the value space (Thomke 1998). From an organizational standpoint, certain models analyse the nature of organizations capable of adapting to more or less rugged 'fitness landscapes' (Levinthal 1997). These are in fact particular cases of value management in which the value space is fixed and is independent from the exploration. Generally speaking, design helps to gradually build several value spaces, sometimes with very different dimensions (*see* Chapter 10 and following; in particular, Chapter 13).
- *Options and portfolio of options.* The notion of option is often used to suggest management methods in the context of intensive innovation (*see* in particular O'Connor (2008)). We shall not discuss here the advantages and limitations of the notion of option in managing innovation (Adner and Levinthal 2004b; McGrath, Ferrier and Mendelow 2004). We simply note that value management does not consist of deciding which option to choose in an already existing portfolio but rather building the portfolio itself. A design space is not a space for taking up options but rather for generating options (*see* Chapter 10 and following).
- *Open innovation, user involvement, crowd sourcing.* Several works insisted on the role of sourcing knowledge and ideas outside the firm (von Hippel 1988; Chesbrough 2003). These practices actually correspond to specific design spaces. However, the innovation process with users or with outside 'idea suppliers' also includes a value management process. This value management process is a variable that is often neglected in research. This point is illustrated in Chapter 11.

Bibliography

Abernathy, W. J. and Clark, K. B. (1985). 'Innovation: mapping the winds of creative destruction.' *Research Policy*, **14**, (1), pp. 3–22.

Abernathy, W. J. and Townsend, P. L. (1975). 'Technology, productivity and process change.' *Technological Forecasting and Social Change*, **7**, (4), pp. 379–396.

Abernathy, W. J. and Utterback, J. (1978). 'Patterns of industrial innovation.' *Technology Review*, **2**, pp. 40–47.

Abernathy, W. J. and Wayne, K. (1974). 'Limits of the learning curve.' *Harvard Business Review*, September–October, **52**, (5), pp. 109–118.

Adner, R. and Levinthal, D. A. (2001). 'Demand heterogeneity and technology evolution: implications for product and process innovation.' *Management Science*, **47**, (5), pp. 611–628.

(2004a). 'Real options and real tradeoffs.' *Academy of Management Review*, **29**, (1), pp. 120–126.

(2004b). 'What is *not* a real option: considering boundaries for the application of real options to business strategy.' *Academy of Management Review*, **29**, (1), pp. 74–85.

Aggeri, F., Pezet, E., Abrassart, C., and Acquier, A. (2005). *Organiser le développement durable. Expériences des entreprises pionnières et formation de règles d'action collective*, Vuibert & ADEME, Paris.

Aghion, P. and Howitt, P. (1992). 'Un modèle de croissance par destruction créatrice.' *Technologie et richesse des nations*, D. Foray and C. Freeman, eds., Economica, Paris, pp. 177–212.

(2006). 'Joseph Schumpeter Lecture. Appropriate growth policy: a unifying framework.' *Journal of the European Economic Association*, **4**, (2–3), pp. 269–314.

Ahuja, G. and Lampoert, C. M. (2001). 'Entrepreneurship in the large corporation: a longitudinal study of how established firms create breakthrough inventions.' *Strategic Management Journal*, **22**, pp. 521–543.

Akrich, M., Callon, M., and Latour, B. (1988). 'A quoi tient le succès des innovations, premier épisode: l'art de l'intéressement, deuxième épisode: l'art de choisir les bons porte-parole.' *Gérer et Comprendre, Annales des Mines*, June and September, pp. 4–17, 14–29.

Alexander, C. (1964). *Notes on the Synthesis of Form* (15th edition, 1999), Harvard University Press, Cambridge, MA.

Allen, T. J. (1977). *Managing the Flow of Technology* (5th edition, 1991), The MIT Press, Cambridge, MA.

Alter, N. (2000). *L'innovation ordinaire*, PUF, Paris.

(2002). 'Les innovateurs au quotidien: l'innovation dans les entreprises.' *Futuribles*, **271**, pp. 5–23.

(2003). 'Innovation organisationnelle entre croyance et raison.' *Encyclopédie de l'Innovation*, P. Mustar and H. Penan, eds., Economica, Paris, pp. 71–88.

Amabile, T. M. (1996). *Creativity in Context*, Westview Press, Boulder, CO.

(1998). 'How to kill creativity.' *Harvard Business Review*, September–October, pp. 77–87.

Amabile, T. M., Barsade, S. G., Mueller, J. S., and Staw, B. M. (2005). 'Affect and creativity at work.' *Administrative Science Quarterly*, **50**, (3), pp. 367–403.

Amabile, T. M., Conti, R., Coon, H., Lazenby, J., and Herron, M. (1996). 'Assessing the work environment for creativity.' *Academy of Management Journal*, **39**, pp. 1154–1184.

Aoussat, A., Christofol, H., and Le Coq, M. (2000). 'The new product design – a transverse approach.' *Journal of Engineering Design*, **11**, (4), pp. 399–417.

Argyris, C. and Schön, D. (1978). *Organizational Learning*, Addison-Wesley, Reading, MA.

(1996). *Organizational Learning II*, Organizational Development Series, E. H. Schein and R. Beckhard, eds., Addison-Wesley, Reading, MA.

Arrow, K. J. (1962). 'The economic implication of learning by doing.' *Review of Economic Studies*, **29**, pp. 155–173.

Ayçoberry, A. (1962). 'Le verre dans la vie moderne, conférence faite le 11 janvier 1962 à la société des ingénieurs civils de France par M. Ayçoberry, nouveau président.' *Mémoires de la société des ingénieurs civils de France*, **113**, (3), pp. 17–32.

Babbage, C. (1830). *Reflections on the Decline of Science in England and Some of its Causes*, B. Fellowes, London.

(1833). *Traité sur l'économie des machines et de manufactures*, E. Biot, trans., Bachelier, Paris.

Backman, M. and Segrestin, B. (2005). 'Drug design strategies: the new challenge of discovery departments in pharmaceutical companies.' *12th International Product Development Management Conference*, Copenhagen.

Bailyn, L. (1985). 'Autonomy in the industrial R&D lab.' *Human Resource Management*, **24**, (2), pp. 129–146.

Baldwin, C. Y. and Clark, K. B. (2000). *Design Rules, Volume 1: The Power of Modularity*, The MIT Press, Cambridge, MA.

(2006a). 'Between "knowledge" and "the economy": notes on the scientific study of designs.' *Advancing Knowledge and the Knowledge Economy*, B. Kahin and D. Foray, eds., The MIT Press, Cambridge, MA, Chapter 18.

(2006b). 'Modularity in the design of complex engineering systems.' *Complex Engineered Systems: Science Meets Technology*, D. Braha, A. A. Minai and Y. Bar-Yam, eds., Springer, New York, pp. 175–205.

Barley, S. R. (1996). 'Technicians in the workplace: ethnographic evidence for bringing work into organization studies.' *Administrative Science Quarterly*, September, pp. 404–441.

Barney, J. (1991). 'Firm resources and sustained competitive advantage.' *Journal of Management*, **17**, (1), pp. 99–120.

Barrois, C. and Lindemann, M. (2004). 'Stratégies d'innovation et développement des activités. Le cas du pneu intelligent.' Ecole des Mines, l'option Ingénierie de la Conception, in partnership with Michelin, Paris.

Bass, F. M. (1969). 'A new product growth model for consumer durables.' *Management Science*, **15**, pp. 215–227.

Basso, O. (2004). *L'intrapreneuriat*, Gestion, Economica, Paris.

Baumol, W. J. (2002). *The Free-Market Innovation Machine: Analyzing the Growth Miracle of Capitalism*, Princeton University Press, Princeton, NJ, and Oxford.

Beer, J. J. (1958). 'Coal tar dye manufacture and the origins of the modern industrial research laboratory.' *Isis*, June, **49**, (2 (156)), pp. 123–131.

Ben Mahmoud-Jouini, S. (2004). 'Management des connaissances et des apprentissages dans les entreprises multi-projets: le cas des stratégies d'offres innovantes.' *Faire de la recherche en management de projet*, G. Garel, V. Giard and C. Midler, eds., Vuibert FNEGE, Paris, pp. 161–188.

Benghozi, P. J., Charue-Duboc, F., and Midler, C. (2000). *Innovation Based Competition & Design Systems Dynamics: Lessons from French Innovative Firms and Organizational Issues for the Next Decade*, L'Harmattan, Paris.

Benner, M. J. and Tushman, M. L. (2002). 'Process management and technological innovation: a longitudinal study of the photography and paint industry.' *Administrative Science Quarterly*, **47**, pp. 676–706.

Benusiglio, D. (1966–1967). 'L'intégration de la recherche scientifique à l'entreprise.' *Sociologie du travail*, **4/66** and **1/67**, pp. 64–98, 338–367.

Best, K. (2006). *Design Management. Managing Design Strategy, Process and Implementation*, Ava Academia, Lausanne.

Bhide, A. (1992). 'Bootstrap finance: the art of start-ups.' *Harvard Business Review*, November–December, **70**, (6), pp. 109–117.

(1994). 'How entrepreneurs craft strategies that work.' *Harvard Business Review*, March–April, **72**, (2), pp. 150–161.

Björkman, H. (2005). 'Learning from members. Tools for service development and strategic change in trade unions' (thesis), Stockholm School of Economics, Stockholm.

Blackler, F. (1995). 'Knowledge, knowledge work and organizations: an overview and interpretation.' *Organization Studies*, **16/6**, pp. 1021–1046.

Blanco, E. (1998). 'L'émergence du produit dans la conception distribuée, vers de nouveaux modes de rationalisation dans la conception de systèmes mécaniques' (thesis), Laboratoires Sols, Solides, Structures (3S) et Cristo, Grenoble.

Boden, M. A. (1990). *The Creative Mind. Myths and Mechanisms*, Weidenfeld and Nicolson, Great Britain.

Boirel, R. (1961). *L'invention*, Presses Universitaires de France, Paris.

Booth, H. (1831). 'N°1: chemin de fer de Liverpool à Manchester, notice historique.' *Annales des Ponts et Chaussées, mémoires et documents relatifs à l'art des constructions et au service de l'ingénieur*, **1**, (1), pp. 1–92.

Booz, E. G., Allen, J. L., and Hamilton, C. L. (1982). *New Product Management for the 1980s*, Booz, Allen and Hamilton, New York.

Boyer, R. (1988). 'L'impact macroéconomique des changements structurels dans le contexte des années quatre-vingts et quatre-vingt dix.' CNRS/CEPREMAP, Memo, Paris.

Bresnahan, T. F. and Trajtenberg, M. (1995). 'General purpose technologies: engines of growth?' *Journal of Econometrics*, **65**, (1), pp. 83–108.

Brock, W. H. (1997). *Justus Von Liebig, the Chemical Gatekeeper* (paperback edition 2002), Cambridge University Press, Cambridge, UK.

Brown, J. K. (1995). *The Baldwin Locomotive Works 1831–1915, A Study in American Industrial Practice*, Studies in Industry and Society, P. B. Scranton, ed., The Johns Hopkins University Press, Baltimore and London.

Brown, J. S. (1991). 'Research that reinvents the corporation.' *Harvard Business Review*, **69**, (1), pp. 102–110.

Brown, J. S. and Duguid, P. (1991). 'Organizational learning and communities-of-practice, toward a unified view of working, learning and innovation.' *Organization Science*, **2**, (1), pp. 40–57.

(1998). 'Organizing knowledge.' *California Management Review*, **40**, (3), pp. 90–111.

Brown, S. L. and Eisenhardt, K. (1995). 'Product development: past research, present findings, and future directions.' *Academy of Management Review*, **20**, (2), pp. 343–378.

(1997). 'The art of continuous change: linking complexity theory and time-paced evolution in relentlessly shifting organizations.' *Administrative Science Quaterly*, **42**, pp. 1–34.

Buderi, R. (2000). *Engines of Tomorrow: How the World's Best Companies Are Using Their Research Labs to Win the Future*, Simon & Schuster, New York.

Burgelman, R. A. and Rosenbloom, R. S. (1989). 'Technology strategy: an evolutionary process perspective.' *Research on Technological Innovation, Management and Policy*, JAI Press Inc., Greenwich, CT, pp. 1–23.

Burns, T. and Stalker, G. M. (1961). *The Management of Innovation*, Social Science Paperback, Tavistock Publications, London.

Bush, V. (1945). 'Science, the endless frontier: a report to the President on a program for postwar scientific research.' Reprinted 1960, National Science Foundation, Washington, DC.

Callon, M. (1986). 'Some elements for a sociology of translation: domestication of the scallops and the fishermen of St-Brieuc Bay.' *Power, Action and Belief: A New Sociology of Knowledge*, J. Law, ed., Routledge and Kegan Paul, London, pp. 196–229.

Callon, M., Méadel, C., and Rabeharisoa, V. (2000). 'L'économie des qualités.' *Politix*, p. 32.

Cattell, R. B. and Butcher, H. J. (1968). *The Prediction of Achievement and Creativity*, Bobbs-Merrill, New York.

Chamberlin, E. H. (1953). *The Theory of Monopolistic Competition*, Harvard University Press, Cambridge, MA.

Champagnat, S. and Lafrance, C. (1999). 'De la signature olfactive au concept de bioclimatisation: l'élaboration d'un nouveau champ d'innovation chez PSA Peugeot-Citroën.' Ecole des Mines, option Ingénierie de la Conception, Paris, p. 23.

Chapel, V. (1997). 'La croissance par l'innovation intensive: de la dynamique d'apprentissage à la révélation d'un modèle industriel, le cas Téfal' (thesis), Ecole des Mines de Paris, Ingénierie et Gestion, Paris.

Chapelon, A. (1952). *La locomotive à vapeur* (2nd edition), Baillère, Paris.

Charpy, M. G. (1919). 'Essais d'organisation méthodique dans une usine métallurgique.' *Bulletin de la Société d'Encouragement pour l'Industrie Nationale*, May–June, pp. 572–606.

Charue-Duboc, F. and Midler, C. (2000). 'Renewing research management in project-oriented organizations – the case of a global vaccine firm.' *Innovation Based Competition & Design Systems Dynamics: Lessons from French Innovative Firms and Organizational Issues for the Next Decade*, P.-J. Benghozi, F. Charue-Duboc and C. Midler, eds., L'Harmattan, Paris, pp. 221–238.

Chesbrough, H. W. (2003). *Open Innovation: The New Imperative for Creating and Profiting from Technology*, Harvard Business School Press, Boston, MA.

Chevenard, P. (1933). 'L'installation et l'organisation d'un laboratoire sidérurgique moderne.' *Mémoires de la société des ingénieurs civils de France*, September–October.

Christenson, C. M. (1997). *The Innovator's Dilemma. When New Technologies Cause Great Firms to Fail*, The Management of Innovation and Change, M. L. Tushman and A. H. Van de Ven, eds., Harvard Business School Press, Boston, MA.

Christenson, C. M. and Raynor, M. E. (2003). *The Innovator's Solution. Creating and Sustaining Successful Growth*, Harvard Business School Press, Boston, MA.

Christenson, C. M. and Rosenbloom, R. S. (1995). 'Explaining the attacker's advantage: technological paradigms, organizational dynamics, and the value network.' *Research Policy*, **24**, pp. 233–257.

Christianson, J. K., Hansen, A., Varnes, C. J., and Mikkola, J. H. (2005). 'Competence strategies in organizing product development.' *Creativity and Innovation Management*, **14**, (4), pp. 384–392.

Clark, K. B. and Fujimoto, T. (1991). *Product Development Performance: Strategy, Organization and Management in the World Auto Industry*, Harvard Business School Press, Boston, MA.

Cochoy, F. (1999). *Une histoire du marketing, discipliner l'économie de marché*, Textes à l'appui, série anthropologie des sciences et des techniques, M. Callon and B. Latour, eds., La Découverte, Paris.

   (2002). *Une sociologie du packaging ou l'âne de Buridan face au marché*, Sciences sociales et sociétés, PUF, Paris.

Cohen, W. M. and Levinthal, D. A. (1990). 'Absorptive capacity: a new perspective on learning and innovation.' *Administrative Science Quarterly*, **35**, pp. 128–152.

Cohendet, P. (1998). 'Information, connaissances et théorie de la firme évolutionniste.' *Economie de la connaissance et de l'organisation*, B. Guilhon, P. Huard, M. Orillard and J. B. Zimmermann, eds., L'Harmattan, Paris.

Conner, K. (1991). 'A historical comparison of resource-based theory and five schools of thought within industrial organization economics: do we have a new theory of the firm?' *Journal of Management*, **17**, pp. 121–154.

Conner, K. and Prahalad, C. K. (1996). 'A resource-based theory of the firm: knowledge versus opportunism.' *Organization Science*, September–October, **7**, (5), pp. 477–501.

Cooper, A. C. (1966). 'Small companies can pioneer new products.' *Harvard Business Review*, **44**, September–October, pp. 162–171.

Cooper, R. G. (1976). 'Introducing successful new industrial products.' *European Journal of Marketing*, **10**, (6), pp. 300–328.

   (1990). 'Stage-gate systems: a new tool for managing new products.' *Business Horizons*, May–June, pp. 44–53.

   (1997). 'Fixing the fuzzy front end of the new product process. Building the business case.' *CMA Magazine*, October, pp. 21–23.

Coriat, B. and Weinstein, O. (1995). *Les nouvelles théories de l'entreprise*, Références, Le Livre de Poche, Paris.

Cropley, A. (2006). 'In praise of convergent thinking.' *Creativity Research Journal*, **18**, (3), pp. 391–404.

Cusumano, M. A. and Selby, R. W. (1995). *Microsoft Secrets: How the World's Most Powerful Software Company Creates Technologies, Shapes Markets, and Manages People*, The Free Press, New York.

Cyert, R. M. and March, J. G. (1963). *A Behavioral Theory of the Firm*, Prentice-Hall, Englewood Cliffs, NJ.

d'Aveni, R. and Gunther, R. (1994). *Hypercompetition: Managing the Dynamic of Strategic Maneuvering*, Free Press, New York.

Daft, R. L. (1978). 'A dual-core model of organizational innovation.' *Academy of Management Journal*, **21**, (2), pp. 193–210.

Daft, R. L. and Weick, K. E. (1984). 'Towards a model of organizations as interpretation systems.' *Academy of Management Review*, **9**, (2), pp. 284–295.

Dahlsten, F. (2004). 'Hollywood wives revisited.' *European Journal of Innovation Management*, **7**, (2), pp. 141–149.

Damanpour, F. (1991). 'Organizational innovation: a meta-analysis of effects of determinants and moderators.' *Academy of Management Journal*, **44**, (3), pp. 555–590.

David, A. and Hatchuel, A. (2007). 'From actionable knowledge to universal theory in management research.' *Handbook of Collaborative Management Research*, A. B. Shani, S. A. Mohrman, W. A. Pasmore, B. A. Stymne and A. Niclas, eds., Sage, Thousand Oaks, CA, pp. 33–48.

David, A., Hatchuel, A., and Laufer, R. (2000). *Les nouvelles fondations des sciences de gestion, éléments d'épistémologie de la recherche en management*, Fnege, Vuibert, Paris.

David, P. A. (1985). 'Clio and the economics of QWERTY.' *American Economic Review*, **75**, (2), pp. 332–337.

Dell'Era, C. and Verganti, R. (2009). 'Design-driven laboratories: organization and strategy of laboratories specialized in the development of radical design-driven innovations.' *R&D Management*, **39**, (1), pp. 1–20.

Deloitte, Touche and Tohmatsu (2005). 'Mastering innovation: exploiting ideas for profitable growth.' A Deloitte Research Global Manufacturing Study.

de Tarde, G. (1903). *The Laws of Imitation*, E. C. Parsons, trans., Holt, New York.

Dickinson, H. W. (1936). *Matthew Boulton*, Réédition de 1999, TEE Publishing, Leamington Spa.

Diehl, M. and Stroebe, W. (1987). 'Productivity loss in brainstorming groups: towards the solution of a riddle.' *Journal of Personality and Social Psychology*, **53**, pp. 497–509.

Dooley, K. J. and Van de Ven, A. H. (1999). 'Explaining complex organizational dynamics.' *Organization Science*, **10**, (3), pp. 358–372.

Doumas, B. (2004). 'Implémentation de la théorie C-K dans le cadre de la gestion d'ontologies. Un outil d'aide à la conception innovante.' Institut de Recherche en Informatique de Nantes et Dassault Systèmes, graduate dissertation, 'C-K theory and the management of ontologies', Paris.

Drucker, P. (1985). *Innovation and Entrepreneurship: Practice and Principles* (reprint 2002), Butterworth-Heinemann, Oxford.

DTI (2004). *The 2004 R&D Scoreboard: The Top 700 UK and 700 International Companies by R&D Investment*, DTI, London.

Duchamp, R. (1988). *La conception de produits nouveaux*, Hermès Science, Paris.

Dyson, J. and Coren, G. (1997). *Against the Odds: An Autobiography*, O. B. Books, London.

Eisenhardt, K. M. (1989). 'Making fast strategic decisions in high-velocity environments.' *Academy of Management Journal*, **32**, (3), pp. 543–576.

Eisenhardt, K. M. and Brown, S. L. (1998). 'Time pacing: competing in markets that won't stand still.' *Harvard Business Review*, **76**, March–April, pp. 59–69.

Eisenhardt, K. M. and Martin, J. A. (2000). 'Dynamic capabilities: what are they?' *Strategic Management Journal*, **21**, (10/11), pp. 1105–1121.

Eisenhardt, K. and Tabrizi, B. (1995). 'Accelerating adaptative processes: product innovation in the global computer industry.' *Administrative Science Quarterly*, **40**, pp. 84–110.

Elmquist, M. and Le Masson, P. (2009). 'The value of a "failed" R&D project: an emerging evaluation framework for building innovative capabilities.' *R&D Management*, **39**, (2), pp. 136–152.

Elmquist, M. and Segrestin, B. (2007). 'Towards a new logic for front end management: from drug discovery to drug design in pharmaceutical R&D.' *Journal of Creativity and Innovation Management*, **16**, (2), pp. 106–120.

(2008). 'Organizing open innovation in practice: a case study of an environmental innovation project in the automotive industry.' *IPDM*, Hamburg.

Encaoua, D., Foray, D., Hatchuel, A., and Mairesse, J. (2001). 'Les enjeux économiques de l'innovation, bilan scientifique du programme CNRS.' CNRS, Rapport du programme CNRS 'enjeux économiques de l'innovation', Paris.

Engwall, M. and Svensson, C. (2001). 'Cheetah teams.' *Harvard Business Review*, **79**, January, pp. 20–21.

Eris, O. (2004). *Effective Inquiry for Innovative Engineering Design*, Kluwer Academic Publishers, Boston, MA.

Etzkowitz, H. (2002). 'The triple helix of university–industry–government implications for policy and evaluation.' Working paper 2002–11, number 29, Institutet för studier av ut bildning och forskning.

Etzkowitz, H. and Leydesdorff, L. (2000). 'The dynamics of innovation: from national systems and "mode 2" to triple helix of university–industry–government relations.' *Research Policy*, **29**, pp. 109–123.

Fairbank, J. F. and Williams, S. D. (2001). 'Motivating creativity and enhancing innovation through employee suggestion system technology.' *Creativity and Innovation Management*, **10**, (2), pp. 68–74.

Farson, R. and Keyes, R. (2002). 'The failure-tolerant leader.' *Harvard Business Review*, **80**, August, pp. 65–73.

Fauconnier, G. and Turner, M. (1996). 'Blending as a central process of grammar.' *Conceptual Structure, Discourse, and Language*, A. Goldberg, ed., Center for the Study of Language and Information (CSLI), [distributed by Cambridge University Press], pp. 113–129.

Fayol, H. (1917). 'De l'importance de la fonction administrative dans le gouvernement des affaires.' *Bulletin de la société d'encouragement pour l'industrie nationale*, November–December, pp. 225–267.

(1918). *Notice sur les travaux scientifiques et techniques de H. Fayol*, Gauthier-Villars, Paris.

Felk, Y., Le Masson, P., Weil, B., and Cogez, P. (2009). 'Absorptive or desorptive capacity? Managing advanced R&D in semi-conductors for radical innovation.' International Product Development Management Conference, Enschede, the Netherlands.

Finke, R. A. (1990). *Creative Imagery: Discoveries and inventions in visualization*, Erlbaum, Hillsdale, NJ.

Fiol, C. M. and Lyles, M. A. (1985). 'Organizational learning.' *Academy of Management Review*, **10**, (4), pp. 803–813.

Foray, D. (2000). *L'économie de la connaissance*, La Découverte, Paris.

(2003). 'Les nouvelles formes d'innovation dans l'économie de la connaissance: explications, expressions et enjeux.' *Encyclopédie de l'Innovation*, P. Mustar and H. Penan, eds., Economica, Paris, pp. 497–518.

Forty, A. (1986). *Objects of Desire*, Thames & Hudson, London.

Franke, N. and Shah, S. (2002). 'How communities support innovative activities: an exploration of assistance and sharing among end-users.' *Research Policy*, **1380**, pp. 1–22.

Fredberg, T. (2007). 'Real options for innovation management.' *International Journal of Technology Management*, **39**, (1/2), pp. 72–85.

Fredberg, T. and Piller, F. T. (2006). 'The paradox of strong and weak ties.' Academy of Management Conference, Atlanta, GA.

Fredriksson, B. (2003). 'Engineering design – theory and practice.' International Conference on Engineering Design '03, Stockholm.

Freeland, W. E. (1920). 'Coordination of sales with scientific production.' *Bulletin of the Taylor Society*, **5**, (5), pp. 202–207.

(1926). 'Progress towards science in marketing, application of scientific method in sales, organization, budgets and operations, physical distribution and advertising.' *Bulletin of the Taylor Society*, **11**, (4), pp. 207–213.

Freeman, C. (1988). 'Japan: a new national system of innovation?' *Technical Change and Economic Theory*, G. Dosi, ed., Pinter, London, pp. 330–348.

Fromonot, F. (1998). *Jorn Utzon et l'opéra de Sydney* (Edition originale: Jorn Utzon, architetto della Sidney Opera House, Electa, Milan, Documents d'architecture), Gallimard, Paris.

Garçon, A.-F. (2004). *Entre l'etat et l'usine: l'Ecole des Mines de Saint-Etienne au XIXème siècle*, Presses Universitaires de Rennes, Rennes.

Garel, G. (1998). 'Le co-développement: une transformation de l'organisation du développement du produit et du process.' *La politique du produit*, Paris, B. Nicolas, J. M. Pointet and J.-C. Thénard, *Les cahiers de recherche du GIP – Mutations industrielles*, **76**, 15 October 1998, pp. 161–172.

(2003). *Le management de projet*, Repères, Editions La Découverte, Paris.

Garel, G. and Rosier, R. (2006). 'Définir et gérer les technologies à haut potentiel: vers un management de l'exploration.' Fifteenth International Conference on Strategic Management (AIMS), Annecy-le-Vieux.

Gawer, A. (2000). 'The organization of platform leadership: an empirical investigation of Intel's management processes aimed at fostering complementary innovation by third parties' (thesis), MIT, Sloan School of Management, Cambridge, MA.

(2009). *Platforms, Markets and Innovation*, Edward Elgar, Cheltenham, UK, and Northampton, MA.

Gawer, A. and Cusumano, M. (2002). *Platform Leadership: How Intel, Microsoft, and Cisco Drive Industry Innovation*, Harvard Business School Press, Boston, MA.

(2008). 'How companies become platform leaders.' *MIT Sloan Management Review*, **49**, (2), pp. 28–35.

Gawer, A. and Henderson, R. (2007). 'Platform owner entry and innovation in complementary markets: evidence from Intel.' *Journal of Economics & Management Strategy*, **16**, (1), pp. 1–34.

Gaynor, G. H. (2002). *Innovation by Design: What It Takes to Keep Your Company on the Cutting Edge*, Amacom, New York.

Geels, F. W. (2004). 'From sectoral systems of innovation to socio-technical systems: insights about dynamics and change from sociology and institutional theory.' *Research Policy*, **33**, (6/7), pp. 897–920.

Gibbons, M., Limoge, C., Nowotny, H., Schwartzman, S., Scott, P., and Trow, M. (1994). *The New Production of Knowledge: The Dynamics of Science and Research in Contemporary Societies*, Sage Publications, London.

Giget, M. (1998). *La dynamique stratégique de l'entreprise: innovation, croissance et redéploiement à partir de l'arbre des compétences*, Dunod, Paris.

Gilfillan, S. C. (1970). *The Sociology of Invention* (1st edition 1935), The MIT Press, Cambridge, MA.

Goldenberg, J. and Mazursky, D. (2002). *Creativity in Product Innovation*, Cambridge University Press, Cambridge, MA.

Goodman, N. (1978). *Ways of Worldmaking*, Hackett Publishing Company, Indianapolis, IN.

Grebel, T., Krafft, J., and Saviotti, P. P. (2006). 'On the life cycle of knowledge intensive sectors.' *Revue de l'OFCE*, Special Issue, June, pp. 63–85.

Gruber, W. H. and Marquis, D. G. (1969). 'Research on the human factor in the transfer of technology.' *Factors in the Transfer of Technology*, W. H. Gruber and D. G. Marquis, eds., The MIT Press, Cambridge, MA.

Guellec, D. (1999). *Economie de l'innovation*, Repères, J.-P. Piriou, B. Colasse, P. Combemale, F. Dreyfus, H. Hamon, D. Merllié and C. Porchasson, eds., La Découverte, Paris.

Guellec, D. and Ralle, P. (1993). 'Innovation, propriété intellectuelle, croissance.' *Revue économique*, **44**, (2), pp. 319–334.

(1995). *Les nouvelles théories de la croissance*, Repères, J.-P. Piriou, La Découverte, Paris.

Guilford, J. P. (1959). 'Traits of creativity.' *Creativity and its Cultivation*, H. H. Anderson, ed., Harper, New York, pp. 142–161.

Gwynne, P. (1997). 'Skunk works, 1990s-style.' *Research Technology Management*, **40**, (4), p. 18.

Hage, J. T. (1999). 'Organizational innovation and organizational change.' *Annual Review of Sociology*, **25**, pp. 597–622.

Hage, J. T. and Meeus, M. (2006). *Innovation, Science, and Industrial Change: The Handbook of Research*, Oxford University Press, Oxford.

Hagedoorn, J. (2001). 'Inter-firm R&D partnerships: an overview of major trends and patterns since 1960.' *Research Policy*, **31**, pp. 477–492.

Hamel, G. and Prahalad, C. K. (1994a). 'Competing for the future.' *Harvard Business Review*, **72**, July–August, pp. 122–128.

(1994b). *Competing for the Future: Breakthrough Strategies for Seizing Control of Your Industry and Creating the Market of Tomorrow*, Harvard Business School Press, Boston, MA.

Hannan, M. T. and Freeman, J. (1989). *Organizational Ecology*, Harvard University Press, Cambridge, MA.

Hargadon, A. and Sutton, R. I. (1997). 'Technology brokering and innovation in a product design firm.' *Administrative Science Quarterly*, **42**, (4), pp. 716–749.

Hartmann, M. and Hassan, A. (2006). 'Application of real options analysis for pharmaceutical R&D project evaluation – empirical results from a survey.' *Research Policy*, **35**, pp. 343–354.

Hatchuel, A. (1994). 'Apprentissages collectifs et activité de conception.' *Revue Française de Gestion*, June–July–August, pp. 109–120.

(1995). 'Les marchés à prescripteurs.' *L'inscription sociale du marché*, A. Jacob and H. Vérin, eds., L'Harmattan, Paris, pp. 203–225, Collection Logiques Sociales.

(1996a). 'Comment penser l'action collective? Théorie des mythes rationnels.' R. Damien and A. Tosel, eds., Les annales littéraires de Besançon, Besançon.

(1996b). 'Les théories de la conception.' Cours de l'Ecole des Mines, option Ingénierie de la Conception, Paris.

(2001a). 'Linking organization theory and design theory: collective action in design worlds.' European Conference in Organization Science (EGOS), Lyon, France.

(2001b). 'Quel horizon pour les sciences de gestion? Vers une théorie de l'action collective.' *Les nouvelles fondations des sciences de gestion*, A. David, A. Hatchuel and R. Laufer, eds., Vuibert FNEGE, Paris, pp. 7–43.

(2002). 'Towards design theory and expandable rationality: the unfinished program of Herbert Simon.' *Journal of Management and Governance*, **5**, (3–4), pp. 260–273.

(2004a). 'Créativité et conception, outils et organisations de la conception innovante.' *Renault – Rendez-vous de la technologie*, 19 October, Renault, Guyancourt.

(2004b). 'Histoire des révolutions de la gestion des entreprises.' *Problèmes économiques, la documentation française*, **2**, (852), pp. 43–48.

(2006). 'Du raisonnement de conception. Essai sur le "forcing" en théorie des ensembles.' *Les nouveaux régimes de conception*, A. Hatchuel and B. Weil, eds., Vuibert, Paris, pp. 133–149.

(2009). 'A fundationalist perspective on management research: a European experience and trend.' *Management Decision*, **47**, (9), pp. 1458–1475.

Hatchuel, A., Chapel, V., Deroy, X., and Le Masson, P. (1998). 'Innovation répétée et croissance de la firme, analyses empiriques et conditions théoriques.' Ecole des Mines, Paris.

Hatchuel, A. and Le Masson, P. (2001). 'Innovation répétée et croissance de la firme: microéconomie et gestion des fonctions de conception.' *Cahier du CGS n° 18*, Ecole des Mines, CGS, Cahier, programme CNRS 'Enjeux économiques de l'innovation', Paris.

(2004). 'L'évolution des activités et des parcours d'ingénieurs: faut-il renoncer à l'idée de métier?' *Renouvellement des dynamiques de métiers*, Ecole des Mines de Paris, 5–6 February.

(2006). 'Growth of the firm by repeated innovation: towards a new microeconomics based on design functions.' 11th International Schumpeter Society, Nice-Sophia-Antipolis, France.

Hatchuel, A., Le Masson, P., and Weil, B. (2004a). 'C-K theory in practice: lessons from industrial applications.' 8th International Design Conference, Dubrovnik, 18–21 May.

(2004b). 'The management of science based products: managing by design spaces.' 11th International Product Development Management Conference, 20–22 June, EIASM and School of Business Studies, Trinity College, Dublin, pp. 727–743.

(2005a). 'Activité de conception, organisation de l'entreprise et innovation.' *Travail, entreprise et société. Manuel de sociologie pour des ingénieurs et des scientifiques*, G. Minguet and C. Thuderoz, eds., Presses Universitaires de France, Paris, pp. 97–120.

(2005b). 'The development of science-based products: managing by design spaces.' *Creativity and Innovation Management*, **14**, (4), pp. 345–354.

(2006a). 'Building innovation capabilities. The development of design-oriented organizations.' *Innovation, Science and Industrial Change: The Handbook of Research*, J. Hage and M. Meeus, eds., Oxford University Press, New York, pp. 294–312.

(2006b). 'The design of science-based products: an interpretation and modelling with C-K theory.' 9th International Design Conference, Dubrovnik, 15–18 May, D. Marjanovic, **1**, 33–44.

(2008). 'Studying creative design: the contribution of C-K theory.' *Studying Design Creativity: Design Science, Computer Science, Cognitive Science and Neuroscience Approaches*, Aix-en-Provence, 10–11 March.

(2009). 'Design theory and collective creativity: a theoretical framework to evaluate KCP process.' International Conference on Engineering Design, ICED'09, 24–27 August, Stanford, CA.

Hatchuel, A. and Molet, H. (1986). 'Rational modelling in understanding and aiding human decision-making: about two case-studies.' *European Journal of Operational Research*, **24**, pp. 178–186.

Hatchuel, A. and Weil, B. (1992). *L'expert et le système, gestion des savoirs et métamorphose des acteurs dans l'entreprise industrielle*, Economica, Paris.

(1995). *Experts in Organization: A Knowledge-Based Perspective on Organizational Change*, L. Librecht, trans., Studies in Organization: Innovation, Technology and Organizations, A. Francis, ed., Walter de Gruyter, New York.

(2000). 'Critique de l'apprentissage organisationnel: les enseignements des activités de conception.' *Conception et dynamique des organisations: sait-on piloter le changement?*, Université des HEC, Lausanne, 17 March.

(2002). 'La théorie C-K: fondements et usages d'une théorie unifiée de la conception.' *Colloque sciences de la conception*, Lyon, 15–16 March.

(2003). 'A new approach of innovative design: an introduction to C-K theory.' *ICED'03, August*, Stockholm, Sweden.

(2007). 'Design as forcing: deepening the foundations of C-K theory.' International Conference on Engineering Design, Paris.

(2009). 'C-K design theory: an advanced formulation.' *Research in Engineering Design*, **19**, pp. 181–192.

Hauser, J. R. and Clausing, D. (1988). 'The house of quality.' *Harvard Business Review*, **66**, May–June, pp. 63–73.

Helfat, C. E. and Raubitschek, R. S. (2000). 'Product sequencing: co-evolution of knowledge, capabilities and products.' *Strategic Management Journal*, **21**, (10/11, special issue The Evolution of Firm Capabilities), pp. 961–979.

Henderson, R. M. and Clark, K. B. (1990). 'Architectural innovation: the reconfiguration of existing product technologies and the failure of established firms.' *Administrative Science Quarterly*, **35**, pp. 9–30.

Herath, H. S. B. and Park, C. S. (1999). 'Economic analysis of R&D projects: an options approach.' *The Engineering Economist*, **44**, (1), pp. 1–35.

Hilaire-Pérez, L. (2000). *L'invention technique au siècle des Lumières*, L'évolution de l'humanité, J.-C. Perrot, P. Boutry, J.-Y. Grenier and H. F. Berr, eds., Albin Michel, Paris.

Hindle, B. and Lubar, S. (1986). *Engines of Change: The American Industrial Revolution, 1790–1860*, Smithsonian Institution Press, Washington, DC.

Hirt, O. (2003). 'The compromise pre-requisites: establishing the conditions for design concepts deployment. The Renault "Design Fundamentals" process.' 3rd European Academy of Management, Milan, 3–5 April.

Holbrook, M. B. and Hirschman, E. C. (1982). 'The experiential aspects of consumption: consumer fantasies, feelings and fun.' *Journal of Consumer Research*, **9**, pp. 132–140.

Hounshell, D. A. and Smith, J. K. (1988). *Science and Corporate Strategy: Du Pont R&D, 1902–1980*, Cambridge University Press, Cambridge, MA.

Howells, J. (2005). *The Management of Innovation and Technology*, Sage, London.

Hughes, T. P. (1983). *Networks of Power: Electrification in Western Societies, 1880–1930*, Johns Hopkins University Press, Baltimore, MD.

Iansiti, M. (1993). 'Real-world R&D: jumping the product generation gap.' *Harvard Business Review*, **71**, (3), pp. 138–147.

Imai, K., Nonaka, I., and Takeuchi, H. (1985). 'Managing the new product development process: how Japanese learn and unlearn.' *The Uneasy Alliance: Managing the Productivity Technology Dilemma*, K. B. Clark, R. H. Hayes and C. Lorenz, eds., Harvard Business School Press, Boston, MA.

Jacobides, M. G., Knudsen, T., and Augier, M. (2006). 'Benefiting from innovation: value creation, value appropriation and the role of industry architectures.' *Research Policy*, **35**, (8), pp. 1200–1221.

Jansson, D. G. and Smith, S. M. (1991). 'Design fixation.' *Design Studies*, **12**, (1), pp. 3–11.

Jaruselski, B., Dehoff, K., and Bordia, R. (2005). 'The Booz Allen Hamilton Global Innovation 1000: money isn't everything.' *Strategy and Business*, Winter, (41), p. 15.

Jeantet, A. (1998). 'Les objets intermédiaires dans la conception. Elements pour une sociologie des processus de conception.' *Sociologie du travail*, no 3/98, pp. 291–316.

Jewkes, J., Sawers, D., and Stillerman, R. (1958). *The Sources of Invention*, Macmillan & Co. Ltd, London.

Joerges, B. and Shinn, T. (2001). 'Instrumentation between science, state and industry.' *Sociology of the Sciences*, P. Weingart, ed., Kluwer Academic Publishers, Dordrecht.

Johnson, S. C. and Jones, C. (1957). 'How to organize for new products.' *Harvard Business Review*, **35**, (3), pp. 49–52.

Joly, P.-B. (2001). 'Les OGM entre la science et le public? Quatre modèles pour la gouvernance de l'innovation et des risques.' *Economie rurale*, **266**, pp. 11–29.

Jonash, R. S. and Sommerlatte, T. (1999). *The Innovation Premium: How Next Generation Companies Are Achieving Peak Performance and Profitability*, A. D. Little, Perseus Books, Reading, MA.

Jones, C. I. (1995a). 'R&D-based models of economic growth.' *Journal of Political Economy*, **103**, (4), pp. 759–784.

(1995b). 'Time series tests of endogenous growth models.' *Quarterly Journal of Economics*, May, pp. 495–525.

Jovanovic, B. (1982). 'Selection and the evolution of industry.' *Econometrica*, **50**, pp. 649–670.

Karsenti, B. (1993). 'Présentation du livre "Les Lois de l'Imitation" de Gabriel de Tarde.' *Les Lois de l'Imitation*, J.-M. Vincent, ed., Editions Krimé, Paris, pp. vii–xxvi.

Kazakçi, A. (2009) 'A formalization of C-K design theory based on Intuitionistic Logic.' *ICORD.*

Kazakçi, A. O. and Tsoukias, A. (2005). 'Extending the C-K design theory: a theoretical background for personal design assistants.' *Journal of Engineering Design,* **16**, (4), pp. 399–411.

Khurana, A. and Rosenthal, S. R. (1998). 'Towards holistic "front ends" in new product development.' *Journal of Product Innovation Management,* **15**, pp. 57–74.

Kim, W. C. and Mauborgne, R. (1997). 'Value innovation: the strategic logic of high growth.' *Harvard Business Review,* **75**, January–February, pp. 103–112.

  (2000). 'Knowing a winning business idea when you see one.' *Harvard Business Review,* **78**, September–October, pp. 129–137.

King, R. (2000). *Brunelleschi's Dome: How a Renaissance Genius Reinvented Architecture,* Walker & Company, New York.

Klepper, S. (1996). 'Entry, exit, growth, and innovation over the product life cycle.' *American Economic Review,* **86**, pp. 562–583.

  (1997). 'Industry life cycles.' *Industrial and Corporate Change,* **6**, (1), pp. 119–143.

Klette, T. J. and Griliches, Z. (2000). 'Empirical patterns of firm growth and R&D investment: a quality ladder model interpretation.' *The Economic Journal,* **110**, (April), pp. 363–387.

Kline, S. J. and Rosenberg, N. (1986). 'An overview of innovation.' *The Positive Sum Strategy: Harnessing Technology for Economic Growth,* R. Landau and N. Rosenberg, eds., National Academy Press, Washington, DC, pp. 275–305.

Koch, W. (1908). 'Die Organisation der Westinghouse Electric and Manufacturing Company in Pittsburgh.' *Technik und Wirtschaft, Monatsschrift des VDI,* I, pp. 453–459, 493–505.

Koen, P., Ajamian, G., Burkart, R., Clamen, A., Davidson, J., D'Amore, R., Elkins, C., Herald, K., Incorvia, M., Johnson, A., Karol, R., Seibert, R., Slavejkov, A., and Wagner, K. (2001). 'Providing clarity and a common language to the "fuzzy front end".' *Research/Technology Management,* **44**, (2), pp. 46–56.

Kohn, K. (2005). 'Continuous change in mature firms' (thesis), Chalmers University of Technology, Department of Project Management, Fenix Research Program, Gothenburg.

König, W. (1999). *Künstler und Strichezieher. Konstruktions- und Technikkulturen im deutschen, britischen, amerikanischen und französischen Maschinenbau zwischen 1850 und 1930,* Suhrkamp Taschenbuch Wissenschaft, Suhrkamp Verlag, Frankfurt am Main.

Kotler, P., Keller, K. L., Dubois, B., and Manceau, D. (2006). *Marketing Management,* Pearson Education, Harlow, Essex.

Kozinets, R. V. (2002). 'The field behind the screen: using netnography for marketing research in online communities.' *Journal of Marketing Research,* **39**, (February), pp. 61–72.

Kristensson, P., Magnusson, P., and Matthing, J. (2002). 'Users as a hidden source for creativity: findings from an experimental study on user involvement.' *Creativity and Innovation Management,* **11**, (1), pp. 55–61.

Krogh, G. V., Ichijo, K., and Nonaka, I. (2000). *Enabling Knowledge Creation: How to Unlock the Mystery of Tacit Knowledge and Release the Power of Innovation,* Oxford University Press, New York.

Lakhani, K. R. and Panetta, J. A. (2007). 'The principles of distributed innovation.' *Innovations: Technology, Governance, Globalization*, **2**, (3 (summer)), pp. 97–112.

Landau, R. and Rosenberg, N. (1985). *The Positive Sum Strategy: Harnessing Technology for Economic Growth*, National Academy Press, Washington.

Lander, D. M. and Pinches, G. E. (1998). 'Challenges to the practical implementation of modelling and valuing real options.' *Quarterly Review of Economics and Finance*, **38**, (Special Issue), pp. 537–567.

Lane, P. J., Koka, B. R., and Pathak, S. (2006). 'The reification of absorptive capacity: a critical review and rejuvenation of the construct.' *Academy of Management Review*, **31**, (4), pp. 833–863.

Lapeyronnie, G. and Macaire, M. (2002). 'Conception et stratégie d'innovation: confort thermique et qualité de l'air dans l'automobile. Travail dirigé par Armand Hatchuel et Benoit Weil.' Ecole des Mines, option Ingénierie de la Conception, Paris.

Laufer, R. (1993). *L'entreprise face aux risques majeurs. A propose de l'incertitude des normes sociales*, Logiques sociales, L'Harmattan, Paris.

Laurent, G. and Kapferer, J.-N. (1985). 'Measuring consumer involvement profiles.' *Journal of Marketing Research*, **22**, (1), pp. 41–53.

Lave, J. and Wenger, E. (1991). *Situated Learning: Legitimate Peripheral Participation*, Cambridge University Press, Cambridge, MA.

Lawler III, E. E. and Mohrman, S. A. (1985). 'Quality circles after the fad.' *Harvard Business Review*, January–February, pp. 65–70.

Layton, E. T. (1971). *The Revolt of the Engineers. Social Responsibility and the American Engineering Profession*, Case Western Reserve, Cleveland, OH.

Le Bail, N. and Oussaïffi, Y. (2004). 'L'impact des modèles sémiotiques en conception innovante.' Ecole des Mines de Paris, option Ingénierie de la Conception, Paris.

Le Châtelier, H. (1930). 'La science et l'industrie.' *Génie Civil*, November, 50th anniversary issue.

Le Masson, P. (2001). 'De la R&D à la RID: modélisation des fonctions de conception et nouvelles organisations de la R&D.' Thesis in Management Science, under supervision of Benoît Weil, MINES, ParisTech.

Le Masson, P., Hatchuel, A., and Weil, B. (2007) 'Creativity and design reasoning: how C-K theory can enhance creative design.' International Conference on Engineering Design, ICED'07, Paris.

   (2009). 'Platforms for the design of platforms: collaborating in the unknown.' *Platforms, Market and Innovation*, A. Gawer, ed., Edward Elgar, Cheltenham.

Le Masson, P. and Magnusson, P. (2002). 'Towards an understanding of user involvement contribution to the design of mobile telecommunications services.' 9th International Product Development Management Conference, Sophia Antipolis, France, European Institute for Advanced Studies in Management and Ecole des Mines de Paris, 2, 27–28 May, pp. 497–511.

Le Masson, P. and Weil, B. (2008). 'La domestication de l'innovation par les entreprises industrielles: l'invention des bureaux d'études.' *Les nouveaux régimes de la conception*, A. Hatchuel and B. Weil, eds., Vuibert-FNEGE, Paris, pp. 53–69.

Le Moigne, J.-L. (1995). *Les épistémologies constructivistes, que sais-je?*, Presses Universitaires de France, Paris.

Lefebvre, P. (1998). 'Formation des grandes entreprises et innovations dans les relations de travail: coordination hiérarchique, gestion de la main d'oeuvre, paternalisme (France, XIXème siècle)' (thesis), Paris IV, Sociologie, Paris.

Leifer, R., McDermott, C. M., O'Connor, G. C., Peters, L. S., Rice, M. P., and Veryzer, R. (2000). *Radical Innovation. How Mature Companies Can Outsmart Upstarts*, Harvard Business School Press, Boston, MA.

Leifer, R., O'Connor, G. C., and Rice, M. P. (2001). 'Implementing radical innovation in mature firms: the role of hubs.' *Academy of Management Executive*, **15**, (3), pp. 102–113.

Lenfle, S. (1997). 'La gestion des projets d'innovation en amont des filières industrielles: l'exemple d'Usinor.' *Ecole Nationale des Ponts et Chaussées*, Université de Marne la Vallée DEA Organisation et Pilotage des Systèmes de Production, Mémoire de DEA, Paris.

(2008). 'Proceeding in the dark. Innovation, project management and the making of the atomic bomb.' Ecole Polytechnique, Centre de recherche en gestion, Working paper no 08/001, Paris.

Lenfle, S. and Midler, C. (2000). 'Managing innovative projects in upstream industries – the case of a French steel group.' *Innovation Based Competition & Design Systems Dynamics: Lessons from French Innovative Firms and Organizational Issues for the Next Decade*, P.-J. Benghozi, F. Charue-Duboc and C. Midler, eds., L'Harmattan, Paris, pp. 193–217.

Leonard, D. and Rayport, J. E. (1997). 'Spark innovation through empathic design.' *Harvard Business Review*, **75**, November–December, pp. 102–113.

Leonard, D. and Sensiper, S. (1998). 'The role of tacit knowledge in group innovation.' *California Management Review*, **40**, (3), pp. 112–132.

Leonard, D. and Swap, W. (2000). 'Gurus in the garage.' *Harvard Business Review*, **78**, November–December, pp. 71–80.

Leonard-Barton, D. (1992). 'Core capabilities and core rigidities: a paradox in managing new product development.' *Strategic Management Journal*, **13**, pp. 111–125.

(1995). *Wellsprings of Knowledge*, Harvard Business School Press, Boston, MA.

Leonard-Barton, D. and Sviokla, J. J. (1988). 'Putting expert systems to work.' *Harvard Business Review*, **66**, March–April, pp. 91–98.

Leser, E. (2004). 'La mutation de Kodak, un cas d'école de rupture technologique.' *Le Monde*, 8 October (Entreprises-industrie), p. 14.

Letté, M. (1998). 'Henry Le Châtelier (1850–1936) et la constitution d'une science industrielle, un modèle pour l'organisation rationnelle des relations entre la science et l'industrie au tournant des XIXème et XXème siècles, 1880–1914' (thesis), Ecole des Hautes Etudes en Sciences Sociales, Histoire des Sciences et des Techniques, sous la direction de Jean Dhombres, Paris.

Levinthal, D. A. (1997). 'Adaptation on rugged landscapes.' *Management Science*, **43**, (7), pp. 934–951.

Levitt, B. and March, J. G. (1988). 'Organizational learning.' *Annual Review of Sociology*, **14**, pp. 319–339.

Lint, O. and Pennings, E. (2001). 'An option approach to the new product development process: a case study at Philips Electronics.' *R&D Management*, **31**, (2), pp. 163–172.

Loch, C. L., De Meyer, A., and Pich, M. T. (2006). *Managing the Unknown*, John Wiley & Sons, Hoboken, NJ.

Loch, C. L., Solt, M. E., and Bailey, E. M. (2008). 'Diagnosing unforseeable uncertainty in a new venture.' *Journal of Product Innovation Management,* **25,** pp. 28–46.

Lorsch, J. W. and Lawrence, P. R. (1965). 'Organizing for product innovation.' *Harvard Business Review,* January–February, **43,** (1), pp. 109–120.

Lundvall, B.-A. (1985). *Product Innovation and User–Producer Interaction,* Aalborg University Press, Aalborg, Denmark.

(1999). 'National business systems and national systems of innovation.' *International Studies of Management & Organization,* **29,** (2), pp. 60–77.

MacCormack, A., Verganti, R., and Iansiti, M. (2001). 'Developing products on "internet time": the anatomy of flexible development process.' *Management Science,* **47,** (1), pp. 133–150.

Maclaurin, W. R. (1953). 'The sequence from invention to innovation and its relation to economics growth.' *Quarterly Journal of Economics,* **67,** (1), pp. 97–111.

Magnusson, P. (2001). 'Customer involvement beyond chanting: towards an understanding of how to organize for beneficial customer co-development in new service innovation.' 17th EGOS Colloquium, 'The Odyssey of Organizing', 5–7 July 2001, Lyon, France.

(2003). 'Customer-driven product development: experiments involving common users in the design of mobile services' (thesis), Fenix Research Program, Stockholm School of Economics, Department of Business Administration, Stockholm.

Mairesse, J. and Sassenou, M. (1991). 'Recherche-développement et productivité: un panorama des études économétriques sur données d'entreprises.' *L'évaluation économique de la recherche et du changement technique,* J. deBandt and D. Foray, eds., Les éditions du CNRS, Paris, pp. 61–96.

Malerba, F. (2006). 'Innovation, industrial dynamics, and industry evolution: progress and the research agenda.' *Revue de l'OFCE,* Special Issue, June, pp. 21–46.

Malinvaud, E. (1993). 'Regard d'un ancien sur les nouvelles théories de la croissance.' *Revue économique,* **44,** (2), pp. 171–188.

Mansfield, E. (1981). 'How economists see R&D.' *Harvard Business Review,* **59,** November–December, pp. 98–105.

March, J. G. (1991). 'Exploration and exploitation in organizational learning.' *Organization Science,* **2,** (1), pp. 71–87.

March, J. G. and Olsen, J. P. (1975). 'The uncertainty of the past: organizational learning under ambiguity.' *European Journal of Political Research,* **3,** pp. 147–171.

Maslow, A. H. (1987). *Motivation and Personality* (3rd edition), Addison-Wesley Publishing Company, New York.

McGee, D. (1995). 'Making up mind: the early sociology of invention.' *Technology and Culture,* **36,** (4), pp. 773–801.

McGrath, R. G. (2001). 'Falling forward: real options reasoning and entrepreneurial failure.' *Academy of Management Review,* **24,** (1), pp. 13–30.

McGrath, R. G., Ferrier, W. J., and Mendelow, A. L. (2004). 'Real options as engines to choice and heterogeneity.' *Academy of Management Review,* **29,** (1), pp. 86–101.

Mees, C. E. K. (1916). 'The organization of industrial scientific research.' *Science,* **43,** (1118), pp. 763–773.

Mees, C. E. K. and Leermakers, J. A. (1950). *The Organization of Industrial Scientific Research* (2nd edition), McGraw-Hill, New York.

Mensch, G. (1975). *Das technologische Patt*, Umschau Verlag, Frankfurt. (English edition: 1979, *Stalemate in Technology: Innovations Overcome the Depression*, Ballinger Publishing Company, Cambridge, MA.)

Meyer, M. H. and Dalal, D. (2002). 'Managing platform architectures and manufacturing processes for nonassembled products.' *Journal of Product Innovation Management*, **19**, pp. 277–293.

Meyer, M. H. and Lehnerd, L. (1997). *The Power of Product Platforms*, The Free Press, New York.

Meyer, M. H. and Mugge, P. C. (2001). 'Make platform innovation drive enterprise growth.' *Research Technology Management*, **44**, (1), pp. 25–40.

Meyer-Thurow, G. (1982). 'The industrialization of invention: a case study from the German chemical industry.' *Isis*, **73**, (268, September), pp. 363–381.

Midler, C. (1993). *L'auto qui n'existait pas, management des projets et transformation de l'entreprise*, InterEditions, Paris.

(2000). *Les partenariats interentreprises en conception: pourquoi? comment?*, ANRT, Paris.

(2004). 'Expansion des produits, des usages, des marchés et dynamique du système de conception: l'exemple de la voiture communicante.' *Les nouveaux régimes de la conception*, Colloque de Cerisy, 14–20 June, A. Hatchuel and B. Weil.

Miller, J. (1995). *Lockheed Martin's Skunk Works* (revised edition). Midland Publishing Ltd, Leicester.

Miller, W. L. and Morris, L. (1999). *Fourth Generation R&D: Managing Knowledge, Technology, and Innovation*, John Wiley & Sons, Inc., New York.

Minguet, G. and Osty, F. (2008). *En quête d'innovation. Du projet au produit de haute technologie*, Business, économie et société, D. Ménascé, ed., Hermès-Lavoisier, Paris.

Minguet, G. and Thuderoz, C. (2005). *Travail, entreprise et société: manuel de sociologie pour ingénieurs et scientifiques*, Sciences sociales et sociétés, Presses Universitaires de France, Paris.

Mintzberg, H. (1979). *The Structuring of Organizations*, Prentice-Hall, Englewood Cliffs, NJ.

(1982). *Structure et dynamique des organisations*, P. Romelaer, trans., Editions d'organisation, Paris.

Moore, G. E. (1996). 'Some personal perspectives on research in the semiconductor industry.' *Engines of Innovation: U.S. Industrial Research at the End of an Era*, R. S. Rosenbloom and W. J. Spencer, eds., Harvard Business School Press, Boston, MA, pp. 165–174.

Morris, C. R. and Ferguson, C. H. (1993). 'How architecture wins technology wars.' *Harvard Business Review*, **71**, (2), pp. 86–96.

Mullen, B., Johnson, C., and Salas, E. (1991). 'Productivity loss in brainstorming groups: a metaanalytic integration.' *Basic and Applied Social Psychology*, **12**, pp. 3–23.

Myers, M. B. and Rosenbloom, R. S. (1996). 'Rethinking the role of industrial research.' *Engines of Innovation: U.S. Industrial Research at the End of an Era*, R. S. Rosenbloom and W. J. Spencer, eds., Harvard Business School Press, Boston, MA, pp. 209–228.

Nagai, Y. and Taura, T. (2006). 'Formal description of concept-synthesizing process for creative design.' *Design Computing and Cognition '06*, J. S. Gero, Springer, pp. 443–460.

Nagai, Y., Taura, T., and Mukai, F. (2008). 'Concept blending and dissimilarity. Factors for creative design process – a comparison between the linguistic interpretation process and design process.' Design Research Society Biennial Conference, Sheffield, 16–19 July.

Nakamura, L. I. (2001). 'Education and training in an era of creative destruction.' Federal Reserve Bank of Philadelphia, Working Paper No. 00–13R, March.

Nelson, R. R. and Winter, S. G. (1973). 'Toward an evolutionary theory of economic capabilities.' *The American Economic Review*, **63**, (2), pp. 440–449.

(1982). *An Evolutionary Theory of Economic Change*, The Belknap Press of Harvard University Press, Cambridge, MA, and London.

Neuhaus, F. A. (1910). 'Technische Erfordernisse für Massenfabrikation.' *Technik und Wirtschaft, Monatsschrift des VDI*, **3**, (10), pp. 577–597, 649–660.

Nonaka, I. (1990). 'Redundant, overlapping organization: a Japanese approach to managing the innovation process.' *California Management Review*, Spring, pp. 27–38.

(1994). 'A dynamic theory of organizational knowledge creation.' *Organization Science*, **5**, (1, February), pp. 14–37.

Nonaka, I. and Takeuchi, H. (1995). *The Knowledge Creating Company: How Japanese Companies Create the Dynamics of Innovation*, Oxford University Press, New York.

O'Connor, G. C. (2008). 'Major innovation as a dynamic capability: a system approach.' *Journal of Product Innovation Management*, **25**, pp. 313–330.

O'Connor, G. C. and de Martino, R. (2006). 'Organizing for radical innovation: an exploratory study of the structural aspect of RI management systems in large established firms.' *Journal of Product Innovation Management*, **23**, pp. 475–497.

OECD (1981). *La mesure des activités scientifiques et techniques, méthode type proposée pour les enquêtes sur la recherche et le développement expérimental. Manuel de Frascati 1980*. OECD, Paris.

(1994). 'Définitions et conventions de base pour la mesure de la recherche et du développement expérimental (R-D). Résumé du Manuel de Frascati 1993.' *OECD/GD (94) 84*, OECD, Paris.

Olilla, S., Norrgren, F., and Schaller, J. (1998). 'Political skills in leading product development projects.' 5th International Product Development Management Conference, Como, Italy, EIASM.

Orr, J. (1990). 'Sharing knowledge, celebrating identity: war stories and community memory in a service culture.' *Collective Remembering*, D. S. Middleton and D. Edwards, eds., Sage, Beverly Hills, CA, pp. 169–189.

Osborn, A. F. (1957). *Applied Imagination* (1st edition), Charles Scribner, New York.

Pahl, G. and Beitz, W. (1977). *Konstruktionslehre* (English title: *Engineering Design*), K. W. Arnold Pomerans, translator, é. a. K. Wallace, Springer Verlag, édition anglaise: The Design Council, Heidelberg, version anglaise: London.

(2006). *Engineering Design: A Systematic Approach*, K. Wallace, L. Blessing and F. Bauert, trans., Springer, Berlin.

Pakes, A. and Ericson, R. (1998). 'Empirical implications of alternative models of firm dynamics.' *Journal of Economic Theory*, **79**, pp. 1–45.

Panofsky, E. (1975). *La perspective comme forme symbolique*, Les éditions de minuit, Paris.

Parnes, S. J. and Meadow, A. (1959). 'Effect of "brainstorming" instructions on creative problem solving by trained and untrained subjects.' *Journal of Educational Psychology*, **50**, pp. 171–176.

Paulus, P. B. (2000). 'Groups, teams, and creativity: the creative potential of idea-generating groups.' *Applied Psychology: An International Review*, **49**, (2), pp. 237–262.

Paulus, P. B., Brown, V. R., and Ortega, A. H. (1999). 'Group creativity.' *Social Creativity in Organization*, R. E. Purser and A. Montuori, eds., Hampton, Cresskill, NJ.

Paulus, P. B. and Dzindolet, M. T. (1993). 'Social influence processes in group brainstorming.' *Journal of Personality and Social Psychology*, **64**, pp. 575–586.

Pavitt, K. (1992). 'Some foundations for a theory of the large innovating firm.' *Technology and Enterprise in a Historical Perspective*, G. Dosi, R. Giannetti and P. A. Toninelli, eds., Clarendon Press, Oxford, pp. 212–228.

Penrose, E. T. (1959). *The Theory of the Growth of the Firm* (4th edition 1968), Basil Blackwell, Oxford, UK.

(1960). 'The growth of the firm. A case study: the Hercules Powder Company.' *Business History Review*, **34**, pp. 1–23.

Perlitz, M., Peske, T., and Schrank, R. (1999). 'Real options valuation: the new frontier in R&D project evaluation.' *R&D Management*, **29**, (3), pp. 255–269.

Peters, T. J. and Waterman, R. H. (1982). *In Search of Excellence*, Harper & Row, New York.

Peychès, I. (1951). 'La recherche industrielle privée.' *Mémoires de la société des ingénieurs civils*, **104**, pp. 327–342.

Piller, F., Koch, M., Möslein, K., and Schubert, P. (2003). 'Managing high variety: how to overcome the mass confusion phenomenon of customer co-design.' European Academy of Management 2003, Milan, 3–5 April, 21.

Polanyi, M. (1958). *Personal Knowledge: Towards a Post-Critical Philosophy*, University of Chicago Press, Chicago, IL.

Prahalad, C. K. and Ramaswamy, V. (2000). 'Co-opting customer competence.' *Harvard Business Review*, **78**, January–February, pp. 79–87.

Prevéraud, J.-F. (2005). 'La conception innovante.' *Industrie et Technologie*, **867**, pp. 50–56.

Rabeharisoa, V. and Callon, M. (1998). 'L'implication des malades dans les activités de recherche soutenues par l'association française contre les myopathies.' *Sciences sociales et santé*, **16**, (3), pp. 41–65.

Reich, Y., Shai, O., Subrahmanian, E., Hatchuel, A., and Le Masson, P. (2008). 'The interplay between design and mathematics: introduction and bootstrapping effects.' 9th International Conference on Engineering Systems Design and Analysis, Haifa, Israel.

Reinertsen, D. (1994). 'Streamlining the fuzzy front-end.' *World Class Design to Manufacture*, **1**, (5), pp. 4–8.

Renouard, Y. (1949). 'Les hommes d'affaire italiens aux Moyen-Age.' *Econcomies, Sociétés, Civilisations*, Armand Colin, Paris.

Riedler, A. (1916). *Emil Rathenau, und das Werden der Grosswirtschaft*, Verlag von Julius Springer, Berlin.

Rip, A. and Kemp, R. (1998). 'Technological change.' *Human Choice and Climate Change*, S. Rayner and E. L. Malone, eds., Battelle Press, Columbus, OH, Vol. 2: Resources and Technology, pp. 327–399.

Rittel, H. W. J. (1972). 'On the planning crisis: systems analysis of the "first and second generations".' *Bedriftsokonomen*, **8**, pp. 390–396.

Robinson, A. G. and Stern, S. (1997). *Corporate Creativity: How Innovation and Improvement Actually Happen*, Berrett-Koehler Publishers Inc., San Francisco, CA.

Rogers, E. M. (1983). *Diffusion of Innovation* (3rd edition), The Free Press, New York.

Roll, E. (1930). *An Early Experiment in Industrial Organization, Being a History of the Firm of Boulton and Watt, 1775–1805* (new impression 1968), Frank Cass and Company Limited, London.

Rolt, L. T. C. (1960). *George and Robert Stephenson: The Railway Revolution*, Longman, London.

Romer, P. (1986). 'Increasing return and long term growth.' *Journal of Political Economy*, **94**, pp. 1002–1037.

(1990). 'Endogenous technical change.' *Journal of Political Economy*, **98**, (5), pp. S71–S102.

Rosenbloom, R. S. and Spencer, W. J. (1996). 'Introduction: technology's vanishing wellspring.' *Engines of Innovation: U.S. Industrial Research at the End of an Era*, R. S. Rosenbloom and W. J. Spencer, eds., Harvard Business School Press, Boston, MA, pp. 1–9.

Rosier, R. (2007). 'Stratégies et organisations des processus d'exploration: le cas de la pile à combustible chez Axane/Air Liquide' (thesis), Paris-Est Marne la Vallée, Sciences de Gestion, Paris.

Roussel, P. A., Saad, K. N., and Erickson, T. J. (1991). *Third Generation R&D: Managing the Link to Corporate Strategy*, Harvard Business School Press, Boston, MA.

Ruffat, M. (1996). *175 ans d'industrie pharmaceutique française, histoire de Synthélabo*, La Découverte, Paris.

Salomon, J.-J. (1992). *Le destin technologique*, Situations, J.-P. L. Dantec, ed., Balland, Paris.

Sanderson, S. and Uzumeri, M. (1995). 'Managing product families: the case of the Sony Walkman.' *Research Policy*, **24**, (5), pp. 761–782.

Schneider, M., Tejeda, M., Dondi, G., Herzog, F., Keel, S., and Geering, H. (2008). 'Making real options work for practitioners: a generic model for valuing R&D projects.' *R&D Management*, **38**, (1), pp. 85–106.

Schön, D. A. (1990). 'The design process.' *Varieties of Thinking. Essays from Harvard's Philosophy of Education Research Center*, V. A. Howard, ed., Routledge, New York, pp. 110–141.

Schön, D. S. (1969). 'Managing technological innovation.' *Harvard Business Review*, May–June, (3), pp. 156–162.

Schot, J. and Geels, F. W. (2007). 'Niches in evolutionary thoeries of technical change. A critical survey of the literature.' *Journal of Evolutionary Economics*, **17**, pp. 605–622.

(1932 [2005]). 'Development.' *Journal of Economic Literature*, **43** (March 2005), pp. 108–120.

Schumpeter, J. (1942). *Capitalisme, socialisme et démocratie*, G. Fain, trans., Payot, Paris.

(1964). *Business Cycles: A Theoretical, Historical and Statistical Analysis of the Capitalist Process*, McGraw-Hill, New York and London.

Segrestin, B. (2003). 'La gestion des partenariats d'exploration: spécificités, crises et formes de rationalisation' (thesis), Ecole des Mines, Sciences de gestion, Paris.

(2005). 'Partnering to explore: the Renault–Nissan alliance as a forerunner of new cooperative patterns.' *Research Policy*, **34**, pp. 657–672.

(2006). *Innovation et coopération inter-entreprises. Comment gérer les partenariats d'exploration?*, Editions du CNRS, Paris.

(2009). 'Collaborative innovation capabilities: developing platforms through "design games".' 16th International Product Development Management Conference, University of Twente, Enschede, the Netherlands.

Seidel, V. (2006). 'Crafting novel product concepts: concept shifting and the radical development process.' 13th International Product Development Management Conference, Milan, EIASM and Politecnico di Milano, **3**, 1325–1339.

(2007). 'Concept shifting and the radical product development process.' *Journal of Product Innovation Management*, **24**, (6), pp. 522–533.

Shafirovich, E., Salomon, M., and Gökalp, I. (2003). 'Mars Hopper vs Mars Rover.' Fifth IAA International Conference on Low-Cost Planetary Missions, 24–26 Septembre 2003, Noordwijk, the Netherlands, ESA SP-542, 97–102.

Shai, O., Reich, Y., Hatchuel, A., and Subrahmanian, E. (2009). 'Creativity theories and scientific discovery: a study of C-K theory and infused design.' International Conference on Engineering Design, ICED'09, 24–27 August, Stanford, CA.

Shinn, T. (2002). 'The triple helix and new production of knowledge: prepackaged thinking on science and technology.' *Social Studies of Science*, **32**, (4), pp. 599–614.

(2006). 'New sources of radical innovation: research technologies, transversality, and distributed learning in a post-industrial order.' *Innovation, Science and Industrial Change: The Handbook of Research*, J. Hage and M. Meeus, eds., Oxford University Press, New York, pp. 313–333.

Sieg, J. H., Wallin, M. W., and von Krogh, G. (2009). *Managerial Challenges in Open Innovation: A Study of Innovation Intermediation in the Chemical Industry*, European Academy of Management, Liverpool.

Simon, H. (1995). 'The scientist as problem-solver.' *Complex Information Processing: The Impact of Herbet Simon*, D. Klahr and K. Kotovsky, eds., Lawrence Earlbaum Associates, Hillsdale, NJ.

(1969). *The Sciences of the Artificial*, MIT Press, Cambridge, MA.

Simon, H. A. and Kulkarni, D. (1989). 'The processes of scientific discovery: the strategy of experimentation.' *Models of Thought*, H. A. Simon, ed., Yale University Press, New Haven, CT, pp. 356–382.

Simon, H. A., Newell, A., and Shaw, J. C. (1979). 'The processes of creative thinking.' *Models of Thought*, H. A. Simon, ed., Yale University Press, New Haven, CT, pp. 144–174.

Simondon, G. (1958). *Du mode d'existence des objets techniques* (Third edition 1989), L'invention philosophique, F. Laruelle, Aubier.

(2005). *L'invention dans les techniques. Cours et conférences*, edited and presented by Jean-Yves Chateau, Seuil, Paris.

Smiles, S. (1874). *James Brindley and the Early Engineers*, TEE Publishing, Warwickshire.

Smith, S. M., Ward, T. B., and Schumacher, J. S. (1993). 'Constraining effects of examples in a creative generation task.' *Memory and Cognition*, **21**, pp. 837–845.

Sobek, D. K. (1996). 'A set-based model of design.' *Mechanical Engineering*, **118**, (7), pp. 78–81.

Sobek, D. K., Liker, J. K., and Ward, A. C. (1998). 'Another look at how Toyota integrates product development.' *Harvard Business Review*, **66**, July–August, pp. 36–47.

Solow, R. M. (1956). 'A contribution to the theory of economic growth.' *Quarterly Journal of Economics*, **70**, pp. 65–94.

(1970). *Growth Theory. An Exposition*, Oxford University Press, Oxford.

Stalk, G. and Hout, T. M. (1993). 'Time-based results.' *Boston Consulting Group – 'Perspectives'*, **356**, (January), pp. 1–2.

Starkey, K., Barnatt, C., and Tempest, S. (2000). 'Beyond networks and hierarchies: latent organizations in the U.K. television industry.' *Organization Science*, **11**, (3), pp. 299–305.

Stasser, G. and Birchmeier, Z. (2003). 'Group creativity and collective choice.' *Group Creativity: Innovation through Collaboration*, P. B. Paulus and B. A. Nijstad, eds., Oxford University Press, New York, pp. 85–109.

Stephenson, G., Stephenson, R., and Locke, J. (1831). 'N°V: comparaison des machines fixes et des machines locomotives mises en mouvement par la vapeur sur les chemins de fer, ou réponse au rapport de M. James Walker.' *Annales des Ponts et Chaussées, mémoires et documents relatifs à l'art des constructions et au service de l'ingénieur*, **1**, (1), pp. 257–317.

Stewart, D. D. and Stasser, G. (1995). 'Expert role assignment and information sampling during collective recall and decision-making.' *Journal of Personality and Social Psychology*, **69**, pp. 619–628.

Stewart, T. A. (1996). 'The invisible key to success.' *Fortune Magazine*, August 5.

Storey, J. and Salaman, G. (2005). *Managers of Innovation: Insights into Making Innovation Happen*, Management, Organizations and Business Series, J. Storey, ed., Blackwell Publishing, Oxford.

Suarez, F. F. and Utterback, J. M. (1995). 'Dominant designs and the survival of firms.' *Strategic Management Journal*, **16**, pp. 415–430.

Suh, N. P. (1990). *Principles of Design*, Oxford University Press, New York.

Sundgren, M. and Styhre, A. (2003). 'Intuition and pharmaceutical research: the case of AstraZeneca.' Fenix Research Program, Chalmers University of Technology, Gothenburg.

Susskind, C. and Inouye, A. (1983). 'Le rapport de 1937.' *Culture Technique*, **10**, pp. 99–117.

Sutton, J. (1997). 'Gibrat's legacy.' *Journal of Economic Literature*, **35** (March), pp. 40–59.

Sutton, R. I. and Hargadon, A. (1996). 'Brainstorming groups in context: effectiveness in a product design firm.' *Administrative Science Quarterly*, **41**, (4), pp. 685–718.

Takeuchi, H. and Nonaka, I. (1986). 'The new new product development game.' *Harvard Business Review*, **64**, January–February, pp. 137–147.

Teece, D. J. (1986). 'Profiting from technological innovation: implications for integration, collaboration, licensing and public policy.' *Research Policy*, **15**, (6), pp. 285–305.

Teece, D. J. and Pisano, G. P. (1994). 'The dynamic capabilities of firms: an introduction.' *Industrial and Corporate Change*, **3**, (3), pp. 537–556.

Teece, D. J., Pisano, G. P., and Shuen, A. (1997). 'Dynamic capabilities and strategic management.' *Strategic Management Journal*, **18**, (7), pp. 509–533.

Thélot, C. and Vallet, L.-A. (2000). 'La réduction des inégalités sociales devant l'école depuis le début du siècle.' *Economie et Statistiques*, **334**, (2000–4), pp. 3–32.

Thomke, S. H. (1998). 'Managing experimentation in the design of new products.' *Management Science*, **44**, (6), pp. 743–762.

 (2001). 'Enlightened experimentation, the new imperative for innovation.' *Harvard Business Review*, **79**, February, pp. 67–75.

 (2003a). *Experimentation Matters. Unlocking the Potential of New Technologies for Innovation*, Harvard Business School Press, Boston, MA.

 (2003b). 'R&D comes to services: Bank of America's pathbreaking experiments.' *Harvard Business Review*, **81**, April, pp. 70–79.

Thomke, S. H. and Fujimoto, T. (2000). 'The effect of "front loading" problem-solving on product development performance.' *Journal of Product Innovation Management*, **17**, (2 March), pp. 128–142.

Thomke, S. H., von Hippel, E., and Franke, R. (1998). 'Modes of experimentation: an innovation process and competitive variable.' *Research Policy*, **27**, pp. 315–332.

Thurston, R. H. (1878). *A History of the Growth of the Steam Engine*, Appleton, New York.

Tidd, J., Bessant, J., and Pavitt, K. (1997). *Managing Innovation: Integrating Technological, Market and Organizational Change*, John Wiley & Sons, Chichester.

Todorova, G. and Durisin, B. (2007). 'Absorptive capacity: valuing a reconceptualization.' *Academy of Management Review*, **32**, (3), pp. 774–786.

Toulemonde, G. and Tuchendler, A. (2000). 'Innovation répétée et conception systématique dans une PME: le cas des "Outils-Malins".' Option Ingénierie de la conception, Ecole des Mines de Paris et société, Avanti SA, Paris.

Tracy Kidder, J. (1981). *The Soul of a Machine*, R. M. Vanalo-Villaneau, trans., Atlantic Little Brown, Boston.

Tranfield, D. and Starkey, K. (1998). 'The nature, social organization and promotion of management research: towards policy.' *British Journal of Management*, **9**, (4), pp. 341–353.

Trigeorgis, L. (1993). 'Real options and interactions with financial flexibility.' *Financial Management*, **22**, (3), pp. 202–226.

(1996). *Real Options: Managerial Flexibility and Strategy in Resource Allocation*, MIT Press, Boston, MA.

Tseng, M. M. and Piller, F. T. (2003). *The Customer Centric Enterprise: Advances in Mass Customization and Personalization*, Springer, Berlin.

Tushman, M. L. and Anderson, A. D. (1986). 'Technological discontinuities and organizational environments.' *Administrative Science Quarterly*, **31**, pp. 439–465.

Tushman, M. L., Anderson, P., and O'Reilly, C. (1997). 'Technology cycles, innovation streams, and ambidextrous organizations: organization renewal through innovation streams and strategic change.' *Managing Strategic Innovation and Change: A Collection of Readings*, M. L. Tushman and P. Anderson, eds., Oxford University Press, New York, pp. 3–23.

Tushman, M. L. and O'Reilly III, C. A. (1996). 'Ambidextrous organizations: managing evolutionary and revolutionary change.' *California Management Review*, **38**, (4), pp. 8–30.

Usher, A. P. (1929). *A History of Mechanical Inventions*, McGraw-Hill, New York.

Utterback, J. (1994). *Mastering the Dynamics of Innovation*, Harvard Business School Press, Boston, MA.

Utterback, J. M., Vedin, B.-A., Alvarez, E., Ekman, S., Walsh Sanderson, S., Tether, B., and Verganti, R. (2006). *Design-Inspired Innovation*, World Scientific, New York.

Valéry, P. (1957). 'Une conquête méthodique.' *Oeuvres, Gallimard, Bibliothèque de la Pléiade*, Paris, pp. 971–987.

Van de Ven, A., Polley, D. E., Garud, R., and Venkataraman, S. (1999). *The Innovation Journey*, Oxford University Press, New York, Oxford.

Van de Ven, A. H., Angle, H., and Poole, M. S. (1989). *Research on the Management of Innovation: The Minnesota Studies*, Ballinger/Harper & Row, New York.

Varnes, C. J. (2005). 'Managing product innovation though rules. The role of formal and structured methods in product development' (thesis), Copenhagen Business School, School of Technologies of Managing, Copenhagen.

Varnes, C. J. and Christianson, J. K. (2006). 'The ignorance of information at gate meetings.' 13th International Product Development Management Conference, Milan, EIASM and Politecnico di Milano, 3, 1519–1536.

Verganti, R. (2008). 'Design, meanings, and radical innovation: a metamodel and a research agenda.' *Journal of Product Innovation Management*, **25**, (5), pp. 436–456.

Vitruve (1673). *Les dix livres d'architecture de Vitruve, corrigés et traduits nouvellement en François avec des Notes et des Figures*, C. Perrault, translator, Coignard, Jean-Baptiste, Paris.

Vitruvius (1999). *Ten Books on Architecture*, I. D. Rowland and T. Noble Howe, eds., Cambridge University Press, Cambridge, UK.

von Hippel, E. (1977). 'Has your customer already developed your next product?' Working paper from MIT Sloan School no 865–76.

—— (1978). 'Successful industrial products from customer ideas.' *Journal of Marketing*, January, pp. 39–49.

—— (1982). 'Get new products from customers.' *Harvard Business Review*, **60**, March–April, pp. 117–122.

—— (1988). *The Sources of Innovation*, Oxford University Press, New York.

von Hippel, E., Thomke, S., and Sonnack, M. (1999). 'Creating breakthroughs at 3M.' *Harvard Business Review*, **77**, September–October, pp. 47–57.

von Stamm, B. (2003). *Managing Innovation, Design and Creativity*, Wiley, Chichester.

Ward, A. C., Liker, J. K., Cristiano, J. J., and Sobek, D. K. (1995). 'The second Toyota paradox: how delaying decisions can make better cars faster.' *Sloan Management Review*, **36**, (3), pp. 43–61.

Ward, T. B. (1994). 'Structured imagination: the role of category structure in exemplar generation.' *Cognitive Psychology*, **27**, pp. 1–40.

Warren, J. G. H. (1923). *A Century of Locomotive Building by Robert Stephenson & Co.* (2nd edition 1970), Andrew Reid, Newcastle.

Weick, K. E. (1998). 'Improvisation as a mindset for organizational analysis.' *Organization Science*, **9**, (5), pp. 543–554.

Weil, B. (1999). 'Conception collective, coordination et savoirs, les rationalisations de la conception automobile' (thesis), Ecole Nationale Supérieure des Mines de Paris, Ingénierie et gestion, Paris.

Weisberg, R. W. (1992). *Creativity Beyond the Myth of Genius*, W. H. Freeman Company, New York.

West, J. (2003). 'How open is open enough? Melding proprietary and open source platform strategies.' *Research Policy*, **32**, pp. 1259–1285.

West, J. and Gallagher, S. (2006). 'Challenges of open innovation: the paradox of firm investment in open-source software.' *R&D Management*, **26**, (3), pp. 319–331.

Wheelwright, S. C. and Clark, K. B. (1992). *Revolutionizing Product Development: Quantum Leaps in Speed, Efficiency, and Quality*, The Free Press, Macmillan, Inc., New York.

Whitley, R. (2000). 'The institutional structuring of innovation strategies: business systems, firm types and patterns of technical change in different market economies.' *Organization Studies*, **21**, (5), pp. 855–886.

Wideman, R. M. (1992). *Project and Program Risk Management*, Project Management Institute, Newton Square, PA.

Woodward, J. A. (1965). *Industrial Organization: Theory and Practice*, Oxford University Press, Oxford.

Zahra, S. A. and George, G. (2002). 'Absorptive capacity: a review, reconceptualization, and extension.' *Academy of Management Review*, **27**, (2), pp. 185–203.

Zand, D. E. (1974). 'Collateral organization.' *Journal of Applied Behavioral Science*, January, pp. 275–283.

Index

Note: Page numbers in *italic* indicate Glossary entries

28260115R00261

Made in the USA
Lexington, KY
11 December 2013